ISBN 978-1-334-01900-5
PIBN 10741007

1 MONTH OF
FREE
READING

at
www.ForgottenBooks.com

By purchasing this book you are eligible for one month membership to ForgottenBooks.com, giving you unlimited access to our entire collection of over 700,000 titles via our web site and mobile apps.

To claim your free month visit:

www.forgottenbooks.com/free741007

FRATERNITY

A COMPILATION OF

HISTORICAL FACTS AND ADDRESSES
PERTAINING TO FRATERNALISM
IN GENERAL AND THE FRA-
TERNAL SYSTEM IN
PARTICULAR.

HELPFUL AND TIMELY SUGGESTIONS FOR ORGANIZERS
AND ADDRESSES ON VARYING OCCASIONS AND
CEREMONIES IN BOTH LOCAL AND SUPREME
BODIES.

PUBLISHED BY
THE FRATERNAL MONITOR
ROCHESTER, N. Y.
1910

/‾

INTRODUCTION

It is not the purpose of this publication to set forth the origin of Fraternity or to follow the winding paths it has followed in its onward and upward progress. The subject is so broad and far-reaching that it would be presumptuous to attempt to give more than a given phase of its adaptation and development within the covers of a single book. Those who would go deeper into the subject should betake themselves to the encyclopædias or to those studies on sociology which may be said to run along parallel lines.

The origins, purposes and derivations of Fraternalism may all be said to, in a general way, hinge upon the conditions prevalent at such times. Adaptations and improvements have very properly kept pace with the ever-changing order of things. Fraternalism is a growth. The societies are all inter-related in one form or another and, therefore, that which is worthy of preservation in one organization possesses an interest for others operating in what may be termed kindred fields.

It is not claimed that there is anything new or original in this publication. Its purpose is that of reflecting the best fraternal thought and effort. The addresses reproduced are intended to broaden the horizon of the fraternal view; to show what those who have stood on its watch-towers think of it and its possibilities; to sound notes both of warning and encouragement to those upon whom the burden of proper representation may devolve, and to show to the world that Fraternalism is the embodiment of Humanitarianism.

The Brotherhood of Man is the paramount cry to-day. Both the rich and the poor—the high and the low—are giving heed to its call. Fraternity is the rallying centre—the pivotal situation. If its exponents are alive to their opportunities—if they can give proof of the faith that is in them—the Cause of Man will rise to a higher and better plane. And, if this publication—setting forth fraternal purposes and accomplishments—is of assistance in strengthening Fraternal Faith and increasing Fraternal Efficiency, it will have accomplished that for which it was intended.

HISTORICAL SKETCH

Reference to the fraternal societies of this country is necessarily of a general nature. Many of the organizations not furnishing insurance as a special feature are so inter-related, or their data are so scattered, that anything attempting to give full and detailed information would require more space than can be here given to this subject. Only the principal societies are referred to. The circle of fraternal operation gradually widens as it extends down into those small local and special organizations which owe their existence to the general principle upon which fraternalism or co-operation rests.

The various Masonic bodies in the Western Hemisphere number over 2,000,000 members. The Independent Order of Odd Fellows have in their American organization, which is not in affiliation with an English order entitled the Manchester Unity of Odd Fellows, about 1,500,000 members. The Knights of Pythias have over 700,000 members. The Order of Good Templars have about 675,000 members. The Grand Army of the Republic has 220,000 members. The Improved Order of Red Men has 475,450 members. The Woman's Relief Corps —an auxiliary to the Grand Army of the Republic—has about 170,000 members. The Order of the Eagles has over 300,000 members. The Ancient Order of Hibernians numbers about 325,000 members. The United Confederate Veterans has approximately 75,000 members. The Benevolent and Protective Order of Elks has over 300,000 members. Such other organizations as the United American Mechanics, the Sons of Veterans, the

Ancient Order of Foresters, the Foresters of America, the Ancient Order of Druids, the Knights of the Golden Eagle, and many others, may be safely estimated to have at least 2,000,000 members, so that the entire membership of the many fraternal societies not furnishing insurance as a special feature may be approximately given at 9,000,000.

What are known as the fraternal beneficial societies—those furnishing insurance as a special feature—have a membership of approximately 8,000,000. They are receiving new members at the rate of one million a year and their net increase may be safely computed at from three hundred to four hundred thousand members annually. The amount of insurance protection they carry approximates the stupendous total of $9,000,000,000, and they are paying about $100,000,000 each year to the beneficiaries of their members. Their assets are nearly $150,-000,000, and the movement begun a number of years ago in the way of determining by actuarial computation the present value of their future liabilities has resulted in a rapid increase in such assets.

Since organization these societies have paid fully $1,500,000,000 in benefits. If to this total are added the benefits paid by the social societies for sickness and temporary relief—this sum approximates $500,000,000—it will be seen that during the comparatively brief period of about forty years the fraternal system has disbursed to its members and their dependents the tremendous sum of $2,000,000,000. This work may very properly be said to be in its infancy and, therefore, it is but safe to assume that succeeding years will show even greater results as to the amount of good done members and their dependents.

With these general statements as setting forth the vastness of the fraternal system and the important part it is destined to play in working out economic and social conditions, the case as to the standing of the system and the proportions it has attained is rested. The succeeding pages will be devoted to addresses delivered by the great fraternal thinkers and speakers of the past few years. These, coupled with carefully prepared papers setting forth fraternal needs and purposes, cannot but constitute a great source of inspiration for those who may be called upon to address fraternal bodies and gatherings on regular and special occasions.

It has been the central purpose in the compilation of the material herein submitted to have it cover as wide a range of fraternal operation as is possible. To this end addresses of an upbuilding, admonitory and encouraging nature are reproduced. In addition, there are other topics considered and, all in all, it is believed that the following pages will be found to be a fair presentation of what fraternalism is, what it can do and why it has won for itself such a strong place in the affections and confidence of the people.

AMERICAN FRATERNITY

A. CHISHOLM, OTTAWA, ONTARIO

Far-reaching and masterful have been the forces and influences which have laid the foundations and reared the pillars of American brotherhood. Its main strength lies in those elements which weld communities into a compact and harmonious aggregation. "There are some words," writes Henri-Frederic Amiel in his "Journal," "which have still a magical virtue with the mass of the people; those of State, Republic, Country, Nation, Flag, and even Church." These words apply with peculiar force to every State in the American Union. The mottoes of its forty-eight states loudly proclaim the principle and spirit of true brotherhood. In Pennsylvania's state motto, "Virtue, Liberty, and Independence," there are equal rights for every honest and law-abiding citizen. In Georgia's motto, "Wisdom, Justice, and Moderation," there are liberties and privileges for all men, regardless of creed or class. In Missouri's and Kentucky's watchword, "United we Stand, Divided we fall," there is sounded a note of loyalty and fellowship which rings true to the death. In the motto of Delaware, "Liberty and Independence"; of Vermont, "Freedom and Unity"; of Illinois, "National Union, State Sovereignty"; of Louisiana, "Justice, Union and Confidence"; of Nevada, "All for Our Country"; of Oregon and Idaho, "The Union"; of New Jersey, "Liberty and Prosperity"; of Florida, "In God We Trust"; and of Dakota, "Liberty and Union, now and forever, one and inseparable";—in all these mottoes there rings out clearly and distinctly the one dominant keynote of staunch and steadfast brotherhood; a brotherhood that ever seeks to uphold and defend the right, to help the helpless, uplift the down-trodden, and render equal justice to all.

The literal fulfillment of these mottoes of justice and equity, fraternity and freedom, will prove a wall of fire around the people who practice and profess them. The principles they enunciate have ever dominated the lives of America's greatest citizens, and proved the strongest bulwarks of their rights and liberties. It was in the spirit of these mottoes of the States that America extended a welcome to the millions who flocked to the World's Fairs at Philadelphia, Chicago, Buffalo and St. Louis, for these exhibitions voiced, in a peculiar sense, the sentiment of American cordiality, hospitality and fraternity. It was in this spirit of friendship and fraternity that Britons and Americans gathered at the Jamestown Exhibition, and bade the world behold the golden fruitage and the imperishable triumphs of three hundred years of Anglo-Saxon brotherhood and Anglo-American supremacy.

About thirty-five years ago there gathered in the city of Philadelphia a vast multitude from every land to behold what was probably, up to that time, the most remarkable of World's Fairs. Waving above the noble pile of exhibition buildings might be seen the flags of all nations, and high over all floated the ample folds of the Star Spangled Banner. Underneath this banner the people of every nation received a greeting which proved the depth and wholeheartedness of America's welcome. That welcome from the American people had in it the warm throb and thrill and firm grasp of American brotherhood.

Seventeen years ago, again on American soil, there assembled from all nations, people of every tongue to behold in the city of Chicago a world's fair greater and more wonderful than that which dazzled the millions which in 1876 flocked to the Quaker City. These peoples from every nation came hither to witness contests that drew no blood, competitions which dealt no wounds and inflamed no passions; but rather to behold a rivalry whose noblest aims and triumphs were those of peace and good will. Once more to the people of every land America extended the hand of friendship and hospitality, once more she displayed the ample evidences of her spirit of splendid brotherhood.

At this Chicago Fair of 1893 were heard voices that spoke for the world's joy and for the world's good; voices that rang out clearly their messages of peace, their brave words of liberty, independence and freedom; voices of manly courage, unshaken trust, high soaring faith; but strongest and bravest of all were the voices that spoke in the World's Parliament of Religions for the Brotherhood of Man and the Fatherhood of God. Such words as came from the lips of men like Hon. Charles Carroll Bonney, President of the World's Congress Auxiliary, Rev. John Henry Barrows, D. D., the Chairman of the General Committee on Religious Congresses, Dr. Schaff, and Dr. Pentecost, can never be forgotten by those who heard them. Some of these words have been carried to every corner of the earth to keep aglow the fires of world-wide friendship and fellowship. These voices in the Parliament of Religions struck the chord of universal peace and good will, and not the least impressive among them was that of the Rev. Dr. Frank Bristol, who in one of his addresses said:

Since this Parliament opened all thoughtful, serious men have been living in a larger world of faith and hope. Little things have been diminishing, and great things have been growing greater. Never was there such a bright and hopeful day for our common humanity along the lines of tolerance and universal brotherhood. And we shall find that by the words these visitors have brought to us, and by the influence they have exerted, they will be richly rewarded in the consciousness of having contributed to the mighty movement which holds, itself, the promise of one faith, one Lord and Father, one Brotherhood.

At this notable gathering Spain found eloquent repre-sentation in Pastor Fliedner, of Madrid. He was grateful to America for the reception she had given to him and his countrymen; he had met with kindness and friendship on every hand; and these are the words in which he expressed his gratitude to the American people:

From Spain, which discovered America, I tender a farewell greeting to those who have made America what it is to-day; to the sons and daughters of the Pilgrim Fathers who left their homes in England and Scotland, in Holland and Germany, and came to this country and here established liberty from the Atlantic Ocean to the Pacific Shore; to them I say farewell. They brought liberty to America because they knew the fountain of liberty, even the liberator of mankind, the author of the brother-hood of man, yea, God manifest in the flesh, light of freedom shining into the darkness of slavery. Spain has been down-trodden for centuries by ecclesiastical and political oppression, but now it has regained liberty, and therefore it says its farewell, rejoicing that it is free in that freedom with which Christ makes all men free. God bless free America.

Not less impressive and memorable were the words uttered by Dr. Barrows, the Chairman of the General Committee on Religious Congresses, at one of the meet-ings of the Parliament. Dr. Barrows laboured day and night for the success of the Congresses, and his person-ality was everywhere and at all times in evidence. In the following utterance he conveyed to his hearers the real message and meaning of the Parliament which had brought people together from every part of the civilized world:

I thank God for the friendships which, in this Parliament we have knit with men and women beyond the sea, and I thank you for your sympathy and ever generous appreciation, and for the constant help which you have furnished in the midst of my multiplied duties. Christian America sends her greetings through you to all mankind. We cherish a broadened sympathy, a higher respect, a truer tenderness to the children of our common Father in all lands, and, as the story of this Parliament is read in the

cloisters of Japan, by the rivers of Southern Asia, amid the
universities of Europe, and in the isles of all the seas, it is my
prayer that non-Christian readers may in some measure dis-
cover what has been the source and strength of that faith in
divine fatherhood and human brotherhood which, embodied in an
Asiatic peasant who was the Son of God and made divinely
potent through Him, is clasping the globe with bands of heav-
enly light.

In the two volumes edited by Dr. Barrows which tell
the complete story of the World's Parliament of Religions,
one sees a work of monumental industry. It is a work
every page of which glows with the flame of world-wide
fraternity; and no silver trumpets of peace ever rang out
to the world a clearer note than is heard in almost every
sentence of the sixteen hundred pages contained in these
two volumes. The address of President Bonney was one
of the most memorable delivered at the Parliament. He
spoke to all peoples and for all time when he said, in rela-
tion to the meetings of the Congress, "What many men
deemed impossible God has finally wrought. The religions
of the world have actually met in a great and imposing
assembly; they have conferred together on the vital ques-
tions of life and immortality in a frank and friendly spirit,
and now they part in peace with many warm expressions
of mutual affection and respect. . . . And now fare-
well; a thousand congratulations and thanks for the
co-operation and aid of all who have contributed to the
glorious results which we celebrate this night. Hence-
forth the religions of the world will make war, not on
each other, but on the giant evils that afflict mankind.
Henceforth let all throughout the world, who worship
God and love their fellowmen, join in the anthem of the
angels: 'Glory to God in the highest; peace on earth,
good will among men.'"

To the success of the Chicago World's Fair the lady
delegates from the United States and Great Britain con-

tributed in no small degree. By voice and pen, by precept and example they gave to the exhibition the full strength of their personality. Some of them displayed a tact and administrative genius which were alike the praise and admiration of all with whom they came in contact, while both in speech and in verse they manifested an intellectual stature rarely surpassed at any one of the congresses. Memory recalls the Commemoration Dedicatory Ode from the pen of Miss Harriet Monroe of Chicago, in which the forces that have made for America's greatness and brotherhood are recounted, and in which she tells the world how,—

> Clan on clan,
> The embattled nations gather to be one,
> Clasp hands as brothers 'neath Columbia's shield,
> Upraise her banner to the shining sun.
> Along her blessed shore
> One heart, one song, one dream,—
> Man shall be free forevermore,
> And love shall be supreme.

Others will recall the poem on "The World's Parliament" composed by Laura Ormiston Chant, which proved that while some of the women of the Parliament could delight great audiences by their powers of speech, others were able to entrance their hearers by the spell of their verse. But speech and song alike at the Chicago World's Fair breathed the all-pervading note of brotherhood. The address of Mr. H. Dharmapala, of Ceylon, of David James Burrell on "What Christianity has wrought for America;" of Shaku Soyen on "Arbitration Instead of War;" of Dr. G. D. Boardman, on "Christ the Unifier of Mankind," and at least a hundred other addresses on topics bearing on Christian unity and fellowship—all struck the key-note of American brotherhood and world-wide fraternity. Said Mr. Boardman in part:—

Every human being in distress, and whom I can practically help, whether he lives in Chicago or Pekin, is my neighbour. As a matter of fact the locomotive and the steam engine ánd the telegraph are swiftly making all mankind one vast physical neighbourhood. . . . Now do you not see that when every human being—American, Asiatic, European, African, Islander—regards and treats every other human being as his own neighbour, all mankind will indeed become one blessed unity.

If ever great and notable event in the history of a nation gave true expression to the pulsations of humanity and fraternity throbbing in the blood of the people, that event was the dedicatory celebration of the Chicago Exhibition. The dedicatory ode of Harriet Monroe, the dedicatory oration of Henry Watterson, of Kentucky, the Columbia oration of Chauncey M. Depew, the inauguration speech of Archbishop Ireland, (in many respects an unmatched production,) and the noble utterances of Mrs. Potter Palmer on behalf of the Women's branch of the World's Congress Auxiliary—all were vibrant with the note of international goodwill, all gave imperishable expression to the soul and sentiment of American friend ship and American hospitality. From Henry Watterson of Kentucky came words which voiced America's greeting to all the nations of the earth, and he did so in a manner which would have well become the lips of a Wendell Phillips or a Daniel Webster. Although it is now many years since that address was delivered, its enkindling forces are as strong to-day as they were at the hour in which they were delivered. Mr. Watterson said in part:—

This vast assemblage speaks with a resonance and meaning which words can never reach. It speaks from the fields that are blessed by the never-failing water of the Kennebec and from the farms that sprinkle the valley of the Connecticut with mimic principalities more potent and lasting than the real; it speaks in the whirr of the mills of Pennsylvania and in the ring of the woodcutter's axe from the forests of the lake peninsulas; it speaks from the great plantations of the south and west teeming with staples that insure us wealth and power and stability, yea, and from the mines and forests and quarries of Michigan and Wisconsin, of Alabama and Georgia, of Tennessee and Kentucky, far away to the regions of silver and gold that have linked Colorado and the Rio Grande in close embrace, and annihilated time and space between the Atlantic and the Pacific; it speaks in one word from the hearthstone in Iowa and Illinois, from the home in Mississippi and Arkansas, from the hearts of seventy millions of fearless, freeborn men and women, and that one word is "Union."

There is no geography in American manhood. There is no section to American fraternity. . . We have come here not so much to recall by-gone sorrows and glories as to bask in the sunshine of present prosperity and happiness, to interchange patriotic greetings and indulge good auguries, and above all to meet upon the threshold the stranger within our gates, not as a foreigner, but as a guest and friend, for whom nothing that we have is too good. From wheresoever he cometh we welcome him with all our hearts, the son of the Rhone and the Garonne, our god-mother France, to whom we owe so much, he shall be our Lafayette; the son of the Rhine and the Moselle, he shall be our Goethe and our Wagner; the son of the Campagna and the Vesuvian Bay, he shall be our Michael Angelo and our Garibaldi; the son of Arragon and the Indies, he shall be our Christopher Columbus, fitly honoured at last throughout the world.
All nations and all creeds be welcome here; from the Bosphorus and the Black Sea, the Viennese woods and the Danube plains; from Holland dyke to Alpine crag; from Belgrade and Calcutta, and round to China seas and the busy marts of Japan, the isles of the Pacific, and the far away capes of Africa—Armenian Chris_tian and Jew—the American, loving no country except his own, but loving all mankind as his brother, bids you enter and fear not; bids you partake of these fruits of 400 years of American civilization and development, and behold these trophies of a hundred years of American independence and freedom.

These words of Henry Watterson fitly and eloquently represent the fraternal spirit of the American nation, and if any one should ever entertain a lingering doubt as to the sincerity and cordiality of that spirit, let the words of Henry Watterson silence his doubts for ever; and let him find additional proof in the story of the Pan-American Exhibition at Buffalo, or of the still greater World's Fair at St. Louis, the magnitude and splendor of which have perhaps never been surpassed.

Many pens have portrayed the dazzling scenes, the gorgeous displays, the innumerable wonders of American World's Fairs, but better than the magnitude and splendor of these historic exhibitions, better than the wealth and brilliance of their displays, is the heart of kindness that beats under American banners, the flame of loyalty that burns on the altars of American homes, and the blood of brotherhood that throbs in the veins of the American people.

The strength and compass of American fraternity are seen in its deeds of Christian and fraternal benevolence; in the gifts that ennoble and uplift the citizenship of the country; in the vast sums which are given yearly in aid of the poor and suffering, in the cause of religion and education. America's chief glory lies not in her princely palaces, in her commercial triumphs, her scientific achievements, or her colossal industries so much as in her abundant provision for the relief of the distressed, for the support of the unfortunate in homes and hospitals, and in acts which have brought comfort, health and blessing to multitudes. These are and must ever remain the most enduring monuments of a country's greatness—this is brotherhood in its highest, noblest aspects.

Washington gloried not more in a splendid victory of arms than in an act of kindness to a poor man. Lincoln's delight was not so much in the conquest of the South as in the emancipation of the slave. The angel of peace was to Lincoln a far more beautiful sight than the triumphant gods of war. Jefferson, McKinley and Garfield bequeathed to posterity the heritage of a noble example, the memory of kind, brotherly deeds, and these are the most valuable, the most imperishable bequests that can be left to any people. Perhaps the finest spectacle in the whole Civil War was, that of Grant and Lee, at the end of the conflict, shaking hands with each other as brothers, as enemies no more.

If we may judge great men by their words, uttered in the presence of many witnesses, or printed on the imperishable page, then would we like to judge William McKinley by the tribute he has paid to his predecessors in office. Of General Grant he once said: "He was great in life, majestic in death. He needs no monument to perpetuate his fame; it will live and glow with increased lustre so long as liberty lasts, and the love of liberty has a place in the hearts of men." It is a trite saying that from admiration to emulation is but a step. It is certain that there was much in common between McKinley and Lincoln. Both admired what was truly commendable and noble in manhood; both scorned to be mean, unjust, unfair; courage flashed from every act and word in the lives of both men. Lincoln had no greater admirer than McKinley, who has said of him —"Lincoln, the martyr of liberty, the emancipator of a race, may be buried from human sight, but his deeds will live in human gratitude for ever." And of Washington Mr. McKinley has also said:—"And so, too, will the nation live, victorious over all obstacles, adhering to the immortal principles which Washington taught and Lincoln sustained."

McKinley and Garfield were alike in many respects. No two men ever loved their country more; no two men would have sooner died for the honour of the nation and the glory of an unsullied, unstained banner. Both have uttered words which it is the delight of the young and old to repeat, and which will be quoted in the schools, acade_ mies and books of the world until the end of time. There is nothing finer in the utterances of Lincoln or Garfield than the words contained in their inaugural addresses. In one of these McKinley said:—"Our faith teaches that there is no safer reliance than upon the God of our fathers, who has so singularly favoured the American people in every national trial, and who will not forsake us so long as we obey His commandments and walk humbly in His footsteps."

The stately monuments which the American people erected to the memory of Grant and Lee have been looked upon and admired by millions, because they are the enduring embodiments of the nation's respect and gratitude; but the following words from the lips of McKinley will last as long as the most enduring monument:—

The army of Grant and the army of Lee are together. They are one now in faith, in hope, in fraternity, in purpose, and in an invincible patriotism. And, therefore, the country is in no danger. In justice strong, in peace secure, and in devotion to the flag, all are one. God bless and prosper the American home and the American people. Upon these rest the strength and virtue and permanence of our nation, which we pray our heavenly Father to ever have in His sacred keeping.

We are speaking to-day of the dead rather than of the living; but it may be said of one prominent living American, Theodore Roosevelt, that he has spoken in the language of fraternity to many nations, nations at war and nations at peace, with no uncertain sound. Benjamin Harrison was a really great man and one of the striking proofs of his greatness was his magnanimity. No man was ever more ready than Harrison to say a good word for another, and he knew Theodore Roosevelt better than most men. He pronounced him to be a forceful, energetic, and resourceful man of business; but what he most admired in Roosevelt was his indomitable courage. "He is forceful to the backbone" wrote Benjamin Harrison of

Roosevelt. . . . "there are many who believe that he is too aggressive, but Mr. Roosevelt makes strength of character an object. To him it is the deed and not the word; the American people love a man who does things. They love a man of capability and honesty. Theodore Roosevelt is better known to every man, woman, and child, because he has always won his fights in the open, and not by secret scheming and combining with the opposition." This is a remarkable tribute from one man to another. But we like best to think of Roosevelt to-day as our brother man; as the true lover of peace and fraternity. Herein we see him at his best. It was the fraternal element of his character that made him the peacemaker between Russia and Japan, that won for him the Nobel Peace Prize, and that enabled him to perform one of the most splendid services ever rendered to the cause of international peace.

As we have tried to estimate William McKinley, Abraham Lincoln, and George Washington by their own words, so would we like to measure the strength and character of the ex-President of the United States by the following notable passage from his own pen:—

Finally, remember to stand for both the ideal and the practical. Remember that you must have a lofty ideal as Abraham Lincoln had, and that you must try to achieve it in practical ways as he tried to achieve it during the four years that he lived and worked and suffered for the people, until his sad, patient, kindly soul was sent to seek its Maker. Remember, also, that you can do your duty as citizens in this country only if you are imbued through and through with the spirit of brotherhood; the spirit that we call Americanism. You can do no permanent good unless you feel, not only in theory, but also in practice, that fundamentally we are knit together by close ties,—the closest ties,—the ties of morality, of fellow feeling and sympathy, in its broadest and deepest sense. We cannot live permanently as a republic; we cannot hold our own as the mightiest commonwealth of self-governing free men upon which the sun has ever shone, unless we have it ground into our souls that we know no class, no section; that east, west, north and south, our people, whatever may be their occupations, whatever their conditions in life, stand shoulder to shoulder, striving for honesty, for decency, for all the fundamental virtues and morals that make good American citizenship.

It was the passionate love of Wendell Phillips for all things manly, fair, and beautiful that made him the true nature's nobleman he was, and gave him such a supreme mastery over the minds and hearts of his hearers. It was his intense fraternity, embodied in golden words, which made his presence and his speech irresistible. What was said of John Knox can truthfully be affirmed concerning Wendell Phillips:—"He never feared the face of man." The oratory of Phillips displayed the polish of a Burke and the fire of a Webster. His patriotism blazed in almost every word; and he yielded to no man in love of the American banner. His manhood had the strength of the lion and yet the gentleness of the lamb; but the best of Lincoln, the best of Jefferson, and the best of Washington, was also the best of Wendell Phillips, the kindly attitude of the man to all ranks and races; and perhaps he never uttered nobler words than these:—

I believe in the possibility of justice, in the certainty of union. Years hence, when the smoke of this conflict clears away, the world will see under our banner all tongues, all creeds, all races, one brotherhood, and on the banks of the Potomac the Genius of Liberty, robed in light, four and thirty stars for her diadem, broken chains under her feet, and an olive branch in her right hand.

Thus did Wendell Phillips predict the "one brotherhood" of a day to come; and it is with such courageous heart and tongue that men like him have appealed to great audiences and swayed them as great tempests sweep the ocean billows. With such words of brotherhood did Washington, Jefferson, Lincoln and Webster move their countrymen to deeds of love and glory, to achievements of kindness and fraternity. In such words, and in such a spirit, have the best of the American poets sung their songs of freedom and patriotism, of liberty and independence. In such strong and kindly voices have Longfellow and Lowell, Halpine and Stoddard, Whittier and Whitman given to the world the inspiriting melody of their immortal verse. Theirs has been in speech, in song and in story the voice of true comradeship, the song of best brotherhood; theirs the glad and sympathetic note which has cheered many a gloomy pathway, lightened many a heavy burden, and banished the clouds of darkest sorrows. These voices of American brotherhood have helped men to win great victories in the struggle of life, and given heart and hope to many a despairing wayfarer. They have nerved the soldier in the long and dreary march and the sailor in his silent watches on the lonely deep. They have comforted the pioneer and the missionary in their weary marches through home and foreign lands; and they have enabled men and women to fight more bravely than ever for their country and their country's flag. American fraternity has inspired the spirit and the song of Memorial and Decoration Days, and recalled memories which have made beautiful the lives of departed soldier and sailor. American fraternity has been a shield and refuge to the oppressed and the afflicted; it has been a wall of fire around the widow and the orphan. It has presented object-lessons of love and tenderness to the nation's millions. It has taught men and women the wisdom of forethought and thrift, and the noblest lessons of family life. American fraternity has helped to burst the shackles of slavery; it has made the heart of the captive leap for joy, and throb with abounding gratitude to his deliverer. It has brought to the forsaken and disconsolate glad memories of home and fatherland. It has com-

pelled men to do their best and bravest in the hour of
peril and danger, and reminded them of the words con-
tained in the national motto: "In God We Trust." It
has also impressed upon the American people the true
meaning of that message of comradeship which inspired
the American poet Charles G. Halpine to write these
noble lines :—

> Comrades known in marches many,
> Comrades tried in dangers many,
> Comrades bound by memories many,
>   Brothers ever let us be.
> Wounds or sickness may divide us,
> Marching orders may divide us,
> But whatever fate betide us,
>   Brothers of the heart are we.
>
> Comrades known by faith the clearest,
> Tried when death was near and nearest,
> Bound we are by ties the dearest,
>   Brothers ever more to be.
> And if spared, and growing older
> Shoulder still in line with shoulder,
> And with hearts no thrill the colder,
>   Brothers ever we shall be.
>
> By communion of the banner,
> Crimson, white, and starry banner,
> By the baptism of the banner,
>   Children of one church are we.
> Creed nor faction can divide us
> Race nor language can divide us,
> Still, whatever fate betide us,
>   Children of the Flag are we.

ORIGIN OF FRATERNAL BENEFIT SOCIETIES

BY C. H. ROBINSON

Long before the dawn of history it was the custom of our savage and barbarous ancestors of the Teutonic, Celtic, and Gothic tribes, to indulge in funeral feasts, which often became wild orgies. The shadow of these primitive conditions remains in the "wake" for the dead, still observed to some extent.

Some historians have formulated the theory that as the tribes became more intelligent and civilization advanced, these feasts, by process of evolution, became gilds in the nature of burial clubs, which, again, in the centuries of advancement, took on the features of benefit societies, substituting instead of the wild feast for the dead, a provision for his decent burial, and a donation to his dependent family.

Others have attempted to trace the origin of Fraternals to the Roman burial societies, which certainly existed as early as the reign of the Emperor Hadrian, 117 to 128, A. D.; thence down through the trades gilds which flourished throughout Christian Europe in the Middle Ages, and which, it is claimed, have had their final development in the Friendly Societies of England and the Fraternal Benefit Associations of America.

For my own part, I am inclined to believe that such societies of the present day owe their origin neither to the funeral feasts of the savages, the burial clubs of the Romans, nor the trades gilds of the Middle Ages, but are of pure Anglo-Saxon origin, and arose from the same self-governing spirit which prompted the early organization of "Hundreds," the "Wiggengamote" and the Town Council composed of elders or aldermen. This spirit has been characteristic of the Teutonic peoples from the earliest times.

So long as the only social organization of the community was that of the tribe and family, man's need for co-operation in securing his safety, his relief in case of misfortune and his decent burial at death, was satisfied by the family and tribal customs and laws; but, as the tribes separated; as the Saxons, Angles and Jutes in England became commingled by blood and association with the conquered Danes, Britons and others who had preceded them as inhabitants of the country, the tribal governments were broken up and family relations dissolved by the dispersal of the original families, and ties of actual kinship could no longer dominate the community. There were still, however, wants, social and economic and, to supply these, artificial kinships in the nature of sworn brotherhoods soon began to be organized; and these subsequently developed into Gilds with rules for contributions and for benefits.

Of the organization of the earliest of these brotherhoods or Gilds, no record has come down to our day, but it is certain that they existed in great numbers before there was a King of England, for they are recognized as established institutions in the books which contain the oldest of the relics of the English laws.

The laws of Alfred the Great; of Ina, Athelstan, and Henry I., reproduce still older laws, the origin of which is lost in the mists of the past, but in the laws of these kings the existence of the Gilds is treated as a well known fact, and, in them it is taken, as a matter of course, that every one belonged to some Gild.

In their inception, most of the Gilds were no doubt merely for conviviality and good fellowship. Social intercourse, however, almost invariably enlarges the human sympathies. The men who met together simply to crack

jokes and sing songs over their beer, began gradually to
feel some interest in the happiness and prosperity of each
other. If one of their number suffered affliction, the
charitable impulses of his more fortunate brethren were
stimulated by the discussion that naturally grew out of
the case; and not merely sympathy, but substantial pecun-
iary assistance was early afforded; and thus, by progres-
sive steps from humble beginnings, the great Friendly
Societies of England and the Fraternal Insurance Organ-
izations of America have been developed.

These societies have done so much for their members
by the benefits conferred in sickness; by increasing their
self-respect and independence; by death benefits paid to
widows and orphans, thus decreasing the expenditures of
public charity, and by general fraternal help, that they
now have very strong claims upon the community whose
interests they have so largely promoted.

To suggest some of the evidence on which is based
the opinion of the writer that the English Gilds are of
pure Anglo-Saxon origin, and that they were the progen-
itors of our modern Friendly Societies and Fraternal
Insurance Orders, is the object of this paper. In its com-
pilation I have been greatly indebted for the historical
facts to the following authors: Mr. Toumlin Smith,
whose work on the History of English Gilds, now out of
print, I was so fortunate as to secure in London; Mr. E.
W. Brabrook, former Chief Registrar of Friendly Socie-
ties, in his book entitled "Provident Societies and Indus-
trial Welfare;" and to the Friendly Societies Manual by
Mr. Charles Hardwick. From all these works, as the best
authorities on the subject to which I have had access, I
have necessarily made lengthy quotations.

While, as stated before, the commencement of the
earliest gilds is lost in the dimness of the past, and remains
quite unknown; some very early ones have left records of

their rules and customs which are available to the delver after origins. Indeed, the evidences of these societies in the old English (Anglo-Saxon) times, convincingly proves that the principle of association for mutual help in the affairs of life—commonly but mistakenly thought to be modern—is found, in name and in fact, in the English laws of nearly 1,200 years ago. It existed then, and has since continued a very living spirit in England and America, through all the changes of age and circumstance, to the present time, and this spirit bids fair to greatly enlarge the scope of its beneficiary operations for the future.

Among the laws of Ina, a Saxon king who reigned from 688 to 725 A. D., are two touching the liability of the brethren of a Gild in the case of the killing of a thief. Among those of Athelstan whose reign extended from 924 to 940, A. D., may be found the following: "And we have also ordained respecting every man who has given his 'wed' (meaning initiation oath), in our Gildships, if he should die, that each gild-brother shall give a fine loaf for his soul, and sing fifty psalms, or get them sung, within thirty days." The loaves of bread thus contributed were sold and the proceeds used to pay the priests for saying masses and singing psalms for the repose of the dead. In those days all social organizations were also deeply religious in character, and the rules of all the early societies provided for attendance upon religious worship on the part of the members, and for procuring prayers for the souls of those who should die. The chaplains of many of the societies were regularly ordained priests, and it is curious to notice that while the members might drink beer in unlimited quantities, and their meetings were usually occasions for this, in many societies the rules prohibited the Chaplain of the Gild from frequenting public houses.

The constitution of the Gild of Exter, which existed

in Anglo-Saxon times is given in Turner's History of the Anglo-Saxon as follows: "This assembly was collected in Exter, for the love of God, and for our soul's need, both in regard to our life here, and to after days, which we desire for ourselves by God's doom. Now we have agreed that our meetings shall be thrice in the twelve months; once at St. Michael's Mass, the second at the time of St. Mary's Mass, after mid-winter, and the third time on All-Hallows Mass-day after Easter. And let each Gild-brother have two sesters of malt (otherwise beer), and a sceat of honey. And let the mass-priest (Gild chaplain), sing two masses, one for living friends, the other for the departed; and at the death of a brother each man sing six masses or six psalters of psalms, and at death a five-pence. At a house-burning, each man one penny. If any one neglect the day, for the first time three masses, for the second five, and for the third time let him have no favor, unless his neglect arose from sickness or his lord's need. If any one "misgreet" another (call him names), let him make "boot" (amends) with thirty pence. Now we pray for the love of God that every man hold this meeting as we have rightly agreed upon, God help us thereunto."

The word Gild is of Saxon origin, and one of its meanings was "a rate payment;" later it came to mean a payment in money, from which we have the word "gold." This shows that a regular payment of dues was required by these societies at a very early time.

All the gilds, whether religious, social or trades, rested upon another solemn principle; they were sworn brotherhoods between man and man, established and fortified by a solemn oath or pledge, which was the "wed." The obligation taken by a candidate for admission in a modern fraternal is the survival of the ancient wed or pledge of brotherhood.

The fraternal order of to-day is then a lineal descendant of the Social Gild, which was founded upon the wide basis of brotherly love, mutual aid and moral comeliness without distinction as to calling or class, while the trades unions are probably the off-spring of the merchant or trade gilds, which were of much later origin.

A noticeable fact in the history of the Social Gilds is, that nearly all of them admitted to membership both men and women, showing the early recognition of the equality of the sexes in such societies, and it is stated that a candidate, after being obligated, was saluted by all the members with a kiss of peace. The participation of the ladies in this doubtless rendered this part of the initiation less monotonous than the present adjournment of the lodge for a few minutes that the brethren may shake hands with the new member, but the modern custom is doubtless a survival of the kiss of peace salutation.

These ancient societies also had an initiation fee, but it varied greatly in kind and amount. The Gild of St. Benedict required six shillings eight-pence, about $1.70 of our money, but as money had then more than three times its present purchasing power, the actual fee in present coin value, was more than $5.00. St. George's Gild of Norwich had six shillings eight-pence for men and three shillings four-pence for a woman. In that of Stretham, every newcomer was required to pay two pounds of wax and a bushel of barley. The dues were paid weekly, monthly or quarterly as the rules might require, and no member was entitled to any privileges or benefits while his dues were delinquent. In addition to the dues and membership fees as sources of income, it was quite common for wealthy members to make donations or to leave the society a sum by will; indeed, in some of the societies the member obligated himself to bequeath something to the Gild, if he made a will at all.

These gilds held regular weekly, monthly or quarterly meetings besides an annual Gild-day, when the brethren and "sistern," clad in their hoods or "livery," assembled at the church bearing lights, which then played a conspicuous part in all ceremonies whether religious or civic, and there made the prayers for the dead enjoined by their rules, and to consecrate by these acts of faith that brotherly love and peace which they were sworn to cherish. After making their offerings they went their way; perhaps to a "morn-speech" or meeting at which the Gild-boox would be audited and the money in the "Box" inspected, or, if this were not the custom, they met in good fellowship at the Gild-house around the festive board.

The practical mutual charity of the gild-spirit may be seen in the way they expended their funds. Care for the fitting burial of deceased members at the cost of the Gild was constantly taken. Help to the poor, the sick, the infirm and the aged, is shown by their records; assistance to members who suffered losses or robbery, and to those overtaken by misfortune, if this were not through their own fault or mismanagement, were prominent features in their rules. Weekly payments to poor and unfortunate members are frequently specified in their records. Sometimes such were to be visited, and they were frequently entertained at the houses of their more wealthy brethren. In some cases loans of money were made from the Box or treasury, upon security; in others, free loans or gifts are recorded as made to young members of either sex to enable them to travel in search of employment; and in the Ludlow Gild, the rules provided that on her marriage "any good girl of the Gild" should have a certain marriage portion given to her from the Box, if her father were unable to provide it. Also brethren who were cast into prison were to be visited and aided to get free.

Their charities were not always confined to their members. The Gild-merchant of Coventry "kept a lodging house with thirteen beds" to lodge poor travelers, and the governor or matron were to wash the feet of the guests. In the Lincoln Gild it was provided by the rules that "on Gild-day as many poor persons as there were brothers and sisters in the Gild were to be fed with ale, bread and fish or meat." Sometimes the gild funds were used to repair roads or churches.

Many of the early societies had uniforms or "liveries" which must be worn by the members on Gild-days or in public processions.

Each Gild was, for the most part, confined to a single town or city, and in government they were, therefore, democratic; the rules being adopted or changed and the funds disposed of by a majority vote of the members. The presiding and other officers were chosen by ballot on Gild-day of each year, and, any refusing to serve were fined. No one was admitted to membership unless of good character, and, "if a member became a brawler or thief," he was expelled. They also encouraged industry. One Gild had this rule: "If any man, being of good state (in good health) and use hym to ly long in bed, and at rising of his bed he will ne (not) work, ne (nor) keep his house (support his family), and shall go to the tavern to wyne, to ale, to the wrasling (wrestling), or to the scheating (skating), and in this manner falleth poor, and left his catell in defaut for succor (will not properly feed his domestic animals) and wish to be holpen (helped) by the fraternity; that man shall never have good, ne (nor) help of the companie, neither in this life, ne (nor) at his death: (No masses shall be said or psalms sung for his soul,) but shall be put off forevermore of the companie."

One brother was not allowed to "belie" or wrong another; if he did he was fined by the Gild. Unruly

speech at the meetings was forbidden and peaceable and
civil conduct at the feasts strictly enjoined. If a dispute
should arise between one brother and another, it was the
duty of all the members to do what they could "to bring
them at one" (reconcile them), and induce them to settle
the quarrel; and not until this was tried by the Council
of Conciliation, could the disputants go to law.

As to what we call ritualistic or secret work, there is
little trace of it in the earlier times, although the use of
uniforms or liveries, and the enacting of plays or pageants
on Gild-days, seems to anticipate its introduction. It is
more than probable that emblematic initiations, signs,
grips, etc., were adopted later after the societies had
spread to more than one town, for the two-fold purpose
of rendering the initiations more impressive, and to pro
tect such gilds from imposters. They were probably bor-
rowed or imitated from one or more of the orders of chiv-
alry, the Masons, or some of the numerous secret societies
which sprang up all over Europe after the Crusades. A
recent writer describing an initiation into what is now one
of the most prominent of the Friendly Societies, says:
"The candidate for membership, a hundred years ago, on
being led to the ante-room, was carefully blindfolded and
after passing the outer and inner guard, he felt a peculiar
awe steal over his senses, in consequence of the solemn
and death-like silence which at the time prevailed. Soon
his perverted sense of hearing became fearfully awakened
by the rattling of huge iron chains and the unmeaning
sound of men's voices. In this stage of the initiation; that
is provided he was not tossed and tumbled about among
brush-wood, or soused over head in a large tub of water,
the bandage was removed from his eyes, and the first
object that caught his visual organs was the point of a
naked sword close to his heart. As soon as he could with.
draw his attention from the Worthy Warden and his

blade, his eyes rested upon a large transparency of Old Mortality, whose ghastly grin would be enough to freeze the warm blood in his veins, while every part of the room was filled with symbols of both holy and profane things, the meaning of which but few could explain. The dresses of the officers were in keeping with the rest of the mummery. The ceremony being over, each member pledged the newly initiated brother in a brimming glass for which the new brother had the honor of paying. (Suggests the eleven cents of the Buffaloes, does it not?) Momus now presided, and the deep wrought fears of the novice were soon drowned in the loud laugh, or the boisterous chorus of a Bacchanalian song."

The same writer says that all this mummery has long been abandoned by the reputable orders, and rational advice substituted in its stead.

My subject is by no means exhausted. I might occupy your time for an hour or more in reproducing here the unique and often amusing rules for the transaction of business; for the conduct of members; for the accumula tion and disbursement of funds; the quaint character of the benefits sometimes paid; their odd liveries or uniforms, and the humorous or pathetic records found in the minutes of the meetings of these old time ancestors of our societies, but a consideration of the time which may properly be used in the presentation of a historical paper of this character, warns me to omit further details.

I trust, however, that the historical facts which with some labor and pains I have collected for your entertainment may be of use to those who may wish to delve into the history of our societies for use in public or other addresses.

I trust also, that considering these old societies with their mutual aid; their benefits to members in sickness, old age and distress; their funeral or death benefits; the obligations administered to candidates at initiation; their requirement for the payment of an initiation fee; the collection of regular periodical dues; the suspension of benefits to a member while delinquent, and their general, although often grotesque similarity to the objects and methods of our own societies, will incline you all to agree with me, that both the English Friendly Societies and our own insurance orders are the natural outgrowth or evolution of the Social-Gilds of the Anglo-Saxon times.

THE ENDORSEMENT OF THE CHURCH *

TEXT—GENESIS XLI.

35. And let them gather all the food of those good years that come, and lay up corn under the hand of Pharaoh, and let them keep food in the cities.

36. And that food shall be for store to the land against the seven years of famine, which shall be in the land of Egypt, that the land perish not through the famine.

37. And the thing was good in the eyes of Pharaoh, and in the eyes of all his servants.

BRETHREN: The words of my text were the words of Joseph, the president of the first life insurance company the world ever saw. Pharaoh had a dream that distracted him. He thought he stood on the banks of the river Nile and saw coming up out of the river seven fat, sleek, glossy cows, and they began to browse in the thick grass. Nothing frightful about that. But after them, coming up out of the same river, he saw seven cows that were gaunt and starved, and the worst look-

---

* The Rev. T. DeWitt Talmage, who died April 12, 1902, delivered a sermon on making provision for the future which should be handed down to coming generations alike as a guide to action and a warning against improvidence.

ing cows that had ever been seen in the land; and in their ferocity of hunger they devoured their seven predecessors.

Pharaoh, the king, sent for Joseph to decipher these midnight hieroglyphics. Joseph made short work of it, and intimated that the seven fat cows that came out of the river were seven years with plenty to eat; the seven emaciated cows that followed were seven years with nothing to eat. "Now," said Joseph, "let us take one-fifth of the corn crop of the seven prosperous years, and keep it as a provision for the seven years in which there shall be no crop."

The king took counsel, and appointed Joseph, because of his integrity and public spiritedness, as the president of the undertaking. The farmers paid one-fifth of their income as a premium. In all the towns and cities there were branch houses. This great Egyptian life insurance company had millions of dollars of assets. After a while the dark days came, and the whole nation would have starved if it had not been for the provision they had made for the future. But now these suffering families have nothing to do but go up and collect the amount of their life policies. The Bible puts it in one short phrase: "In all the land of Egypt there was bread." I say this was the first life insurance company. It was divinely organized. It had in it all the advantages of the "whole life plan," of the "tontine plan," of the "endowment plan," and all the other good plans.

We are told that Rev. Dr. Anhate of Lincolnshire, England, originated the first life insurance company in 1688. No; it is as old as the corn cribs of Egypt, and God himself was the author and originator. If that were not so I would not take your time and mind in a Sabbath discussion of this subject. I feel it is a theme vital, religious, and of infinite import—the morals of life and fire

insurance. It seems to me that it is time for the pulpit to
speak out. But what does the Bible say in regard to the
subject? If the Bible favors the institution, I will favor
it; if the Bible denounces it, I will denounce it. In addi-
tion to the forecast of Joseph in the text, I call your atten-
tion to Paul's comparison. Here is one man who, through
neglect, fails to support his family while he lives or after
he dies. Here is another man who abhors the Scriptures
and rejects God. Which of these men are the worst?
Well, you say the latter. Paul said the former. Paul
says the man who neglects to care for his household is
more obnoxious than a man who rejects the Scriptures.
*"He that provideth not for his own, and especially those
of his own household, is worse than an infidel."*

Life insurance companies help most of us to provide
for our families after we are gone. But if we have the
money to pay premiums and neglect it, we have no right
to expect mercy at the hand of God in the judgment. We
are worse than Tom Paine, worse than Voltaire, and
worse than Shaftsbury. The Bible declares it; we are
worse than an infidel. After the certificate of death is
made out, and the thirty or sixty days has passed and the
officer of a life insurance company comes into the bereft
household and pays down the hard cash on an insurance
policy, that officer is performing a positively religious rite,
according to the Apostle James, who says: "True religion
and undefiled before God and the Father is this: to visit
the fatherless and the widow in their affliction."

When men think of their death they are apt to think
of it only in connection with their spiritual welfare, and
not of the devastation in the household which will come
because of their emigration from it. It is meanly selfish
for you to be so absorbed in the heaven to which you are
going that you forget what is to become of your wife and
children after you go. How can you go out of this world,

not leaving them a dollar and yet die happy? You can trust them in the hands of the God who owns all the harvests and the herds and the flocks, but if you could not pay the small premium on a policy, and thus insure their comfort for years after your departure, what kind of a reception can you hope for among the Father's elect? *"He that provideth not for his own, and especially those of his own household, is worse than an infidel."*

The great indifference of many people on this important subject accounts for much of the crime and pauperism of this day. Who are these children sweeping the crossings with broken brooms and begging of you a penny as you go by? Who are these lost souls gliding under the gaslights in thin shawls? Ah! they are the victims of want, and in many of the cases the foresight of the parents and grandparents might have prevented it. God only knows how they struggled to do right! They prayed until the tears froze on their cheeks; they sewed on the sack until the breaking of the day, but they could not get enough money to pay the rent, they could not get enough money to clothe themselves decently; and one day in that wretched home the angel of purity and the angel of crime fought a great fight between the empty bread tray and the fireless hearth and the black-winged angel shrieked, "Aha! I have won the day."

Say some men, "I believe what you say—it is right and Christian, and I mean sometime to attend to this matter." My friend, you are going to lose the comfort of your household in the way the sinner loses heaven— by procrastination. The sky is clear and the sea is placid to-day, but how will it be to-morrow? Do you know if you are strong enough to weather a gale? I see all around me the destitute and suffering families of parents who meant some day to attend to this Christian duty. But on a rainy day the man of the household gets his feet wet; then comes a chill, and a delirium, and the doleful shake of the doctor's head, and the obsequies. If there be anything more pitiable than a woman, delicately brought up, and on her marriage day by an indulgent father given to a man to whom she is the chief joy and pride of life until the moment of his death, and then that same woman going out with helpless children at her back to struggle for bread in a world where brawny muscle and rugged soul are necessary—I say, if there be anything more pitiable than that, I don't know what it is.

And yet there are good women who are indifferent in regard to their husband's duty in this respect. And there are those positively hostile, as though a life insurance subjected a man to some fatality. There is in this city to-day a poor woman keeping a small candy shop, who vehemently opposed the insurance of her husband's life, and when application had been made for a policy of $10,000 she frustrated it. She would never have a document in the house that implied it was possible for her husband ever to die. One day his life was instantly dashed out. What is the sequel? She is with annoying tug making the half of a miserable living. Her two children have been taken away from her in order that they may be clothed and schooled, and her life has become a prolonged hardship.

Oh, man! before forty-eight hours have passed away appear at the desk of one of our great life insurance companies, have the stethoscope of the physician put to your heart and lungs, and, by the seal of some honest company, decree that your children shall not be subjected to the humiliation of financial struggle in the dark days of your demise!

It is a mean thing for you to go up to heaven while they go to the poor house. You, at death, move into a mansion river front; and they move into two rooms on the fourth story of a tenement house in a back street. When they are out at elbows and knees the thought of your splendid robe in heaven will not keep them warm. The minister may preach a splendid sermon over your remains, and the quartet may sing like four angels in the organ loft; but your death will be a swindle.

You had the means to provide for the comfort of your household when you left it, and you wickedly neglected it.

"Oh," says some one, "I have more faith than you; I believe when I go out of this world the Lord will take care of my family." Yes, he will provide for them. Go to Blackwell's Island; go through all the poorhouses of the country, and I will show you how God often provides for the neglected children of neglectful parents—that is, he provides for them through public charity. As for myself, I would rather have the Lord provide for my family in a private home, and through my own industry and paternal and conjugal faithfulness.

"But," say some men, "I mean in the next ten or twenty years to make a great fortune, and so I shall leave my family, when I go out of this world, very comforta ble." How do you know you are going to live ten or twenty years? If we could look up the walk of the future we would see it crossed by pneumonias, and pleurisies, and consumptions, and colliding trains, and runaway horses, and breaking bridges, and funeral processions. Are you so certain that you are going to live ten or twenty years that you can warrant your household any comfort after you go away from them?

Besides that, the vast majority of men die poor. Only two out of a hundred succeed in business. Are you certain that you are going to be one of the two? There are men who die solvent who are insolvent before they get under the ground, or before their estate is settled. How soon the auctioneer's mallet can knock the life out of an estate? A man thinks the property worth $15,000. Under a forced sale it brings $7,000. The business man takes advantage of the crisis, and he compels the widow of his deceased partner to sell out to him at a ruinous price or lose all; or the administrator is ordered by the surrogate to wind up the whole affair. The estate was supposed at the man's death to be worth $20,000; but after the indebtedness has been met, and the bills of the doctor and the undertaker and the tombstone cutter have been paid, there is nothing left.

That means the children are to come home from school and go to work.

That means the complete hardship of the wife—turned out with nothing but a needle to fight the great battle of the world. Tear down the lambrequins, close the piano, rip up the axminster, sell out the wardrobe and let the mother take a child in each hand and trudge out into the desert of the world! A life insurance would have hindered all that.

A PYTHIAN ADDRESS

GEORGE B. GRIGGS

Man is a social as well as a selfish being. He is both vicious and virtuous. Vice and virtue were innate with his creation, and have ever been the fountain from which flowed the necessities, desires and fancies of the human race. Necessity gave birth to secrecy—virtue to fraternal organization.

If history be true, the first organization of secret societies antedates the birth of Christ, and perhaps the very inception of historic literature. The early periods of secret fraternalism were sorely pressed by the galling yoke of Church and State. The Church, over all, was supreme. Kings and monarchs trembled at her command. To carry a secret within one's bosom was a sin against the priestly power. The Church assumed absolute control, not only of men's temporal conduct, but also of their destiny beyond the grave.

It was decreed by a kind Providence that right and justice should prevail and, with all the combined, opposing powers of Church and State, there grew into the hearts and soul of men a mystic fraternalism that lived and prospered within the very shadows of the Church, and even entwined itself, like creeping ivy upon a deserted castle, around the very thrones of mighty kings.

Around the mystic shrines of fraternalism were promulgated the sciences, philosophy and human happiness. From those shrines emanated teachings of a higher order —teachings that have made men and women better, purer, noble and truer, paving the way to freedom of thought.

While those secret and fraternal societies were paving the way for freedom of thought and speech, civil and religious liberty, the Church and State were inventing the wheel and rack for the torture and death of the citizen who dared to be free. Overarched by despotism, the silver star of human liberty could not be seen in the smoky heavens of blighted hope. Every manifestation of intellectual thought was suppressed, and every pure conception of human accord was bedimmed by the breath of priestly power. I call to witness the generations of time that the ancient political and religious powers have been the strongest prisons, the most tyrannical sovereigns and the most cruel prisoners of the mind and soul of man.

Hoary time holds in its hands the history of ages gone; when war was the occupation of nations; when the citizen was the soldier; when the scientist was the prisoner;

when the religious thinker was the heretic, and when poetry was the song of victors and triumphant marches.

No longer do men cherish such love of war, nor are they given to such boastings of victory. Universal strife is giving away to universal brotherhood. When the Goddess of Liberty weeps, the English lion moans and the German Eagle droops its head in sorrow. The walls of ancient cities are transformed into temples of learning, and the battleships of nations into commercial conveyances.

But what has brought about this wonderful change? What is the cause? Can the force or power which has wrought this change be any of the vices of mankind? Where may we find the key that unlocked the doors to this glorious transformation?

Come with me. Let us go back, back, back through the flight of centuries into the mystic ages, long before the manger of Bethlehem was a cradle. Here is the ancient Syracuse, the capitol of that beautiful Sicilian island in the Mediterranean Sea. Syracuse is in all her glory,—war and strife are the only virtues—chaos reigns within her walls, and human blood flows in her streets like the tides of the restless sea. Here we find, in this charnel house of crime, vice and misrule, the living example of the virtues that have brought about this wonderful transformation, this change in the conditions of the world. It is the example of the friendship between Damon and Pythias.

Damon was a senator, Pythias a soldier, in Syracuse. They had been schoolmates and boys together. For some supposed conspiracy against the throne King Dionysius decreed that Damon should die. Damon pleaded to be permitted to see his wife and child before his death, but the request was refused. Pythias, the childhood companion of the doomed man, begged the tyrant to grant the request of Damon, and offered himself as a hostage and a pledge for Damon's return. Listen to his pleading: "Let Damon go and see his wife and child before he dies. Put me in chains, place me in his dun geon as pledge for his return, and let me die if he do not return."

Standing there at the foot of the throne, in prophetic vision, Pythias glanced down the winding corridors of time and saw tyrant and monarch replace tyrant and monarch. He also saw a beautiful garland of friendship slowly evolving itself into a mighty scepter of power, rising higher and higher, only to strike a shattering blow to the thrones of the old world. He saw the selfishness of man slowly melting away from the hearts of men and nations, and the dawn of a glorious, fraternal concord in all things. He saw an age of universal peace, when war would become arbitration, and when poetry would be the song of civilization, sung by a united world to the cadence of free thought and free speech. Cheered by this vision, he begs the tyrant to grant the request. Hear him:

"As thou art a husband and father, hear me; for four hours respite Damon. Do but this, and may the gods build up thy greatness as high as their own heavens."

The respite was granted, and Pythias was taken as pledge for Damon's return. When the hour of execution arrived, Damon had not returned. The excited mob now taunt Pythias with the seeming falseness of his friend, but he would not hear their taunts. Proclaiming the fidelity of Damon, Pythias turns to his executioners, to meet his fate. At the last moment, as the headsman's axe is raised to strike the fatal blow, Pythias rushes into the scene, and saves his friend. The shouts of derision from the crowd were now turned to praise of the mystic tie of friendship that bound these two friends. The tyrant looked on in wonderment and, as he looked, the cruel purpose of the hour passed away, and Damon's life was spared. To this glorious example of friendship the ages have looked with fondest admiration, radiating from behind the prison walls of old Syracuse, down through the centuries, like a beacon light, revealing such unbounded faith, such unparalleled friendship, such remarkable fidelity, it still beams upon the pathway of mankind, leading to a better and more peaceful life.

That example of a virtue is the kind that has crumbled the thrones of the old world. It is that kind of virtue that makes our lives happy and our homes bright. May kind Providence speed the day when true friendship shall sit as a monarch upon his throne in the heart of every man, guiding, ruling and directing his life.

CHARITY

Friendship carries with it an element of charity and benevolence. Charity, as taught by our fraternal orders, is charity toward the frailties of human nature. True it is, that this virtue is more preached than practiced—more admired than preached. It is a virtue that is calculated to soften the hearts of men and mellow the asperities of human nature. It is the substratum of philanthropy, the main pillar of earthly felicity—the brightest star in the Christian's diadem—the connecting link in the golden chain that reaches from earth to heaven. It spurns the scrofula of green-eyed jealousy—the canker of self-tormenting envy—the typhoid of boiling revenge—the cholera of damning ingratitude. It is the sunbeam of living light which sheds its rays into the wilderness of man's perverted nature, evangelizing and fraternizing him and crowning him with simple love and good will for all mankind.

BENEVOLENCE

Benevolence, coupled with friendship and charity, forms the grandest triune of all the other virtues possessed by man. Benevolence is the celestial quality of one's nature, imparting to the giver consolation, and instilling in the recipient the most sacred gratitude of the soul. It falls like the dews of heaven upon the withered flower, invigorating the better nature of man, and calling forth an approving smile of heaven. Benevolence never opens, but rather heals, the gaping wounds of misfortune; never ruffles, but rather calms, the troubled heart.

What are these three great virtues, and why do I mention them? They are the foundation stones upon which rests the noble structure of Pythianism, and because our membership is required to practice these virtues. In this society, every member is bound by a sacred vow to a recognition of these virtues and to their practice and culture. This very night thousands of men and women are being inspired by these vows to nobler and better lives. What myriad choirs; what hosts of orators; what hallelujas; what marching throngs; what bands of music would be required to proclaim the honor or to shout the glory that is justly due to the promulgators and doers of this great good in the wicked world about us!

THE ORDER

The great order of Knights of Pythias is a secret, fraternal organization. Upon the three great virtues heretofore mentioned, the structure is reared. Within its walls there is no room for hostility nor enmity. It is a society of peace and good will, and its members are ever mindful of the blessedness of peace-making. When hostility enters a mans' heart there is no room for a Pythian virtue. Such a man is cruelly disturbed and is filled with a score of passions—hate, canker, enmity, ingratitude, all breed ing a tornado of maddened action—a whirlwind of impul sive passion that unfits him to bear the name of brother.

The Order, being founded upon those three great vir tues, seeks to impress upon the minds and instill into the

hearts of its members the beauty and the benefits of a
truly Pythian life—of being noble, brave, and true to
every trust imposed, morally, socially or otherwise. It
teaches its members to be industrious, sober, reliable, and
upright in all the walks of life. It teaches and commands
confidence in a brother—forbids the slanderous tongue
to malign. It demands that men shall respect the virtue
of women, and protect the family of a brother as he would
his own. It teaches men to be good husbands, fathers and
citizens.

He who has learned through Pythianism to be honest,
brave and true, is the most happy man. If we but live
truly Pythian lives, then let come old age or death, they
will each come as the beautiful, rich autumn after a glor-
ious summer. Aye, if the heart has been truly pure, it
will have learned that there is something better beyond
this vale of tears. Faith will have grown into our lives
as the blossom upon the bud, and as the flower upon the
slowly lifting stem.

SENTIMENT AND LIFE INSURANCE

BY MOORE SANBORN

The strongest thing in the world is a true sentiment.
Mountains can not hem it in, dykes can not stop its flow-
ing, distance can not long separate it from its goal of
good. It is a leaven of civilization, and at the same time
a lever lifting the world. Egotistic, practical people, who
sneer at sentiment as a jelly-like something quivering in
a lake of tears, are bias brained, with stigmatic eyes and
logic askew.

All history, rightly read, reveals the triumph of sentiment wherever man has trod the bloody way. Conscious or sub-conscious, it has stirred in silence, or at times in storm in all the variant ways of life where man has struggled upward. The love of God—a sentiment—has inspired all the religions of the world. The love of country—a sentiment—has written all the heroic annals of patriotism. The love of our fellows—a sentiment—has pushed all doctrines of the rights of man, all flowering beauties of educational effort and sociological endeavor, up into the sunlight. The love of home, of wife and weans, of father and mother—sentiments all—are the dynamos of the common and countless sacrifices, heroisms and struggles which sublime and transfigure human life.

No man ever traveled far—except downward—without some splendid sentiment nesting at the core of his being, driving him on and ever on. No member of the so-called sentimental sex ever existed, save in some foul shape like Milton's Portress of Hell,

> Which seemed a woman to the waist, and fair,
> But ended there, with many a scaly fold,
> Voluminous and vast.

who did not live by sentiment as surely as by oxygen.

The power of every living romance; the strength of every deathless song; the beauty of every great poem; the exaltation of every noble life lies in its expression of some sentiment and the world will not willingly let die. Look upon one of the great masterpieces of an artist— sentiment wielded the brush and mixed the colors for its creator. Read a great book upon whose pages the play and passion of human aspiration is portrayed, and you will know that sentiment gripped the thought of him who wrote it. Study the story of a great man's career—let it be that of Washington or Lincoln, whom all the world honors, if you please—and before you have ended, his personality shall be seen as saturated with a sentiment close of kin to the sacred. We sometimes boast that ours is a practical age, filled with the strident cries of commercialism, forgetting that those on whose shoulders we stand were moved by high and true sentiments as they planned and toiled for days and men unborn. More than this, we are so busy with our buying and selling, our getting and gaining, that we have no time to think how all that is best in our unmatched modern life is conserved and enlarged by the perpetuity of the sentiments dominating our ancestors. Gravitation is no more essential to the placing of the planets than right sentiment is to the stability of all that our race prizes as best and highest. The healthy optimism on which growth, progress, and power are predicated, is fed and sustained by sentiments stronger than steel and more enduring than brass.

SENTIMENT IS ALL-POWERFUL IN THE BEST BUSINESS

Life insurance has been called "the best business in the world," and it is so, if it is a business at all, because it is most completely infused by sentiment. Sentiment is its life blood, its eyes, its hands, its feet, its tongue, its thought.

Actuaries tables, legislation, plans and modes of application and operation, are only the staging about the real structure. To guard the home and those who dwell therein is the end and aim of all its work. To make sure provision for those we love, is the unselfish cause of its supply and demand. It has grown like religion and democracy to be an important factor in the world's work, because sentiment has focused so much of its power and beauty upon it. Its policy or certificate is the ripened product of sentiment as truly as were the Psalms of David, the Magna Charta, or Lincoln's Proclamation of Emancipation.

FRATERNALISM CONTRASTED WITH OLD-LINE INSURANCE

While it will be granted by all students of life insur_

ance that sentiment is the causative force behind all its phenomena of expansion, few of my readers probably will utter a ready "Amen" to the assertion that the province where it finds its finest and fullest fruition is in the fraternal beneficial societies. Commercial life insurance, as practiced by the companies usually termed "corporations for profit" could not have flourished, without a sense of the solidarity of mankind, as well as the desire to protect the dear and dependent from the wrinkling worries of want.

On these unshaken foundations their multiplied millions have been gathered. They have lamentably failed, however, to translate the spirit of the sentiments, to which they owe their being, into their work. Their officers have often been like kings, above the power of suffrage to reach them, and drawing their revenue from the people, never mixing with or knowing them. Their agents and managers usually pride themselves on being business men and, pursuing an occupation made possible by sentiments high and true, they spend their strength and time on ratios, dividends, and scores of other arguments as remote from the purpose of life insurance as the Equator is from the pole.

The tools with which they work, their literature and expressed ideals, are in the main as coldly commercial as the harvesting of ice on a Wisconsin lake. The spaces of the Seven Seas seem to separate their methods of work and their schemes for success from the warmth of personal interest and the transforming force of association to reach a common goal.

The life insurance company says to the public "Buy of me and I will pay," and it keeps its legal contract and *does no more; for those who pay its price.* A child of human brotherhood, it shows no disposition to honor its parentage, only so far as it is legally bound to do. It sells something a buyer needs, and considers its full duty ended when the goods are delivered. It is a business, not a social program, nor a flower of altruism.

Using the mathematics of mortality with scrupulous exactitude, it purchases expensive financial service, gath ers its millions, if sufficiently aggressive, becomes a power in the marts of money, planning and caring as little for the persons who purchase its policies as the railroads do for those who buy their tickets. Even in the mutual companies, in theory belonging to and operated by their policy holders, practically the same ideas and methods are followed as in stock companies, the only discernible difference being that in one an annual "slate" is elected by the use of a few proxies, and in the other by a few stockholders.

Policyholders expect nothing beyond the letter of their contracts, have no personal interest in the management of the company to which they pay their money, and frequently do not even take the trouble to remember its name.

THE VAST DEVELOPMENT OF FRATERNALISM

How different in all but cause are the fraternal societies, which in the brief period of two score years have grown to closely rival the far older companies in number of members, benefits scattered, and promises pledged. Within the coming decade, unless all signs fail, they will be doing more good, even when measured by the standard of dollars and cents, than the legal reserve companies with their world wide operations and their hundreds of millions of accumulations. Within a score of years the fraternal beneficial orders have paid over a billion dollars to their members and their families. The ideals and sentiments on which all life insurance is based dwell as an overmastering force in the fraternal orders and *nowhere else*. In them there is no line of demarcation drawn between the cause and the effect. In true humanitarianism their work follows the spirit of the Man of Nazareth, who "went about doing good," adopting the Good Samaritan as its patron saint.

The fraternity has its secret signs, passwords, grips, and ceremonies, as a bond of union, but its teaching of emphasis is always the brotherhood of man. It is in the same business as the churches, the schools and the hospitals. Whether its ritual is literary mincepie, or a monument of striking and sonorous rhetoric, it teaches beautiful and uplifting truths that cannot fail to enrich and ennoble the characters of those who hear it repeated.

A LODGE A PLAYGROUND AND CLUB

Providing monetary relief in the day of disability or death, its incidental benefits of good fellowship with its troop of blessings, pass the power of any statistician to compute. The lodge is a playground, a training school, and a social club. In its atmosphere of a "lend-a-hand" society, moral backbone is manufactured, harmless enjoyments cluster, the wings of caste are singed, and cheer and companionship are freely dispensed to those who need their gracious ministrations. Where the question is always publicly asked: "Does any one know of a member who is sick or in distress," it will easily be seen that much good is done that is never advertised.

The order makes its appeal to those who believe in brotherhood and in co-operation for mutual protection and relief. It promises no dividends, fosters no schemes of wresting profit from misfortune, and avoids all attempts at financial aggrandizement. By mutual agreement, through mutual control, it promises to pay; but it also offers food for the dramatic instinct, and by drill, debate, social enjoyments, lectures, and the opportunity of mingling on terms of equality with a great number of men and women in the lodge room, it adds to the zest and pleasure of life. There is no cure for a grouch equal to the fraternal goat.

The splendid sentiments permeating a fraternity are noble school-masters training millions of men and women to be better than they otherwise would be. Ties that bind during life are insisted upon. Loyalty in helping to bear one another's burdens here and now, is the spirit broadening and blessing the members of all the sister-brotherhoods.

BROTHERLY ATTENTIONS TO SICK AND UNFORTUNATE

Let the member of an order fall sick; to his bedside come his fraters to minister to his wants; flowers are sent; the worries and burdens of the anxious family are shared; the reality of the high teachings of the familiar ritual finds appreciated illustration. The sick man dies; his faithful comrades watch by his bier; attend to the sad details of mourning necessity; follow him to his last resting place; place floral tributes on his coffin; "weep with those who weep," recite by the grave the words that breathe the common hope of the bereaved; and later bring to the desolated home the money benefit, for which the company would have charged a far higher price, and would probably have paid by sending through the mail. The company pays the cash it promised; so does the order, but to it adds the precious bonus of personal care, sympathy and affection,

The fraternal society is a miniature republic; it cherishes a representative form of government, and does its utmost to emphasize the fact of joint ownership and control. It tries to keep its members fully informed of all financial transactions, and matters of importance to the work of the craft, usually publishing a journal for that purpose, that is sent to all members without charge or at cost. The average member of one of our great orders knows more about "Our Order" than the great cross examining ability of Governor Hughes was able to learn of some of the companies which were inquired into by the Armstrong commission.

Having been for years in the executive councils of old line companies, with hosts of friends and acquaintances, whom I honor for their integrity and ability, engaged in the building up of legal reserve life insurance, I have no stone to throw at them or their business, nor would I withhold uttering a word of praise for the wonderful achievements and untold benefits of American life insurance. Its triumphs of expansion rightly find place among the most valuable and honorable economic forces of the past century. Viewed from the standpoint of a financier or a lover of his race, its work has been a marvelous application of the finest form of financial co-operation.

But to end as I began; the strongest thing in the world is a true sentiment, and because the fraternal insurance orders carry such sentiment into all their work and the companies do not, and by their very nature cannot, I believe the former offer the ideal system of life insurance, a system that will grow to be as correct mathematically as it seeks to be fraternally. When the day comes, as come it will, in which the great fraternities put themselves on an adequate basis of payments; collecting what is absolutely required to carry out the benefits provided in their certificates, continuing their economical administrations, and the leadership of true hearted men, who join with clergymen, educators, and scientists, in a willingness to sacrifice something of monetary reward, to help on the common good, they will have won the field of insurance endeavor.

Sprinkling the desert of work-a-day monotony with oases of good cheer, and a comradeship whose loyalty lasts through life and beyond death, it will be fitted to serve as the perfect vehicle by which sentiments creating insurance necessity can do their splendid work. "Founded on the deep needs of human nature, cemented by the purposes of an all wise Creator, it was born not for a day, but for all time." Yea—

> 'Till the sun grows cold,
> And the stars grow old,
> And the leaves of the Judgment Book unfold.

FRATERNITY—A TOAST

GEORGE R. ALLEN

Standing before you this evening, holding to the back of this friendly chair for reassurance, I glance at my *menu* and wonder as I have been wondering for some three weeks past, what I shall say in your presence to-night.

The verse supplied by you, Mr. Toastmaster, is comprehensive enough and if I am to speak of the various thoughts suggested by it, I must fashion after the Vermont schoolboy who, being required to write a composition dealing in detail with the several days of the week, wrote this: "On Monday father and I went hunting and shot a bear. This supplied us with meat enough for Tuesday, Wednesday, Thursday, Friday, Saturday and Sunday."

I am conscious of a sort of fellow feeling for the Pennsylvania farmer, well-to-do, but economical, who had worn the same suit of butternut for church and going to town and weddings and funerals and festive occasions generally, until the waistcoat bore varied samples of his good wife's skill; trouser patches bore silent testimony to years of service, the coat resembled Joseph's, and over them all hovered the delicate aroma of his homely occupation.

John's folks were back from Kansas on a visit on this

day in question and upon his return from town would be at the old homestead. So, while walking along the street our friend concluded to follow his wife's oft-repeated request and get a new suit. It was accordingly purchased and, driving homeward after nightfall, the good man fell to thinking how surprised mother would be to see him dressed other than in the bedraggled "butternut." When he reached the bridge spanning the creek a mile eastward of his house, he stopped, quickly divested himself of the old suit, threw it over the railing to the stream below, and reached back into the spring wagon for the new suit. But, to his mingled surprise and consternation, that bundle had bounced out during the homeward drive. Mother was, indeed, surprised at father's appearance when he stepped shivering on the porch ten minutes later

But, speaking of Fraternity, I read on my card:

> God hath made mankind one
> Mighty Brotherhood;
> Himself their Master and the
> World His Lodge.

Some four thousand years ago a tiller of the soil, incensed because his sacrificial fruits were rejected and the firstlings of the herdsman's flock accepted, in anger struck the other child of his parents to the earth, and in response to the question of the Lord's said:

> Am I my brother's keeper?

Mankind from that day to this has grappled with that question. The warrior rulers of historic empires, Babylonia, Persia, Egypt, Macedonia, Rome, all trampling with fearful tread upon their subject's rights, held valueless the life that thwarted their ambition. But Assurbanipal, Cyrus, Rameses, Alexander, and the Caesars, with all their mighty genius, were each alike unable to write across the golden, dawning skies of progress a decree forever banishing responsibility for our brother. Because He whom we as Masons adore placed in the beginning in the human heart a well-spring of affection that bade defiance to despotic mandate.

Even while these lived and reigned, wise men were pondering deep upon the mysteries of nature, selecting and handing down through chosen successors principles of life and living whose logical fruition within these walls at this convocation we have been pleased to receive.

The philosophy of the world has given no uncertain answer to the question. The Persian Magi, the Egyptian Priesthood, the Grecian Mysteries—each in error, groping in darkness, crawling toward the light—were battling for the cause of the "oppressed against the oppressor," of "toleration against intolerance," of "light against darkness." Or at least were forging the weapons that in other hands, in other lands, in other ages, would deal mighty blows for humanity.

Fraternity—a brother love—not the earthquake or the tempest, but the still small voice. It is the most powerful force known in all the earth.

Fraternity is not concerned with length of service, but with its quality. Not hand service, not head service; not lip service, but with all of these making what we call heart service. I would not be misunderstood. Fraternity does not follow service. It precedes it. As the grain of wheat falls into the earth and perishes, followed by the growing grain, so is fraternity the sinking away of self, the uplifting of another. Service is neither the warp nor woof of fraternity, but its proof.

A brother's love cannot be hedged about or circum-scribed by rivers, or mountains, or mighty oceans, or state lines; nor yet by race, religion, or degree of civilization. Witness to this our own beloved order, powerful in two hemispheres, prominent in fifty governments, a living, vital, palpitating force that in some form antedated the pyramids, and will exist when Macauley's New Zealander views the mounds that mark the site of England's capital and speculates upon the barbarians that once peopled those ruined walls.

And order that has always stood and stands now with flaming sword, the guardian of the mysteries of light and liberty; whose traditions are sacred to the memory of the Wise King and the fidelity of our first Grand Master; whose effort has always been for the capture and execution of "Ignorance," "Intolerance," and "Tyranny," the assassins of "Wisdom."

Masonry, and I refer to no single rank or rite, early learned and has always practiced the true fraternity that vaunteth not itself. Love seeks not to disclose each good deed done, but likes best the affection of a brother helped.

Within a stone's throw of this Temple a costly building is being erected, dedicated ostensibly to the public, through the generosity of a single individual. But over the door must be carved, under the terms of the gift, the doner's name, and each book plate must bear his imprint. This building is one of scores made possible by this man's wealth, but in each like terms prevail.

Yesterday the public prints said that this man so feared to be called into the presence of the Great Architect of the Universe that the word death might not be uttered in his presence. Is he with his millions striving to buy peace for his soul? Is he placing a dollar mark upon love?

These book palaces, thus erected by a manufacturing prince with his individuality thus forcibly thrust into the face of this and all succeeding generations, are not monuments of self-abasement, but of colossal egotism; they stand as memorials of supreme selfishness, differing in degree, but not in kind, from the Great Pyramid at

Ghizeh. Books are no more to us, if as much, as were "onions and garlic" to Khufu's toiling myriads.

It is as if in that priceless parable before referred to we read that before the Samaritan would care for the wounded man, and pay for his lodging at the inn, by contract a marble shaft must pierce the sky at the "rocky defile" bearing on its base name and date and detail; and a bronze tablet with appropriate inscription be placed upon the walls of the hostelry.

MEMORIAL DAY ADDRESS *

It is a worthy custom that we recognize to-day in this meeting of the members of this Society to scatter flowers on the graves of those who have gone to their long rest, and as I was thinking of this day and of a subject appropriate for the occasion, this thought occurred to me as one worthy of elaboration: While the ties of home are more binding than those of any fraternity, and while the duty that rests upon the members of the family to keep the grave green is a sacred one, yet the service rendered by the fraternities in this respect is even more permanent than that which can be rendered by the members of the family.

I wonder how many here to-day are situated as I am. No one of my immediate family resides at the place of our birth, nor does any member of my father's family reside at the place of their birth. In this country we move about so that the graves of the family are after awhile deserted. The children often find homes in different and distant parts of the country, and the care of the grave, excepting

---

* Extracts from the address of the Hon. WILLIAM JENNINGS BRYAN at Lincoln, Nebraska, on the occasion of the Modern Woodmen of America's Memorial Day exercises, June 7, 1908.

when one of the family returns, is left to strangers. In
Mexico they rent a place for the coffin for five years, and
if at the end of five years the vault is not re-rented, the
bones are piled up in a place set apart for that purpose,
and after awhile the bone room is the largest part of the
cemetery.

We remember that in that great play that immortalizes
Joe Jefferson, when *Rip Van Winkle* came back after a
few years, he found that he was entirely forgotten. I
once went to an old grave yard in Chicago that had been
used less than one hundred years before, and I found it
deserted and neglected. ·The tombstones had fallen down
and there was no evidence of any care. It is strange how
rapidly the current of life sweeps on.

The fraternity is not made up so much of individuals
as it is of generations. Its life links the generations
together. One hundred years from now the graves of the
Neighbors who have passed away this year will be marked
with flowers by those who are then members of the fra-
ternity. Just pause and think what that means.

It is appropriate that man's work should be remembered
by those with whom he works, for man's work is a work
with, among and for his neighbors. What a man does
alone in this world is very little; what he does in conjunc-
tion with others is very large. A school is not founded
by an individual: it is founded by a group of individuals.
The school system of this country was not built up by one
person or by one family, but by all the people working
together. Government is not the work of an individual:
it is the work of people united and acting together. The
church is not the work of one person; it is not the work
of the pastor: it is the work of the members working with
the pastor. And so I might take up department after
department of the work in which we are interested, and
show that the great work which we do in business, in

society, in the church, in government and in every occu-
pation and profession is the work that we do together,
walking side by side, laboring shoulder to shoulder.

Thus does humanity bear the burdens of the world;
thus, one in purpose, we carry forward the civilization of
the world. Man by himself is insignificant, and a gener-
ation by itself is not very important when we measure it
against history. Yet, without this individual work, each
doing his part, there could be no society. It is proper,
therefore, that we, the members of this fraternity, should
thus recognize the relation that we bear to each other and
perpetuate the memory and deeds of those who have done
their part in the accomplishment of that which is being
accomplished.

Take away one drop of water from a stream and its
absence would not be known; but a multitude of these
drops make the stream. If you visit the Grand Canyon of
the Colorado, you will find that the river has cut its way
down through almost a mile of rock. Standing on the
bank and looking down, you see the river about 4,500 feet
below, as it struggles in its course to the sea. If you
descend its banks, you will find layer after layer of stone,
the softer stone at the top, the harder stone as you go
down. As you approach the river you find 1,500 feet of
solid granite, and for ages that stream has been cutting
its way through those layers of rock. Every drop of
water that has passed through the chasm has left a record
of its work. While no one drop of water made a per-
ceptible change, yet all of these drops together have been
necessary to accomplish what is recognized as one of the
wonders of the world. And just as important in the
writing of history and in shaping the course of events are
these small and almost imperceptible beings whom we
call brothers. Everyone has his part and without every
one history would not be just what it is. It is proper,

therefore, that we do our work together, who contribute a common service, should on each Memorial day, drop some flowers upon the graves of our departed brothers as a recognition of that relation that binds us together— as a recognition of our appreciation of what the dead have done.

What are they doing who belong to these fraternities? They are teaching the important lessons of life. In the lodge room and the Camp we learn that the heart shapes the destiny of man, and that the heart's purposes and the heart influences are the important things in this life. When we meet together we leave that artificial society which builds distinctions upon birth, or upon education, or upon wealth.

In the lodge room and in the Camp, we do not ask a man who his father *was;* we simply inquire what he *is.* We do not ask what his *father* has done; *we* simply ask if *he* is ready to do the work that falls to him; we do not ask whether he has received a diploma from some institution of learning; we simply ask him if he has studied the science of "How to live;" if he recognizes the ties that bind him to mankind. We do not ask him how many acres of land he possesses; we ask him whether he is possessed of the spirit of brotherhood and whether he counts all as entitled with him to the benefits of civilization and to the helps that come therefrom. The lodge room and the Camp help to draw us together; they help to unify the world; they help to teach the spirit of brother hood.

I am glad to be with you on this day. I am proud of my membership in this great fraternity, the greatest fraternity of its age in all the world and in all history. So far as we know, no organization of men bound together by the ties of fraternity has ever grown so large or exerted so great an influence in a quarter of a century.

The fact that it has grown and is still growing, proves that it is founded upon the rock and that it has met the needs of the people.

It is an honor to be one of this army of a million men. These men represent the best that is in this land. They represent the common people of this country, and the common people constitute probably 95 per cent. of our total population. There are a few who · have accumulated vast wealth and who do not consider themselves of the masses, and you may find a few criminals who have forfeited their right to be counted as members of this great brotherhood of the common people; but the common people from whom the membership of our society comes are the ones who constitute the nation's strength. In peace they are the builders of the country—in war they are the country's bulwark.

We bring our floral tribute to those who, once with us, have been taken from us, but who shall be long remembered. We stand as it were, on this middle ground: Looking back, we recall the day when they were among us, and we scatter flowers over their graves as evidence that they are not forgotten; and, turning from their graves, we look into the future and think, as we must on an occasion like this, that soon our work shall be done; that soon we shall be gathered with them in that life that never ends, our work on earth left to those following us.

To-day we may find some consolation in the thought that, as we remember those who have died, so, when our days are numbered, those who still live and still act together as members of our Society will lay flowers upon our graves and, in so doing, indicate that they remember us and appreciate our work.

FRATERNITY

H. S. HUDSON

My friends, I am a believer in Fraternity—a follower of happiness—and a friend of joy. I am an optimist. I had rather stand with my naked eyes turned toward the burning sun, hoping its rays might penetrate my soul and drive the chill from my heart, than be a pessimist, groping with trembling hands and troubled face through the slough of despond. I want to see the day come when all will be believers in the Brotherhood of Man; when all humanity will be worshippers at the shrine of brotherly love; when human affection will reach from the cottage on the street to the mansion on the hillside and back again; when luxury will stop to put a flower on the brow of care; when wealth will wipe the tears from off the cheeks of poverty; when ignorance will seek and see the light of knowledge and cruel and thoughtless words will no longer bruise the hearts of little children.

Some day fraternity will make sunshine enough in the world to drink up the tears of grief. It will take fear from out the human heart, and place the badge of courage upon the weeping form of widowhood. It will take the hands of avarice and greed from off the home, and bid the wide and startled eyes of orphanhood to no longer fear the darkening clouds of adversity. It will be a leveler of all distinctions and, standing by the sarcophagus of rich and poor alike, it will teach that "kind words are more than coronets and simple faith than Norman blood."

Fraternity has illuminated the Valley of Death with the beaming stars of Hope and, in all the desert wastes of life, it has found the paths that lead to the oasis of eternal happiness. Fraternal organizations have made the best of all the better instincts of mankind. They have taken the pity of one human heart and added it to that of many others. They have taken the good will of one human being and placed it with a multitude of others. They have concentrated joy and happiness, kind words and good deeds and, with these marshalled hosts, have waged ceaseless and relentless battle against all the hordes of misery and death.

Fraternity is strenuous labor for the right. It is the splendid effort that vies with the school and the church to do the most towards the betterment of mankind. It is the teachings of the Christ not uttered by the lips but performed by the hands. It is not the work of the doctor who suggests, but that of the Good Samaritan who performs; not the kindly word, but the thoughtful act; words tremble but a moment on the lips and are lost into nothingness. Deeds are the act of the heart performed through the hands and are as eternal as the universe; like the morning sunshine laden with the perfume of flowers they touch every life with hope, bring forgetfulness of yesterday and courage for tomorrow.

Fraternity is non-sectarian and non-political and, where the church cannot scale the wall of prejudice, Fraternity walks unhindered. It teaches knowledge school masters never knew and instructs multitudes who never cared for the unmeaning hieroglyphics of science, the philosophy of right living.

Fraternity is the eternal enemy of selfishness and, for my part, I had rather live my life among those who live happy in the present, and hopeful in the future—men whose generous hearts and helping hands fill the sky with sunshine and the air with melody—than to be a pampered son of arrogant wealth, clad in the garments of nobility; fed in the lap of luxury; living in gorgeous palaces; drinking the nectar of the gods; but feeling in my breast the emptiness of life, and holding in my conscience the memory of selfish acts and ungenerous deeds.

Selfishness is a murderer yet unhung. It has incited every riot, and committed every crime since first the morning stars sang together. It has murdered men and women and children; given birth to every slander; seared the cheek of virtue; robbed the cradle and the grave and devastated the hearthstone of happiness. Selfishness is the embodiment of evil. Fraternity is the home of love. One promotes misery, the other fosters happiness. There is a gulf between the two as impassable as the line of demarkation between Heaven and Hell. Where one is the other cannot be, and I had rather have upon my limbs the manacles of public degradation than to have upon my heart the chains of public and private selfishness. I had rather live in a dungeon, with only a memory of God's soft sunshine, the birds, the flowers, the trees, but with a full measure of pity in my heart, than to live in a palace, unmindful of the cry of distress; the pinched lips of poverty; the grief stricken children, their eyes swimming in tears, and the heart-broken cry of bereft parents.

I would rather have in my heart the precious joy of one kindly act than to have in my pocket the golden coin of selfishness. Fraternity and fraternal organizations have touched the sleeping conscience of all civilized peoples and aroused them to potent action; fraternal organizations may not have builded the magnificent piles of iron and steel and granite that are monuments of commercial greed and selfishness, but they have builded and protected homes wherein "faint dreams like shadowy vales divide the billowed hours of love," and were all the money that has been expended for fraternal benefits and for the preservation of homes gathered together in one mass, it would astound the civilized world. It would build a city of homes the beauty and extent of which

would seem like a fairy tale to the most imaginative phil-
anthropists.

If there is a person within the reach of my voice, who
is absolutely sure that he will lay aside enough of this
world's goods to protect his home, his wife and children
from the calamity that may come out of the future, to
him I have nothing to say. To this man the history of
the world and the experience of mankind are as nothing
when compared to his own egotism. Who is sure of the
future? Who can pierce the veil that hides to-morrow,
and who can say that he is absolutely sure that there will
be a to-morrow? Cities that represented the wealth and
elegance of their time have vanished in smoke. Moun-
tains that reared their tawny heads to the starlit skies
have been leveled to the earth from which they sprang.
Manly men who felt within their veins the rich red blood
of youth have fallen beneath the iron rule of destiny and
become spiritless masses of clay. Then who knows
that he is exempt from the common destiny that
guides us all? Who can say with any degree of certainty
that he can lay aside enough to protect his family from
unforeseen calamity? No one, unless he be possessed
with the vision of a prophet, and I have not met many of
these people lately.

You know not many years ago there was a great preju-
dice against orders and once in a while you find people in
this enlightened age who view them with suspicion. I
know in my youthful days, and that is not so many years
ago, I used to think every man that I knew to be a Mason
was a sort of a side partner of the devil. Some people think
so yet. They knew there was a goat nearly as large as
an ordinary cow, and hobgoblins and mysterious words
and signs and, by deduction, which is a line of reasoning.
employed by detectives who never catch anybody, they
concluded that the order was in some way inimical to

their best interests. And even to this day there are people who view with suspicion what they are pleased to term secret societies. But the world has progressed and just as it has discarded the crooked stick for the modern plow, just as the superstitions of the past have faded before the light of knowledge, just as the piano has super seded the tom tom as a musical instrument, so has the world progressed and the modern fraternal and insurance organizations of to-day, profiting by the mistake of the past, have entered upon a wider field of endeavor, and a more complete method of procedure until to-day ours is the only flag that has in reality upon it "Liberty, Fraternity and Equality," the three grandest words in all the languages of men. "Liberty!"—Give to every man the fruit of his own labor. "Fraternity!"—Every man in the right is my brother. "Equality!"—The rights of all are equal.

I have said these fraternal organizations add to the sum of human joy and, after all, the happy man is the successful man. Happiness is wealth, and that man is a millionaire who has no fear for the future comfort of those whom he honors and esteems.

To protect the home which contains those we love is a duty every honorable man acknowledges and assumes. Every act in the life of man testifies more eloquently than words eternal fealty to this duty. Every cent placed in a savings bank, every dollar invested in stocks and bonds, every life and fire insurance policy,—every hour spent in labor—every stroke of the pick—every furrow turned by the plow—all the weary moments spent in poring over books—every call to arms—every drum beat and call of bugle—all the battle fields which contain the martyred dead—every monument to heroism, and all the pages of history speak most eloquently of man's defense of the home, and the man who will not defend the home that has

cared for and protected him is a dirty scrub who contam-
inates the air he breathes.

> The wretch, concentered all in self,
> Living shall forfeit fair renown,
> And, doubly dying, shall go down
> To the vile dust from whence he sprung,
> Unwept, unhonored, and unsung.

The man of wealth insures his life as a plain business
proposition, but the man who labors for his daily bread,
and the man without a bank account, the man whose life
is one unending round of toil, should insure his life not
only as a business proposition but as a plain, unmistak-
able duty as well. Among a thousand workingmen, per-
haps one-third have homes, and one-fourth a bank
account, two-thirds or three-fourths live from day to day,
from week to week, unable to save more than a pittance
from their daily wages. The man in this condition, who
neglects to insure his life to protect his home or his family,
is criminally negligent, and fear and remorse will make a
hell of his death bed.

Young men, insure your lives, protect your homes,
do something for those who have done and are doing
so much for you. There is no reason why you should
not insure your lives, and every reason why you should.
It is a mark of prudence. It signifies business sagacity.
It places you in touch with the business men of your com-
munity. Fraternal life and life insurance broadens your
mental horizon, and makes you a man in the eyes of men.

An organization of this kind represents the best
impulses of mankind. It arouses the loftiest sentiments
and the noblest ambitions in every human soul. It is a
builder of stronger nations; of greater empires; of
humanitarian communities, and it furnishes to us the
source of that intense patriotism, that optimistic hopeful-
ness of the future which characterizes the American

people. It appeals to every heart that has touched the cross of human suffering. It is the many-hued bow of promise shining through and over all the clouds of sorrow. It is the word of hope heard above the clamor of the mob. It is the crimson light that ushers in the tawny head of morning. It is Fraternity.

THY NEIGHBOR

H. C. EVANS

How insignificant all things else become in comparison with a brave, industrious man who stands upright in the image of God; who lives and loves and perpetuates the human race; who with honest purpose bares his breast and squares his shoulders for the duties and responsibilities of life. A man who is not only making a living, but who is making a life. Such men constitute the body politic of fraternalism.

Fraternalism has its inception in the divine command: "Love thy neighbor as thyself." At least eight different times, in these exact words, is this commandment given. Holy Writ designates it as the second great commandment, and likens it in importance to the first, and declares that "on these two commandments hang all the law and the prophets."

The poet tells that the angel, in writing down the names of those who loved the Lord, wrote first the name of him who loved his fellow-man. No word in our language save those relating to our immediate home and family is dearer than the word "neighbor." To those who live, or have lived, in a quiet country neighborhood, where peace and quiet reign and the golden rule is the law of action, the word has a special endearment. It is in such a neighborhood that a favor is asked as a right, and a benefit is bestowed as a duty. Such a people fully comprehend the divine direction, "Every man shall borrow of his neighbor, and every woman of her neighbor."

Fraternalism does not proscribe or give limitations to the word "neighbor." Fraternalism has eliminated space and remoteness of residence. If you have doubt as to who your neighbor is, you may have the answer:

> Thy neighbor? 'Tis the fainting poor
>   Whose eye with want is dim,
> Whom hunger sends from door to door—
>   Go thou and succor him.

If you still have doubt, we point you to the greatest authority known among men—the definition given by the Saviour of man.

In 'one of his journeys a certain lawyer questioned Christ as to his duties. Christ gave him the two supreme commandments: "Love the Lord, thy God, with all thy soul, with all thy strength, and with all thy mind, and thy neighbor as thyself."

The lawyer—lawyer-like—asked: ˉ

"Who is my neighbor?"

The answer was given in the story of the good Samaritan:

After carefully studying the laws of architecture and temple building by which foundations are made firm; by which towers are made secure and domes perfect, Ruskin declared that the laws of architecture and temple building are in reality the laws of character building.

As the architect takes the component parts, stone, iron and wood, and rears them into a building, either strong and beautiful, or weak and offensive, so man builds his character. Ruskin says:

1. The soul is a temple more majestic than any cathedral.
2. Principles are foundation stones.
3. Habits are columns and pillars.
4. Facilities are master builders.
5. Every thought drives a nail.
6. Every deed weakens or makes strong some timber.
7. Every holy aspiration lends beauty as every unclean thing lends defilement—the whole standing forth at last builded either of passion or of purposes more precious than gold.

Buildings fall and become uninhabitable because the architect puts lying stones in the foundation; because the architect substitutes painted columns of plaster for marble, and time soon exposes the ugly lie; because the builder puts lying tiles upon the roof. Ships are wrecked upon the rocks because a smith puts a lying link in the anchor's cable.

THE WORLD CONQUERING FORCE*

Some years ago, on a steamer from Hong Kong to Bombay, I fell into conversation with an educated, traveled Parsee, who was somewhat of a philosopher. We had just left China, with its tangled mass of humanity, overflowing to all the nations of the earth; and we talked of the race problem in the Orient, with its myriad complexities and the forebodings they bring as to the final clash between Mongolian and Caucasian.

---

* An address delivered by the Hon. LEE W. SQUIER, President of the Associated Fraternities of America, at the dedication of the Temple of Fraternity on the Louisiana Purchase Exposition grounds, St. Louis, Missouri, October 24, 1903.

"You Anglo-Saxons," said he, "are destined to rule the world. My father was an astrologist—a student of the stars of the moral firmament that guide our poor humanity in the bitter blackness of the world's live-long nights.

"Men, tribes and nations, like Greece under Alexander, Rome under Julius Cæsar, France under Napoleon, have followed a star, that century after century has flamed athwart the heavens like a comet—War. But this star ever sets, leaving men and nations no nearer the goal of universal sovereignty than when it first arose on the black ness of the night.

"Others, like ancient Babylon, Assyria, Egypt, Athens, Rome, under Augustus Cæsar; like the Italian civic principalities of the Middle Ages; like Germany and France of the present time, have followed another star, that ever and anon shines with a glory of brightness—Mental Culture. But this star, though shining with varied brightness adown the centuries has made but little impression upon the world's universal night.

"Others have followed the star that 'makes the darkness light about them'—all nations seeming to take delight in this effulgent constellation. My own nation of India," continued this scion of ancient learning and devotion, "has for centuries trod the narrow path of light radiating from this star—Religion. We have ever basked in its pale, yellow light, delving into the mysteries it has shown us of origin, existence, duty and destiny, with the fond hope that with these mysteries solved, we should be hailed and reverenced as the natural, undisputed leaders of the world's progress unto the perfect day.

"But alas! we have no leadership. Our learning, our piety, our devotion have gone for naught. India is forgotten. But wherever you Anglo-Saxons go, there fades the night, there dawns the day. You are marching around this world, transfigured in a golden light that leads you to universal supremacy. It is wonderful. It is splendid. But it is a mystery. I bow in ignorance and awe. I would like to walk in your light."

A few weeks later, I stood on the crest of a hill in Palestine where "Shepherds watch their flocks by night" now as they did nineteen hundred years ago. On that sacred, historic soil, amidst those craggy, jutting limestone rocks, looking down on the olive trees of the valley, the voices of the Past seemed to whisper to me the name of the star that is leading our Anglo-Saxon race to such speedy and splendid world conquest. And I longed to shout across the lands and seas to my Parsee philosopher the solution of the mystery before which he bowed in ignorance and awe.

I seemed to hear the Divine voice, the still small voice in the Garden of Eden, in the midst of the gloom caused by the first murder, "Where is thy brother?" In answer how pitiful is the excuse of war, selfishness, ignorance and bigotry—"Am I my brother's keeper?"

Again from far off Egypt, midst the strife among the brickmakers, I seemed to catch the echo of the divine law-giver's exclamation, "Ye be brethren. Wherefore do ye strive?"

Again amidst the strife and barbarity of civil war, in the Holy Land on which I stood, I seemed to hear the voices of David and Jonathan in their secret midnight love-feasts between the opposing camps, whispering the common language of eternal brotherhood, in their love that surpassed the love of woman.

And again it seemed to me as I stood on that hill-top, not many miles from the blue waters of the Mediterranean, that from the ruins of the not far distant city of

Syracuse, came the echo of the voice of the old Dionysius,
the tyrant, as he expatiated on the amazing brotherhood
of Damon and Pythias, and because of their fidelity the
one to the other, asked that he be admitted to the sublime
fellowship.

And then, as I stooped and looked into the stone recess
called a manger in the ruins of the stable of an inn, it
seemed to me that the light of the star, which the wise
men of the East followed, illumined anew the sacred spot
where the Son of God took upon himself the form of man,
because, "He was not ashamed to call us brethren."

The spell was upon me. I followed this star of
Heaven, tracing the steps of this Elder Brother as he
went up and down the land of promise, teaching and
exemplifying the truths of universal brotherhood. I
lingered where tradition says He taught the lesson of the
Good Samaritan; I went into that upper room where tra-
dition says He washed the Disciples' feet and gave them
that divine example of the elder brother, doing the most
menial service, because of the brother-heart within Him.
I tarried on the hill where they say He gave that match-
less Sermon on the Mount, in which He announced the
rule of conduct in the brotherhood he was founding—
"Whatsoever ye would that men should do unto you, do ye
even so to them." I pondered over the place where it is
said He was asked, "Lord, when saw we thee an hungered
and gave thee meat? When saw we thee athirst and gave
thee drink? Or naked and clothed thee? Or when saw
we thee in prison and visited thee?" And I seemed to
hear His summing up of all charity, its source and sub-
stance—"Verily I say unto you, that inasmuch as ye have
done it unto one of the least of these, my brethren, ye have
done it unto me."

Thus I saw how the star in the East, the star of uni

versal brotherhood, arose upon the blackness of the world's universal night.

Bishop Berkeley once said, "Westward the star of empire takes its way." I followed it. I traveled over Europe and thought of the guilds among the serfs; of the brotherhoods among the squires and knights and of the varied societies among the craftsman and tradesman of the Middle Ages for protection and help amidst danger and suffering. I went across to England and saw the light of this star of universal brotherhood shining even more brightly in the hundreds of friendly societies with their century records of grand achievements. Then westward still I turned my face, towards my native land, which I had not seen for years; and here I find millions of my fellow men organized under the inspiration of our divine Brother and crowding the years full to overflowing with their compliance with His requirement, "Inasmuch as ye have done it unto one of the least of these, my brethren, ye have done it unto me."

"Westward the star of empire takes its way." Here on the grounds dedicated by the greatest nation to commemorate the addition to our national domain and the development of a mighty empire, we to-day dedicate a temple that shall stand to the world a material expression of that mighty principle of brotherhood which has made our nation the greatest among the peoples of history.

These material expressions are of inestimable value. The mind of man is so constituted that it can grasp the spiritual only through the material, the ideal through the real. Emblems and symbols are an inspiration to his faith, a help to his devotion.

Hence come pilgrimages. I have witnessed in all parts of the world the magic effect of religious, scientific, political and educational pilgrimages. I have seen caravans of devotees creeping through the sands of the desert, crawling over rugged mountains, unmindful of torrid heat and frigid cold in turn, pushing on and ever on to visit some poor little shrine, to pray and dream beneath the shadow of some crumbling temple and thence return, over the same weary wastes, with higher aspirations, nobler resolves and steadier purposes in life. At sundown I have witnessed a whole city full of people stop all work, business and pleasure, and like one man fall on their face toward Mecca and pray, as a magic name rang from tower, turret, mosque and minaret, "Allah! Allah!" I have seen a poor Russian peasant, clothes threadbare and tattered, feet shoeless and bleeding, face pinched and body starved after six months' walking from his native village to the Holy Land to visit the ruins which somehow symbolize the foundations of his faith; and in deepest sympathy have I looked at his rags and suffering and asked him, "Is it worth it all?" And instantly, a light almost divine shone from those sunken eyes and illumined that wan face as he answered, "Worth it all? I would travel twice as far and go through thrice the privations, just to kiss the stones on the streets of the Holy City."

Yes, the material symbol is an inspiration to faith. The outward emblem is a proof of the inner reality. On leaving Japan some years ago, there was presented to me a box, finely inlaid with choice woods and beautifully decorated—a model of construction and beauty. On opening it, I found within a smaller box, also perfect in its beauty and construction. Within this, I found another; and so on until I had opened nine of these splendid works of art. The tenth was a little cube which I could hold in my hand. It was likewise a perfect structure. But on opening it, I found within a precious stone upon which was graven the image of the Mikado.

On these grounds the world will find magnificent art palaces and splendid buildings showing forth the triumph of the world's progress towards the true light of perfect civilization. It is significant that these great buildings all cluster around this hill, and that the center of all this magnificent display is this Temple of Fraternity—the precious jewel bearing the image, in its meaning, of the Son of God, our Elder Brother. This Temple will illustrate the work which the brotherhood of man has accomplished, through hospitals, the relief of the distressed, the rescue of the perishing, the care of the dying. This temple is the material emblem of that force in modern civilization, which in the end triumphs over war, selfishness, ignorance, superstition and bigotry. This temple is but a symbol of the countless homes which have been reared and saved in the sacred name of Fraternity. How proud will be the multitudes that visit this Temple. Proud that they are brothers; grateful for the epoch in the history of the world in which the work of Fraternity is first symbolized in an appropriate and special palace like this. With what inspiration will they return to their homes and firesides, their towns, and villages, their lodges, camps and councils. The world-conquering force of Fraternity will receive from these pilgrimages to this Temple a mighty impetus and increase of its beneficent influence, which will soon envelop and enfold all races and nations.

As I stood by the recently excavated corner-stone of King Solomon's temple on Mount Moriah, in imagination I saw the members of the first operative lodge of our universal brotherhood toiling ceaselessly day after day, month after month and year after year, until at length that great temple was completed in all its majesty and glory—the wonder of the world. Without sound of hammer or chisel was it reared. Silently, like a divine-mystery, it arose to its glory. This Temple, which the fraternal hosts are building on these grounds, will be but a symbol, a material expression, of that immaterial temple of Fraternity built by the life and heart of the millions following the star of universal brotherhood, shining brighter and brighter unto the perfect day—a temple not made by hands, eternal in the heavens.

PYTHIAN JUBILEE ADDRESS

HON. ALBERT J. BEVERIDGE

Brothers: It would be indeed a stony heart and a dull mind which would not be keenly sensible of the far too partial words which our Grand Chancellor, brother Merrill E. Wilson, whom we all admire and who deserves our admiration, has used in introducing me. No man can look upon this amazing audience without sincere pride in his membership in this Order. I can not but think that this mighty assemblage is not an accident; I can not but feel that there are profound reasons at the bottom of this Order's existence. It is these reasons which most interest me to-night, and which, with your permission, I will use as the theme of my address.

All of human life and history are stages in the development of the noblest things in the character of man. All war is merely murder which does not in some form serve civilization. All industry is merely selfishness if the shuttle does not weave into the fabric of prosperity a strand of the finer qualities of the human heart. All education is mechanical and lifeless which does not work out in the soul of the student the true, the beautiful and the good. Civilization is not civilization if it does not produce as its principal result men and women who are unselfish, sweet and truthful.

It is upon this fundamental verity that our Order is founded. We have taken the best of human conceptions and made them the reason and principle of our existence. Friendship! Charity! Benevolence! Concentrate all the thought and effort of the past and these three things are the best and final product. It is the vitality and glory of our organization that, taking these for our creed, we have made it our business to spread them by systematic, organized effort. So it is that our Order is a twentieth century propaganda of righteousness.

This is why we have grown so signally and so soundly in so brief a time. I do not say that all of our hundreds of thousands have carefully thought this out, and, on well reasoned conclusions, become our brothers; but I do say that it is the instinctive recognition of these fundamental truths which is drawing the Nation's young manhood to us. For this Nation is a good nation; a nation of good men and women; God-fearing, believing, hopeful, charitable. The heroes of the American Republic have been not necessarily its ablest men; but always they have been types of its best men.

The great virtues we seek to make practical. As I understand this Order its whole spirit is unselfishness. We seek to reduce the eternal truths to actual living and doing. We do this by the methods of the time. The principal characteristic of the nineteenth and twentieth centuries is organization. Men are banding together; that means fraternity. Industries are consolidating; that means the application of universal system to business, and in the end makes for industrial peace. So we Knights of Pythias obey the spirit of the times and organize with military solidarity and discipline, not for war, but for brotherhood. Even the gospel of the Master can reach the masses of men only through the careful organization of the church. And so we see that even religious discipline constantly becomes more rigid, while creeds steadily become more tolerant.

Think what it means to this Nation to have more than half a million of the flower of young manhood dedicating their lives in a practical way to these generous and fraternal ideals. Think what it means to have these lofty views of life and conduct forever written upon their consciences by a profoundly impressive ritual! Think what it means to have this ritual—this dramatic instruction in the highest conceptions of the human character—strengthened by a solemn oath. Think what it means to have all this followed by a continuous and permanent reminder of its meaning through the work of each night at the lodge room and through the powerful teaching of our daily walk!

Speaking merely of the effect upon the Nation, the Republic would be better off if there were a hundred such organizations as the Knights of Pythias. Every order which makes men live better lives also makes the Nation to which they belong live a better life. The great, ancient, universal Masonic Order, the powerful, vigorous, beneficent Order of Odd Fellows and all kindred associations which teach men brotherhood are pillars of strength to the Republic.

The beginnings of secret orders were in the cause of liberty and to fetter the hand of tyranny. They began with the close association of the best minds who dared not freely express their thoughts, in order that in the safety of the secret chamber they might have that intellectual freedom denied them in the open. At a period in the world's history when learning itself was treason, the sciences were cultivated and the world's accumulated knowledge was preserved by secret organizations. So, while they did not produce free institutions, free institutions were the realization of their original purpose. Thus, organizations like our own, or like any one of those that I have named whose foundation stones are loyalty to our free government and that broad human charity that would extend fraternity all over the globe, are elements of strength in sovereignties of the people. But where secret organizations are formed for other purposes, where they become propagandas of anarchy rather than of liberty, of destruction rather than of human friendship, their very secrecy makes them all the more evil.

What a republic needs and what it must have if it is going to endure, is the habit of calm thinking among its citizens, a broadness of mental view, a largeness of conception of what life is for and the real purpose of the nation in the world's work and in history. Our Order gives this; and therefore is a source of strength to the Republic. Every other order that does the same is another spring from which flows life-giving and perennial streams throughout the land.

No human mind can estimate the far-reaching effects of a single good man's daily deeds among his fellows. The deed does not die with itself. It sets all the universe in motion. It inspires other acts kindred to itself, and these in turn produce still others. How much more, then, does a great order benefit our land, and, indeed, all humanity? Its work is not the righteous living of a single life. Its labors for the higher things embrace the combined and organized efforts of hundreds of thousands.

So it is that not Newton, or Hamilton, or any mathematician who ever lived can compute the benefit to mankind wrought by the great Order of which we are proud to be members. So it is, too, that we are not content to confine the blessings of this Order to ourselves alone. We reach out a loving and helpful hand to every man of

spirit, character and fine impulses throughout the whole
United States, for the Knights of Pythias are as yet exclu-
sively American. Our six hundred thousand men are of
our own land and blood and tongue. Our Order was
founded while civil war made men forget for the moment
that friendship, charity and benevolence, which we pro-
posed to preserve, restore and cherish. So we are an
American Order, blood-baptized and consecrated to peace
and good will among men. A million members is our
mark to-day; millions of members will be the mark we set
for to-morrow. And all this, not for power, or lust of
gold, or armaments, or even for the material construc-
tiveness of peace. No, all this only for the spread and
strengthening of pure and beautiful character among the
children of men!

A LODGE OF SORROW*

JOHN A. LODOR

This is one of our festive days, and we are wont to
commemorate it in honor of one of our Patron Saints.
With us, however, it is a day of mourning—a day set
apart to pay the last tribute of fraternal affection to the
memory of our brethren, whom death has clasped in his
icy embrace during the present year.

The day itself—our custom of observing it—and the
special purpose for which we are now convened, all com-
bine to remind us of the beautiful and significant Egyptian
custom of placing a skeleton at the head of the festal
board. There, in the midst of life, and mirth, and feast-

---

*An Address commemorative of their Fraternal Dead of
1860, delivered before Halo Lodge of Cahaba, Alabama, Decem-
ber 27, 1860.

ing, sat the ghastly herald and emblem of Death. Silent and motionless amid the general joy, most eloquently it reminded those present of their mortality, and uttered, in language not to be misunderstood, the mournful Truth, that there is a time for all things, and among them a time to die. No flight of fancy—no stretch of imagination was required to comprehend the force of the lesson taught by that grim monitor. It was the stern prototype of Death, presiding over an assembly in which mirth, joy, love, youth, beauty, age, wit, genius, rank and wealth, though all were there, yet each one for himself, bowed in homage before that symbol, whose presence announced the fact, felt and recognized by all, that they too must die.

Our festive day is turned into a day of sorrow. We, too, have a skeleton in our midst, and he points with his long, bony, fleshless finger, to the vacant places in our fraternal circle—most unfeelingly he presses upon our bleeding hearts, causing them to flow afresh in remembrance of the loved and lost, whom his Grand Master, Death, has taken from among us.

But a twelve month since, within the precinct of our lodge, our ranks were filled—our mystic circle was complete. We entered upon the New Year, with the future spread out before us, bright with all the gilding of Hope. No dark cloud was visible in our sky—no note of danger was heard upon the wind—no shadow of gloom appeared to warn us of the approach of Death, or startle us by his proximity. In the vigor of youth—in the pride of manhood—in the strength of age—united by our mystic tie—hand in hand and side by side, we entered the year together. Now, at its close, we pause to look around us, and note the events which have marked its flight. Place after place is vacant by our side—our circle is broken—our brethren are gone—our lodge room is draped in sable weeds, the mute symbol of our grief, and when we ask for our absent brothers, we bow our heads in sorrow as the mournful dirge rings in our ear and imparts their fate— tells us that the silver cord is loosed—the golden bowl is broken—the pitcher is broken at the fountain—and the wheel is broken at the cistern.

Once, twice, thrice, yea, even six times, has the shaft of the insatiate archer stricken down a brother by our side. Again and again were we called upon to suspend our daily labor, and bury our dead. Again and again was impressed upon our heart and reiterated in our ear, the solemn lesson that from earth we came, and unto earth we must return again.

It is not for those who had lived their three score years and ten—not those whose heads were silvered o'er by age, for whom we are called upon to mourn. It is for the young and middle aged. For those to whom life opened with apparently a lengthened vista, and whose future was sparkling and bright with all the rainbow hues of Hope.

Death is at all times terrible, even when he gathers into the coffers of the grave, those who, like the ripened harvest, had passed through the spring, summer, autumn, and advanced into the winter of life: but oh! how startling it is to see those who had just entered upon its spring, laid in the silent tomb, and know that their career is ended ere it is well begun. * * * * *

One after another we have seen our brethren gathered to the tomb, and we have mourned for them and for ourselves. Now, this dear friend—this dear brother, is added to the number. Verily, the cup of our affliction is filled— filled to the brim, and in all its bitterness we are compelled to drain it to the dregs.

Would that we could do justice to his memory, and properly express the high meed of praise so justly his due. We can only say

None knew him but to love him
Nor named him but in praise:

That his loss to his family—his host of friends, and this community, is irreparable. A place is left vacant that will not soon be filled. A bright light of the fireside—the social circle—the sick chamber—and the lodge room, is utterly extinguished, and the sad wail of lamentation for his death, vibrates and finds an echo in every heart.

Sad was the fate of our friend and brother, and deeply do we regret it. Kindly will we remember him, until our hearts have ceased to beat their

"Funeral marches to the grave."

And now our task is almost ended. We have not the temerity to inquire why, oh why! are we thus afflicted? We try to yield with humble submission to the will of Him who doeth all things well, satisfied that it is for some wise purpose He has inculcated these sad lessons of mortality upon us. It may be as a warning to us, to set our house in order—a notice to us, to prepare for that dread hour when we too must enter the dark valley of the shadow of death. It may be an unpleasant, yet surely not an unprofitable reflection, to remember the Egyptian custom to which we have already alluded. We stated, we had a skeleton at our festal board. It was an error, for we have six—six vacant places are by our side—six voices from the tomb are ringing in our ear—six grassy mounds tell us the saddest of all sad stories—that of man's mortality. Clear and distinct as did the Egyptians impress the idea of death upon themselves, it is yet more clearly and vividly impressed upon us. To them it was presented in a single view—to us, in varied forms. Youth and beauty—manhood in its strength, and wisdom in its pride—to-day they are ours, to-morrow, they share the bed of the earthworm.

Alas! for the pomp and vanity of human life. What is it all worth, when we view its termination?

'Tis the glance of an eye, 'tis the draught of a breath
From the blossom of health, to the paleness of death,
From the gilded saloon, to the bier and the shroud,
Oh! why should the spirit of mortal be proud?

How frail the tenure by which human life is held— how often we witness its abrupt and awful termination? Untold examples are ever before us, in the chapter of casualties, by which we see in an instant all ranks lev- elled—all distinctions done away. Young and old—rich and poor—the proud and the humble—the prince and the peasant—the master and the slave, all with their lives, yield obedience to the despot, Death, and at his command, assume their places among "the pale nations of the dead." Over the living, Death reigns supreme.

All nature tells man the story of dissolution. On every page of her volume it is illustrated. In every form it is presented to view, and pressed home upon him in every manner. Even the spider's web affords us a lesson on which we may muse and meditate. Who has not looked upon it with surprise and admiration, as he noted the numerous gossamer threads, radiating from a given centre, with the most beautiful regularity, in every direc- tion, and these are crossed and recrossed, over and over again, by many parallel lines, which to wondrous beauty gives it greatest strength. How light, how airy, how artistic, and how beautiful this web! and yet it is the frail- est of all frail things; a wave of the hand, and it is brushed out of existence for ever. It finds its parallel in human life. Youth is its radiating point; the ties of home, country, kindred, love, friendship, wealth, beauty and power, are a few of its radiating lines—the warp of life. The pleasures, joys and amusements which surround us, interwoven as they are with myriad hopes and fancies, are the parallel lines—the woof in the mystic web which combine to make life beautiful and existence desirable. Should the finger of death touch it, in a moment it turns to ashes; but if for a time it escapes such a fate, as anticipations end in disappointment, as hopes fade away, as joys perish and give place to grief, as pleasure is supplanted by sorrow, as friends and kindred fall by our side, thread by thread of the web is broken, its beauty destroyed, its strength gone, the wreck of a once young and hopeful life, toils on with a sad and heavy heart, craving only a sweet slumber in the bosom of our mother Earth—a resting place, where the wicked cease from troubling, and the weary are at rest.

While our brethren have passed away to their long home, while we commemorate their virtues and their worth, and embalm their memory in our hearts, we have yet another duty to perform, and it is one we must not, dare not, ignore. It is to remember kindly the sorrowing kindred, the fathers and mothers, sisters and brothers, the widows and orphans of our deceased brethren.

While we mourn over our loss, we must remember theirs. It is heavier than ours. The manly form, on which the father and mother leaned with confidence to sustain their faltering footsteps to the grave, he whom they would have near them in their last hour, to close their eyes in death, and shroud them for the tomb, has gone before them, and they are left in all the dreariness of a desolate old age, to pursue the weary remnant of life's journey, alone, to the grave. Have we no sorrow— no sympathy for such a grief as theirs? The brother and sister, whose hearts were filled with fraternal love for him who had been nourished at the same maternal fount, who had shared all the joys and sorrows of childhood, the hopes of youth and manhood, have seen the form of him they loved laid in the bosom of our common mother. Again, we ask, have we no tears, no sympathy for such a grief as theirs? The widow and the orphan, how shall we speak of them? How shall we measure their loss and their grief? The husband wedded in early manhood, he, who, before God's holy altar, had sworn to love, cherish, and protect the trembling and fragile form by his side, who had traveled along the path of life her safe protector and her guide, whose heart had beat in unison with hers, and shared her every joy and care, is now no more. The oak is stricken down by the thunderbolt, and the ivy is left without a support, clinging still, not to the oak as in days gone by, but, to the sweet memories of the past— the shadow, merely, of a shade. The widow is left desolate, broken hearted and alone. The orphans, poor, little, helpless innocents! The father, in whose smile they lived, whose presence made their young hearts bound with joy, whose labor furnished them food and raiment, who guided their youthful steps through the perils of childhood, and whose pride, as well as duty, it was to educate them for their future usefulness, is gone, forever gone. They have no father save Him in heaven. Again we ask, have we no tears to shed for them—no sympathy for such a grief as theirs? May God in His mercy help the widow and the orphan! May He be a Husband to the widow, and a Father to the fatherless.

If there be a single Mason present who has forgotten or neglected his duty, we admonish him at once to clear away the rubbish that chokes up the fountain of charity in his heart. Smite its adamantine walls, even as Moses smote the rock in the wilderness, and let its pure, sweet waters gush forth free and unrestrained. Every heart has within it the elixir of life, the fountain of perpetual youth; give it, oh! give it fair play, and its owner will never shrink into the avaricious miser, whose God is seen on every coin he grasps.

One by one, have our brethren gone to the tomb. They have finished their pilgrimage on earth, and now inhabit the silent city of the great King, Death. We are traveling the selfsame path they trod, and our journey has the same destination. Every second draws us nigher unto it, and at any moment we may arrive there. No human power can avert it. It is the crowning point of human life, the moment, at which man stands upon the verge of two worlds, when he takes a swift, rapid and comprehensive view of his past career, and endeavors to comprehend its just value as a preparation for that eternal world on which he is about to enter. With the certainty of our destination before us, with the knowledge of our speedy arrival there, it surely behooves man to prepare to meet his destiny. And how shall we prepare? We do not propose to trench upon the province of those whose duty it is "to point to heaven and lead the way," but, as a mason, we feel at liberty to point to that God in whom every mason heretofore declared he put his trust, to those great lights to be found upon our every altar—the Holy Bible; that inestimable gift of God to man, the rule and guide of our faith, is there; there too, we learn to square our actions with all mankind, and circumscribe and keep our passions within due bounds. In a nutshell, our whole duty is placed before us, and the injunction is ours, to perform it with regularity.

The standard of Masonry is a high one; but, oh! how few live up to it, how many fall below it—and some, we say it "more in sorrow than in anger," there are some, whose lives are a libel upon the institution of Freemasonry. Hold up before you, my brethren, the mirror of Truth, and scrutinize your image as reflected in it; test it by plumb, square and level, and satisfy yourself, if you can, that you still stand before your brethren and the world the just and upright mason you once appeared to be. If the examination be unsatisfactory, at once repair your moral and masonic edifice; repair the wrong you have done yourself and your brethren. Let the Cardinal Virtues be ever your guide. They are Temperance, Prudence, Fortitude and Justice—the Masonic North, South, East and West. Let these bright virtues mark your lives, your habits and your conversation. Let Temperance be your North Star; ever behold it, beautifully represented upon the masonic chart by a youthful virgin leaning against a broken column, with a pitcher of Water by her side—Water, cold Water, be it observed, pure, sweet and fresh as that found by Hagar in the desert.

Each of these virtues will impart their own impressive lesson, and lead us straight into the beautiful path of a mason's life. However sadly we may have erred heretofore, however widely we may have wandered from the true path, we shall yet find that our brethren will cast the mantle of Charity over us, and become oblivious to our faults, our follies and our sins; even as we have cast it over the memory of our departed brethren, and have forgiven and forgotten theirs. Their voices, sweet with the tones of Brotherly Love, strong in the power of Truth, will come to our Relief, and guide us back to the path of rectitude. When the fraternal grasp is given, and the strong arm thrown around a wayward or an erring brother, to support his weak and faltering footsteps, when good counsel is whispered in his ear, when his most hidden thought is safely deposited in a brother's faithful breast, when he remembers that on bended knee a voice is raised to heaven in his behalf, surely, with such aids as these, such love as this, the wayward and the erring will no longer refuse to return to the path of duty, of safety, and of honor. It is a broad, clear and beautiful way, embellished with shade trees and flowers, and the air is fragrant with sweet perfume. It leads us through all the chambers of our mystic Temple, where we are taught the great lesson how to live, onward to the Temple of Christianity, where we are taught that other lesson, how to die. For full well we know

> 'Tis not the whole of life to live
> Nor all of death to die.

Here again we must pause, or encroach on the province of others. By traveling the path we have feebly endeavored to point out—by learning the all-important lessons how to live and how to die, we may take the acacia, our own beautiful emblem of immortality in our hand, and while yielding obedience to Death, we can still enter the tomb and find its dark precincts illumined by the Christian's Hope—its portal, but the door opened for us to a better and brighter world than this. Thus we fondly hope our brethren have found it; thus we hope that we may find it, for

> Death's but a path that must be trod
> If man would ever pass to God.

MASONIC IDEALS*

GEORGE R. ALLEN

If you will kindly permit me to use the language of the New England minister, I suggest to you that, if you forget everything else I may say in your presence to-night, do not forget the excerpt which I quote found

---

* Response to toast at banquet of Kansas City, Kansas, Masonic lodges.

upon the program placed by your plate. It comes from
Mrs. Browning, one of those rare women who seem in
some way to have caught the gleam of poetic vision in
rare degree. She realized and voiced the truth that the
mind of man controlled his destiny. Her language is
this :

> 'Tis not what man does that exalts him,
> But what he would.

Masons ought of all men to be the most responsive to
the thought of the controlling power of ideals. The
splendid bodies of men that in all ages have exercised a
more or less controlling power over the affairs of the
world have been those whose ideals have been formulated
and imparted to them in part by the followers of those
who in the building of the Temple gave the world the
splendid ideals which we know as speculative Masonry.

And yet, while our worthy toastmaster has spoken of
the value of ideals in the speculative and abstract, and
we have heard something of the wonderful power and
influence of the Rite, I think there is something more in
ideals than that. When you make the final analysis of all
those things that yield tribute to our every day comfort,
they are but the ideal of some man, somewhere, sometime,
who moulded all his powers of body and mind round a
single concrete conception, which was to him his ideal.

And yet something more than mere life is required
to enable the fruit of ideals to manifest itself. Capacity
to profit and reap benefit must be within or ideals are as
barren of benefit as the wastes of the desert. One of the
farmers of our Kansas fields may place his choicest calf
in a pasture with blue grass knee deep; he may in these
days of general prosperity ransack the art galleries of the
world and rob them of their treasures, and hang on each
fence post surrounding that pasture a masterpiece of

painting; he may group the statuary of ancient Greece and Italy along its streams and beneath its shade trees; he may place the literature of all the ages within convenient access, and that calf will remain but a calf.

But with that farmer's child it is different. Give the boy or girl the ennobling and uplifting influence of painting and statuary, of books and all the softening and civilizing tendencies that work for good, and you develop the powers of body and mind that make the individuality what it was intended to become. And in this is found the secret of the tremendous influence of our order. Whatever the world owes to Masonry, it owes because Masonry as an institution has never been satisfied with the products of a day and generation. We live more to-day in a year than our ancient brethren lived in a century. And yet, whatever we have that is worthy of preservation is but itself the product of the ideals for the perpetuation of which was formulated this noble order whose devotees we are.

If you are inclined to think that Masonry has reached its zenith, that the future ages will know nothing more of the order than we now know, permit me to suggest that possibly those who met first upon the tessellated pavement may have been of like opinion, and we know now how weak and feeble, indeed, must have been their conception of life, living, and its attendant responsibilities compared with those we enjoy. Not a single inscription upon the walls of the Masonic Lodge but that is pregnant with meaning; not a device upon our regalia or paraphernalia but that has its own meaning and symbolizes its own ideals to our mind.

I am reminded of a story of an old southern negro who tells his experience in a haunted house. It runs something like this: "Mars John axed me tother day ef

I wuz borned to see evul, and I sed I spected I wuz, coz I had seed a powful sight of it in my day. En den he says 'Jim' sez ze, 'ef you'll go an spen' de night in dat house whar dat ol' Simpson woman died at las' week, I'll give yo five dollars in the mornin'.' I sed, 'Yassur, I'll do dat in er minit'. I've done hearn of hants and hantees but I never heard yit, what da dun hut nobody. So long 'bout night, I git me some lite wood and a lamp an' I goes over dar, and goes in and builds me a fire and lights 'e lamp, and was jes a settin' dar athinking how easy I gwine mak' dat ar five dollars, when I heard a noise at de do'. When I luk aroun', I seed a big black cat a comin' in. He was just about dat high, an' he had his tail sticking up in the air, jus' like a broom han'le. He walk erround me en I foller him wid my eyes, en den he jump on de table and look at me, en say: 'Mister dey aint nobody here but you and me, is dey?' I sez, 'No sur, en de aint gwine to be nobody but you here in a minit' Wud dat I runned outen de house, en down thro the frunt yard, en tuk the gate wid me, and after I went fru dat, I runned erbout er ten mile, when I gotten out uv bref, and wuz layin' down on de groun' tryin' to git me bref back, when erlong cum er man whut had his haide cut off, en he had his haide under his arm, so, en he walk all erroun' me en look at me an say, 'Hi dar, Nigger, but you suttinly kin run some.' I sez, 'Yessur, but you aint seed nothun' yit; jes' watch me now.'"

And thus, my brethren however much we may glorify the achievements of our order in the past; however much we may feel that its accomplishments in this day and generation are of the highest order, we must remember that in all the years that shall follow, we may say, and our successors may say, to the world, "You aint seen nothin' yit; just watch me now." This great and puissant society must in the future as in the past stand in the very forefront of progress, striving continually to live up to the ideals that have made it rock-ribbed; whose every touch has been that of life.

I said in the beginning that Masonry was an ideal; that its chief glories are idealic; that it proves it worth to live by the fruits of its existence scattered broadcast upon every hand. It claims nothing of the divine in its origin. It does not now seek, and it never in its history sought to supplant the church. It wages no warfare with any institution of mankind that seeks the elevation of the race. It joins hands with every effort for the enlightenment of mankind. It stands as the foe of all those things that tend to degrade men. It stands for purity of life, for freedom from evil, for abhorrence of every wrong deed. It knows no darkness but only light.

No man can live as high a life as his Masonic ideals inculcate. In this is found one of the reasons for the perpetuity of the order. If it were possible for you or me, or for any brother anywhere, under any circumstances, to measure in full degree within the compass of human life the full teachings of the order, Masonry would die to-morrow. Indeed, it would have died ages ago. Masonry stands as the chief exponent of esoteric teachings on non-sacred origin. It asks only of the world the privilege of promulgating its doctrines along its own lines, which are "friendship, morality and brotherly love." It concedes the weaknesses of men, and seeks to sustain them against their own evil inclinations. It asks from the world naught in return for the blessings conferred by its existence save the privilege of promulgating its beneficent existence.

The Temple, in the erection of which our order had its legendary inception, and upon the tessellated floor of which our first brethren were accustomed to meet, was an ideal. Splendid example of eastern architecture. Its golden walls and brazen columns, its porticoes and spacious courts teeming with the national life of a busy people. Real though it was to the Kingdom of Israel, it was yet in the larger sense but an ideal. Erected under the direction of Deity as a place that should symbolize His care for His people and contribute to their national life by creating a centre around which their choicest memories might cluster and for the preservation of which they might brave the most desperate conflict, it was repeatedly destroyed by the rude hand of war, and as often arose, phoenixlike from its ruins. Perhaps not for a thousand years has it been possible for a living person to place his hand upon a single stone, of all the rocks of earth, and say with assurance, "This was once a stone in the wall of the magnificent Temple." And yet no person of thought can be found anywhere who will say that the Temple of Solomon was ever at any period in the history of the world a more potent influence for good than it is in these opening years of the Twentieth century. And why? Because it is and was an ideal, marking a milestone upon the path of human progress.

Little did Jebus think, when in the infancy of the race, he selected that smooth piece of volcanic rock upon the summit of Moriah as the foundation of the crude altar he erected, and around which his sons and daughters and bond servants gathered for some form of barbaric worship, that that spot of ground should become the most noted one in history. He and his have perished, his name remembered only through the transforming and vivifying power of an ideal, with the formation of which he had nothing to do. It has become eternal.

That Temple is eternal, not because Solomon, King

of Israel, builded it, or because Hiram, King of Tyre, assisted in its construction, or because the most skillful artisan of his time, "skilled to grave in gold and silver, in iron and brass, and to find out every device that should be put to him drew its plans upon the trestle board." It is eternal because of the idea it was designed to illustrate, the ideal it symbolized in the larger sense. That Temple marked the setting of the sun of Polytheism, or many Gods; it marked the dawning of the idea of monotheism, or one God, the great central force in nature, the Creator and Preserver of his universe. The idea symbolized by it, expressed in a phrase is, "The Fatherhood of God; the Brotherhood of man"; expressed in a word it is Equality.

No conception of the unity of the race is comprehensible that involved the idea of plural force in creation. A single central power, responsible to its creatures, is necessary to fulfill the natural law of creator and creature. The Supreme Architect is possible only as we conceive his unity of being and his singleness of purpose. What mind can understand two fathers in a natural sense?

We who stand to-day as the successors of those early brethren who formulated the ideals under which we work, and to which we acknowledge allegiance cannot lose sight for a moment of their true significance. Opportunities and responsibilities have increased hand in hand. The ideals of the founders of the art have been realized only in part. In one sense they can never be realized, because they are as limitless as eternity itself. The institution they gave the world must stand at all times in the very forefront of progress planning for and accomplishing greater things in the future than it may have enjoyed in the past.

Masonry is conservative, but if I read its ideals aright I understand that it countenances no dead line the cross-

'ing of which is death. Upon the contrary I understand that the Mason who truly gathers the lessons his lodge would teach him must be one who knows no rest, no satisfaction with things done, who catches a gleam of the transforming power of the high ideals placed before him, and lets each succeeding day in his life mark some fruit of the teachings whose devotee he is.

RESPONSE TO ADDRESS OF WELCOME

HON. JACK BEALL

I came for a little while to sit at the feet of the men who have founded this Order, who have been with it during the years of its growth, to learn from them, and not with any thought or expectation of instructing or entertaining anyone else. I was on the program last night, and think it would be better for some of those brothers who then had no opportunity to address this convention to do so rather than myself.

I am very much gratified to learn of the encouraging state of this fraternal organization. I am a great believer in these organizations for more reasons than one. I believe in them because I believe that they teach a great and important lesson that this country needs to learn now, needs to understand now as, perhaps, it never needed it before; that the world ought to understand as it has never understood it before—that, in spite of difference in class, if there be classes, or difference in station of life; in spite of differences of vocations and professions; in spite of all these things, we all, at last, belong to the same great family—brothers in truth and in fact—and our destiny is indissolubly linked and connected one with the other. I believe that it is important that this lesson be taught and impressed, and taught and impressed again, upon the hearts of the American people. I believe in these organizations for another reason—because they give protection to those who are most in need of it.

Not only do we as members of the organization contribute our part to the upbuilding of the organization, but the organization in turn helps and strengthens us, making all of us better citizens, making all of us better husbands, better wives, better fathers, better mothers, better brothers, better sisters, better in every way.

I heard a story one time of an ancient city that employed a cunning artist to create a statue of the most beautiful woman of the land. It was erected in a public place and stood there a thing of grace and of beauty. One day a little, ragged, unkempt girl came to the public square and looked with admiring eyes upon the figure. Her dress was torn, her hair unkempt, her face dirty. The next day she came back and looked again at the figure and her face was cleaner. She came again and her dress was tidy and neat. She came again and her hair was combed. She came again and again, and as the years went by and that girl grew to womanhood, it was said that she resembled all the features and form of that beautiful statue of the most beautiful woman of the land. The influence of that inanimate thing left its impress upon the heart of that little girl as years went by; she modeled herself after it and became like it. So it is in these great fraternal organizations. When we contemplate the great principles that underlie and support them, when we devote our minds to the consideration of their beautiful teachings, the spirit and sentiment of them permeate our own being, and we, unconsciously perhaps, learn to model our lives more and more after them and become filled with the spirit that animates these great organizations.

I believe in them because they are helping to make this old world of ours better than it has ever been before. I believe the world is getting better; I believe that there is more charity now among men than ever was before; I believe there is more consideration and love for our fellow-man. I believe there is a greater disposition to extend the helping hand to those who are down, to lift them up to a higher and purer atmosphere than they have ever lived in before. I believe this condition is largely true because this spirit of fraternityship is being taught and instilled into the hearts of all of our people. The lesson is being learned that it is not wealth, that it is not power, that it is not high position, that it is not social prestige that is to determine the status of humanity in the future, but it is the higher and truer things—greatness of mind, of ideals, of aspirations, of hopes, that are to uplift and to make this world better.

The very essence of all fraternal organization is the spirit of love taught by Him who died upon the cross. He taught the sublime and divine lesson that the world is beginning to recognize, to understand, to endorse and live up to.

I heard another story; read it somewhere, of a mother, a great lady of the land, who was about to start upon a long journey. She had three sons. She asked them to give her before she left them some token of their affection and love. One of the sons brought to her a beautiful tab_ let of marble, with her name chiseled upon it. Another brought her a piece of finest gold, with her likeness engraved upon it. The third son came to her and said· "Mother, I have no tablet of marble, no likeness of gold to give to you, but I have a heart; upon that heart your name is written and your likeness engraved; that heart, full of affection, will follow you wherever you may go and be with you wherever you repose." So it is in this world of ours to-day. It is affection that fills the heart of man towards his fellowman; that is making the world greater and better than it has ever been before. It is not the towering monuments that we erect to those who have done great deeds; it is not the great institutions that men, endowed with great wealth, have been building, that are doing the great work in uplifting humanity and inspiring it with nobler ideals and higher actions. It is the golden thread of sympathy and love and affection that reaches from one heart to another, reaches from one brother down into the depths, touches and is twined about the heart of the fallen one, lifting him up, making the world more beautiful than it has ever been before.

From the depths of my heart I say to you may the God of mercy look with favor upon these great fraternal organizations that are lifting up His fallen children and instilling into their hearts purer ideals and inspiring their lives with nobler ambitions than ever before.

FIVE ELEMENTARY CHARACTERISTICS

ABB LANDIS

Nothing is more significant of the standing and importance of the fraternal beneficiary societies than the recognition of them as competitors by the regular life companies and the attention accorded them by the insurance commissioners.

Further evidence of the importance of fraternal beneficiary societies is the existence of some two hundred of them, with more than seven million members and promised benefits exceeding eight billion dollars.

In these circumstances it is appropriate to have a clear and comprehensive presentation of the distinguishing characteristics of fraternal beneficiary societies, together with some references to their history, their strength, their weakness, their opportunities, their relation to the State and to society, and in what particulars they differ from or resemble charitable and benevolent organizations, pure fraternal orders, open assessment associations, and the regular legal reserve life companies.

All of these subjects cannot be fully treated in one paper of moderate length. In this first paper it is thought best to consider the "Five Elementary Characteristics" of fraternal beneficiary societies, which may be designated:

> Co-operation,
> Fraternity,
> Constitution,
> Object, and
> Permanency.

CO-OPERATION

In order to form a society, the first and absolute requisite is *co-operation* of a number of persons.

The very essence of co-operation is mutuality. Unless aims, purposes, interests, efforts, and management are upon a mutual basis, there can be no effective co-operation for the general good of the association, whether in a social, fraternal, or financial way.

Co-operation means *the act of working together to one end;*

> *combining for a certain purpose;*
> *joint endeavor;*
> *concurrent effort.*

These definitions, in their widest sense and in their

application to co-operation in a fraternal beneficiary society, signify the combined activities of many persons under a voluntary system of mutual helpfulness.

"Work together" is the literal meaning of *co-operation;* and it obviously fails when there is "pulling apart," or division, dissension, disorganization, or desire to forward selfish designs to the detriment of the general membership.

Complete co-operation is the fundamental and foundation principle upon which societies are based. It is the first and absolutely requisite elementary characteristic of mutual association.

FRATERNITY

Second to co-operation and mutual association there must be *fraternity* in a *fraternal* beneficiary society. Without *fraternity* the society would be as the play of "Hamlet" with the role of the eccentric Dane omitted.

Fraternity is not proved an existent fact by formal greeting as a brother. There must be sincere regard for the welfare of others and unfeigned pleasure in their fellowship.

Individual interest may (and it does) influence the lawyer, the doctor, the merchant, the grocer, the tailor, the butcher, the barber, the regalia manufacturer, and other craftsmen, to seek association and personal acquaintance with each other and with wage earners and breadwinners generally through the medium of the lodge room; but the desire for private gain and advancement must be subordinated to that of mutual good; otherwise the name "fraternity" will be a cloak for deception and sordid selfishness.

Fraternity must be coupled with *co-operation* if *joint endeavor* is to be most effective.

In a purely business enterprise it is possible to have successful *co-operation* by mutual agreement among persons who are entire strangers to each other, and no mutual ties to bind them together except the provisions of a written contract or by common patronage. Instances of such are fire, marine, and life insurance companies; building and loan associations; savings and commercial banks; etc. Mutuality in such institutions is confined to *concurrent effort,* with no other end in view than the accomplishment of an individual purpose only obtainable through combination and co-operation.

Fraternal co-operation is the perfection of mutual association in *joint endeavor* and *concurrent effort.*

Co-operation supplemented by *fraternity* gives added power to mutual association, as demonstrated in the popularity and vitality of beneficiary and friendly societies.

Members of fraternal beneficiary societies are not strangers, though they have never met. They know and recognize each other by virtue of the bonds and vows of *fraternity.* As citizens of the same country will march under a common flag to a common death for pure patriotism, so members of the same fraternity will stand by their society and their associates through pure love and loyalty. In this lies the superior strength of the fraternal beneficiary societies over those co-operative organizations where the fraternal bond is missing. Members of these societies have a higher aim and a nobler purpose than that of mere personal gain, financial advantage, or·conservation only of family interests. Philanthropy, charity, benevolence, and all of the higher traits of human nature are developed by *fraternal co-operation.*

Since, in our state of interdependency of interests, it is impossible for a full and rounded man to live for himself alone, the highest attainment and the consummation of an ideal relationship result when he is placed in association with his fellows under conditions which enable all to work together harmoniously as brothers in a common cause.

Fraternal consideration is the exemplification of the Golden Rule, and necessarily must exert a powerful influence toward the perfection and effectiveness of any mutual and co-operative activity and effort.

CONSTITUTION

There must be organization and system and intelligent direction in any joint endeavor, according to well-defined rules and well-digested regulations, if certain and continued success is assured.

It is as an army without a general, a State without a Governor, for a society to have no directing and controlling power. But, to be thoroughly and mutually co-operative, the authority for directing the affairs of the organization should be consonant with prescribed provisions clearly set out in a *constitution* framed to give the fullest expression to the will and intent of the members.

There can be organization, system, and direction without a constitution prescribing rules and regulations for the guidance and restraint of managing officials, as in the case of a life insurance company; but invariably the government and control of the organization become oligarchic and autocratic when the power of officials is not limited and restricted by constitutional provisions, the violation of which annuls their authority and renders void any act that is *ultra licitum*.

A constitution is an absolute necessity for a fraternal beneficiary society intending to have a representative form of government with supreme control retained by the members; indeed, in most of the States a fraternal beneficiary

society could have no legal standing without a constitu-
tion. The advantage and benefit of such are so patent
that specifications are not here required.

OBJECT

Without some definite *object,* some fixed purpose,
there could be no basis for mutual and fraternal *co-opera-
tion.* This is a self-evident fact which needs no elabora-
tion. However, most societies have more than one object;
and there is room for discussion when there is multiplic-
ity of purposes. In a later paper the proper objects of
fraternal operation will be reviewed. It is now pertinent
to indicate the comprehensive scope of the average
beneficiary society by quoting from the declaration of
principles of a grand lodge of one of the oldest and larg-
est of these organizations:

OBJECTS.

1. To unite white male persons—regardless of nationality,
political preferences, or denominational distinctions—into a
fraternal brotherhood, the members of which recognize and believe
in the existence of a Supreme Being, the Creator and Preserver of
the universe.

2. The adoption of such secret work and means of recogni-
tion as will enable the members to make themselves known to
each other wherever the order may exist.

3. To embrace and give equal consideration to all classes and
kinds of labor, mental and physical; to endeavor to improve the
moral, intellectual, and social condition of the members; and, by
wholesome precepts and fraternal admonitions, to inspire a due
appreciation of the realities and responsibilities of life.

4. To hold lectures; read essays; discuss inventions and
improvements; encourage research in art, science, and literature;
and, when practicable, establish and maintain libraries for the
improvement of the members.

5. To create funds in aid of the members during sickness or
other disabilities, and, generally, to care for the living and bury
the dead.

6. To pledge the members to the payment of a stipulated sum to such beneficiary as a deceased member may have designated—subject, however, to such restrictions and upon such conditions as the laws of the order may prescribe.

PERMANENCY

Were the fraternal beneficiary societies, like the open assessment associations, to pass out of existence, one of the most potent influences for good would be lost to the human race.

It were a useless fear to anticipate such a catastrophe. It would be as reasonable to predict the failure of the church, to prophesy the subversion of human nature and the eradication of all kindness and sympathy and love from the heart, as to set a limit to the future existence of the fraternal beneficiary system.

The germ of fraternal co-operation was planted so long ago and its roots have become so imbedded and interwoven into the very fabric of human institutions that with its destruction would disappear the established order of our social and civil customs.

That individual societies have failed and that others may fail will not be disputed. Such failures are not a discouragement, nor do they presage the failure of the fraternal beneficiary system.

Final success and improved methods and perfected operation are built upon the ruins of previous effort.

We learn from mistakes and profit by errors.

By the mariner who has wrecked his vessel upon the hidden rock we are directed into the channel; by the man who has tried and failed we are warned against impractical schemes.

Improvement and progress and development follow failure.

Servile imitation is the reward of success.

In every line of mutual co-operation there have been failures. Hundreds and thousands of them! Mutual insurance companies of every description! Savings banks, building and loan associations, and all manner of co-operative enterprises!

Nothing has come perfected from the human brain. The heart moved men to friendly thought of their unfortunate associates, and the mind imperfectly devised ways and means of relief. Trial and experience, experience and failure, failure and improvement, improvement and progress, progress and perfection! Such is the slow development of man's strenuous endeavor; such is the course to the goal from the beginning to the end of his thinking.

Of course there have been failures of fraternal beneficiary societies, as there have been failures of life insurance companies. The insurance system is not yet perfect, nor are men infallible; and there will be more failures of societies and companies—all of which means improvement and progress and ultimate perfection.

Failures are unfortunate circumstances in respect of those who thereby must suffer and sacrifice. For the great majority they are most important events in teaching how to avoid errors and how to correct mistakes.

Human progress always gives pain to somebody. To move forward, the halting and the lame and the weak must be pushed aside or trampled under foot. Even the word of God has come to the hearts of the unconverted through means of the sword, the ax, the guillotine, the torch, and the horrors of the Inquisition.

A few failures, more or less, signify nothing as to the *permanency* of the fraternal beneficiary system. However, there is this consolation to its advocates: Fewer failures have occurred among fraternal orders than among any other kind of mutually co-operative organizations.

The strength of *fraternity* has sustained them in trials that would have wrecked and ruined other co-operative institutions without the fraternal spirit to support them.

As a truth, it should not be said that any fraternal society has ever "failed," because *failure* is generally construed to mean financial loss. Where these societies have gone out of existence there has been no financial loss. Every member has received all that he has paid for. He has had his protection, and he has only paid for his protection. Millions in funds have not been accumulated to be lost by failure, as in the cases of the failures of the "old-line" companies. It must also be remembered that when one of these societies goes out of existence, it leaves no young men with dependent young wives and children without protection; for there only remain the aged, the great majority of whom have no dependents, and their assessments generally are paid by others as a matter of speculation. If "failure" is to be construed to mean financial loss, then it must not be said that any fraternal society has "failed," but that its existence has ended in decay, dissolution, death.

Where societies have become extinct—"failed," if you please—the minimum of injury has resulted, invariably preceded by the accomplishment of untold good.

There was the American Legion of Honor. It "failed" after twenty-six years of operation and after the distribution of forty-three million dollars for the support of widows and the maintenance and education of orphan children. It "failed," but not before making a glorious and imperishable record; it "failed," but not in dishonor; it "failed," but not without teaching an invaluable lesson concerning methods and plans for perpetuating similar organizations now turning toward *permanency*.

No, "failure" should not cause discouragement;

defects in methods of operation should not produce despondency; while criticism should be turned to profit and competition should whet determination for improvement and success.

CREATIVE FRATERNALISM

(From THE FRATERNAL MONITOR.)

In talking with a fraternalist who is a recognized leader in our institutions, existing conditions and their trend came up for review. THE MONITOR suggested that too much turmoil and agitation were conditions precedent to efforts of a progressive nature and that results along this line were minimized in this way.

It was observed that too much consideration was given to matters of a detail nature and not enough to those having to do with the system in its entirety. Internal situations were allowed to dominate rather than those having as their central purpose results for the performance of which organizations exist and for which members identify themselves with them.

In other words, there is not enough of creative fraternalism in evidence. There is not that comprehensive view manifested which gives details their proper place and which makes the ends aimed at the main consideration. Briefly, to use a Biblical phrase, "we strain at a gnat and swallow a camel." Is it not worth our while to give at least passing attention to this view?

DIFFICULTIES EXAGGERATED.

Are we not making the burden of our songs matters of a comparatively insignificant nature? Are we not impeding the onward progress of our great system by attempting to thresh out details which carry with them a solution for the problems they create? In the language of Newton, are we not playing along the shores of fraternal operation while the great ocean of its possibilities lies before us? Should we not set sail on this ocean duly equipped for the voyage we have in view and possessing as an inherent power that liberty of action permitting us to conform to conditions as they present themselves?

It was a man of ripe experience who observed to his son that, "I have had to contend with many difficulties in my life, but the majority of these never happened." So it is in the conduct of our fraternal institutions. They may plan in a manner covering the most remote of details and they meet all sorts of fancied difficulties in advance, but in actual operation they will find that the majority of the things for which they have made provision "never happened."

What we need to-day is a creative fraternalism—a fraternalism which has as its central purpose the promotion of the best interests of its members and the protection of its dependents. We need a fraternalism that realizes that the future is fraught with problems of an uncertain nature; we need a fraternalism that has as its central purpose the solution of such problems in the best possible manner; we need a fraternalism that does not cavil at technicalities and does not brook opposition in carrying out the purposes for which it exists.

AVOID PETTY TRAMMELS.

When one ponders over the comprehensive purposes for which our institutions exist, he cannot but be impressed with the difficulties bound to arise in the way of forecasting their future or of deciding their limitations. In a degree, they are republics to themselves, organized for mutual well-being and behoof, and they should possess powers sufficiently broad to permit them to adapt themselves to the ever-changing order of things. They should not be limited to hard and fast rules· which may be applicable to-day and obsolete to-morrow. They should not be so hemmed in by petty trammels and environments that they are able to perform in but a limited way the purposes for which they exist.

THE MONITOR believes that we have given too much attention to matters having to do with the internal affairs of individual societies. It believes that these have been given too broad publicity. It is of the opinion that conditions in common with all institutions of human creation—in common with humanity, for that matter—have been given a degree of publicity that makes them assume abnormal proportions as compared with other affairs of life. It believes that, in a degree, those who have been on the watch-towers have had the perspective of their vision so distorted that they could see but difficulties and obstacles to overcome rather than the glorious promise awaiting those who have the courage to do and persevere.

THE HABIT OF CRITICISM.

The habit of criticism, in common with all other habits, grows with use. By dwelling upon one particular feature or subject, one becomes so permeated with its importance that there is danger lest he allow this to overshadow in his own mind that of other elements or considerations having equally as much to do with the proposition in its entirety.

The fraternal system is so broad and comprehensive that it requires a broad and comprehensive mind to even grasp its possibilities. One inclined to a particular line or adaptation is apt to regard these as paramount to all others.

There is need for specialists in fraternal work. The service they have to perform is an important one. Likewise, it is important that they be limited to the special field on which they have particular information and that they be not allowed to have this obscure other situations or considerations equally as important.

There is a tendency on the part of the specialist to magnify the importance of that to which he gives particular attention. Other factors are not accorded that thought to which their importance entitles them. He loses sight of general conditions. His particular aim is to set forth accurately that which is under his particular observation. Whether or no other elements equally as important are given their due share of attention in the general proposition is something concerning which he has but a hazy idea.

The fraternal proposition is a many-sided one. It has divers and diverse interests to employ and harmonize. No particular one will work out successfully unless the other receives the attention to which its importance entitles it. All must be considered as regards their relation to the whole, and it is just as much an error to neglect one at the expense of the other as it is to neglect all of them.

A CREATIVE SPIRIT.

What is needed to-day, above all things else, is a creative spirit in fraternal ranks—a spirit which embraces the general purposes and possibilities of the cause and which makes the various elements interwoven with it to do their proper share of service in bringing efforts to a successful issue.

There is needed that spirit of earnestness and enthusiasm which brushes aside obstacles created either by actual conditions or by a biased view of them. It needs a spirit of accomplishment which judges the proposition by its results rather than by the various elements interwoven with it. It needs a spirit which brooks neither unnecessary restraint or delay—a spirit which carries opposition before it or makes it do service in its behalf.

As has been said, there is danger lest the various problems we have encountered in the onward march of our system become so distorted and exaggerated that they become a serious menace to the future. Such conditions have existed in all undertakings and, unless the abnormal is experienced, will continue to be in evidence in one form or another in the future.

We should only regard them in the light of factors having to do with strengthening and adding to the effectiveness of our undertaking. At no time and under no circumstances should they be regarded as a bar sinister to progress, or as an element that menaces existence.

THE MONITOR does not wish its observations to be interpreted as a criticism on fraternal exponents generally, or as a reflection on the progress they have made. On this latter score the results themselves are in evidence. They show progress of a most pronounced nature. They set forth attainments eclipsing all previous efforts. They set forth in most emphatic terms what can be accomplished when criticism and earnest efforts are put forth.

NO OCCASION FOR PESSIMISM.

There are those in a more or less envious frame of mind who point to progressive effort in terms of criticism. They forecast the time when it will be impossible to keep up such ratio of progress, and otherwise they evidence that critical and captious spirit utterly out of joint with the tenets of fraternalism. It is to such that these comments are directed. There is no occasion for a pessimistic attitude or for carping criticism. Rather, the time is here when we should set our faces resolutely forward and when we should look toward present accomplishments and future prospects rather than toward past difficulties.

We need creative fraternalism. We need those who have the mind and power to plan even greater things for the future. We need those so thoroughly entrenched in the principles of fraternal operation that they regard each difficulty met and overcome as but a stepping stone to greater accomplishments. It is such who have made the present magnificent fraternal record possible. These are the ones who will bring about greater results as the years roll on.

STRONGER THAN EVER.

Much of the criticism with which fraternal operation has been visited the past few years is due to the pessimistic notes sounded by many of its champions and leaders. The opponents of fraternalism get the basis for their attacks from such an attitude. They enlarge upon results and use their imaginations to picture ends of a most disastrous nature. Largely, their arguments are based upon those of fraternal exponents who have allowed their ardor to cool and who have interpreted their own misgivings as conditions indicative of future trouble.

We have but to look at fraternal achievements to realize how utterly at fault are those who mould their prophecies along such lines. The system has gone forward by leaps and bounds. It was greater, larger and stronger a year ago to-day than it was a year prior to this. It is stronger and better fitted for its undertaking to-day than it was ever before in its history. Each month adds to its strength and to the good accomplished. What we need are those who can use present conditions as a basis upon which to build a greater and broader fraternalism.

PROTECTION AS FURNISHED BY THE ANNUITY SYSTEM OF INSURANCE

BY A. T. STEVENS

As Fraternalists we are all deeply interested in the one great central idea and purpose that has called our organizations into being, and that is the best plan and method of furnishing the fullest possible measure of aid and protection to the members of our societies, and their beneficiaries.

Fraternalism in the United States has a wonderful record to its credit, in its brief existence of about a third of a century almost *one billion dollars* having been paid in benefits to members, their widows, orphans and other beneficiaries. No man can ever tell the amount of misery and suffering this money has prevented, nor words express the good that has been accomplished by it, and yet we are still inquirers, still striving to attain to greater perfection in furnishing complete protection to the loved ones of our own families, and to the families of our brother members. And we find that to this end the various societies are devising new plans and methods, as experience develops the need of improvements upon the older ones in use.

WHAT IS LIFE INSURANCE PROTECTION?

We often hear and use the words "Life Insurance" and "Protection," but what do we understand by "Life Insurance Protection?" As commonly understood to-day it means that a man takes out a policy of insurance, or certificate with a Fraternal society, on which he makes payments of so much each year, or each month as long as he lives and then at his death, his wife or other beneficiary will receive from the company or society the amount of money called for in his policy or certificate, and it is a very common expression often heard, that "Mrs. A. or Mrs. B. has insurance protection to the amount of $1,000 or $5,000."

This expression is correct and proper as to the amount of insurance, and also to the extent of the amount named "Mrs. A. or Mrs. B. is presumed to be protected," but does this satisfy the fraternal heart that "Mrs. A." or "Mrs. B." is, or can be fully and permanently protected even with this amount of insurance money? Does it not rather raise in our minds the question whether the "Life Insurance Protection" we desire for the loved ones of our household can be measured or secured by the thousand dollars unit value? If not, is there any other system or method by which greater protection can be assured?

We believe that it is the sincere desire of every man who procures "Life Insurance Protection" for those dependent upon him, that the protection shall be as nearly as possible similar to that he has furnished to them during his life time. He would if he could so arrange that his loved ones should never know want, and should never become dependents upon any persons or charitable institutions, but should be always cared for by the provisions he is able to make in their behalf. It was from such feelings as these that the "System of Protective Life Insurance" was evolved, and it is only by carrying out as near as possible these desires that the fullest measure of protection can be assured to the beneficiaries.

ONLY TWO WAYS.

Generally speaking, there are but two ways of making payment of insurance money to the beneficiary. One is that form which is in most common use in this country, where at the time of the death of the policy or certificate holder, there is paid over to the beneficiary in one lump sum the amount called for in the policy or certificate held by the insured. This payment completes the transaction so far as the society or company is concerned, they having fully complied with all the requirements and terms of the insurance contract. Insurance money paid over in this way may properly be termed as "provided capital." That is, the insured has left for the benefit and protection of the beneficiary a fixed amount of money which if sufficient to invest may produce an income for the support and maintenance of the beneficiary, or which if used by proper and careful management, may supply her needs and wants.

The other form is known and designated as "annuity" or "income" payments; under this plan the beneficiary does not receive one large sum upon the death of the insured, but only receives a certain specified amount required to be paid at that time, and thereafter at certain stated periods, either annually, semi-annually, quarterly or monthly, covering a number of years or during the life of the beneficiary, will receive these stated amounts until the conditions of the certificate or policy have been fulfilled.

When the payments to be made on any "annuity" certificate are for a certain number of years or months, it is designated as a "Limited Annuity Certificate." If the payments are to be made during the life of the beneficiary it is known as a "Life Annuity Certificate," or as designated by the insurance companies a "Continuous Installment Policy."

We have learned by experience that under no system or plan can the fraternal societies furnish insurance or protection below cost, and the system of annuity insurance is not exempt from this demand for "adequate rates of contribution."

Some of the chief objections that are urged against the plan of protective insurance that furnishes in one large amount a sum of money or "capital" for the beneficiary are

While it places in the hands of the beneficiary a sufficient amount of money to provide for a livelihood for a time at least, it does not and cannot ensure that the beneficiary will always be provided for and protected by this money. The beneficiary may live for many years, or by reason of physical disability may be barred from earning a livelihood, and the amount of the insurance money may not be sufficient, even with the most economical use, to furnish the required protection.

In many cases this "precious insurance money" has been lost by ill-advised investments, sometimes wasted by extravagant living, or false ideals, sometimes loaned to impecunious friends or relatives, without security, and no possible hope of its ever being repaid, and in many other ways it has been lost or dissipated. It matters not by what means this "protection" is lost or squandered, in each and every case it fails to accomplish that for which the provider intended it; the provider is gone and the provision can never be made again. The loss of insurance money received by beneficiaries in large amounts, are not in rare and exceptional cases, but are sufficiently numerous to cause Fraternalists to give this subject serious consideration, and if possible find a remedy. In fact, so many instances have occurred that only a few years ago a former insurance commissioner of one of our largest States, in making a plea that there be added to his office a bureau for the investment of insurance money of the beneficiaries of the State, made this statement: "That of all moneys received from insurance companies, the beneficiaries have within five years from the time of receiving it lost or parted with the greater portion of it."

ANNUITY LIFE INSURANCE PROTECTION.

Without going into a detailed history of the "annuity" or "income" system of protective insurance, how natural and fraternal was its beginning, born of love and sympathy going out to the helpless widows and orphans of brother fellow-craftsmen, with a true desire to render them aid and assistance. How simple, effective and lasting was the remedy suggested and applied.

The wages of fellow-workmen had ceased with their death, and these widows and orphans needed *the wages* for their sustenance and support. This was the condition that confronted these men, and the hearts of the living fellow-workmen answered, "We will join ourselves together, and contribute from our earnings, and pay over to these helpless and dependent ones the amounts necessary for their comfortable support, at just such times as the provider brought to them his wages; in this way we will always know that they are provided for, and then when we are called away by death our living brothers will see to it that our own loved ones are also cared for."

This was the birth of "True Fraternalism." There were no eminent actuaries to mystify these pioneers of "Protective Life Insurance" with puzzling figures, and estimates, no supervision of insurance departments nor other impediments to hamper them in their good work of love and benevolence, and as the years rolled by they grew in power and strength and numbers.

There are well authenticated records of "Widows' and Orphans' Aids," "Widows' Funds," "Guilds," and other societies that have practiced this plan for almost two centuries, furnishing "permanent protection" to the widows, orphans and other dependents of deceased mem_ bers, which not only proves that this system antedates all other plans for the protection of the "home and family," but also demonstrates that these societies had learned the true secret of fraternalism.

How many thousands or millions of dollars were paid to beneficiaries by these earliest pioneers will never be known, as it was not a part of their business to keep a strict account of what any one beneficiary received, *but it was their chief business* to see that not one of those whose welfare depended upon them should ever be neglected or forgotten.

The larger number of present-day "Annuity Societies" are located in England and Scotland, although there are many in France and Germany and some in other European countries. Some of these societies claim existence for several hundreds of years. A number of the British societies have fairly intelligible statistics, covering from seventy-five to one hundred and twenty-five years. The general plans of these societies are similar, the rates of contribution and amounts of benefits varying with the different societies, according to their purposes and objects. Provisions are made by these societies for the payment of the following benefits:

Annuities for life will be paid to a father, a mother, a wife (unless she remarries), or a physically disabled child.

Children who are not physically disabled may be provided "Annuities" until they become of legal age.

For other beneficiaries the "Annuities" are limited to a certain number of payments, or years.

Provisions are also made for the member himself in case of total disability, or old age, usually one-half of the amounts to be paid to the beneficiary after his death, for total disability, and the full amounts as an old age disability.

"Annuity" benefits are estimated at so much each year, and payments are made on account of them, either annually, semi-annually, quarterly, or monthly, according to the rules of the different societies.

Some of the Scotch societies claim records of "Annuitants" who have received benefits for more than half a century, many "Annuitants" who have been paid for more than forty years each, and a vast number who have received benefits for shorter varying periods, and we believe that it has never been intimated or reported that one of the least of these beneficiaries has ever been overlooked or neglected.

The "Annuity System" as practiced in England and Scotland was, we believe, introduced into this country about twenty-five years ago under the Fraternal Plan, and the certificates issued contained all the provisions of the British societies. Other societies have been organized in recent years which contain many features of these societies, with some variations in the provisions made to the beneficiaries; one of these features is to issue a "Limited Annuity Certificate" to every member which calls for a certain number of stipulated payments covering a number of months or years, and in cases where "Life Annuities" are granted, the "Life Annuity Certificate" is issued. Supplementary to the "Limited Annuity Certificate," that is, there will be paid on account of the "Limited Certificate" a certain number of payments to all alike, this gives a specific amount of insurance on the installment or income plan, and then where a "Life Annuity Certificate" is held in connection with a "Limited Certificate" the payments on account of the "Life Annuity Certificates" commence after the payments have all been made on account of the "Limited Certificates," provided that the beneficiary be then living, and in case of a widow, she still remains the widow of the certificate holder. These societies are constantly growing in popular favor. Some of the older societies have added "Annuity" or "Installment" certificates, and others have provided that the insured, or beneficiary under any certificate may, if they so option, have the amount of the certificate paid in "installments" covering a period of years.

In addition to these movements among the Frater nal Societies, the Old Line Life insurance companies have been conducting a campaign for some years in favor of insurance on the "Annuity" or "Continuous Install ment" plan, and by these things we observe that this system of protection is receiving much attention in the insurance world.

Many incidents could be related from experience where the insurance on the "Annuity" plan has been an unmixed blessing to the beneficiaries. It has often saved the widow from being the target of an adventurer, as there could be no money he could get his hands on, as by remarrying the widow would lose the income. It has proved to be the one thing only, that many widows could count on, even when they supposed that they had other resources that would not fail them, because there was no way that any person could deprive them of this sacred protection.

ARGUMENTS IN FAVOR OF ANNUITY INSURANCE PROTECTION.

There are many arguments in favor of "Annuity" or "Income" insurance for protection, but we shall only briefly state a few of them.

First, it is the most natural form of protection in the world. The insured, who has always protected the loved ones by his salary or wages is called away by death, but the demands for food, and fuel, and clothing and the other necessaries of life, still continue with his family; the society steps in to replace the provider, and there is paid over to the widow a certain amount of money—not a large sum—with which she is to provide the necessaries of life for a month, or perhaps for three months, or six months. She understands that this money is to take the place of the wages formerly brought home for these purposes by her husband, and she knows just what to do with it. She does not need to advise with any person as to its use, and so provisions are made until the time when she receives another amount equal to the first, and for the same purpose, and to provide for the same length of time, and so it goes on, sometimes for years, sometimes during the life of the beneficiary. "Pay-day" comes not once, but many times, and the dependent ones are protected and cared for.

Second, the "Annuity System" is the most elastic form of protection known, and enables a father, a husband, or children to provide just the protection they desire for the loved ones; "life incomes" for a father, a mother, or a wife; "incomes" for children, to furnish the means for their care and education, until they are equipped to fight in the battles of life; "incomes" for other dependents for the term of years desired.

Third, the insurance money cannot be lost or wasted, bringing distress and disaster to those dependent upon it. If one installment should not be rightly used, it will only be a short time until another installment is received, making it utterly impossible to suffer much from ill-advised or foolish extravagance, such as would be the case if the insurance money were in one large sum, and should be lost or wasted.

Fourth, the "Income" is the golden ideal of every true man, and if he plans and labors to any purpose at all in life, it is to reach a time,—perhaps in old age,—when by his labor and thrift he shall himself enjoy an "Income" without being obliged to toil from day to day. And if a husband, the anticipated joy is greater by the thought that *his wife,* who has stood so nobly with him in the battles of life, shall enjoy with him this surcease from toil and labor; and when the true husband realizes that death may prevent him from ever enjoying this "Income," how natural it is for him to try to make sure that if he fails to realize the golden dream, he will at least provide so that his wife may enjoy the "Income."

Fifth, "Life Annuity" protection makes the beneficiary independent, and forever takes away the bitter thought that the loved ones shall become dependents, or a charge upon any persons or charity, even though they live to a very old age.

Sixth, more insurance can be provided at the same cost where the payments are made to the beneficiary on the "Annuity" or "Installment" plan than can be furnished in one lump sum payable at the death of the insured.

Seventh.—Under the "Annuity System," that fraternal feeling that goes out to the brother member is kept alive by being in constant touch with his beneficiary after his death, sometimes for many years, and the fraternal spirit may be often invoked, or shown in many ways,— by counsel, or advice, or other service, and often smooth out for the dependent ones, many of the rough places in the journey of life.

Much more could be said in favor of the "Annuity System" of protective life insurance, and we sincerely believe it to be worthy of the greatest consideration by the fraternal societies of our country, for we believe that our organizations are destined to work out and develop the best and highest forms of protective life insurance the world has ever known.

A CASE IN POINT

BY CHARLES H. COONS

This is a brief chapter from the life story of three men—a wise man, a wiser man and one not so wise. Since I do not pretend to be a student of philosophy you will have to draw your own conclusions as to which was which.

I have named my three men, Brown, Black, and Green—not because I think it will add color to the narrative, however. Nomenclatorial perfection is hardly to be expected in a homely homily like this.

I presume you have all read of the thrifty German citizen who wanted the street railway company to increase the fare to ten cents. He said he would save more money when he walked. This was left-handed and illogical reasoning; but a whole lot of people get their thinking caps on crooked occasionally. Wait until you read about Brown. But, as the novelist would say, we are digressing.

Brown owned and operated a swell shoe-shop on a swell thoroughfare. The panes of plate glass were a little larger than any on the block. The electric lighting for the roomy show windows was conspicuously elaborate and good. Suspended over the sidewalk was a massive sign with large letters of fire. The windows were undeniably "dressed" by expert hands. Within were rows upon rows of boxes carefully arranged upon shelves of solid oak. The floor was handsomely carpeted and the long tiers of seats cushioned with costly leather.

The cashier's window was like that of a bank—the kind of bank that frowns upon a small depositor. The brass was burnished daily by a negro in full uniform.

When Brown was not strolling about surveying the luxurious surroundings with pride and self-satisfaction he was seated at his great mahogany desk in the private office. An air of elegance pervaded the entire place, a fact which could scarcely escape the notice of the customers. Possibly some of them may have thought Brown was accumulating wealth rather rapidly and that when they purchased shoes at his establishment they were contributing as much to the brass fixtures and the liveried negro as to the real value of the footwear.

A square below and on the opposite side of the ave nue Black kept another shoe store. The electric lights in his show windows were not so numerous as his neigh bor's and there was no flaring, fiery sign to illumine the darkness of night. On either side of the entrance appeared the proprietor's name in modest gilt letters. The goods in the windows were tastefully arranged, though there was no regal display of purple plush. Each article bore a neat, plain pricemark to catch the public eye. Within were comfortable accommodations for patrons. The clerks were neither unadept nor discourteous, even when they were busy, which was nearly the entire time. There was a snug little office at the rear, but the burnished brass and the concomitant burnisher were not in evidence. The customers were satisfied and Black was wont to remark that his large increase in trade was due to this fact—the purchasers told their friends.

Now let us see about Green. An honest, every-day business man, he has made friends as well as a competence, and he has enjoyed life. For years he has bought his shoes of Brown. He could not have told you why, except that it had become a habit with him. Brown was not an intimate friend—barely a business acquaintance, in fact. Furthermore, his prices were too high and Green knew it. Possibly he may have taken a little pride in his ability to pay $8 for a pair of shoes, though he would hardly have admitted it. More likely he would have passed it off by saying "Brown needed the money."

One day Green was waiting for a car at Black's corner. It was raining steadily and he took to the friendly shelter of the shoeman's awning. He had thrown Black for some time in a casual way—had served with him on a Board of Trade committee on one occasion. By the way, Brown did not belong to that body, thought Green. "By Jove," he mused; "that pair of shoe marked $4 looks exactly like the pair I have on. Wonder if I am paying twice too much to Brown." He stepped into the store. Black greeted him personally and in a cordial manner and —sold him the shoes.

"You can't beat them, I don't care where you go," said Black. "The style and fit are perfect and I will guarantee the wearing qualities. Good-day, Mr. Green." Green went home and told his wife. "Catch Brown giv ing any personal attention to *his* customers," she said; "he is too fond of the gilt cage you have been paying for during the past ten years!"

Six weeks later Black and Green chanced to meet. The former extended his hand. "How are they wearing?" he asked. "Fine; couldn't be better," replied Green, putting out one foot for inspection. "Let's go and get a cigar," he added. It was evident Brown had lost a customer.

Some time after Green was passing Brown's store just as the proprietor came out. Both nodded. "By the way," called Brown; "it has been quite awhile since I saw you in the store. Anything wrong with the last pair?"

"No," answered Green; "I bought the last pair else_ where. Was stricken with a little fit of economy as it were. I gave up $4 and saved $4. Paid a visit to your neighbor Black."

"You'll be sorry for your bargain counter arrangement," retorted Brown; "That fellow can't sell goods at those prices and live. It is an utter impossibility. He can't pay his help."

"You may be better posted as regards his business than I am," said Green, with a little acerbity; "but I am willing to wager he pays his bills. He does business enough, that's certain, and if he gives everyone the value he gave me that accounts for it. It has just dawned on me that people won't always pay two prices for anything, Mr. Brown. They eventually get wise, same as I did."

Brown lost his temper. "I tell you he can't last. The sheriff is bound to get him. My prices are right and he ought to have better sense than to cut away below me. He—"

"Hold on!" cried Green, angry in spite of himself; "I want to tell you a thing or two. I passed over your remark about 'bargain counter' and paid no attention to your imputation of Black's dishonesty. But your last sentence lets the cat out of the bag and shows plainly what you are kicking about. Black has tread on your toes because he has dared to cut under your prices. He sells cheaper than you and because he does not rob the public he is no good. Who pays for the swell fixtures in your store? Who pays for the liveried lackey? I do, Mr. Brown, I and the other fools! And because an honest chap is willing to make a dollar on a pair of shoes instead of hogging five his stuff is no good and he is a crook! And if I ever again pay you $8 for a pair of shoes you ought to sell for $4 you can set me down as a truant from some school for the weak-minded. I hope I have made myself plainly understood. Good-day, Mr. Brown."

But Mr. Brown did not deign to answer. He had now lost a friend, as well as a ·customer!

MORAL.

No doubt you have all heard about Mrs. O'Toole, who had a very deaf husband. When she heard he had been arrested she said she was very glad because he would get his "hearing" in the morning.

"Old-Line" Brown is the Mr. O'Toole of my story. He is deaf to the rights of his patrons and those who would become patrons if they did not know they would have to pay *twice too much* for the goods.

"Fraternal" Black represents Mrs. O'Toole. He knows Brown is meanly jealous of him and outspokenly malicious because of honest business competition. He is always glad for a "hearing" on the merits of the case.

"Insuring Public" Green stands for the judge and his understanding and decision is proper and in keeping with fact and logic.

If anyone gives you the old story that only the exorbitant priced system of insurance is safe tell them the story of Brown, Black, and Green.

BRITISH BROTHERHOOD

A. CHISHOLM, OTTAWA, ONTARIO

In no country in the world have the fraternal orders taken deeper root than in the British Isles. Even in the early age of Pict and Scot, Saxon and Celt, a spirit of strong fraternity prevailed which stood them in good stead in the hour of danger and battle. The whole history of Freemasonry, Oddfellowship, and other leading fraternities in Great Britain furnishes an imperishable proof of the steadfastness and rapidity which have characterized the growth of these fraternities on British soil. The fraternal societies of England and Scotland will compare in strength with those of any kingdom or continent; and they all stand for the true, the upright, the just and the houorouble in manhood and in nationhood. There is not a pledge nor a watchword, not a sign nor a symbol in the fraternal societies of Great Britain which does not appeal to man's better nature, which is not calculated to inspire his highest ideals. Wherever the words Liberty, Benevolence and Concord are heard, wherever the square and compass convey their lessons of Faith, Hope and Charity; wherever the words Friendship, Love and Truth cheer the heart and brighten the pathway of the brother in adversity; wherever the passwords and watchwords of the fraternal orders knit Britons together as steel is welded to steel or iron to iron; wherever, in brief, the insignia and the music of British fraternalism are seen and heard, there, too, shall be found the greeting and the grasp of truest sympathy, the smile of·loyal comradeship, the marks of a friendship that is true, faithful and generous to the core.

The most powerful chord that vibrates to-day in the song of British national life is that of Brotherhood. Take that one chord out of the national music, and the strain seems pulseless and cold. It is this deep-seated, wholehearted spirit of kinship, knitting together Britain and her Colonies, which, more than any other element, contributes to the unity and solidity of the Empire. That Empire is a great human chain composed of many millions of living links. It is this sentiment of brotherhood which makes the Empire great in peace, and terrible in war, which makes it impossible for a slave to tread on British soil; which inspired these memorable words of John Philpot Curran:

I speak in the spirit of the British law, which makes liberty commensurate with, and inseparable from, British soil; which proclaims even to the stranger and sojourner, the moment he sets his foot upon British earth, that the ground upon which he treads is holy, and consecrated by the genius of Universal Emancipation.

It was this love of freedom and this recognition of the claims of brotherhood which constituted the greatness, the nobility and the fearlessness of men like Hampden and Pym, Cromwell and Wilberforce. What these men were ready to do and dare in their day, Britons now living are prepared to do should occasion arise. The valor which a few years ago adorned the prestige of British arms on the banks of the Modder and Tugeulo, and at Kimberley, Mafeking and Ladysmith, was not one whit different from the courage which won Magna Charta for the British people, and gave the Declaration of Independence to the American nation. The flame of brotherhood that glows to-day in the breast of a Chamberlain or a Roberts, a Roseberry or a Kitchener, is of the same temper and spark as that which roused the lion in Cromwell, and King Richard, and enabled Cranmer Ridley and Sir Thomas More to walk cheerily to their heroic deaths. The great Indian Empire is maintained to-day by the spell and power of British brotherhood. The fire of British guns and the stroke of British swords have done much to win British territory in India, but the sceptre of British kindness and the spirit of British conciliation have done much more to solidify and strengthen the foundations of that vast Empire. Every citizen within its broad boundaries who proudly asserts "I am a Briton" is covered by the shield of British brotherhood, in the same way as he who declares "I am an American" has behind him the strength of a nation of more than ninety millions of people.

Edmund Burke never uttered anything finer than these words :—

Our hold of the Colonies is in the close affection which grows from common names, from kindred blood, from similar privileges and equal protection. These are ties which, though light as air, yet are strong as the links of iron.

The Dominion of Canada will always cherish the remembrance of men who have represented her brotherhood ideals, men like Sir John A. MacDonald, Hon. Alexander Mackenzie, Hon. Joseph Howe, Hon. D'arcy Magee, Hon. George Brown, Sir Wilfrid Laurier, and a score of others whose names gleam on the page of Canadian history; but there passed away, on American soil not long ago, another Canadian, a man of Indian blood, whose memory the Dominion of Canada will treasure with equal pride and lasting respect. This illustrious man, Dr. Oronhyatekha, will always rank among the foremost of great Canadians, but especially as one of the truest and best types of British brotherhood. No more convincing proof of the esteem in which he was held by Americans (as well as by his own countrymen) could be adduced than the fact that some years ago he was chosen to fill the honoured position of president of the National Fraternal Congress, which then met in the city of Boston. It was a significant tribute to the greatness of this man that he was elected to preside at a meeting which represented fraternal societies numbering millions of members and a total insurance in force of over four billion dollars!

Few men have had a more unique history than this famous Indian chief. Born in the province of Ontario some sixty-eight years ago, a full-blooded Indian of the Mohawk tribe, educated in Canadian, American and English schools, he rose to a position of eminence which made his name familiar to fraternal circles throughout the world. In his lifetime he mingled with many of the leading men of his own and other countries, contracted friendships with people of every rank, from the king on the throne to the humblest citizen, and achieved distinction by abilities rarely matched, and by a personality which converted enemies into friends, his bitterest opponents into his warmest allies. He lived to obtain the highest degrees and honours in the gift of the societies to which he belonged, and none of these was greater in his estimation than his election to the presidency of the National Fraternal Congress at Boston. Perhaps no words ever uttered by him at a public gathering are more memorable than those contained in his presidential address on that occasion. They constitute the best evidence of the brotherhood spirit that animated his whole career, and dominated every act and word of his prominent life. Although he had delivered many similar discourses in his lifetime, yet one is prone to turn to the words of his address to the National Fraternal Congress at Boston as the most typical and forceful that can be cited to illustrate the character and sentiments of the man. At this Boston meeting Dr. Oronhyatekha said in part:

Does not your heart swell with a just pride, and your blood course through your veins with increased volume and force when you think of these figures and remember that you have had a part in this great work, and that your own contributions have made up in part the millions that have been distributed among the helpless and afflicted by the fraternal benefit societies? But when you come to estimate the relief given to the sick in the way of free medical attendance and free medicines, the watching and nursing by the bedside of the sick, the help given to fellow-members in distress, in money and in kind, in the securing of employment, in the payment of dues and assessments to prevent suspension, and in the moral and material aid given in a hundred different ways, known only to the lodge men and the lodge women, all of which, if estimated in dollars and cents, would amount to a far larger sum than the millions given in the schedule as having already been paid to the aged and disabled members, and to the widows and orphans of the land, you must be more than mortal if your heart does not bow in thankfulness to the Supreme Being, in that you have had a part in such a heavenly work. A system that brings forth such results is worthy of the attention and consideration of the world's best minds.

These are the words of a man who devoted many of the best years of his life to the cause of world-wide fraternity, who, as Mason, Forester, and Good Templar, opened the big heart and the broad hand of brotherhood to his fellowmen, did his utmost to shed light and happiness upon the homes of the widow and orphan, and at the same time to tighten the bonds of unity, goodwill and fellowship which bind the people of the British Empire to those of the American Commonwealth. And he did his work, and fought his battle, in a spirit which seldom failed to command the respect and the admiration of the British and American people.

In the Memorial which was framed by the Executive Council of the Order of which Dr. Oronhyatekha was Supreme Chief, a remarkable tribute was paid to his memory by the faithful band of brothers who were associated with him in his great work. That tribute contained the following words, as noble as ever were recorded in honour of a distinguished man:

No granite pile need be erected to keep his memory green, for he hath carved his monument with his own hands and fashioned it with his masterful brain out of a more enduring material—the hearts of that numberless throng who have felt his brotherly touch. "He lives in glory, and his speaking dust has more of life than half its breathing moulds." He put aside his well-formed life's ambitions to acquire fame in a noble profession, in response to the call to an unselfish duty made by his fellows, and with his own hands rocked the fraternal cradle that contained the infant organization that struggled for life and which was destined to make his name all but immortal. A fit summary of his life would be found in those eloquent words of another: "This brave and tender man in every storm of life was oak and rock, but in the sunshine he was vine and flower; he was the friend of all heroic souls; he climbed the heights and left all superstition far below, while on his forehead fell the golden dawning of a brighter day; he loved the beautiful, and was with colour, form and music, touched to tears; he sided with the weak, the poor and wronged and lovingly gave alms; with loyal heart and with the purest hand he faithfully discharged all trusts." On Sunday evening, March 3rd, 1907, at Savannah, Georgia, as the sun went to rest, this tired child of the North went home to the rest he had so well earned.

But Dr. Oronhyatekha was only one link in the great chain of British brotherhood. One finds to-day, on every shore of the British Empire, this spirit of brotherhood represented in the St. George's, St. Andrew's and St. Patrick's societies. These societies are constantly cherishing those ideals, and maintaining with solicitude the traditions which have ever made for the strength and stability of fraternity. At the same time they keep ever green and beautiful the fondest recollections of home and motherland. In the lodge rooms of these societies the Englishman, Scotchman, or Irishman never fails to find the greeting and the welcome which assures him he is among friends; never fails to find there the flag of his country, and hear the songs of native land. There, too, he will be seen wearing the jewels and badges of British brotherhood. In these halls, by song and speech and story will be kindled in his bosom the stirring recollections, the undying memories that are associated with the Rose of England, the Thistle of Scotland and the Shamrock of Ireland.

The spirit of British brotherhood glows in almost every page of the nation's annals. About a hundred years ago it spent twenty millions sterling for the abolition of the slave trade. It moved the hand of William Wilberforce to strike his hardest blows in the British Parliament for the abolition of slavery. The triumph of Wilberforce won the applause of the British nation and an honoured burial in Westminster Abbey.

It was the spirit of British brotherhood which incited John Howard to visit the prisons of Great Britain and Ireland, and to endure hardships and bring about reforms of the greatest magnitude and influence. It was this spirit of brotherhood which impelled him to visit the lazarettos of Europe, and to die the most glorious of deaths in an act of devotion to his suffering fellowman. Men like Carlyle and Dickens, Wilberforce and Gladstone achieved triumphs which startled the whole world, not so much by the brilliance of their intellects as by the dynamic forces of brotherhood which inspired every word they wrote or spoke.

When all the world beheld the continent of Africa steeped in hopeless darkness, a Scotch lad, imbued with the missionary spirit, penetrated the depths of the Dark Continent, and gave his life for the cause of missions in that land. Thus British brotherhood saw one of its greatest missionary triumphs in the life and death of David Livingstone.

Some thirty years ago a man of Canadian birth, who first saw the light in the village of Aylmer, in the province of Quebec, conceived the need of rousing the youth of the churches and cities to a more strenuous religious life. Through the efforts of this one man, (Dr. Francis Clarke,) the Christian Endeavor Movement was born, a movement which now unfurls its banners to the breezes of every country. Over fifty years ago the late Sir George Williams saw there was a work to be done for the young men of London and the Empire, and British brotherhood produced the Young Men's Christian Associations which now girdle the globe with their chains of brotherhood and love.

Over forty years ago the wail and the death struggle of Britain's submerged Tenth reached the ear and the heart of General Booth, and the Salvation Army of to-day, working its triumphs of love and sympathy in every corner of the earth, is the imperishable evidence of the brotherhood of General Booth.

These are but a few of the many great and distinguished names which are synonyms for British brotherhood, of men who have reared the pillars of empire, upon the foundations of righteousness and won a nation's gratitude.

The songs of a country are among the enduring emblems of its spirit of fraternity. British brotherhood produced *Scots Wha Hae, Rule Britannia* and *God Save the King.* If American brotherhood produced Emerson and Longfellow, Washington and Lincoln, and "The Star Spangled Banner," British brotherhood produced Thomas Carlyle, Walter Scott, Robert Burns, and the "thousand-souled Shakespeare."

The bead-roll of Masonic annals glows with the names of some of the world's greatest statesmen, warriors and poets. Not very long ago a concert was given in the Royal Albert Hall, London, in honour of Robert Burns. The audience numbered thousands; the hall was crowded by people of all ranks from all parts of the United Kingdom, including members of the Royal family. The occasion was a marvelous testimony to the worth and the brotherhood of a great Scotsman. And the Masonic fraternity may well take pride in the name and memory of Robert Burns, who, in his day, was one of the greatest and most popular of Scottish Masons. Burns was a member of Lodge Canongate, Kilwinning, No. 2, of the Grand Lodge of Scotland. Until this day there is a place in the lodge room known as Burns' Corner, which is always held sacred to his memory. In this very lodge-room his anniversary was celebrated not many years ago; and on that occasion it was said that "Burns the man was but the husk of Burns the poet, whose spirit had filled the world, and bound nation to nation by extending to infinity the foundation stone of the Masonic Order, 'the Universal Broth erhood of Man.' "

Certain it is that among all the kings, princes, statesmen and illustrious men of the world who have adorned the ranks of Freemasonry, not one of them occupies a higher place than the humble Scottish ploughman who wrote these words:

> A king can mak' a belted knight,
>   A marquis, duke and a' that,
> But an honest man's aboon his might,
>   Guid faith he maunna fa' that:
> For a' that, and a' that,
>   Their dignities and a' that,
> The pith o' sense, and pride o' worth,
>   Are higher ranks than a' that.
>
> Then let us pray that come it may,
>   As come it will for a' that,
> That sense and worth, o'er a' the earth,
>   May bear the gree, and a' that;
> For a' that, and a' that,
>   It's coming yet, for a' that,
> When man to man, the world o'er
>   Shall brothers be, and a' that!

At the yearly gatherings of British fraternal societies there is ever felt the throb of international friendship, and equally honoured and respected by the membership of these societies have been the names of the late King Edward and Theodore Roosevelt. The Atlantic Ocean has never been broad enough to prevent these two rulers from clasping hands across the seas, and sending to each other their messages of hope, faith and friendship. It is this deep-seated, rock-anchored brotherhood of kings, presidents and people which brings more closely together, which knits heart to heart as well as hand to hand, which transmits across the wide seas the sentiments and the melody of unchanging and undeviating fraternity. It is this tie of international fellowship which has bound together, constantly, and indissolubly, the Sons of England, the Sons of Scotland, and the Sons of Ireland to each other, whether living under British or American banners. Hand in hand, and shoulder to shoulder they march and fight together, performing their deeds of mercy and love, weaving their crowns of faith and gratitude, rearing their monuments to the great and good, and singing the praises of the men and women who have rendered heroic service in seasons of storm and stress, in times of danger and death, and this they will continue to do until the end of time.

British and American fraternities are now being knit together by ties stronger than steel. In the nineteenth century four names have pre-eminently represented the brotherhood spirit on both sides of the Atlantic, names revered alike by Britons and Americans. These four names are George Washington, Abraham Lincoln, Robert Burns, and Sir Walter Scott. One of these, the humble ploughman, born on the banks of Ayr, has penned words whose fires of patriotism and fraternity have blazed in the hearts and homes of his countrymen ever since his death. Sir Walter Scott may be said to have struck the note of brotherhood in every one of his books and poems, so completely have they taken hold of the thought and spirit of the British and American people. Abraham Lincoln so perfectly combined in his life and character the ideals of freedom and fraternity that the very mention of his name sends a thrill through the hearts of his countrymen.

George Washington sounded the same depths of humanity and manhood that made Burns, Scott and Lin

coln the darlings of the people; and among all the names
of the present day, the mere mention of which brings
Americans and Britons closer together, none is more
potent than that of George Washington. Washington is
regarded alike by Englishmen and Americans, as the bril
liant statesman, the strong nation-builder; the man who
was the saviour of his country, the magnificent fighter,
the great patriot and the staunch friend. It was the
brotherhood spirit in Washington which impelled him,
when he decided to resign the office of Commander-in-
Chief, to pen these memorable words:

"I now bid a last farewell to the cares of office, and all
the employments of public life. * * * and I make it
my earnest prayer, that God would have you, and the
State over which you preside, in His holy protection; that
he would incline the hearts of the citizens to cultivate a
spirit of subordination and obedience to government—to
entertain a brotherly affection for one another; for their
fellow-citizens of the United States at large, and particu-
larly for their brethren who have served in the field; and,
finally, that he would most graciously be pleased to dis-
pose us all to do justice, to love mercy, and to demean
ourselves with that charity, humility and pacific temper of
mind, which were the characteristics of the Divine Author
of our blessed religion; without an humble imitation of
whose example in these things we can never hope to be a
happy nation." The thread of gold which runs through
these sentences is the same as shines in the utterances of
every great American or Briton who has truly loved his
country and his fellowmen, and who has delighted to
designate a fellow-countryman by the name of "brother."
Washington had long been accustomed to the language
of fraternity. He was a Freemason, and never upon its
distinguished beadroll has there been a nobler name. Lin-
coln, Grant and Roosevelt have in like manner voiced the-

spirit of fraternity; and it is safe to say that every promi-
nent American of recent times has done his utmost by pen
and voice, by precept and example, to bring the British
and American nations nearer to each other, and to bind
them in the strong bonds of brotherhood.

Mr. Andrew Carnegie has written and spoken notable
words in his lifetime. As an eloquent exponent of Anglo-
American friendship he has rarely been surpassed. It is
the fraternal spirit in this man, as it is the fraternal spirit
in Lord Strathcona and Lord Mount-Stephen, which
makes them the benefactors of their fellowmen, and the
pride of the country which gave them birth. It is not
their great wealth which has brought them honour and
reputation; it is the consideration they have shown to
their less fortunate and less favoured brothers. The
language of the Scottish bard is as true to-day as it was
a hundred years ago

> The rank is but the guinea's stamp,
> The man's the gowd for a' that.

As long as the torch of brotherhood burns, so long will
the British nation be found bearing that torch, side by
side with the people of the United States, and with every
citizen of the world who is willing to cherish for his fel-
lowman a spirit of kindness, courtesy and sympathy. As
long as American banners stand for the guardianship of
the unfortunate and oppressed, so long will the folds of
the Union Jack be flung to the ends of the earth as the
emblem of justice, of protection to the wronged and the
downtrodden. It is not too much to predict that while
the ages run, these two flags, Starry Banner and Union
Jack, will be found displaying to the world their united
colours as a guarantee of peace, friendship and brother-
hood between the two nations.

That true friend of the British and the American
people, Andrew Carnegie, never uttered nobler or more

stirring sentences than those contained in his address delivered on the occasion of his being presented with the Freedom of the Worshipful Company of Plumbers, about seven years ago. "I stand before you," he said, "as a representative of both the old and the new, being neither exclusively of one or the other, yet of both—a Scottish-American—one my native and the other my adopted country. I like to think of them as mother and wife, both to be greatly loved. Such they are to me. I never see the two flags entwined as I see them before me now without finding the lump in my throat. It is many years since there first floated from our castle in Scotland a double flag, the Stars and Stripes and the Union Jack, sewn together. It floats there now, a symbol heralding, I believe, what is to come. Even to-day the position justifies such a flag. When yachting on the Mediterranean one calm morning I found only a single flag displayed. I said to the captain, "What is the matter with the united flag?" "Sir, there isn't wind enough to-day. In calm seas the united flag droops, being heavy." A stiff breeze came in the afternoon, and I came on deck to see the united flag unfurled to the breeze like a thing of joy. It is the day of storm and danger that will bring out that united flag, and woe to those that stand against it.

ANNIVERSARY ADDRESS*

Since that winter's night when you told me of the arcana of Odd Fellowship, I have acquired the right to make a lot of distress signs recognizable in a good many brotherhoods, but none of them are more valued by me

---

* Address delivered by Hon. George R. Allen of Kansas City, Kansas, on the Anniversary of the Institution of the Independent Order of Odd Fellows.

than those given in that first instruction received at the hands of your officers.

I always feel when I am in a gathering of Odd Fellows and their families and associates that I am mingling with men and women who have an adequate conception of the duties and responsibilities of life; those who realize that in this day and generation it is not sufficient for a man merely to so live and act that he may escape the doors of the penitentiary; and at each succeeding eventide congratulate himself that on that day at least society through the law laid no heavy hand upon his shoulder and banished him for his misdeeds from its presence. Rather, that I am in the presence of those who know and realize that the welfare of every individual is closely wrapped up and identified with the welfare of every other individual with whom he associates. That no man, no matter how broad his shoulders and how undaunted his courage, can stem single-handed the adverse currents that beset him without learning that, by uniting his efforts with others and joining hands for the overcoming of obstacles, ordinary and extraordinary, he may struggle with the assurance of splendid success for his portion.

Let me give you this story to illustrate the thought I have in mind: The other day in one of the smaller cities in the southern part of our State one of those weary, disreputable looking fellows who come into town along the railroad track and leave it by the same route—drifting upon the stream of life without thought of anchor or hope of harbor—ragged, dirty, disreputable looking and hungry, the fellow walked up to the door of a house and rapped. Now it chanced that in that house there lived a woman, a good woman, one of those, however, found even in Kansas, whose kindness is flaunted in the face of the unfortunate; who do good merely to be seen and known of men; who have no charity in their heart; no sympathy in their soul; who care nothing for the unfortunate, and do nothing for them except as driven under the lash of public sentiment.

This woman opened the door, looked the poor fellow over from head to foot, heard his request for something to eat, and tried to freeze him with a look, and said, "Stand there, Sir." She then went back into the pantry and in a minute returned with the hardest and dryest piece of bread the house afforded. Just a great, dry, hunk, two weeks old, and she handed the poor fellow a chunk with these words, "Not for my sake nor for thy sake, but for the Lord's sake, do I give you this bread." Now, it happened that the poor unfortunate was one of those fellows, well educated, intelligent, but for some reason, lack of stability, common-sense or other essential wholly unable to successfully fight the battle of life. Without moving he reached out his hand, took the bread, straightened up and in the same tone of voice replied, "Madam, not for my sake nor for thy sake, but for the Lord's sake, put some butter on that bread."

And I am quite certain that when I am mingling with Odd Fellows and their families and associates I am associating with those who are in a sense the butter upon the bread of humanity. Those who are doing their part to alleviate the conditions of those with whom they come in contact; whose endeavor it is to make the world a better and brighter place in which to live.

But I am well nigh forgetting that this is an Anniversary—a sort of birthday festivity. And it is proper that, even at the risk of repetition, something be said about the early days of this society. I have noticed, and so have you that the history of any people, or any movement social or otherwise, is simply in the main a record of the lives and activities of those chiefly concerned. An ultimate analysis reveals—that common-causes and ordinary efforts to check, divert or assauge existing conditions— sometimes lead to results far beyond the wildest imaginings of the pioneers in the movement. This is startlingly true in the history of the magnificent order under whose auspices we are gathered this evening.

At the close of the war of 1812, fought about a third of a century after the war in which we had gained our freedom from the English throne, there existed in this country a deep and bitter prejudice against England and Englishmen. This feeling manifested itself nowhere more than in the city of Baltimore, where the hardships of a predatory warfare had been most grievously felt. Their business prostrate; manufacturers destroyed; their ships, then the best and fastest in the world, had been for more than three years driven from the ocean. The national capital, thirty miles distant had been pillaged and burned by a marauding band.

Under these circumstances the few English emigrants who came were treated more as enemies than as friends. It mattered not that they spoke the same language; held the same forms of religious ceremonies sacred; were imbued with the same love of civil and religious freedom, and in great measure had been subject to the same general form of judicial and governmental administrations. In a word, where all circumstances existed which should lead men to be brothers, and insure kindly welcomings and fraternal greetings the very opposite existed.

At this time and under these circumstances two young English mechanics, one of whom had been in this country but six months, the other a little more than a year, became acquainted. The unjust and repellant treatment to which they had been subjected because of their nationality had burned into their hearts and, smarting under the sting of ostensible inferiority, their friendship quickly became more intimate than is common between strangers upon short acquaintance.

In casting about for a means to make their lives more endurable, if not enjoyable, they determined to find others of their countrymen whose situation was like unto theirs. Individual inquiry having failed, they inserted an advertisement in a weekly newspaper, asking any young Englishmen who cared to do so to meet with them at an Inn, on March 2nd, 1819. At this meeting they were joined by two others who had chanced to read the little notice. These four then parted with an agreement to meet again thirty days later. They advertised another meeting in the same paper for the same place and this time they were joined by the fifth man. These five, after consideration, decided to form an organization for mutual helpfulness patterned after something they had known in their own country.

In pursuance to this agreement these five men met at a tavern named "The Seven Stars" on Second Street, in Baltimore, Maryland, on Monday night, April 26th, 1819, and there formed the first Lodge of the Independent Order of Oddfellows in America.

At that meeting Thomas Wildey, aged thirty-eight, a "coach spring maker" according to his articles of indenture, although he commonly called himself a "blacksmith"; John Welch, aged twenty-eight, a painter and plumber by trade; John Duncan, John Cheatham and Richard Rushworth. These last three are named simply because they chanced to answer the advertisements and enabled the immortal Wildey and Welch to launch their enterprise—washing up from the great city like driftwood from the beach, appearing for a moment and then sinking back into the great sea of humanity and never showing further upon the pages of history. These five men I have named that night issued to all men who cared to comply with its conditions a sort of promissory note by the terms of which they agreed *"To visit the sick, relieve the distressed, bury the dead and educate the orphan."*

Payment upon this note of hand in accordance with its terms and provisions has never been refused in all the years of its existence. No formal protest under hand and seal has ever proclaimed repudiation or dishonor by its makers and endorsers. First and last, from that time to this, within the territorial jurisdiction of the Sovereign Grand Lodge of America, this note of hand has been signed and payment according to its terms and conditions guaranteed by more than two millions of men in all the walks and circumstances of life, and who have bettered themselves, honored their families, and elevated the community in which they lived by reason of the obligations thus assumed. These men have paid upon this obligation, in compliances with its terms and for the purposes named therein more than one hundred and twenty millions of dollars. And have they paid it all? No! No! The obligation still is outstanding. It is not and cannot be wiped out while there lives a man in whose bosom throbs a heart responsive to the solemn vows taken before the altar of Odd Fellowship.

The good book says "there is that scattereth and yet increaseth." This was never truer than when applied to our order. We are never so rich as when acting in compliance with the terms of the original agreement. No man ever impoverished his soul or depleted his purse by good deeds. Odd Fellowship has wrested the old adage, "A fool and his money are soon parted," from its original moorings, set it adrift upon the sea of fraternal endeavor and caused it to read under the searchlight of modern civilization "A fool and his money are never parted. They are one and inseparable."

Beginning with the foundation laid under such cir-

cumstances as have been named, we have erected a super-
structure unexcelled by any. We have builded an insti-
tution whose financial dealing with its beneficiaries is
not that of the bestowal of alms, but the payment of a
debt. The treasury of an Odd Fellows lodge opens in
compliance with the laws of the order. These laws were
placed in operation by the cry of the sick and the afflicted.
And if, because of the exigencies of the particular case
the usual relief is not sufficient, then from the fullness of
their hearts and the sufficiency of their store the brethren
contribute, gladly, aye royally, to the relief of the necessi-
ties. And yet not as charity, but because we realize that
in the highest, the truest, the deepest and the best sense
of the term, we are in truth and in deed our "Brothers'
keeper." Our own possessions in the light of our
brother's need become by that very need both his and
ours. With those principles in the forefront we have
builded a fraternal society, the largest in the world. No
other in ancient history or modern approaches its
number.

This great, puissant institution, to which you and I so
proudly claim allegiance is everywhere—in the East, the
West, the North, the South, on the mountain side, by the
river and upon the plain; in city, town and hamlet, quietly
and without ostentation—going about and doing good—
wherever sickness and distress exist; wherever lips are
parched with fever's fire, or the brow racked with pain;
wherever the mourner lingers, and lingering clings to the
couch of the loved dead; wherever the orphan follows the
pathway of the student, and wherever the widow strug-
gles for bread, and clothing. There you find this society
and you find it working out its destiny along the magnifi-
cent lines planned for it by its founders, those plain men
who toiled by day and pondered by night over cruel injus-

tice that made them practical outcasts in a land of freedom.

You can number the dollars expended in all these ways; you can show from our records the members visited; you can state with accuracy the interments made; you can count the orphans educated and the widows assisted, but you can never, never, until the recording angel shall strike the final balance upon the pages of God's eternal record tell all the good this order has accomplished.

If you are inclined to think, when you consider the magnificent record of Odd Fellowship, that the institution has reached its zenith; that future years can know nothing more of us than the present, and that those who follow us will work along no broader lines than those we know, permit me to suggest that those brethren whose activity was in the first twenty-five years of our history may have been of like opinion, and we now know how meagre and feeble, indeed, were their achievements compared with those of the present decade.

Institutions of mankind are as much the product of environment and the subject of evolution and growth as are the families of the vegetable or animal kingdom. The law of the survival of the fittest is as absolute and as inevitable as the law of gravitation. Just so certainly as the rock thrown upward will descend again to earth, will the unfit die. This law stands in dual capacity—the pitiless executioner of every unworthy movement, the generous benefactor of all that deserves to live.

Odd Fellowship claims no divinity in its origin. It permits no rivalry with the church. It seeks not to supplant in the heart of any man that service which every individual owes to the Christian religion. It asks only of the world the privilege of promulgating its own doctrines along its own lines, which are: "To visit the sick;

relieve the distressed; bury the dead, and educate the orphan." It asks from the world naught in return for the blessings conferred by its existence, save the privilege of continuing its beneficent course.

In conformity with the decrees of this law this order need only to maintain the high ideals that have marked its past to enable it to live forever. But if it shall stand in the future where it now stands, it must be found upon the right side of every question of moral and civil responsibility and significance. In its early history it took giant strides toward the right and reaching its goal, stood firmly, as Tennyson says, "Four square to every wind that blew."

Its birthplace an Inn, on a side street, its sponsors practically ostracised because of the accident of birth, when one of its early members was taunted with bacchanalian associations, it banished refreshments from its lodge room. Driven from its hall over a tavern because of this stand, its founder, the immortal Thomas Wildey, opened the doors of his own home for its refuge, and from that day to this the subordinate lodge has been the champion, defender and protector of the Christian home.

> As the cord unto the bow is,
> So unto man is woman;
> Though she draws him, she obeys him,
> Though she bends him, yet she follows,
> Useless each without the other.

This thought so beautifully expressed by the New England poet, was early recognized by Odd Fellows. Lodge life was not more complete without some opportunity for the pleasures of social intercourse with the "angels of earth" than would be the home without their presence there. More than fifty years ago the great auxiliary whose symbols and insignia are the bee hive, dove, lily, typifying industry, innocence, and purity, came into existence. Through this feature it has been the privilege of Odd Fellows to have something of the beauty, the sacredness and the refining influence of the home and family circle brought into the lodge room, and so real has the benefit proven that there are now nearly 400,000 members in the Rebekah branch.

And the motto of our order, "Friendship," "Love" and "Truth," those noble and inspiring words! In the stern battle of life, the banner of Odd Fellowship, bearing in letters of gold upon its broad and shapely folds these words pregnant with meaning, for devotion to which in the ancient days of chivalry armed knights wearing in helmet fair lady's favor, their hearts filled with love of king and country, were wont to go down cheerfully to death, float before us at once, an inspiration and an incentive.

That magic banner is to the great hosts whose membership is joined in indissoluble union by the magic three linked chain what the "White plume of Henry of Navarre" was to the French soldiery of his day. While that plume waved amid the smoke and shriek and the sound of carnage in the very forefront of the fight, his followers knew defeat was impossible and victory must crown their efforts. While the banner of Odd Fellowship waves triumphant from the castlements of 20,000 subordinate lodges, each the rallying place for a band of members, pledged, joined in solemn compact for the finer and better things of life, there will be no going backward, no losing of high ideals.

> Howe'er it be it seems to me,
> 'Tis only noble to be good,
> Kind hearts are more than coronets,
> And simple faith than Norman Blood.

FRATERNALISM—A MEMORIAL ADDRESS

EDWARD NEWTON HAAG, LL.B.

At the close of the Russian-Japanese war, when the victorious hosts returned to that wonderful Oriental land of beauty and marvelous achievement on the part of its almost Lilliputian inhabitants, one of the great commanders, following a custom dating back to a remote antiquity, delivered an oration to the spirits of those who had freely given their lives in defense of their country and to maintain its honor. He addressed them as being present and taking a prominent part in the memorable services. To us, who until recently have been taught to believe otherwise, this was a strange and startling procedure. Who shall say, however, that the spirits so addressed were not in reality present and fully cognizant of what was taking place? It is said that, contrary to what might have been supposed, there was rejoicing and a manifestation of pride on the part of the relatives and friends of the departed. They had shown themselves worthy of a lasting place not only in the shrines commemorating their memory and their deeds of heroism and devotion, but also in the hearts and minds of all future generations.

In each home thus honored and blessed by having had one or more of its members selected as worthy of such preferment there was erected a miniature shrine, which will be carefully guarded by succeeding generations, with ever increasing reverence. Those families which are not thus represented in the Pantheon of heroes deem it a misfortune, and believe that they are blessed in a lesser degree than their neighbors or friends who had this enviable distinction conferred upon them by the gods.

It is right and proper that we should honor the mem-

ory of departed heroes. No nation will endure which does
not cherish their deeds and set before the rising genera-
tion for emulation their noble example. America is the
"Land of the Free and the Home of the Brave" to-day,
with all its splendid possibilities, because its ·sons have
ever stood ready to defend its honor. There are victories
won in the everyday walks of life, however, which are
no less heroic than those achieved on the field of battle.
This is a trite saying, but the truth of it is too often over-
looked. Many a man or woman, who never receives
special recognition nor expects it, makes a record for self-
sacrifice and devotion to all that is best and noblest which
will live through all eternity, and which contributes
toward the betterment of humanity to a far greater degree
than we can imagine.

Scientists, theologians, physicians and thoughtful per-
sons in general who give consideration to such matters
are just beginning to recognize to some slight degree the
tremendous influence one mind has upon another. The
very fact that we wish well to our fellow-men, and that
our heart and mind are actuated by an impulse for good,
undoubtedly helps those about us and makes the toilsome
pathway of life seem the brighter.. There are some peo-
ple whose very presence repels, while others scatter joy
and sunshine all about them. If you are blessed with
goodness and other desirable qualities, the chances are
that you cannot keep them to yourself, even if you should
desire to do so. The undesirable person, on the contrary,
whose thoughts are intent upon self and individual gain,
no matter at what expense it may be to others, is usually
soon found out and checkmated. Those who do good to
others whenever the opportunity presents itself and wish
them well receive not only the reward of a clear con-
science, but are also blessed with one of earth's choicest

gifts—many friends. It has well been said: "To make friends, be one."

It is not given to us mortals to know just what the future life has in store in the way of blessings and rewards. We see as "through a glass dimly," but, if you will pardon my venturing to have an opinion on so momentous a question, I would say that personally I believe the world is growing better day by day and year by year in no small degree by reason of the spiritual pres ence and influence of good men and women who have gone before. Only that will be saved which is worth saving. Those traits of unselfishness, benevolence, love and devotion to what is good and right each in themselves have the attributes which will make them live through all eternity. I believe that the dear departed ones, whose memory we have assembled to commemorate, are with us to-night in spirit, and are happier because when upon earth they did their Fraternal duty toward their loved ones by making provision for their protection. We fondly cherish their memory, and it is right that we should do so, but they are not in reality lost to us, but have merely entered upon a higher sphere of usefulness and enjoyment, where we will shortly be able to join them. The Founder of Fraternalism removed the sting of death and largely freed the grave of its terrors. Whether heaven is a specially set apart place, as we have been taught, or whether, as I believe, all God's universe, with its myriads of worlds and wonders and beauties beyond our mortal conception, is the realm of the departed, matters not so much as the fact that we are coming to know more clearly that human life is but a stage of development fitting us for greater enjoyment and usefulness, not only now, but in the hereafter.

Those who are true to the standard of Fraternalism until the Silent Messenger comes achieve a great victory, because they conclusively demonstrate that they are unselfish and possessed of the divine attributes of Him who first taught the doctrine of universal Brotherhood, which has done and is doing so much to regenerate this old world, and to wipe out misery, poverty and sin.

What a tremendous change Fraternalism has wrought through the ages! The old Greek motto, "Let those who have light give it to others," has truly been exemplified in the working out of this noble cause. Great towers with noble spires, beautiful cathedrals, richly adorned and so symmetrical architecturally that they have come down to us as models, were in bygone centuries often erected in the hope of thus appeasing the wrath of an angry Deity, but seldom for the love of God or to further the cause of universal Brotherhood. The sun shone through splendorous windows and was reflected on costly mosaics and rich furnishings and priceless paintings, thus inspiring awe in the worshippers, but how often underneath in the dungeons human beings lay fettered in chains and cried in vain for deliverance from their fiendish persecutors. The few favored fortunates were benefited, but the masses were cursed on account of greed, ignorance and superstition. Fraternalism broke the shackles and revealed the benign face and taught the blessed precepts of the Master. There has come with its development a broader view of the higher laws of love, generosity and friendship. The universal Brotherhood of man is no longer a beautiful sentimental theory, but a living, actual reality. At no time in the history of humanity has the spirit of Fraternity held such universal sway in the hearts and minds of mankind as at present. It leads the march of our advancing civilization. The age is glorified by it. The spirit of Fraternalism is the common property of the world. It makes us more capable of enjoyment and more useful, no matter what sphere of human life we occupy. Everywhere you turn the voice of cordial greeting sounds in the ear, and the warm hand of Brotherly love and friendship is held out to you. Surely the potent power which has greatly contributed to bring about this felicitous and desirable condition is the influence of Fraternal societies upon the people. They have become, to a large degree, the educators of the masses in those sacred laws of humanity and love which will, we doubt not, eventually lead to an ideal state of living and cement the common interests into unity.

Abraham Lincoln once said: "When I am dead I want it said of me by those who knew me best that I always plucked the thistle and planted a flower where I thought a flower would grow." This is the spirit of true Fraternity. If, when we have finished life's journey the world is no better on account of our having lived in it, then it were better that we had never been born. A kindly word of greeting or a pleasant smile does much to lighten many burdens and make them easier to bear. You have no doubt heard of the man who was accosted on the street by a stranger, who said to him: "I want to thank you for the great help you have been to me. You have truly been a friend." The man addressed did not recognize the speaker, and replied: "I don't remember ever having met you. How, then, was it possible for me to help you?" "You are right," replied the other; "but I have passed you on the street many times, and I never saw you when you were not smiling. When I was depressed your smile was like a ray of sunlight on a cloudy day."

Have you ever stopped to think what a tremendous influence the spirit of Fraternalism has upon our Government and all its institutions, and how much it has contributed toward making this the greatest land of freedom the world has ever seen? Have you noticed during recent years how great reforms have come about in the government of the nation, State and municipalities almost like magic? It has been possible because the people are enlightened and love right and justice, because they have learned of its blessings through Fraternalism. Those of us who are enrolled under its banners enjoy a blessing which we do not fully appreciate. Fraternity disseminates sunshine and distributes blessings. It holds the shield of protection over the home and guards the loved ones. It heals the wounds made by an all too cruel world, and not only hears but heeds the cry of the needy and distressed. Its generous and noble heart is ever ready and willing to call back those who have strayed away, to lift up the fallen, to aid the distressed and to elevate humanity in general. It increases the capability for the enjoyment of that which is noblest and purest. It is the "new commandment," and those who impede its progress are not true to that which is best in the human heart. Neither the present nor the future can have much in store for such.

Dr. Lyman Abbot characterizes this as the "Age of Fraternity." He predicts that the spirit of true co-operation and universal Brotherhood, when a common respect for every other man's rights will exist, is rapidly coming about, influencing every sphere of human activity. Co-operation is working wonders, and the tendency in this direction has but begun. Civilization is not being built, as it was in ancient days, for the few, but for the masses. Far better to send our warships, as was recently done, to Sicily on a mission of mercy when nature had wrought such dire destruction than to use them for conquest. Universal education and Brotherhood are moving forward hand in hand. No longer is there so much interest in what contributes to the luxury and extravagance of the few as there is in solving the problem of how all may be made better and happier; not how great wealth may be accumulated by the few, but that the means of livelihood and comfort be given to the many, and that every honest man and upright woman should be able to care for loved ones, and have a fair chance in solving life's problems and meeting its requirements. Poorhouses are being displaced by systems of old-age pensions in France, Germany, England, Australia and, to some extent, in this country. It is a remarkable fact that some of the great aggregations of capital have found it to their financial advantage to promote plans of this kind to take care of the aged and injured. We have come to know that what we formerly thought were necessary burdens are not divinely decreed, but that we can get rid of them through Fraternal co-operation. I predict that the time is not far distant when there will be a universal system of old-age pensions in every civilized country. I should like to give further consideration to this theme of old-age pensions and all that it implies, but time will not permit.

I do not desire to disparage the past. Far from it. The men who made the glory that was Greece and the grandeur that was Rome; Leonidas in the pass; Horatius on the bridge; the 600 who went in at Balaklava; the Pilgrim fathers; the Revolutionary fathers—these men and the rest who fill the corridors of the past are entitled to all honor, but I also believe with Tennyson that "through the ages one increasing purpose runs"—not a decreasing, but an increasing purpose—because I believe that this is the best day and age the world has ever seen. True, we do not have a Shakespeare, a Raphael, no sculptor who can match the miracles of Phidias, no philosopher who can speak with the authority of Plato, but these were the rare exceptions in their day and age, and the masses were downtrodden and ignorant.

The condition of the average man and woman—aye, child—thanks to the power of Fraternalism, is infinitely better than that of those in any preceding age. In the past there was the rule of the few. To-day there is the rule of the many. Then might ruled, and the vast majority were deprived of their liberties, and in reality were slaves—whether designated by that name or not. To-day there is the rule of right—every day growing stronger. Those whom Lincoln loved to call the "plain people" have more of life, liberty and the pursuit of happiness than human beings ever possessed before.

It is for these reasons that I glory not in the past, but in the present, with its noble possibilities and splendid fruits.

There is a great painting which is considered a masterpiece. Some of you may have seen it. It represents the March of the Conquerors through all the ages. The greed of gain and love of conquest is implacably stamped upon the countenance of each of those as they ride ruthlessly over the prostrate forms of their countless victims. As I gazed upon those so-called heroes, who brought such misery and wretchedness into the world, I instinctively placed in contrast with them the founders of Fraternalism and the noble men and women who are carrying forward its standard. Is it any wonder that the world is growing better? Is it strange that it seems to be the mission of America to work out the problems of civilization throughout the World? The lodge-room is and has been, in no small degree, the schoolhouse where we have been taught these noble lessons.

President Roosevelt truthfully said: "This Government will endure just so long as those principles which underlie the Fraternal orders—namely, the protection of the home—are fostered and maintained." Fraternalism offers the greatest possible opportunity to do good. It is the flower which has resulted from the tears and sighs and longings of the widows and orphans and down-trodden of all ages. Its sweet perfume not only pervades the world, but, I have no doubt, reaches to the very throne of the Creator.

Have you ever stopped to think that most people, after they attain the age of forty years, find their greatest pleasure in benefitting others?

It does not matter so much what we achieve, whether it be in the cause of Fraternalism or any other direction, so long as we are engaged along proper lines and do our best. I take it that in the hereafter we will not be judged so much by what we have accomplished as by the honesty, sincerity and zeal of our efforts. The great difficulty with many persons and why they never accomplish anything worth while is because they are always waiting for some great opportunity, forgetting that many of the brightest and enduring events of history were achieved by men and women when they were scoffed at and derided, and when all looked dark and dreary.

Glancing hastily at the business world, even the most casual observer knows that it is a day of great changes. Combinations of capital have come to practically control and monopolize many of the leading industries. Railroads, steamship lines, manufacturing industries of all kinds, Old Line Insurance companies and the necessities of life are controlled by trusts and selfish syndicates to a degree that is well calculated to make one pause and ask as to what the ultimate result will be. Many of these movements undoubtedly tend strongly toward enslaving the masses. Fetters are being placed upon them which, unless they are broken, will mean greatly lessened opportunities for the vast majority during coming generations. There is a growing intelligence, however, as has been stated, and the people are thinking and acting. They have the remedies in their own hands, if they will but avail themselves of them. If the over 7,000,000 of Fraternalists in this country and the more than 30,000,000 of their dependents fully awake to the responsibility which devolves upon them to assert their citizenship and exert their combined influence through legislation and in every other legitimate way, they could speedily accomplish the desired results. Such pressure could be brought to bear that no official would dare to disregard the wish of this vast aggregation of liberty-loving, patriotic, frugal, right-thinking and acting people, who believe in the "live and let live" policy and the greatest good to the greatest number. I entreat you as Fraternalists to remain true to your noble standard, and thus protect not only your own best interests, but those of your children and future generations.

The lodge-room and Fraternal effort in general, as exemplified in such a splendid manner by our own beloved Order, teach the lessons which fit us for the emergency when it comes, as it did the other day when John R. Binns —"Jack" Binns—the wireless operator way up on the smashed and dismantled deck of the Republic, remained at his post for nearly thirty hours, much of the time in total darkness, and not knowing but that every minute the vessel would plunge to the bottom, with engines stopped and only storage batteries, the lever of his transmitter broken, nevertheless sent the flash which brought relief and saved upward of 2,000 human lives. Scarcely had the two vessels crashed into each other, when, undismayed and undaunted, this poorly-paid, unknown hero, with no hope of reward, and who afterwards dismissed it all as an ordinary occurrence, with the emphatic statement: "I merely did my duty; what the h— did you expect I would do?" sent the wireless message into space which informed operators hundreds of miles distant that a direful calamity was threatened. When the faint signal of his instrument was caught by an operator more than one hundred miles distant it was as follows: "The vessel is sinking, but I am going to stay at my post." Truly, as was stated by Mr. Boutell in introducing a resolution of recognition and thanks in Congress, "Binns has given the world a splendid illustration of the heroism that dwells in many who are doing the quiet, unnoticed tasks of life. Is it not an inspiration for all of us to feel that there are heroes for every emergency and that in human life no danger is so great that some 'Jack' Binns is not ready to face it."

Oh, yes, they had their ancient heroes, and we honor them, but we have our Deweys, Hobsons, Funstons, Evanses, Binns and thousands of others who are not fatalists, but plain, everyday, honest American heroes, who prize their life but little in comparison with doing their duty as men. They do that which is noble and right in the sight of God and man as a matter of course, because they are true Fraternalists.

In his weakness and imperfections man has truly accomplished wonders, but let us not forget that during the last hundred years, since the doctrines of Fraternalism began to be more fully recognized and its precepts carried out, more progress has been made than during all the preceding ages of the world. Since then we have had the steam engine, steamship, wireless telegraph and telephones, perfect reproduction of the human voice and the possibility of preserving it in a form which will enable those of future generations to hear the spoken message of the present, transmission of power for long distances, the turning of darkness into brilliant daylight, submarine navigation, the conquest of the air, the conquering of scores of diseases, and innumerable other inventions, discoveries and developments so marvelous that those of bygone ages scarcely dreamed they would ever become a reality.

If to-day we can send a current of thought around this old world in an instant without the use of wires is it too much to hope and believe that the time will come when it will be possible for us to also communicate with those who have gone before? Indeed, are we not already doing so without knowing it? Do they not powerfully influence us for good in some mysterious way of which we can only conjecture? As time and space have largely been annihilated in this earthly sphere, so God's whole universe is rapidly coming into closer sympathy, and what heretofore have seemed like insuperable barriers are one by one being penetrated and set aside. As life has been freed from many of its evils and retarding elements, so I doubt not the last great enemy is, after all, only an entrance gate to a realm of greater possibilities for enjoyment of those blessings which we are told are in store for those who are worthy of such preferment.

We all have our influence, and the smallest wave set in motion expands and widens until it reaches the eternal shore. Surely these developments, these hopes and aspirations will not be lost.

Have you ever noticed as you stood on the shore and cast a pebble into the clear expanse of water how the surface rippled by waves, widening and ever widening until the eye could no longer follow them? We are standing on the shore of life. Will we cast an influence for good by a smile, a pleasant word, a kindly deed or by doing our duty as men and women bravely, whatever our lot may be? Can we doubt that thus the wave of our influence will widen far beyond our knowledge and ultimately reach even the eternal shore? We are told that in the economy of life nothing is lost, no word spoken or written, no act performed or thought conceived by the human brain has ever been lost or ceased to exert its influence. The thoughts, words and deeds of those who have gone before

have made this old world what it is to-day, and so the
world of the future will be what we do to make it better,
nobler and purer.

As the hand-grasp in ancient times signified friend-
ship and freedom from a deadly weapon, to-day it sig-
nifies the bond of universal Brotherhood—of human sym-
pathy and a willingness to do what we can to lighten the
burdens which weigh all too heavy upon the human race.

While Europe is practically an armed camp, with five
millions trained in the science of war, ready to spring at
each other's throats and to rend each other asunder, we
have in this beloved land of ours a peaceful army of
upwards of seven millions of noble men and women
enrolled in the ranks of these Fraternal orders. They
have paid out nearly a billion and a half dollars to widows,
orphans and beneficiaries during the past thirty-five years,
and are pouring out their stream of benevolence day by
day and year by year to beneficiaries. If any of these
orders have had faults, it was that they attempted to do
too much, but how easy it is to correct defects of that kind
where all are willing to bear their just share of the bur-
den and responsibility!

America is the greatest country in the world, because
its people are the most just and enlightened. They fought
the first war the world has ever seen for the cause of
humanity when they broke the cruel hold of Spain on
Cuba, and now, in the fullness of time, when she is able
to govern herself, they have set Cuba free. They con-
quered the Spanish and seized the Philippines, but they
paid the Spanish nation $20,000,000 and have paid
upwards of $1,000,000,000 since to educate and benefit the
natives. They smashed the fleet of the Spaniards at San-
tiago and captured the commanders and their hosts, but
they gave them food and ministered to their wants, treat-

ing them like brothers, and finally sending them home to their ancient shores.

Let it not be forgotten also that the noble men and women who have builded these fraternal institutions are well able to look after their development and care during the years to come. The fraternal system is the true insurance of the people, because it eliminates the features of speculation, investment and profit, and gives protection to the people at actual cost. As such it stands in sharp contrast with old line life, which, whatever may be said in its favor, is conducted largely for the aggrandizement and gain of those who control the system for selfish purposes.

FRATERNAL CO-OPERATION

CARL W. KIMPTON

The Nineteenth Century saw inaugurated, and the Twentieth Century has seen, through fraternal co-operation conducted on the lodge plan, one of the greatest achievements for the benefit of the masses ever realized. The plan and general system of protection to the home and family, at the lowest cost consistent with safety, was like all new efforts, crude in the beginning; but with age and experience the plan has been perfected and the organization has been placed upon a permanent and enduring basis. The bed-rock—the head and corner-stone of these societies—is Co-operative Fraternity. It has very many associates; is based on pure benevolence and charity; is grounded in political, religious and social acts. It remained, however, for those who thoroughly understood and duly appreciated the power of co-operation to place with it fraternity and give to the world the blessings and benefits of the same in a financial sense.

Through the fraternal societies of to-day aid is extended to each other in case of misfortune or distress and society is made better both by precept and example. The lodge room is made a place of pleasure and profit, and justice and honor are exemplified and taught through the ritualistic ceremony.

The little saving for which the industry of the past toiled and on which hopes of the future rested can soon be used. Home comforts vanish, sickness enters, and finally death steps in and takes possession. To meet such cases and be a comforter, fraternal societies have been established and with pure and holy motives and a desire to benefit humanity, claims a place among the list of standard institutions of the century, assuring the man and woman of thought and reason that it is worthy of their personal influence and support.

Issuing policies of insurance by an old line life insurance company is performed for money. Some half dozen men of wealth may be set down as the owners of any one company you may select. If there is money made in writing policies, such profits go into their pockets for they are the proprietors. Persons who become insured or who take out a policy have no voice in the administration of the affairs; no brother or sister is visited nor cheered during sickness by those men who are simply insurance monopolists. Their business is to insure for personal profit; there is no care for the dead nor dying, nor weeping by the bedside of one loved, respected and esteemed and held by bonds of fraternity as a brother or as a sister; their work is for money, profit, gain.

But Fraternity, what of her? Her object is to do good. Look at the pages of history of these fraternal societies. What do they present? Page after page of noble deeds, loving hands and true hearts caring for the members in sickness and in health, love for each other, practically exemplified and set forth in the caring of the widow and orphan and in making the hours of sickness as cheerful as possible and the last moments of life to be passed as the patient waiter is surrounded by those who pledged to him their honor and love and protection. These societies are not monopolies; they are mutual, co-operative fraternities. With one hand they protect and sustain; with the other hand they dispense to all who come within their folds the co-operative earning of a strong partnership. They encourage industry; they stimulate economy; they are helpful in promoting temperance; they prompt their members to practice punctuality and instill in the minds of each member true business principles and bring around one common altar, the rich and the poor, the toilers, as well as those of more or less leisure, and permit them to deliberate on ways and means best calculated to promote their individual happiness.

Our government conducted and carried on through its many departments—such as the Interior, the Navy, the Army, the Treasury, etc., is a grand illustration of fraternal co-operation. Patriotism and with the best interest of "Home, Sweet Home" has made it possible for the United States and its Government to be admired and respected by all the Governments of the World. So the love of home and of the right and of equality of making for the generations, yet unborn, through the principles of civilization—which is fraternity—an enduring and practical institution, which, while mind and memory endure and time rolls on, will stand the test of all opposition and serve the people for the people's good.

IT'S WHAT WE DO

A prominent fraternalist regrets that there are so many in the fraternal field who do not possess a realizing knowledge of the meaning of the term Fraternity. If they do, they do not live up to it and, no matter what they may say, their words have no effect among those who know they are not sincere. Fraternalists should first be true to themselves and the system with which they are identified. Then will they be able to do good to others. It is believed that we will all be judged in the Great Hereafter not so much by what we have accomplished but by the spirit in which we have given our little mite. This creed has been subscribed to by the fraternalist referred to:

> *I* do not fear to tread the paths
> That those I loved before have trod.
> *I* do not fear to pass the gates
> And stand before the living God.
> In this life's fight I've done my best,
> And, if God be God, he knows it well;
> He will not turn his back on me
> And send me down to darkest Hell
> Because I have not prayed aloud
> Or shouted in the market place.
> It's what we do, not what we say
> That gives us mercy in his grace.

The further thought is suggested that, if those in the fraternal field would practice but half what they preach, the members of the fraternal societies would be far happier in trying to live up to this standard, and the outside world look upon the societies in a far different light than it now does.

A VAST BROTHERHOOD

JAMES A. FOSHAY

The fraternal beneficiary society system was inaugurated about forty years ago and has gone on steadily advancing until the membership of the societies to-day is more than six millions, carrying a protection of more than seven billion dollars. Since the organization these societies have disbursed more than $1,050,000,000 and are now disbursing annually about $75,000,000. They have already paid out nearly one-third as much as our government has paid in pensions since the pension system came into existence.

At no period in our nation's history has the brotherhood of humanity been so prominently before the world as it is to-day, protecting as it does the home and the fire side from want and shedding an influence that is upbuilding in its character and patriotic in its nature.

People are seeing a deeper significance in the real meaning of the word "Fraternity" and beginning to realize that all humanity is but one vast brotherhood, more or less dependent upon one another, and that anything detrimental to a single person affects all to a greater or less degree. No longer do we feel that we have a right to stand aloof and say, as was said of old, "I am holier than thou." No longer do we ask with the guilty Cain, "Am I my brother's keeper?" Unbounded love and charity for all mankind is the watchword of the day, and no one can say, "I believe in the brotherhood of any organization," who does not say: "I believe in the brotherhood of man."

GREAT MORAL EDUCATOR

We are convinced that the genuine fraternal spirit universally exercised is the remedy for the present lack of harmony between capitalist and employe, that it is the solution of all social problems, that it will conduce to a nobler and grander philosophy of government than most of us have ever dreamed.

Man is a dependent being, who relies for his success and happiness upon his own efforts, combined with those of his fellows; and when all men labor together in the spirit of true fraternity the right of every man to the fruits of his labors will be granted.

Organized fraternities have grown to be vital to the hearts and homes in the different states of our own country as well as in those of other countries. There is nothing that could take their places. If taken from us the warmth would be taken from the hearthstone and many of the most wholesome virtues taken from the heart.

The true fraternal spirit assists in lifting men into a higher moral atmosphere and instructs them in lessons of honor and generous character. It keeps them from the saloon and gambling table. No one can regularly attend the meetings of these fraternal organizations, wherein the true spirit of morality is taught, and hear the noble lessons rehearsed without becoming a better man or woman, a better parent and a better citizen.

AROUSES FEELING OF KINSHIP

Fraternity is a principle as old as humanity, but the duty of caring for the welfare of one another received its first impetus when the Man of Nazareth emphasized it in such a remarkable degree. And in the centuries that have followed the truths of Christ's teachings have so permeated the minds and hearts of men that true fraternity has become manifested in the relations of individuals, of organizations, and of nations. The large number of charitable institutions throughout the civilized world is an index of its great growth. One of our leading magazines recently contained the thought that the success of the church is not to be measured by the numbers that are added to it, nor by the amount of money contributed, but by the extent to which it is able to instill in the minds of its hearers the true spirit of brotherly love.

From the beginning the word fraternity has been applied to a society, or an association of people working together for their common interest, business or pleasure. We find this thought evidenced in such societies as the fraternal organizations of this city and in others of earlier origin. We find it applied to members of the same profession, as law and medicine, also to associations of students in colleges and preparatory schools. In the fraternities we are made to know and to feel the link of kinship.

EXTENDS HELPING HAND

Organization comes with order. This is true with mankind as well as in nature, and the more perfect the organization the greater the harmony. There may be discordant elements in a society, but if it be perfect in its organization and management, harmony exists. People of different religious and political opinions meet together, but peace abounds in the lodge rooms and there is a reciprocity and fellowship which have the true spirit of fraternity.

We all agree that there is a rule of the universe as to the foundation stone of every perfect principle. Upon this rests right, liberty upon that, and above all is the capstone of unity. "In union there is strength." This caused the Puritan of Massachusetts, the Quaker of Pennsylvania and the aristocrat of the South, each to lay aside his prejudices and join together in forming the continental congress and in laying the foundation for the greatest government the world has ever known. It is in this thought to-day that there is intellectual and moral strength.

In these fraternites the hand of charity is ever distributing. It is soothing the aching heart and wiping the tears from the cheeks of widow and orphan. It is clothing and feeding the dependent ones. How many people would die alone and be lowered into the potter's field were it not for the kind ministrations of true fraternity?

Our most solemn obligations to be fraternal and help ful to our fellowmen, if forgotten when the hand of the helpless is stretched out toward us or the lips of the needy plead for help, can never throw light or hope upon the night whose darkness may terrify the world. The world is calling in a loud voice for the good Samaritan who will stop and bind up the wounds of the afflicted and minister to the wants of him who has fallen by the wayside.

In mankind there is a tendency to make provision for the future of themselves and for those who are dependent upon them. This desire is only a natural one, and when the wageearner is enabled to make this provision, a great source of worry is removed and his chances of success are materially increased.

There is something in fraternity, as represented by the different societies, which touches the heart and brings into practice the teachings of those who are endeavoring to emphasize morality. In these societies we find men and women of the highest intelligence who are distinctively the representatives of their communities, and who are not doing the work merely for monetary gain. We recognize that humanity needs the protection which these societies give. We have been taught the truth, "Bear ye one another's burdens."

AID THE DISTRESSED

It has been demonstrated that such societies are of value in creating thrift among the people, in fostering habits of foresight and self-denial, in making provision for times of need. Fraternal protection gives the member the assurance that in the event of accident, total disability or death, his family will be provided for.

> Hail, holy, happy brotherhood!
> True love and friendship bind in one
> Hearts that are true, sincere and good,
> By thy refining influence won.

It is pleasing to note the growth of interest in these protective organizations. At a recent meeting of fraternal people President Roosevelt said: "Gentlemen, if this government is long to endure, it must be because of a recognition of the fact that the elements which constitute the fraternal societies of America are reckoned with, and kept in mind, in the administration of affairs of this government."

A true fraternal insurance society is formed to give protection and benefits to its members at the lowest possible cost consistent with safety and performance.

It is beyond the estimation of man to realize the extent of the relief given to the sick by free medical attendance, the watching and nursing, and the assistance given to members in distress, both in money and in sympathy, the securing of employment, the assistance in carrying the members to prevent suspension, and in many different cases creating confidence in the hearts of the people. Provisions have been made whereby children can be retained in school, many of whom will grow into stronger men and women because of fraternal helpfulness.

PROMPTLY MEET OBLIGATIONS

In the selection of members of a fraternal protective society not only the local examiner and the supreme medical examiner pass upon the application, but the lodge members themselves, for it occasionally occurs that they have personal knowledge of defects, either in the character or habits of certain applicants, which the doctors may have no means of discovering. The lodge system is especially valuable in that it can make selections, giving attention to the moral qualities of the applicants as well as to the physical and the material, and thus strengthen the society in the character of its risks.

The large army of people carrying fraternal protection in force of more than seven billions of dollars, and the benefits paid last year or more than $1,440,000 a week, cause us to be proud that we have had a part in the great work of distributing these sums among those for whom it has been most helpful.

In fact, fraternal insurance societies, as a rule, have met their obligations promptly and readily. This fact has done much to make them popular. In many cases the members have taken it upon themselves to do the work of deputies, agents or organizers.

AID FOR AFFLICTED

When the great calamity of earthquake and fire came to San Francisco, the grandest and noblest response to the appeals of the afflicted came from the members of the different fraternal organizations, and some of them took steps to pay the dues and assessments of their associates who were stricken. This was done before the request for help fairly reached the supreme offices in the different sections. Not only was money forwarded but the necessaries of life in the form of food, clothing and commodities necessary for the comfort of the people were poured into the laps of the afflicted members of the fraternal orders. Many of these fraternal orders could not boast of their millions of assets, but they could boast of their greater and better assets—the men and women who compose their membership and who have the true spirit of fraternity thoroughly rooted and grounded within them.

WHAT WE STAND FOR

J. E. VAN WINKLE

In the ancient times the great force of organization was for the benefit of the few. ·Retrospect the centuries of the past and you will note that nations had great armies and navies. They had sciences and arts, wealth and letters, kings and palaces. But all these have perished and gone into oblivion. Lying back of the dawn of the christian era were groups of great men. Greece had her Pericles, Socrates, Plato and Eschylus. Rome had her Julius Caesar and a senate of men of uncommon strength. Caesar had been victor in a hundred battles, subdued three millions of people, and in the face of combined opposition seized and held the reins of universal dominion. Before Caesar crouched the warlike Gaul. It was through the force or organization that Alexander became the master of the world. Through the genius of organization Napoleon superseded his adversaries and made the "boundaries of kingdoms to oscillate upon the map."

But these older civilizations, and these rulers of men forgot the people. A few were strong and rich and powerful, but the millions were slaves. A big army and navy does not make a great nation. A king or potentate may have affluence and wealth. He may have the plaudits of his subjects, but it is intermittent and shallow, and rendered under duress. A king with millions of subjects paying him homage may have a kingdom that is lacking in all those essentials which contribute to real greatness. The greatness of a nation must come from the number of happy and prosperous homes throughout the land. Greatness in a nation does not come from the absolute power of a monarch, but in the distribution of sovereignty among a free and intelligent people.

As we review the history of the world we see it dividing itself into three stages. In the first stage power is magnified. Force is deified. The great man is the strong man. In that era Nimrod is the hero after the world's heart. Strength receives the homage of the many. In the second stage power is pushed back a step or two and intellect comes to the front. The great man is the intellectual man. In that era Homer is the favored idol before whom the populace delight to bow. Genius receives the homage of the many. Humanitarianism has inaugurated the third stage. In this era the world is pointed not to Nimrod, not to Homer, but to Christ who taught the world brotherhood, and that humanitarianism that makes the whole world kin. Ever after that it is not power, it is not intellect, but goodness.

What seems strange these three stages of the world history which I have mentioned are paralleled in the individual experience of man as he admires the forces operating the world. What causes the heart of the boy to respond in admiration of David slaying Goliath? Power. Caesar leading the Tenth Legion? Power. Napoleon at the head of the Old Guard? Power. Let the boy pass into young manhood. What causes his heart to respond in admiration as a young man? Shakespeare creating his wonderful characters, and causing his meters to run like the music of the brook and his metaphors to shine like the fields and seas and clouds from which they are drawn. Shakespeare who could arrange the marvellous plots of a striking play, with personages of grand men doing magnificent deeds. Genius. Macauley writing his great history. Genius. Goethe throwing off the marvellous products of his pen. Genius. Let the young man reach his full maturity and become able to sift and weigh and analyze and judge things by the most approved standards. What calls out admiration from the heart of the mature man? John Howard at work among the reeking prisons. Goodness. George Washington sacrificing himself for the American republic. Goodness. Livingstone in the heart of the dark continent, struggling for the elevation of Africa. Goodness. Abraham Lincoln writing the Emancipation Proclamation. Goodness.

I know that goodness has not always been considered the equivalent of greatness, but it must be so considered in the age in which we are living. It was not so considered when the human race was young, but now that the human race is reaching its maturity we must look upon goodness as the acme of all greatness.

Over the gateway of the twentieth century is written in glittering letters the word "Brotherhood." Under the inspiration of this spirit of brotherhood the fraternal insurance societies of our country have enrolled over six millions of people, and have paid to the widow and the orphan more than a billion dollars.

LIFE

H S. HUDSON

Since the world first rolled from the Creator's hand and was peopled with human life, every dawn has seen the miracle of birth, and every dusk the tragedy of a death. In the morning a day is born, glides along to the heyday of Noon, stands for a moment upon the pinnacle of success, then turns its face downward toward the Dusk and finally is wrapped in the mantle of oblivion. Such is birth; such is life; such is death. Between the opening and the closing of the book lies all there is of the thing we call Life. The naked savage who wandered along the banks of the river Nile or made his habitations beneath the shadow of the Pyramids was the product of the same miracle as the chieftain who reigns over him.

The life of a hod carrier is just as mysterious as that of the king who wears purple robes. We cannot fathom the Divinity which quickens the spark of Life, neither can we peer into the Infinity into which it goes. Always the same old questions—sad suggestions. Whence and whither throng our way? We all know that for ages the footsteps of everything endowed with the mystery we call Life have passed down the same highway and onward into the gloom of that bourne from which no traveler ere returns.

We know that a death will follow every birth just as naturally as dusk follows dawn. We know that our own footsteps are following all that have gone before. We know that yesterday is dead and to-morrow is yet to be born. The only tangible, palpitating thing is To-day, and yet many are dissipating to-day, and others are crying from the depths of their souls despair. Oh, God! give me back my yesterday. Yes, all the tragedies were written yesterday. All the deeds that blight, and wither, and kill, are written into the scroll of yesterday. Every compunctious throb of memory is from some deed done, or left undone, yesterday. A word of warning, the right hand of good fellowship—a song, a handclasp—all might have been given yesterday, but to-day is too late; for yesterday is dead and o'er its tomb is written "Of all sad words of tongue or pen, the saddest are these, it might have been," while in the shadow of our neglect we cry, "Oh, God, give me back my yesterday"!

THE DEPUTY

(From THE FRATERNAL MONITOR.)

The demand for high class workers is becoming more and more insistent. The time is past when one could go into the field and secure applications with only a rate card and a small circular. There must be previous preparation and this must be in the way of acquiring information as to the institution to be represented, its plans, its particular field and the advantages it has to offer.

In the past too many have entered upon fraternal field work with no knowledge as to their duties and responsibilities. They relied particularly upon their own personality to secure results. They painted their proposition in rosy colors and, in their hands, it was such a yielding and pliable one that it could be made to fit the wants and needs of everybody.

We have all witnessed the effects of such operation. Members were secured on a basis that verged on the criminal. They did not understand what they were receiving. They accepted the statements of the solicitors rather than the terms of their certificates. They fancied that they had something which was a panacea for practically all the ills human flesh is heir to. When the awakening came they dropped out as rapidly as they had come in but a short time before.

Had these same people been secured on a fair basis, in all probability the majority of them would have remained. The very fact that they had been deceived aroused their suspicions and they felt that the organization was, by implication at least, involved in such deception.

To avoid a repetition of such experience these societies have during the past few years given more attention to the *personnel* of their representatives. They have supplied them with literature setting forth legitimate and proper operation. They have established schools of instruction through which their deputies may have the horizon of their views broadened and alike their opportunities and responsibilities set forth. They have enunciated the cardinal fact that members secured on a wrong basis are an element of weakness rather than of strength.

A FEW "DON'TS"

At the hazard of repeating what practically every one knows, or should know, THE MONITOR submits a few admonitions which should be kept ever in view. It does this on the assumption that prevention is more desirable than is cure—that avoidance of error is far better than overcoming it after it has gained lodgment.

No deputy should work for a society in whose management he has no confidence. He stultifies himself and weakens his self-respect when he does so. He under mines the very foundation on which legitimate effort is based when he is induced by the offer of large commissions to represent that in which he has no confidence.

To have confidence in an institution or system it is necessary that one first have knowledge as to its basis, its purposes and its accomplishments. To have such knowledge it is necessary that one give his subject that study and consideration which necessarily precedes sober and fair judgment. Confidence without knowledge is but a form of blind superstition.

Another "don't" which will stand analysis is that which tells one not to place a contract whose terms and conditions he does not thoroughly understand. The people look to those who present the proposition to them for definite and tangible information as to what it means and what it will do. If the truth is not told, or if this is covered up in a mass of meaningless words, it follows that dissatisfaction is bound to ensue. Misrepresentation is one of the most despicable methods ever employed to attain a given end. This observation is true in all walks of endeavor. He who misrepresents secures business under false pretenses.

CONVINCE YOURSELF FIRST

Do not make statements regarding your own or any other society without first convincing yourself that these are correct. Much of the doubts and skepticisms afloat to-day are due to dishonest or extravagant statements made in the past. We see their untoward results in our general business situation to-day. The confidence of the people has been shaken because they have not been dealt with frankly and openly. This condition has been played upon by designing persons and to-day as a result we are in the midst of adverse conditions which have no valid excuse for existence.

Is not prevention better than the cure? Would it not have been far better for all interests to have avoided those extremes which bring in their wake a reaction just as surely as night follows day? Is not confidence the basis upon which progress and successful operation in all lines of work rest? Without it do we not soon drift on the shoals of unrest, dissatisfaction and ultimate disaster?

THE MONITOR ventures the opinion that there is no institution which can permanently succeed without the confidence and co-operation of those identified with it. It goes further than this. It believes that no nation or people can be prosperous unless they act as an united and cohe sive force in behalf of their own institutions and the inter ests reposed to their keeping.

From this viewpoint, is it not the imperative duty of those standing on the watchtowers of fraternal operation to so conduct themselves that those who look to them for information will have confidence in what they say and do?

Is it not necessary that they act with circumspection and that they make no statements which will not withstand the searchlight of investigation and common sense?

CONDITIONS ARE WHAT WE MAKE THEM

Well has it been said that the wings of opportunity are clipped by Time. If one does not improve them as they present themselves they may never return. One must act promptly and decisively. He must miss no opportunity to impress both upon himself and others the importance of acting in a positive and vigorous manner.

The story is told of two commercial salesmen who arrived in a town on the same train. The one was a sort of negative character who looked upon the dark side of things. When the usual courtesies with his customers were over, he informed each of them that times were very hard, sales were slow, but that he hoped they would buy at least a small order to help him out.

The other possessed a more cheerful and forceful character. In order to convince his customers that everything was moving along prosperously, he showed them that his orders exceeded those during the corresponding months in 1907. He left that town with a good order sheet. Those who had been doubtful as to the future were convinced by the attitude of the salesman and by the fact that others were making provision for the future by laying in stocks of goods.

Does not the above indicate that conditions are about what we make them after all? The first commercial salesman put into the hands of each prospective buyer the weapons of refusal. The results were evident from the start. He defeated himself. The other had a convincing manner of putting things. He encouraged those with whom he came in contact. He showed by his manner that he was successful and he succeeded.

INSPIRE CONFIDENCE

The thought featurized by every institution having representatives in the field is that these must have confidence themselves in order to inspire confidence in others. This self-evident fact is one which cannot be over-stated. Upon it depends the success or failure of both institutions and their representatives. Lack of confidence is a weakening factor. It destroys vitality, quenches vigor and ardor and sows the seed of eventual decay.

The deputy has confidence in his institution and proposition or he would not be representing them. He should make this confidence a breathing and vitalizing force so that it will be known and felt by others. He should remember that no one is going to unite with an institution in which its representative has no confidence and, therefore, it is his manifest duty to instill in his prospect's mind that spirit of confidence which develops into definite and tangible results.

A COHESIVE BUSINESS

It is manifestly in order that the deputy develop his field in a methodical and systematic manner. He should not scatter or alternate between extremes. He should have a given line of effort and this should be so plain that preparation is always made for that which comes later.

A cohesive business is desirable from all viewpoints. It can be kept in line with comparatively little difficulty. It can be made a nucleus upon which other business may be built, and thus it becomes a steadily increasing one rather than of a nature which weakens itself by reason of the looseness with which it is thrown together.

One large local organization is better than a number of small ones. Its affairs will be better looked after. Its very numbers give it strength. Small organizations necessarily have a struggle for existence and this struggle is

reflected in their inability to make that growth character-
istic of the larger one which increases by the very force of
numbers.

THE SUCCESSFUL WORKER

Under the caption "The Successful Life Insurance
Agent of the Future," Mr. Edward A. Woods, in an
excellent communication to the quinquennial number of
The Spectator, suggested the following as a means of
stimulating agents to work more and waste less time.

> Encourage system; induce agents to keep daily reports of
> how their time is spent—if possible, to make daily reports; give
> them valuable help in suggestions and criticisms of their reports
> so that they will feel that the time spent in making them has not
> been wasted; allow no ground whatever for even suspicion that
> their reports will be used to personal advantage of the general
> agent; the one most benefited by the daily audit of the use of
> one's time is the agent himself. * * *
>
> The capital of the life agent is time instead of money. How
> can he know how it has been employed if he keeps no account
> of it? More record and more method will help agents to do
> this. Perhaps as great a cause for idleness as any is the fact
> that the agent after trying a few disheartening cases is too
> played out to initiate new prospects. If he had more definite
> calls assigned to him he would not be so disheartened because,
> if some applications were not secured, there would be plenty of
> prospects from whom he could expect results.

The foregoing is in line with THE MONITOR's expres-
sion of opinion to the effect that there should be syste-
matic effort and that deputies should endeavor to build up
a cohesive business rather than a scattering one. Central-
ization is always more effective than is loose or desultory
effort. He who has a given purpose and who keeps this
ever in view has a better chance of succeeding than does
he who rambles along, ever changing from one extreme
to another.

FRATERNAL INSURANCE AND NATURAL LAW

At its 1904 session in St. Louis, Actuary William Schooling, F. R., A. S., a publicist on the lines of insurance in Great Britain, presented a paper under the above heading. This paper was not in the least controversial. Rather, it emphasized fundamental principles and showed that the fraternal system has a stronger and broader basis than is commonly supposed. He believed that it was but fair to claim for England that it has taught the principles of life insurance to the world.

Actuary Schooling observed that in England there are many friendly societies which have continued for many years, but they are in many respects entirely different from fraternal societies as we know them here. There is only one fraternal society in England and it is hoped that this is the pioneer of widespread fraternal insurance in that country. He called it just fraternal insurance. He believed that it provided what the majority of people want, and in his writings it was his central purpose to spread the knowledge of the true principles of fraternal insurance in the mother country.

THE MONITOR has been requested to reproduce the paper of Actuary Schooling. It regrets that its limited space will not permit it to do so in its entirety. It, however, culls from his address the following which it is believed will be both interesting and instructive.

ADAPTATION AND LIFE INSURANCE

Those of us who are at all acquainted with insurance matters are peculiarly aware of the terrible uncertainty as to the time of death of any individual, but we are equally well aware of the certainty which prevails as to the average duration of life among a large number of people. We know that the death of an individual, especially of a man, commonly involves heavy financial loss, and consequent suffering, for those who are dependent upon him. We know very well, from practical experience, the relief that is afforded by a life insurance policy, but do we recognize in the payment of a claim the operation of a law of nature just as ingenious and just as perfect as that which provides the water ouzel with a thick plumage and strong claws which enable it to obtain food under water that is inaccessible to other birds?

Individuals, by acting in combination, can relieve themselves of the financial uncertainty which results from the uncertain duration of the lifetime of any person. But the Association in which these individuals combine, while it relieves them of uncertainty incurs no uncertainty; the average duration of life being regular, a life insurance institution finds itself in the same situation as the person who buys all the tickets in a lottery, thereby eliminating chance.

Just as the individuals in any species of plants or animals which do not acquire the protective coloring or other characteristics, tending to the preservation of the species, go under in the struggle for existence, so also do individuals of the human species, who abstain from the protection afforded by life insurance, also go under in the struggle for life, or rather it is worse than this; the man who abstains from the protection afforded by natural law working in the social sphere, may thereby cause his wife and family to go under in the struggle for life to the accompaniment of suffering for the individual and detriment to the species or community.

Any individual standing alone is absolutely incompetent, unless he is in the possession of capital, to provide against the financial consequences of the uncertainty of the time of death. He can only do so by acting in combination with others. If it is a question of saving money an individual can do that quite well alone; combination with other individuals may be of little or no direct benefit for such purpose and therefore it seems to me that the primary object of life insurance especially considered from the point of natural law, is protection against the financial consequences of death. Herein *I* think we see a deep natural fundamental reason for the superiority of fraternal insurance to many forms of old line insurance. So far as the old line companies are providing mainly for death protection, they are working in accordance with the natural law which we have been considering and are beneficial in their operations, but so far as they embody investment features involving high premiums, thereby making death protection expensive, they are failing to fulfill in the best way the fundamental natural object of life insurance.

1 fully admit that many of these investment policies are excellent for those who can afford them, but they are saving banks, not insurance, or rather they are partly one and partly the other. We shall see presently that almost every form of old line insurance combines something else with death protection, while fraternal insurance, which to my mind should confine itself to the provision of a sum of money in the event of death, fulfills the natural law of adaptation to circumstances far more perfectly.

THE CHANGE FROM INDEFINITE TO DEFINITE

There is another natural law of the widest possible kind which enforces the same conclusion from another point of view. If we study the evolution of nature as a whole or the evolution of any part of nature, we find progress from lower to higher consisting, among other things, in a change from the indefinite to the definite. Thus from the vagueness of the original nebula there evolves the definiteness of a solar system and its attendant planets and sooner or later on each planet there may come, as there has come on the earth, well defined objects and activities of countless kinds. If we go back to the earthly records of life insurance we find a vague nebulous condition of affairs. The information on the subject was too inadequate for the cost of insurance protection to be known, the consequence was that the premium charged for insuring a given amount at death varied but little, if at all, with the age of the person assured. It was scarcely recognized that age was a factor to be taken into account. Even when some importance was attributed to age, no distinction was made between the purchasers of annuities and the purchasers of life insurance policies. The charges made to both these classes were based upon the mortality of the general population with erroneous, and in some cases, disastrous results. It is now recognized that the rate of mortality among annuitants, among assured lives and among the general population are all different. The primitive indefiniteness has given place to definiteness and exactitude founded upon past experience.

THE BONUS SYSTEM

This primitive indefiniteness gave rise to the system of bonuses. The old Equitable Society of England, which was founded in 1762, felt it necessary to charge premiums sufficiently high to provide to a certainty for meeting claims as they arose. In the course of years it was found that the Society had a surplus beyond all possible requirements for its liabilities, and being a mutual office with no shareholders to take any part of the profit, it was decided to return part of this surplus to the existing policyholders, the distribution being dependent upon the amount and duration of the policies. Thus the bonus system had its origin in ignorance, and, now that primitive vagueness has given place to modern definiteness, the bonus system is retained without the justification of ignorance which was formerly an adequate sanction for so cumbersome a plan. You will see then that it was in consequence of ignorance that the law of adaptation to circumstances, which in the social sphere we call life insurance, worked imperfectly because expensively. The old line companies to an enormous extent still work imperfectly though not availing themselves of the more definite and exact knowledge which is now available.

THE DISCOUNTED BONUS SYSTEM

We have a system in England, I do not know whether it prevails in America, by which although the bonus system is retained the disadvantages of high premiums are avoided. It is commonly called the "discounted bonus" system. A company for instance which has been in the habit of declaring every five years a reversionary addition to its policies at the rate of fifteen dollars a year on each thousand dollars insured takes the present value of this bonus and allows it from the outset as a reduction of premium. If future bonuses are at a higher rate than fifteen dollars per thousand, the difference between the declared bonus and the discounted bonus is given to the policyholder. If the declared bonus is at a lower rate than the discounted bonus, the difference has to be paid by the policyholder in cash or by deduction from the policy when it becomes a claim. The result of this system is to produce rates of premium which are lower than without profit premiums for the same amount of insurance at the same age. Under this system policyholders in a mutual office secure their life insurance benefits at as nearly as possible actual cost, without at any time having to pay much too high a premium; save for the disadvantages of a relatively high rate of expenditure, and save for the fact that the cost of insurance protection is somewhat increased by policyholders having to pay for surrender values, this system is a nearly, but not quite, perfect provision against the financial uncertainty of death. We will consider later this question of surrender values and·

expenses, but in connection with the discounted bonus system, it is important to note that it practically provides the old line companies with a right to levy an assessment if it should be required. An agreed premium is paid from the outset, but it is accompanied by the express stipulation that if future bonuses are smaller than before the policyholder must pay something more than the stipulated premium. To all intents and purposes this is an assessment of a perfectly justifiable and necessary kind.

It seems to me that Fraternal Insurance at its best is the discounted bonus system improved. Fraternal Insurance as it exists in a few cases now, and as it must exist in all societies which are ultimately to survive, charges a level premium which, so nearly as the experience of the past in regard to mortality, and the prospects of the future in regard to the probable rate of interest to be earned upon the funds, enable an opinion to be formed, is the exact cost of insurance protection. If anything happens in the future, such as an unexpected decline in the rate of interest, to upset the calculations upon which the rates of premium are charged, then the members of the Fraternal Society are liable to an assessment, just as discounted policyholders in an old line company are liable to an assessment if the anticipated rate of bonus is not realized. An assessment of this kind, which is entirely different from the system of assessing nearly the whole of the premium according to circumstances, is a necessary provision in order to meet those minor fluctuations which even modern knowledge cannot exactly foresee.

We have seen that in order to fulfill the law of adaptation to circumstances in the most perfect way it is necessary to provide insurance protection at a minimum of cost, and we have seen that in the natural course of progress from indefiniteness to definiteness, from ignorance to knowledge, it has become possible to fix the cost of insurance protection with approximate accuracy. That same process of evolution which partly produces and partly depends upon adaptation to circumstances, which we call life insurance, and which promotes the welfare both of individuals and of the community, is made more perfect in its operation by the contemporary process of evolution from indefinite to definite, from ignorance to knowledge.

THE CHANGE FROM SIMPLE TO COMPLEX.

There is another feature of progress in general which leads to the same conclusion, namely the change from simplicity to complexity. Let us stand in imagination by the camp fire of some primitive tribe and listen to the records of the fighting or the hunting of the local heroes. We are witnesses—did we but recognize it—of the origin of history, the commencement of oratory, the beginning of poetry, the dawn of music, the birth of song, and the earliest of dances. If we trace the development of these primitive records to the stage which they have reached in our own day we arrive at modern journalism, at the work of historians, at the current developments of vocal and instrumental music, and at the present ramifications and developments of local government and of national parliaments. The simplicity of primitive life has developed by the most gradual stages into the vast complexity of our modern environment.

Insurance also exhibits an astounding progress from the simple to the complex. It began with mutual combination for compensation in the event of loss of vessels at sea, it was followed by payments for damage to property by fire, and later on to payments at the death of persons insured. Casualty insurance followed later, until now there is scarcely a contingency that cannot be provided against from a financial point of view by means of insurance. In life insurance, as exhibited by the operations of the old-line companies, the forms of policies are so numerous and so complicated that years devoted to the subject suffice to completely master the whole of the details.

SPECIALIZING

Now we have to notice that throughout the whole of nature the complexity which arises in the course of evolution is always and inevitably accompanied by a process of differentiation. If we go back to a primitive condition of life we find each man building his own dwelling, making his own weapons, obtaining his own food, making his own clothes, and in fact performing for himself all the few functions that were necessary to his condition of life. It is unnecessary to trace the changes that have taken place and which have resulted in the division of labor characteristic of modern existence. Now-a-days one man plays but a small part in the production of one out of many articles of food, in the manufacture of one out of many kinds of weapons. In literature, in journalism, in science, in manufacture, in fact in every department of human activity we see individuals specializing in some one limited direction. This specialization when carried to an extreme may tend to the detriment of the individual, but it is undoubtedly beneficial to the community at large. This process of differentiation, or specialization, has been carried far in connection with insurance. * * *

SPECIALIZING IN DEATH PROTECTION

This being so, specializing in the direction of financial protection in the event of death to the exclusion of all other forms of insurance seems to me the highest and most useful form of insurance that there can possibly be. It is certainly the most necessary for the great majority of people, and it is the form which illustrates far more completely than any other the natural law of adaptation to circumstances to which *I* have previously referred. We shall see presently that Fraternal Orders are far better suited for the provision of death protection in the most effective and the least expensive way, than commercial or old line Insurance Companies.

We have seen that Nature's singularly ingenious method of removing the financial uncertainty of individuals without involving insurance institutions in any uncertainty requires the combination of individuals into an Association. * * *

THE MODERN FRATERNALIST

I. I. BOAK

The thorough-going, up-to-date fraternalist must be a many-sided fellow. It would hardly fill the bill for him to possess those qualities that the old lady considered necessary to become a model chairman; that is, to "look wise, speak but little, think much and give liberally when the hat is passed." No doubt it would be well for him to be equal to all this, but that would hardly put him in the front rank of fraternalists.

Perhaps Emerson was prophetical and had the fraternalist of to-day in mind when he said, "Know a little of everything, and all of something." This injunction is worthy of more than passing notice. It is certainly easy to illustrate. For instance: Many lodge members agree that an occasional smoker is necessary to keep up interest and bring the members out to meetings. This being admitted, let me ask what is a smoker without a boxing bout or two?

There are but few lodge members who object to this form of amusement when properly conducted; so, admitting it to be a necessity, we will also be obliged to admit that we are not all proficient in the manly art. No one would ever think of seeing Joseph Cullen Root and A. R. Talbot dancing around each other, landing corkscrew punches and uppercuts until one of them had to throw up the sponge. If either of these great fraternalists were present at a smoker, he would be expected to deliver a masterly address and, in that capacity, he would surely "deliver the goods," but they would never be expected to put on the mitts.

At such gatherings, it is usually somebody's business to sing a song or two, and I know a lot of top-notch fraternalists whose singing would scarcely be regarded as an unqualified success, unless it would be on the score that *one* effort was such a pronounced success that another song would never be called for. Many other duties are necessary on such occasions and, while admitting it to be unnecessary for any one person to engage in all, or indeed in more than any *one* of such duties, we feel sure that we are right in contending that a fraternalist should be versatile enough to discern when such functions were well performed, or otherwise.

The foregoing, however, is but one phase of a fraternalist's life, and serves to illustrate the necessity of special, rather than varied talents and emphasizes but *one,* and from a fraternalist's standpoint, the least one of the two great thoughts contained in the foregoing quotation from Emerson. Modern industries furnish examples of the same thought. Our large shoe factories are operated without any shoemakers, provided we define the word "shoemaker" as "one who makes shoes," and this definition is the only practical one.

In such institutions a shoe passes through a score of hands before it is complete; every fellow operates his own machine and knows nothing about the other fellow's machine, and perhaps not a man in the factory could make a shoe. The trend of modern usefulness runs to specialties, and all large industries furnish examples of this.

We readily agree that this is "knowing all of something." The other phase of the question, to "know a little of everything," is, I contend, not nearly as easy to attain and, therefore, far less in evidence than the other, and because of this, I feel justified in referring to the *fraternalist* as the "Man of the Hour," *the most useful citizen of the day.* Our captains of industry are specialists; so are the leaders of old line insurance, and, while we do not decry their merits, we feel safe in declaring their usefulness toward their fellowman to be *limited* and ofttimes *questionable.*

To fill the bill as a model fraternalist, one must not only *know,* but *be* a little of everything. He certainly requires a number of natural and God-given qualities, superinduced and developed by cultivation and environment. In his varied duties, he must recognize the Scriptural injunction and "be all things to all men." He must be a "mixer." The needs or desires of men are unknown to the one who does not mingle with his fellowmen. He should be dignified, but not haughty; mirthful at times, but never frivolous; serious, without being sour; he should look on every human being as made in the image and likeness of God, and be more than ready to help the erring one to overcome his shortcomings; never hasty to condemn, or when he does condemn, let his condemnation be directed to the act, rather than the actor; he should place character above intellect and encourage the cultivation of both; he should have the broadest conception of the brotherhood of man; he should ever bear in mind the eternal truth that goodness is measured by usefulness, and that what he *is* speaks louder than what he says; he has a right to be ambitious and aspire to the highest position in the gift of his fellows.

He has no business to expect to reach heights without climbing to them; he should, and does, aspire to *fill* a position and not rattle around in it; he knows well that *the world owes no man that which he does not earn or produce;* he recognizes the everlasting truth that great and noble achievements are the result of earnest and continued effort, and that which is worth having is worth striving for; he knows that character which lives forever was not built in a day; he learns great lessons from the great teacher; he sees the mushroom grown in one night, and in the morn it is naught but a mushroom, one hour of sunshine and it is destroyed and lost forever; he sees stately ships built of hearts of oak and he realizes that it took a hundred years for the great oak tree to grow and develop.

He is right in regarding preparation as a necessary adjunct to the gratification of ambition. He draws a fine, distinguishing line between selfishness and self-preservation. He knows the fellow who thinks of nobody but himself is greedy and miserable, while he who forgets himself and his own interests is unwise. In short, he exemplifies the human side of the Divine Master, for the sweetest and most beautiful synopsis of human greatness is wrapt up in the Savior's inquiry as to the usefulness of *life,* at its close.

And the culmination of *fraternal* ambition, the grandest that mortal mind can conceive of, is to merit that welcome "Well done!" for "Inasmuch as ye have done it unto the least of these, ye have done it unto ME."

A MANY-SIDED PROPOSITION

(From THE FRATERNAL MONITOR.)

Khaled was one of the beneficent genii whom Allah freed from all emotion or prejudice that he might report dispassionately to Allah for final judgment vexed questions arising in the affairs of men.—*Mohammedan Mythology.*

While an arrangement similar to the above may not be workable in fraternal operation at the present time, its imperative need cannot but be admitted by right-thinking persons. The difficulty rests with those whose chief stock in trade is self-exploitation and self-interest. They oppose everything not in harmony with such interests. They have promulgated positive opinions on vexed subjects. The fraternal world, therefore, must defer to these or incur the penalties attendant upon its temerity. They have outlined given plans of operation and those not in harmony with these are declassed by them. They have assumed the functions of dictators and the fraternal world must govern itself accordingly.

Possibly it would be declaring too much if one were to assume that the fraternal proposition is a many-sided one and that there are many adaptations of it. Yet such is the case, and he who stands out for a given adaptation of a particular principle, to the exclusion of all others, may have a hearing temporarily but, in the final analysis, his position will be discredited as being narrow, repressive and unworthy of the possibilities of fraternal operation when exemplified along broad lines. The self-constituted mentor of to-day will to-morrow be regarded as a self-seeker or zealot who could appreciate nothing beyond the horizon of his own views. He will be relegated to the ranks of those who have been tried in the balance of actual results and who have been found deficient under such test.

BIASED OPINIONS UNTRUSTWORTHY

In all walks of life we have had a surfeit of biased opinions and preconceived notions. These are characteristic of those who have given but superficial attention to subjects on which they deliver themselves sagely. They are dangerous for the reason that they fail to appreciate or realize that there are few subjects on which valid grounds cannot be taken by conflicting sides and that it requires experience and a clear head to decide between them.

On the question of adequacy in rates, when considered as an abstract proposition, there can be but one answer. When reduced down to concrete conditions there will be many answers. Everything depends upon the point of view. Everything hinges upon the ends aimed at and the manner in which it is expected that they shall be brought to a successful issue.

We have proponents of the term or step-rate system. We have those who denounce it unqualifiedly. Their conflicting points of view arise from the ideas or interests which dominate them. All depends upon the manner in which they approach the subject and the ends they have in view.

If one desires to create an estate or competence for his dependents, regardless as to whether or no he may live a decade or several decades hence, it is but natural to assume that what is called whole life protection will appeal to him strongly. It is his desire to know and have a rate that will be stable during the period of his connection with an organization. He does not wish to pay a larger sum in the future than he is now paying. He wants to know his obligation and make provision for it. He is not looking so much for the present and its responsibilities as he is for the future and the protection of those more or less dependent upon him after he has reached, or exceeded, his life expectancy. His central purpose is the creation of a given fund or estate after he has departed this life.

The proponent of the step-rate, or term certificate, looks upon the protective insurance proposition as one which gives assurance to his dependents from day to day that there will be provision for them in the event of suddent or unfortuitous events arising. He is the one who has confidence in himself and his earning capacity. If he lives and retains his health the future has no terrors for him. He can meet it and provide for his dependents. It is against the shadow of uncertainty which looms up ever before him that he desires protection. He plans that during his productive years he is incurring greater hazards than he is later on after these have come either to a successful fruition or after he has settled down to the struggle with life as he finds it. He wishes to be protected against the uncertainties of life.

EITHER POSITION TENABLE

Either of the above positions is tenable. Everything depends upon the results desired. All hinges upon the plans and moving impulses of the one who desires to safeguard the future of his dependents.

No real purpose is served by the advocates of one form of protection when they denounce those who favor the other. Each one is feasible and workable. As has been said, everything depends upon the point of view. In the language of Mohammedan Mythology, we should be "freed from all emotion and prejudice" if we hope to solve in a dispassionate manner the "vexed questions arising in the affairs of men."

THE MONITOR has on frequent occasions expressed the belief that there is no reason why a society should not offer either, or both, of the forms of operation set forth above. If an applicant for membership desires a term certificate, no interest is prejudiced if he is given this. If, on the other hand, the applicant desires a whole life certificate, he can secure this on a basis equally as equitable and just as does the one taking out the term certificate. All depends upon the contract. If the same basis for determining rates is employed, it follows that results or their equivalents will be forthcoming. Therefore, each one receives the equivalent of that for which he pays. Results work out in like manner and no one is advantaged at the expense of the other.

HOSTILE ALIGNMENTS

Practically all of the hostile alignments which exist in fraternal operation to-day may be traced to individual ideas or interests. One has personal notions as to the limits beyond which fraternal operation should not go. He may be influenced by the plans of the organization of which he is the accredited exponent. In his desire to be loyal to the interests reposed to his keeping, he not infrequently oversteps these and attempts to apply them to those who have other ideas and who operate along other lines.

A controversy is the result. Each one upholds that with which he is identified. He employs all argument and effort possible in its behalf. Not infrequently he deems it his duty to solicit outside aid and interference. The controversy thus becomes more complicated and the ends aimed at become more obscured.

In the natural order of things there is an alignment of hostile forces and each one deems it to be within the bounds of legitimate effort to employ all means available to further its own interests. Thus, in a greater or less degree, a war of systems or plans is precipitated. This is limited only by the persistency or the ability of the opposing interests to either advance itself or retard the progress of the other.

PRESENT-DAY ANTAGONISMS

The antagonisms existing among fraternal leaders to-day cannot but be regarded with regret by those who have at heart the best interests of the system. These serve no useful purpose. Rather, they afford opportunity for self-seekers and opposing interests to strengthen their contentions. They show to the world that there is something wrong or something misunderstood when there is so much dissatisfaction and so much open hostility among those who are pledged to maintain the best interests of the organizations of which they are at the head and who, as a corollary proposition, are interested in the progress of the system in its entirety.

There is to-day not a battle as to the standard by which fraternal operation shall be gauged. The controversy is as to the means employed to reach or approximate such a standard. There are those who insist that their way is the only way; that the truth is known and that those who temporize with it are evading their full responsibilities. Arrayed against these are those who appreciate that adequacy in rates is essential, but who insist that they are but the servants or subordinates of the interests reposed to their keeping and that, while they can admonish and urge as to duty, they cannot compel their members to take such action as these members alone can take. This substantially is the only point at issue between the conflicting sides.

As arrayed against these are the old-line interests whose adequacy in rates is not questioned. These have been using the dissensions in fraternal ranks to advance their own interests. They have not been slow to point the finger of suspicion at all engaged in this controversy and they have enlisted more or less of public sentiment in favor of their contention.

In evidence of this measures have been presented

before the legislatures of several states, asking for permission to give special contracts and lower rates to members of clubs, labor unions and beneficial organizations in numbers of one hundred or more. This means, if it means anything, that they purpose to take advantage of the present disorganization among fraternal leaders and make it do service in their own behalf.

RESULTS THE PROPER MEASURE

May not one conclusion be drawn without inviting the hostility or antagonism of either side? Are not results the proper measure of operation, rather than standards? If this be admitted, are we not chasing a phantom, and are we not failing to consider properly the substance? If, as the legal permission desired would indicate, the old-line companies are warranted in making special rates for the purpose of disorganizing fraternal operation, would it not be the part of unwisdom to create an arbitrary standard which may place the societies at the mercy of such interests?

If the balance left after caring for current liabilities is sufficient to provide for the future along orthodox lines, have not the full purposes of mortality tables been served? If they are not sufficient for this purpose, does not the results show that such mortality standard is but a warning as to impending evil, rather than a guarantee as to permanence?

The present is an opportune time to face about and aim at results rather than standards. These, as is well understood, are but artificial or guiding lines to show the trend of operation and to warn against danger or to show the results of desirable operation. This being the case, we should lose sight neither of tables nor of results. The one is a standard. The other is a measure. There cannot be a measure without a standard. The two should be employed and neither one should be obscured to advance the other.

Meanwhile the organizations should get together on essentials and should eliminate the question of the interests of individual societies or their exponents.

THE TEMPLE OF FRATERNITY

NOAH M. GIVAN

Almost two thousand years before Christ, Abraham said unto Lot "Let there be no strife I pray thee between me and thee, and between my herdsmen and thy herdsmen, *for we be brethren."* About four hundred years later Moses said to his people, who were slaves and who disagreed, *"Ye are brethren,* why do ye wrong one to another?" These utterances were in striking contrast to the sentiment implied by the question of Cain when he said "Am I my brother's keeper?" I am not my brother's keeper seemed to have been the keynote of the world's character from Adam's fall to the time when wickedness had reached its deepest depths of degradation and the race had to be destroyed by the flood.

A failure to recognize the fact that "we be brethren," a failure to allow the fact to become a part of the ethics of society, was a failure to have imbedded in its structure a principle that would cement and perpetuate it. A community, state, or nation founded upon the vicious doctrine that I am not my brother's keeper, must be of short duration and end in disgrace. The world grew wicked rapidly after Cain's announcement, and "God saw that the wickedness of man was great in the earth, and that every imagination of the thoughts of his heart was only evil continually."

After the destruction of the world by the flood a new order of things was inaugurated, a new doctrine was announced by Abraham and Moses, but it was only prohibitive. It enjoined against strife and wrong doing. It failed to define the duty of helpfulness to others—it was negative goodness, not aggressive righteousness. It was, however, an advance on the old doctrine of Cain. It was the beginning of a reform movement which must develop and grow beyond our time until it shall become a perfect law, form a perfect manhood,—aye, more! shall fit each one as a living stone for that building not made with hands, but made by the silent forces that form Godlike character, and which we look forward to as God's holy temple in the heaven.

As God commanded the old so He has always fostered the new. Growths of reform in government and society are always gradual and, to the impatient, slow, but sure when towards a higher, purer and better life.

David and Jonathan—not of kin—formed a friendship that has blessed the world and contributed mightily to the fraternalism of the present day. Solomon, the son of David, gave form to an organization of helpfulness to the workmen upon the famous Temple that was in advance of Abraham and Moses, and which has grown both in richness of life and in favor with God until it emblazons the world. But it only provided for its members and their families in its inception. Other advance steps were necessary to reach the desired goal.

It was necessary that the homely Samaritan should do a little unostentatious act of kindness and have compassion on one not his kindred, not his nationality, not of his occupation, profession, lodge or church, but to one who was in trouble, with whose people he had no dealings, and thereby teach the world that our neighbors are all mankind, and that we should love our neighbors as ourselves.

From this small beginning of true fraternity which has immortalized the Samaritan man, and made him worthy to be the Prince of all Fraternities, of all ages, past, present and future of all the world, has grown that sentiment of fraternity which has crystalized into an organized brotherhood of millions and millions of men and women who recognize the great doctrine of the brotherhood of man, and who are unselfishly laboring for the uplifting of the race.

It is this great thought that has suggested my subject THE TEMPLE OF FRATERNITY. Not that the invisible sentiment of brotherly love can be materialized into such a Temple, but that the sentiment can be typified by the Temple that is proposed to be built by the Fraternities of the United States in connection with the Great Exposition of 1903, and called the Temple of Fraternity, where all the brethren and sisters of all the fraternal orders may meet and clasp the hand of brotherly love, and learn more of the practical workings of each.

The proposed dimensions and architecture of the building are well known. The name Parthenon, from which it was designed, was from Parthenos the "Virgin," a title of Athena, and was a temple of Minerva the Virgin Goddess of Wisdom and Art. It was built by Pericles about B. C. 438, and stood as a whole until about A. D. 1690. It was of the best material, and is regarded as the finest production of Greek architecture. These qualities made it a firm figure for a newer and greater temple of the best type of manhood and womanhood—The Temple of Fraternity.

What does such a temple represent in the United States? A membership of over 4,000,000 souls in the fraternal benefit societies alone, who regularly and for the most part cheerfully contribute to the protection of the widows and orphans of deceased members. Something over $50,000,000 a year, or about $1,000,000 a week, is thus contributed to this holy cause, chiefly for the protec tion of the *humble* homes of our nation.

What an antidote for discontent and pauperism! Since the beginning of practical fraternalism, now within the memory of some present at this meeting, the statistics show that pauperism has decreased in proportion as fra- ternalism has increased. These fraternal benefit associa- tions are annually contributing enough to support 500,000 people. The vast amount contributed is equal to two- thirds of that raised by taxation for the public care of the poor. These great results have been attained within the past two decades.

"The crowning glory of the Nineteenth Century just passed into history is the fact that fraternalism during that time distributed to its beneficiaries over $515,000,000 and demonstrated in the face of all opposition that safe, sound and reliable protection can be furnished at actual cost. This is the material view of the great work of these orders. The joy that these benefactions have brought to many thousands of our American homes cannot be described on paper. The homes that have been saved, the children that have been preserved to home, school and church life, and thus kept from sin and shame and crime, are shining monuments to the blessedness of fraternalism. But above all, the realization by actual experience to the brethren of these orders, of the truth that it is more blessed to give than to receive, and the fraternal union of rugged and hitherto selfish men in the God-like work of helping others, are the crowning cap stones in the real Temple of Fraternity. God alone, in His infinite wisdom, can estimate the grand results—material, intellectual and spiritual that have grown during the brief period of the existence of fraternalism. * * *

"FRATERNITY APPLIED TO INSURANCE"*

The world at large has not understood as yet the sig-
nificance and the importance of this movement. And this
Exposition will have materially contributed to the wel-
fare of mankind if it advance the interest and increase
the prominence of such a movement. If it shall promote
in any way the growth and reputation of a system which,
in the brief compass of thirty-three years, has paid over
five hundred million dollars to the widows and the
orphans of the common people of America it will have
been a success, even if it shall have failed in every other
respect.

There is no subject concerning which more misrepre-
sentation exists than the subject of fraternal insurance.
It has encountered opposition and criticism from the old
line companies, the most powerful financial forces of the
time. It has caught upon its spotless shield the poisoned
arrows of prejudice and slander. But despite the most
terrible obstacles it has become a permanent and growing
factor in the industrial life of the country. The fact that
only thirty-three years after the establishment of the first
insurance order four million American citizens are
enrolled beneath its banners—banners on which fifteen
million American women and children gaze as upon
sacred ensigns from the skies—gives the lie to calumny
and makes the system worthy of confidence and support.

The nature and importance of life insurance are
almost universally conceded. It is the fraternal system
of life insurance which is not so well understood by the
general public, although it is growing in popularity and
favor at an almost incredulous rate. This system is of

*Extracts from the address of Mr. Morris Sheppard, of the
Woodmen of the World, at the South Carolina Exposition.

comparatively recent development. At the close of the civil war there was not an insurance order in the United States. The old line companies, with decades of experience behind them, monopolized the field. What necessity existed for the fraternal system? What prompted Upchurch in 1868 to organize the great mother fraternity? * * * The object of the founders and apostles of fraternal insurance was to place insurance on a co-operative, non-speculative basis, and thereby to extend its blessings to the struggling masses. The old line companies threatened them, as with a thousand times more emphasis they threaten now, to destroy the proper province of insurance by obscuring it in the glittering mazes of investment and speculation. Fraternalists have felt, and feel to-day, that the central purpose of insurance is the protection of the family and the home when the protector shall have died. We hold that any inducement which diverts from this purpose and directs it to the personal interest of the policyholder himself is dangerous. We hold that, for the sake of his wife and child, it ought to be beyond a man's power to cash his policy, etc.

But the advantages of insurance for the masses through self-government, non-profit organizations, infinite as they are, compose by no means the only beneficent characteristics of the fraternal system. There is yet another characteristic above and below all these, above them a star, below them a pillar—a characteristic without which the success of the system is impossible, with which its triumphs in the past have been won, and its victories in the future are assured—the characteristic of fraternity. Every uplifting impulse of the human heart, every beneficent movement of history, may be traced to the influence of fraternity. Fraternity is Christ embodied in a sentiment, clothed in a principle. He expressed the idea

of fraternity when He said: "Bear ye one another's bur-
dens," the sublimest sentence that ever throbbed on lips
divine. The American Republic is fraternity applied to
government. The fraternal order is fraternity applied
to insurance. Fraternity suggested the rescue of life
insurance from the hands of those who were making it
an instrument of selfish gain. Fraternity suggested that
the mother, the wife and the child could be best protected
by the removal of insurance from the field of speculation
and investment. Fraternity suggested that the common
people gather beneath its wings to secure at cost protec-
tion for their homes. It will thus be seen that the frater-
nal system had its origin in the most laudable and inspir-
ing motives. The assertion will not be denied that its
underlying purposes are pure. Its astonishing progress
is an unquestioned tribute to its integrity and perma-
nence. It has succeeded in bringing insurance within the
reach of the masses, because it has avoided the elements
of investment, profit and large expense.

The members of the true fraternal order are united
by the ties of brotherhood. They assert an active per-
sonal interest in the order's welfare. It is natural and
necessary that they should do so, because they are an
essential, representative part of its very being. They
own the institution. It is of the people, for the people and
by the people. Through the lodge they put the idea of
fraternity into practice. They visit the sick, assist the
needy, and bury the dead. They do not confine their
efforts to the mere payment of dues. This is but half the
fraternal obligation. The member-for-insurance-only is
an imposition. The active members are carrying at least
half of his insurance. The fraternal assessment is paya
ble half in enthusiasm and half in cash. Enthusiasm alone
makes insurance at cost possible. *   *   *

Enthusiasm supplies for the order the expense element

which the company must add in order to defray enormous cost of agencies and the other elements to which allusion has been made. The lodge is the principal agency of fraternalism, the center of enthusiasm. And this saving would exist in favor of one of the fraternal orders should the companies confine themselves to insurance proper and omit the investment proposition entirely. Oh, that every member of every legitimate order would keep religiously in mind the fact that the very life of the fraternal system, with its vast possibilities for good, depends upon the interest and enthusiasm which he as an individual exhibits in its behalf. * * *

The utmost harmony between the orders themselves is essential to continued progress. Co-operation between the orders is as necessary to make the system victorious as co-operation between the individual members of the various orders is necessary to make the individual orders triumphant. They have the same battles to fight, the same enemies to overcome.

FROM CRITICISM TO CONSTRUCTION
(From THE FRATERNAL MONITOR.)

The careful student of events has observed that there are always two stages in the passage of a people from one era to another in the evolution of their business life. These may be termed the critical and the constructive stages. Ordinarily and under healthy conditions, the one follows the other as a result of natural law.

Construction fails to follow criticism when those who have passed through the critical process of self-examination find that "the salt of self-reformation has already gone out of them." In other words, construction is impossible when the ravages of disease or the attempts to expel these have been so drastic as to leave the person or institution under treatment so helpless and exhausted as to be unable to recover.

For a period of several years the fraternal system of this country has been passing through the critical stage of a new era in its existence. As a result of prolonged agitation, participated in by the greatest apostles of fraternal protection, it was declared that the principle employed in the past had reached the limit of its application and that, in consequence, its exponents must conform to present and future needs as set forth.

A CONSTRUCTIVE ERA

With great persistence, and with signal success, the defects in past fraternal operation have been critically exposed. There has been a winnowing of the good and the evil—a separation of the dangerous from the helpful, and a clearer definition of the problem of constructive reform.

Searching scrutiny along lines other than those having to do with fraternal institutions has resulted in a sifting of things that is making history. It has made the old order of things—political, economic and ethical, practically impossible for the future. It has created the necessity for beginning an era of constructive policy

On this point, in the opinion of THE MONITOR, there should be a crystallization of the opinion of fraternal members at this time. The time for analysis only has passed. The need of the present is a constructive program which will gather up apparently divergent and conflicting things and unite them on a basis that will have as its central purpose permanent welfare and will likewise embody these in a safe and sound policy as equitable to all as the inevitable inequalities of general conditions will admit.

Briefly stated, we cannot hope to attain perfection's

height by continuing indefinitely along critical lines. If we confine ourselves exclusively to the consideration of one phase of a proposition, this assumes abnormal propor-tions and we are unable to consider it as regards the rela-tion it bears to the entire proposition. We thus, by our unduly critical policy, defeat the very ends we are aim-ing at.

THE SPIRIT OF OPTIMISM

In our efforts along the lines of construction—and especially at this stage of evolution—we need optimism more than reforms. The latter will follow in due course. We need that spirit of consideration that will impel us to extend a helping hand to sister societies; to be consider-ate of those who possibly have not progressed so far as we have along constructive lines. We should assist them in all ways possible, insisting always, however, that they shall work and bend their energies toward improving their condition.

Have you ever attempted to compute the evils and inequities in the economy of nature? Are not these, from our viewpoint, practically without limit? Is there any-thing which appears to be absolutely perfect?

And so it is with the fraternal system. From the lim-ited vision of the individual it can never be perfect. Its very purpose is to equalize or average imperfections as understood by the individual. Were everything else per-fect, were there no untoward conditions to make provi-sion against, there would be no need for institutions hav-ing as their central purpose the protection of the individ-ual against these.

DISTRIBUTING A HAZARD

One joins a society and dies to-morrow. His benefic-iaries receive one thousand dollars for the payment of one dollar. Another joins to-day and dies sixty years hence.

His beneficiaries receive one thousand dollars for the payment of possibly eleven hundred dollars.

Has the society protecting the beneficiaries of these two members acted unjustly with either? Has it given the dependents of the one dying first an advantage over those of the one who lived perhaps beyond his expectancy? Was this an inequitable contract from the viewpoint of the member who died last?

THE MONITOR believes that there will not be much division of opinion on this subject. The society simply acted as a means of distributing a hazard which the individual did not wish to bear alone. The very existence of such a contingency shows the imperative need of protection and the importance that this be adjusted so that the one who lives up to or beyond his expectancy will assure his dependents the amount of the protection he carries.

THE REAL BUILDERS

The very fact that there have been societies in the past which did not make provision for more than their temporary needs, which did not give to those who had been with them many years unquestioned assurance that payment would be made their beneficiaries according to the terms of their contract, led to what has been termed the period of criticism. This has run its course.

There is to-day no excuse for any member of a fraternal society in the way of saying that he had not been advised as to the evils complained of. Likewise, there is no excuse for one to continue in this stage of criticism indefinitely. As has been said, such a course so weakens the institution criticised that there is danger lest "the salt of self-reformation has already gone out of it."

The work of construction is now in full swing. Those building are looking forward. They have in mind the goal toward which they are striving. Every step forward adds to their earnestness and enthusiasm.

Such workers have passed the period of criticism. They dwelt on this stage of their work only long enough to determine defects and get their bearings. Then they faced themselves in the direction of accomplishment— repinings and explanations as to "what caused it" being left to those who had nothing to engage their attention or occupy their time.

IS LIFE INSURANCE DOOMED?

Some time ago the attention of THE MONITOR was directed toward a paper that would appear before the National Association of Life Underwriters on "Is Life Insurance Doomed?" It did not know what the one to speak on it, Mr. Charles W. Scovel, would have to say. Naturally, this very unusual topic excited attention.

It was explained that by the word "doomed" is not necessarily meant the inquiry as to whether life insurance is doomed to death. Rather, is it doomed to slavery under the lash of many diverse and perverse local statutes, instead of its free, scientific development under Nature's laws of life and death and the world-wide law of supply and demand?

Mr. Scovel asked: "Is it doomed to keep falling behind in the march of human progress instead of keeping up the marvelous stride that has in so few years brought it to the front rank? Is it doomed to be more and more cut up into geographical fragments, doomed to be more and more cut off from all people that do not themselves seek it out, instead of maintaining its rightful place next to Church and State as one of the universal institutions that reach out their hands to serve the individual, the fam ily and the community?

The question was answered by saying that it is thus doomed if its direction is to be dominated by the doctrinaire and the demagogue. The doctrinaire was described as the well-meaning theorist, with a hobby, and the well-meaning layman with the ideal. The demagogue was described as one who regards a public issue as an opportunity to "play politics" for himself or the party. These three were dumped together and Mr. Scovel politely called them "Mr. Reformer."

FREEDOM AND PUBLICITY

THE MONITOR does not believe that the work of construction should be impeded or directed by those whose characteristics are thus described. Rather, it believes that, so far as is possible and consistent with the equities that should obtain between members, the future of these institutions should be allowed to develop along the lines indicated as desirable by their own experience. It does not believe that hard and fast exactions should be required as a part of the work of construction.

What fraternal leaders and members need above all things else is an access of that old-time spirit which swept opposition aside and which scattered discouragement and disorganization whenever and wherever they lifted their baleful heads. It needs the spirit of optimism. Those connected with it should look on the bright side of things for a time at least. Too long have they been looking with critical eyes on things which appeared dark to them. As a result, many things have not since appeared to them in their true light.

Let us get down to first principles in our work of construction. Let us consider each element with reference to its importance in the whole proposition. Let us give each one its due share of consideration, but let us not allow any one to overshadow others equally as important and essential in the great work of constructing a fraternal system that will stand for all time and that will give unquestioned assurance to everyone connected with it that the protection they carry is as safe as anything of human creation can be.

THE FRATERNAL IDEA AND ITS POWER

REV. J. W. VAN KIRK

Comte said, "Ideas govern the world or throw it into confusion." The Czar's idea of his divine right to govern the world threw it into disorder. The ideas of peace and humanity within the masterful mind and heart of President Roosevelt, one of the big brothers of the race, brought order out of confusion, and is now leading the world in the truth and sentiment of brotherhood.

If this age can be said to be conscious of a definite aim and having a predominate purpose, it is that of bettering the conditions of life and infusing a spirit of humanity among all men.

The world is looking at its questions from a new viewpoint, namely, that of humanity. Those who are living in the spirit of the age are not asking, "Am I my brother's keeper," nor "Who is my neighbor," but they are assuming the responsibilities of brotherhood and in sympathy, good will, and practical benevolence are helping to bear the burdens which are so crushing to the less fortunate brother.

Among the many agencies which are at work for bringing in a more humane condition of society are the great fraternal organizations, which, in the United States, embrace in the membership and protection, at least one-half of the population.

If these societies are to operate for the good of humanity, the great principles and spirit which made them possible must ever be kept fresh in the mind and burning in the heart. The real spiritual and ethical content of their teaching must be grasped intelligently, and the sacredness of their sentiments must be consciously felt.

It is only in the present religious and ethical state of society that such a vast system of protection, under the idea and spirit of fraternity, is possible. In Greece, Rome, India, China and Japan, where the people hold a perverted and low conception of God, the sense of humanity in an extended sphere is almost wholly wanting. It is only where men hold a belief in the one living God and Father that a high ethical standard of brotherhood can obtain. A belief in a Father—Creator in whose likeness men are made, is the first or controlling idea which leads men to a belief in, and a practice of universal brotherhood. The philosophy of the family involves the doctrine of parent and child, and where there are two or more children, there is the relation of brotherhood. There is no more sacred relation existing between God and man than that of Father and child, nor do men sustain any higher ethical relation among themselves than that of brothers.

Thus the Fatherhood of God and the Brotherhood of Man is the creed of fraternalism. All fraternities holding to these fundamental ideas are both religious and ethical. Freemasonry, the mother of modern fraternities, is distinctively a religious as well as an ethical institution. Its temples are erected to God, the free, personal, moral and intelligent Governor and Judge of all men. The fraternal world teaches that with God there is no respect of person, and that all stand on an equality before Him. A fraternity is not a religious institution in the sense of a denomination or sect, nor in specifically treating the questions of sin and salvation nor in administering sacraments, but it is a place for true devotion and worship in spirit and in truth. The lodge is also a place for diffusing a spirit of humanity, inculcating righteousness, developing honor and the practice of beneficence. The distinctive work of a fraternity is the making of manhood, the bearing of each other's burdens and the strengthening of the bond of fraternity. The insurance and other material benefits accruing from the fraternity are incidental and secondary to their primary object. Only as a fraternity assists men in building up a religious and ethical character can it show its right to existence and support.

All material interests operated by a fraternity are embodied in these most sacred principles, and under the control of the highest ideals and strongest conviction of duty. The management of such interests is within the sphere of honor where men are prompted by the strongest religious and humanitarian sentiments. It is not for themselves but for others that these funds are to be handled. Within this circle of honor men assume as a sacred trust, the management of the meagre earnings of their brothers who desire to provide a little against the day of need. Thus, if there is any business in the world which has reason to be done in unselfishness and with clean hands, it is fraternal insurance and benefits. The membership of fraternities are to be congratulated that so high a degree of faithfulness has been manifest in the handling of benevolent funds.

But lest we forget and lapse into moral weakness much attention must be given to the great principles and spirit of fraternalism. The teachings of the lodge are embodied in ritualism and symbolism. But these have no power in themselves to promote character, strengthen manhood and develop honor. These forms embody the highest truths of human interests. The content of these teachings need to be amplified, explained and applied. Among those who have these interests at heart there is felt that something more than floor work and putting on of degrees is needed in inculcating the doctrines and sentiments of the lodge. If fraternalism is to fill her high mission of forming character, creating a nobler sentiment of humanity, and being abundant in works of philanthropy she would be much helped and strengthened if

men of high ideals, pure motives and a fine sense of love
to God and man should expound to its members the
spiritual and ethical content of the teachings of the lodge.
It can probably be said of all fraternities what a prom-
inent Mason said of the Craft, that, "It is to be regretted
that Speculative Freemasonry is not more studied and
its teachings, as emblematized by its symbols, better
explained and more largely ventilated throughout the
Fraternity. If its tenets and principles were more fully
known, a better spirit of brotherly union would exist."

This is distinctively an age of humanity. The lead-
ing question of the hour is that of the moral relation of
man to man. The one relation in life which covers the
moral ideal is that of brother to brother. As a principle
by which to rightly adjust men in their various relations
in life the doctrine of the brotherhood of man is the
shibboleth of all who are lovers of their kind and are
seeking to bring in a better state of humanity. A man
can most readily realize his moral obligations to his fel-
low man when he considers them within the relations of
a brother. The fraternities are all built upon the corner-
stone of brotherhood.

FRATERNAL PROTECTION

O. P. GIFFORD, D. D.

"And if any provide not for his own, and especially
for those of his own house, he hath denied the faith, and
is worse than an infidel." 1 Timothy, v. 8.

"Worse than infidel." An infidel is a man who denies
the religion of the age in which he lives. The Christian
religion affirms that God is, that He is Spirit, that "In
Him we live and move and have our being." That He

created and sustains the universe. That Jesus Christ is God manifest in the flesh, "The only begotten Son of God." That the Holy Spirit came into the world to "convict of sin, of righteousness and of judgment, to lead into all truth." That "All have sinned and come short of the glory of God." That man ought to repent of and forsake sin. That God forgives the repentant man. That there is a future judgment, and a life to come. The infidel denies all this. Denies God, Christ, sin, the life to come. "Worse than an Infidel." Can any man be worse than an infidel? Yes, the man who confesses with his lip and denies with his life; the hypocrite; the man who affirms the faith in speech, and denies the faith in act. You have more respect for an infidel than for a hypocrite. John denounced the hypocrite as a generation of vipers, children of the devil. Sailors are safer without a compass than with one that lies. You can trust a man who denies, but who can trust the liar? If a man lets you an office in the top of a building that has no elevator, you expect to climb, but if he has one in that never runs, you lose your temper. The infidel has no elevator, the hypocrite an elevator that does not run.

Before attacking Jericho Joshua issued an order that all property was to be destroyed. Achan stole garments and gold, hid them in his tent, was stoned and burned because he was a hypocrite. Elisha cured Naaman, the Syrian, of leprosy, but gave Gehazi, the Hebrew, leprosy, but Gahazi was a hypocrite.

Peter sent Ananias and Sapphira out to be buried because they lied to the Holy Ghost. Members of the Church, they lived a lie. Neither Joshua, Elisha, nor Peter treated infidels as they treated hypocrites. Christ denounced hypocrites as "Whited sepulchres, full of dead men's bones."

Can anything be worse than a town full of infidels,

denying all that Christianity affirms? Yes, a town full of hypocrites, accepting with the lips, denying with the life.

Judas was the only man who could lead Christ's enemies to his place of prayer, the traitor is more to be dreaded than the open enemy. We honor the man who professes faith and lives it. We have some respect for the man who denies the truth we hold, but only contempt for the man who confesses Christ with his mouth, and denies him in his actions.

Paul found some men in Ephesus who were worse than infidels. Men who confessed Christ, joined the Church, then refused to provide for their own. Christ found such in Jerusalem: Moses said, "Thou shalt honor thy father and thy mother, but ye say, If a man shall say to father or mother, It is Corban, that is, a gift, by whatsoever thou mightest be profited by me, and ye suffer him to do no more for father and mother, making the word of God of none effect through your traditions." When called upon to help father and mother they replied they had given the property of God, dishonored God, by refusing to honor parents, making religion a scapegoat!

Not to make provision for your own is to be worse than an infidel.

A man finds a woman who is to him the one woman in all the world. His love for her arouses her love for him, he gives her his name, social station, promises to endow her with all his wordly goods, puts her at the head of his home, expects her to bear and rear his children. If he leaves her unprovided for, he is worse than an infidel. A man has no right to take a young woman from a home where she is loved, cared for, and neglect her. Of course if he is sick, unable to get work, we pity, otherwise we blame.

It was bad enough when the younger son in the parable went into the far country and wasted his substance in riotous living, but he was unmarried. The married man who pampers his appetites, smokes, drinks, gambles, and leaves his wife with unpaid rent, unfurnished pantry, poorly clothed body, is worse than an infidel. "A man with wife and children hath given hostages to fortune." The man who will not stand by his hostages deserves punishment. Such a man, if an infidel, is mean enough; if a confessing Christian, is superlatively mean, for he wears the mask of hypocrisy over the face of sin.

It is not enough to provide house, food, clothing, for the present, but a man must provide against the future. The word means that, to look ahead, as Joseph did in Egypt—make the fat years feed the lean years. As Jesus did on the cross, providing a home for his mother with John.

Nature teaches the same lesson. The tree packs the germ in food stuff enough to give it a start in life. The bird surrounds the germ in the egg with building material for a body before the shell breaks. Nature is always providing for the future. The germ in seed and egg has an insurance policy to draw on. A man should be as wise as a tree, as provident as a bird.

A man should lay aside something year by year, so that when he drops by the way the widow shall not become a burden upon the community; the children shall not be thrown into the stream to drift or drown. The more careful you have been of them while living, the more reason why you should provide for them after your death, otherwise your care may have unfitted them to struggle.

The best plan thus far devised for safe-guarding the future is Life Insurance. This falls into two classes, Fraternal and Old Line. Either is better than none, but one may be better than the other. I do not stand here to defend or to defame either. Much depends upon organization and management. Bad men will pervert good principles; good men will make the best of bad methods. One method may be capable of more mischief than the other. Granting that both forms are equally good and honorably managed, I can see one advantage in Fraternal Insurance. Old Line is simply and purely business. The child puts in a cent and draws out a chocolate. He gives and gets. On a street car you pay a nickel and get a ride. You must not speak to the motorman or cultivate the conductor. In Old Line a doctor examines you and pockets his fee, and you may never meet again. You are a good risk, send in your check, get your receipt, never see the office nor the officers. The officers may be changed; the machine moves on. You die. The death is proved, the policy returned, the check drawn. You paid money; the family receives money. But, "The life is more than meat, and the body than raiment."

You join a Fraternal Company. You are examined and pass, pay your dues, but belong to a brotherhood. You have social and literary gatherings. You are members one of another. Death comes, money is paid, and sympathy is given. When other brothers died you visited the family. When you pass away, other members of the Fraternity visit your widow and children. You paid money and sympathy. Your family receives money and sympathy. Sympathy is in Insurance what oil is in machinery. Oil is not power, but it helps in the running. Machinery well oiled lasts longer; life lubricated by sympathy wears longer and runs more smoothly. A man is more than a good risk. Insurance ought to mean more than trading checks. The constant danger in a commercial age is that we reduce life to dollars, as the Hebrews reduced jewelry to a golden calf and worshipped it at the foot of Sinai. Old Line may be likened to a hotel. You get what you pay for. Fraternal Insurance to a home. With less variety in the bill of fare, you have more humanity about the board. Old Line is like an incubator, it takes eggs and heat. Fraternal Insurance is like the bird. It gives heat plus maternity. It hatches and broods. Even a chicken knows the difference between an incubator and a hen. Fifty cents with a friend is worth more than twice fifty without a friend. The best part of life is the human part, and that has little play in organized capital.

Provision means more than care for the future of the body. The animal teaches its young how to make the most of life; how to win out in sea or earth, or air. The State compels preparation of the mind, disciplines the head, teaches obedience to authority, and how to live with other children. But the strength of the State lies not in what is taught in the school, but in the home. What is taught in the school means much, but what is taught in the home means more. As the growing boy looks into the future he does not expect to make a school house, but a home. He graduates from the school, but into a home. He expects to be the head of a house; the girl expects to be the mistress of a home, the presiding genius at a fireside. The home is the strength of the Republic. The present home is the mould that will shape the future home. Fathers! Mothers! Are you making the kind of a home you wish to see perpetuated?

In the ark of the covenant of the Hebrew religion the Cherubim bent toward each other, touching wing tips over the Law. The home is the ark of the covenant in the United States. The father and mother should touch lives, bending above it. Why should the mother give her time and strength to the home, and the father bend away from it? Why should the office, the club, the street have such a charm for the father? Isn't your wife the best woman in the world? If not, whose is the fault? You thought once you had the choice of all women, and you chose to suit yourself. What have you done that she isn't as good now as when you chose? Are you a worse man than her father that he gave you the best woman in the world and she has lost value in your keeping?

Aren't your children the best children in the world? Why not? Is it because they take after their father? Isn't your home the best home in the world? Whose fault is it? Have you put yourself into it? Do not let your boy grow up with the idea that home is simply a bed chamber and a lunch room, a sort of repair shop. Are you the kind of husband you wish your daughter to have by and by?

The home is the best fruit of our civilization. Pour upon it the sunshine of your presence. Make provision for the heart needs of your wife and growing children. Give them enough of yourself so that they will miss you when you are gone. So live that your wife will not have to apologize for you to the neighbors and children. Read Burn's "Cotter's Saturday Night," and give such strength to America.

There is another provision to make. Belief in the future is inborn but preparation for the future must be made by each soul for itself. If your children do not see you making provision for your soul, they will grow up and go out unprepared. Why should you be so careful to leave money and sympathy for the living you leave, and make no provision for the life you take away? Every seed falls to the ground prepared to rise to a larger life. Hope leads to preparation. Be as wise as the seed . Many of you men have Christian wives and children. They have provided for the future. Have you? You do not expect the Company to pay your wives and children unless you have made provision. Why should you expect a dividend of life eternal when you have made no deposit of faith? A Christian family would rather have less money and an assurance of reunion, than more money and fear that death will be an eternal separation. Make provision for the deepest needs of the family, the need of you, that the cry of the heart for husband and father may be heard. If Christ makes your wife a better woman, He will make her husband a better man. If He makes your children better boys and girls, He will make you a better father. With Washington, Grant, Lincoln, McKinley, Roosevelt, standing for Christ, there is nothing in the Christian religion to shame you. "Quit you like men, be strong." Make yours a Christian home; be fraternal with your elder brother Jesus Christ.

STRENGTH AND VITALITY OF FRATERNALS

ABB LANDIS

The strength of a man's constitution is often proved by resistance to severe illness. The strength of a bridge is proved by the strain to which it is subjected on the passage of a heavy train. Indeed, generally speaking, the test of strength is resistance to strain and stress. This applies to fraternal beneficiary societies, to life companies, to assessment associations, to any and all co-operative institutions.

Consider how readily banks yield to a "run," or to financial panic, and yet it is a common saying, "As strong as a bank."

Recall the scores of life companies that went down during the decade 1870-1880, when subjected to the test of net valuation under the legal reserve laws.

Think of the large number of open assessment associations which failed, in the decade of 1890-1900, when old mortality began to test the adequacy of their assessment rates and they were put to the strain of readjustment.

Were we to review the insurance history of Great Britain—the home of all manner of insurance schemes and organizations—a similar situation would be revealed of the failure of hundreds of life companies and assessment associations when placed under stress and strain.

By comparison with the relative weaknesses of all other kinds of co-operative effort are discovered the strength and vitality of fraternal beneficiary societies.

The great fraternal system has been tested by the strain of crude business methods, inadequate contributions, the shock of readjustment, and the heavy weight of parasitic and pseudo-fraternal organizations which have taken shelter under the cloak of fraternity to cover the sordid motives of selfish promoters.

As the giant oak, that only bows to the storm that it may lift its branches nearer to heaven and sink its roots deeper into the bowels of the earth, so these great and grand and strong fraternal beneficiary societies, these glorious provident institutions, which scatter charity with a lavish hand to the four corners of the globe, give forth only a tremor when put to the test by the opposing forces of natural law, of mistaken methods, of crude adaptations, as well as subversion of principles in practical operation, of antagonisms and attacks from enemies, of regulation by statute and interference by unfriendly state officials, and, worst of all, by bitter and unjust denunciation and criticism from members whose very membership should have been a guarantee of support and sympathy.

As concrete illustrations of the strength and vitality of fraternal and friendly societies I quote the following instances from a book written by E. W. Brabrook, C. B., for a great many years Chief Registrar of Friendly Societies. The author is discussing "valuation," which discloses weaknesses, and it is considered pertinent to quote his preliminary remarks before the examples showing the wonderful recuperative power of fraternal organizations. While lengthy, the comments are so interesting that I give them *in extenso,* primarily for the concluding paragraphs:—

In the absence of this knowledge, the members of a society, when its funds increase from year to year, sometimes look upon the increase as in itself conclusive evidence that the society is prosperous; but that is not so; the society may be increasing its liabilities to a much greater extent than the increase of its funds, and the test of a valuation may show that it is actually going downhill. So rooted is the idea that the increase of funds must mean prosperity that we have known cases where the members of a society have refused to act upon the report of the valuer, believing that the adverse result which it showed must have been due to a mistake on his part. It would be a most effectual cure for delusions of this kind if the young were taught something of the science of Friendly Society calculations.

There is an error on the other hand that should also be guarded against. The aspect of a valuation is toward the future, not the past. When the valuer declares that such a society has a deficiency of so many thousand pounds, that is not the same thing as saying that somebody has embezzled so many thousand pounds of the society's cash, or that its bank is broken or its investments been depreciated to the same extent. It does not mean more than this: that if the society continues to carry out its existing contracts without modification, and does not take any measures to improve its position, a deficiency will ultimately accrue, of which the present value is so many thousand pounds.

Assuming that the society took the heroic course of raising the money, which is rarely practicable, the result would be, that if the valuer's estimates should turn out to be confirmed by the actual future experience of the society, and if the society admitted no new members, the last member would receive the last pound, and the society would work itself out. The same result would be obtained by diminishing the future benefits to the extent to which the deficiency represents the present value of such benefits— for example, if the valuer found the present value of the future benefits to be 20,000 pounds and the deficiency to be 5,000 pounds, the reduction of the future benefit by an average of one-fourth would wipe out the deficiency. It could in like manner be obtained by increasing the future contributions, or by a combination of both methods. The practical skill and competence of the valuer are greatly tested by the measures he recommends the society to adopt for effecting the necessary adjustment.

Some interesting examples may be given of how a valuation deficiency may be met. A society in Warwickshire had a deficiency of 4,396 pounds. In the course of the next five years it increased its fund from 10,880 pounds to 13,361 pounds, and so reduced its benefits that their present value was diminished from 26,024 pounds to 20,922 pounds or nearly 20% (4s. in the pound). The result was that the next valuation showed a surplus of 2,045 pounds. A society of Middlesex was in the apparently hopeless condition that its funds were 3,720 pounds only, and its valuation deficiency was 5,023 pounds. This society took such vigorous steps for increasing its funds and extending its business, upon properly calculated rates of premium, that in five years it had raised its capita to 10,297 pounds, and though it had increased the value of its estimated future liabilities from 40,282 pounds to 77,333 pounds, the valuation brought out a surplus of 413 pounds. A third society, in Surrey, was in a position that even the most heroic measures would hardly have seemed sufficient to retrieve. Its funds were only 3,471 pounds, yet its estimated valuation deficiency was 18,131 pounds. There could be nothing in such a case short of a drastic dealing with the promised benefits, the value of which was reduced in the next valuation from 22,770 pounds to 9,874 pounds, or more than 50% (11s. in the pound.) The funds were also increased to 4,912 pounds and the valuation showed a surplus of 378 pounds.

These examples may serve to show that the condition of valuation "deficiency" is rarely a hopeless condition. We wrote the following words in 1881, and nothing that has since occurred has shown them to be incorrect:—"A word of caution may be added against forming too hasty conclusions adverse to Friendly Societies if it should turn out that the valuations in many cases show an estimated deficiency in the funds to meet the liabilities. It would be strange if it were otherwise when for the first time scientific tests are applied to contracts that have been in operation without a scientific basis for a long series of years. It must be borne in mind, however, that nothing is more elastic than the contract made by a Friendly Society with its members; no error more easy of remedy, if found out in time, than one existing in the original terms of such a contract. Hence the words 'insolvency,' 'rottenness,' and the like, which we sometimes hear freely used as describing the general condition of Friendly Societies are utterly out of place. Of Friendly Societies in general it may be said that as there are no associations the benefits of which are more important to their members, so there are none that are managed with greater rectitude, and few with equal success."

The recent experience of one of the smaller orders, but yet an important one, having as many as a thousand branches, is another case in point. Its valuation to 31st, December 1891, showed that on the aggregate of all the branches their assets were only 15s. 1d. in the pound of their estimated liabilities.

A valuation to 31st, December 1896, showed that in the aggregate of all the branches their assets were 16s 1d. in the pound of their estimated liabilities. If it is remembered that a deficiency must increase from year to year unless steps are taken to diminish it, it will be seen that most resolute efforts must have been made during the five years to secure this result, which is the more remarkable that the Order has undergone during that time a very unfavorable experience of sickness. The valuers calculate that, taking all things into consideration, the measures adopted were equivalent to an addition of a quarter of a million to the resources of the Order. It has still much to do to attain complete actuarial solvency, for a deficiency of 3s 11d. in the pound is a serious one, but the results here mentioned should encourage the Order to pursue the course of reform it has so successfully commenced.

CARDINAL PRINCIPLES

(From THE FRATERNAL MONITOR.)

How to ginger up one's self and those about him; how to create interest and enthusiasm under adverse conditions; how to train, develop and coach sub-deputies; how to secure and organize workers; how to win the support and co-operation of members; how to meet "objections" and become a good "closer;" how to analyze one's proposition and array its strong points to meet the various requirements of the public—these are among the problems with which both the field man and his superior officers are ever grappling.

It has been said that a good deputy is born—not made. This is simply a generality that means nothing unless it is used to evidence one's natural qualifications. One may have a natural inclination and aptitude for a given calling, but he will fall far short of success if he does not combine with it practical knowledge.

There are certain cardinal principles and guiding lines which must be kept ever in view. These may be extended, built upon and adapted toward the attaining of given ends. The basis, however, remains the same, and this means that one must have more than natural qualifications. He must have zeal, ability, enthusiasm and he must know the subject on which he delivers himself.

PRELIMINARY PREPARATION

A correspondent in this issue of THE MONITOR observes "my chief takes the stand that the best place for deputies to get education is in the field." THE MONITOR concurs in this up to a certain point. It, however, would be manifestly absurd to send a man into the field who had but a hazy comprehension of what he was there for, how he should till it and the implements to be used.

THE MONITOR does not wish to be understood as saying that theory is superior to practice. It is not. One, however, must have a theory or knowledge of his subject before he can put this into practice. He must have a basis upon which to rest his cause. He must understand its various adaptations and he must be able to not only employ these but to outline new plans and methods for himself.

Misdirected effort is perhaps the cause of more failures in field work than anything else. While THE MON

ITOR believes that work is the main essential to success, this is useless if not directed properly. Mere activity, without any definite purpose and without due provision for attaining the ends sought, will accomplish but little. Many a mistaken worker fancies he is doing great things because he is busy early and late. "See what an effort I am making," he says. "Surely, something must be forthcoming soon in the way of results."

MORE THAN BLIND EFFORT NEEDED

THE MONITOR concurs in the idea that something will be forthcoming as a result of work if this is properly directed. Mere blind effort, without preparation or provision, will never enable anyone to retire on the results of previous effort. It requires thinking, planning and a line of action carefully thought out to bring things to pass.

By all means work hard. Use every opportunity that presents itself. One cannot succeed without doing this. Yet, when working, his mind should be working also, and this should direct the physical part in a manner that will cause the latter to put forth its efforts where they will accomplish something.

A moral has been drawn from the story of the "Prisoner of the Chateau D'If," which is worthy of reproduction in this connection. The prisoner was walled up in an underground dungeon and for twenty years he worked at digging a tunnel through which he hoped to escape to fresh air and the companionship of men. His only digging implements were his hands and feet. Every inch and foot of his progress caused him months of painful effort and nerve-destroying watchfulness against discovery.

It is said that after twenty years of such effort he brought up against a wall of granite. He found that everything about him was impenetrable stone. Crazed by the failure of his efforts, he dashed out his brains against the rock, while those who found him saw that, if he had turned but a little to one side with a tunnel half so long, he would have had easy access to the seacoast which would have assured his escape.

Here is an illustration that carries with it its own lesson. It shows almost superhuman effort and persistence. It was no fault of the worker that his energy had been misdirected. He simply worked blindly. Fate was against him. He ran against a wall that he could neither surmount nor penetrate. Failure was his lot.

THE WALL OF MISDIRECTED EFFORT

Too many deputies to-day are running up against the wall of misdirected effort. But a tithe of the energy they expend, were it properly directed, would bring them results beyond their most cherished dreams. Yet they work on blindly, without thinking and without planning as to which forces will produce the greatest results for them. Failure cannot but be their lot.

What is the lesson we should learn from this? We should all see that, while we all work earnestly and unceasingly, we so fortify ourselves with the best implements and tools available that many of the difficulties we encounter can be readily overcome.

A deputy should not only know his society and the contract he presents to the public for consideration, he should know other societies and their contracts. He should know their representatives. He should measure the caliber of those with whom he comes in contact. He should not expend idle or useless ammunition. He should be firmly grounded in the principles of fraternal operation and should be satisfied beyond question as to the integrity of his contracts.

GENERAL INFORMATION NEEDED.

To this should be added a general knowledge of both

fraternal conditions and insurance conditions. He should have a comprehensive knowledge of the world and the people in it. He should be able to adapt himself to existing conditions and he should at all times be both willing and anxious to uphold the system and institution with which he is identified.

Some may say that the above enumeration of essentials to success map out a goodly course of instruction to the deputy. So they do. However, with earnestness and persistence they can be readily acquired and experience will add to them other elements helpful to success.

A general proposition is that a deputy should be vigorous, intelligent, grounded in the principles of the system he represents and a man of standing in his community. Those who succeed will be found to possess such qualities and those who do not can, in a comparatively short time, acquire them and thus command the success which has heretofore been found by them to be elusive and impossible of attainment.

SCHOOLS OF INSTRUCTION

In previous issues THE MONITOR has commended the schools of instruction established by some of the societies. These have performed a most useful service. Their effects are discernible in the progress made by the societies themselves.

It is believed that these schools of instruction, even when they are conducted in the interests of given societies, might well extend their scope so as to include general fraternal conditions and the ethics which should prevail between societies. Herein is an element of weakness which is worthy of careful consideration.

On all hands one hears of the shortcomings of sister societies as set forth by the representatives of others. There seems to be an abnormal craving for something along these lines. Meritorious achievements, good per-

formed, the strengthening of the basis of operation—
these are not touched upon, unless it be as a means of
sounding warnings as to troubles to be met later on.

What can the general public be expected to think of
such methods? By what manner of reasoning is it hoped
to secure or retain confidence in a system or institution
when such reprehensible tactics are employed? Surely,
we have had illustrations galore of the unwisdom of such
narrow, bigoted and unworthy methods. Why, if we
hope to progress and build up permanent institutions, do
we continue along such unworthy lines?

THE SYSTEM GREATER THAN ANY SOCIETY

Every officer, deputy and lay member should bear in
mind that no institution is greater or stronger than the
system of which it is an exponent. Indeed, no society
can do more than work unceasingly toward the high
standards set alike by itself and the system of which it
is an exponent. This being true, it would seem that the
first duty is to proclaim the enduring principles of the
system and then show that the institution is modeled
along such lines and that it is working in harmony with
them.

When once the deputy gets his mind disabused of the
thought that the progress of another institution is antag-
onistic to his own interests, he will have taken a long step
in advance. When next he is impressed with the thought
that this success and the interest occasioned by it can be
employed to good advantage by him, he has taken
another step. When he comes to a realizing sense that
the general prosperity of the fraternal system means a
corresponding degree of prosperity to the institution he
represents and to himself, he will have taken due cogni-
zance not only of general fraternal principles but those
which are regarded to be orthodox in the entire business
world.

It has often been said that the individual societies are but divisions or regiments marshalled under one great cause and that each has a separate and distinct work to perform. When one regiment or division attempts to defeat or handicap the efforts of others, it is a natural sequence that results are neutralized and that no great accomplishment is performed.

STAND FOR THE ENTIRE SYSTEM

So it is with our fraternal institutions. There must be harmony of effort, unity of action and a desire to advance the great and central issues at stake. Individual advancement goes hand in hand with this.

Were fraternal exponents to be duly impressed with the importance of presenting an united front; were they to come to a realizing sense that it is only in this way they can make a permanent success; were they to extend the hand of friendly aid to the exponents of sister societies; were they to proclaim at all times that all institutions employing fraternal methods and principles are worthy of confidence—what an awakening there would be!

Opposition would disappear as chaff before the wind. Those whose duty it is to create doubts and suspicions would have to seek other means of livelihood. The system which is comprised of these individual exponents would enter upon a career of usefulness and prosperity compared to which even the glorious achievements of the past would be but tame and meager.

Deputies have a great work before them in the way of harmonizing the different fraternal institutions and their exponents in the field. Were they to bestir themselves in this direction, they would not only receive an access of confidence on the part of the general public, but they would make themselves better and more effective exponents of the system with which they are identified and for which they are endeavoring to put forth their best efforts.

THE FRATERNAL SOCIETY AS A TRAINING SCHOOL

No one to-day questions the fact that fraternal socie-
ties answer a deep need of man's nature. The fact that
their modern history goes back over a hundred years,
and that these societies are increasing in numbers and
influence is convincing evidence of their importance and
usefulness in man's development. Fraternal organiza-
tions existed centuries ago, and there has perhaps been
no time in history of civilized man when they did not
exist in some form. They are mentioned in the Bible
as flourishing during the period of Roman supremacy.
And among the early Christians such organizations were
frequently formed for mutual protection and encourage-
ment.

The fraternal beneficiary society as it exists to-day
is comparatively a modern institution. It was organized
primarily for the purpose of providing a competent sup-
port for the families of members when death overtook
them. It made its strongest appeal to men of limited
means, providing a method by which they could lay by
from time to time a small amount, such as they could
save from the hard-earned daily wage, for wife and chil-
dren when the husband and father passed to his reward.
The reports of these societies, showing millions of dol-
lars paid out every year, is only one indication of the
splendid way in which they have answered to man's need.

The death benefit is only one of the uses which the
fraternal beneficiary society has met. While this has
been an inestimable boon to thousands of widows and
orphans, it is perhaps not going beyond the mark to say,
that the indirect benefits of these organizations have been
greater than the direct benefit. It is the purpose of this

article to call attention to some of these indirect uses of beneficiary societies.

One of the fundamental characteristics of stable manhood is a sense of responsibility. The men who constitute the backbone of civic and national life are those who recognize the fact that they have duties and responsibilities as well as rights and privileges. The young man who becomes a member of a fraternal beneficiary society obtains certain rights and privileges, but the atmosphere of the organization and the spirit pervading it constantly impress upon him the sense of his responsibility to those who are associated with him and to those who are dependent upon him. His conception of life is clarified, and there is gradually wrought into his character the habit of considering the claims and needs of others. As a member of an organization that is wholly mutual in its aims and methods, and which is dependent upon its mem bers for its success, he comes also to realize its dependence upon him personally, and his responsibility to it. It has always been a tendency of young men to think more of their rights than of their duties, and the fraternal bene ficiary society is bestowing a great benefit upon thousands of young men in educating them to a sense of responsibility.

These societies are also developing in young men the habit of thrift. The regular monthly deposit of a certain sum of money, even though it be a small sum, for the purpose of providing for a future contingency, cultivates the habit of fore-looking. It prevents a young man from becoming so absorbed in present pleasures and present needs that he has no thought for the future. Every time he makes his monthly deposit he is reminded of the necessity of making provision for his old age. He gets the habit of saving. The habit is good not merely because it may save him from ever being a charge upon others,.

but- because of its beneficial influence upon character development. It helps him to become master of self, to put a restraint upon appetite and passion, to develop the great virtue of self-control.

The young man finds also in the meetings of his lodge and in carrying out the plans of his order an opportunity for intellectual development. He is placed upon some committee. He is compelled to exercise thought and ingenuity in accomplishing the work given to him. He must make a report. This requires him to stand upon his feet before his fellows, and express his thought in good language, clearly and to the point. He may be chosen for some office, the duties of which require not only the repeating of a ritual, but occasionally, at least, a prepared talk or extemporaneous remarks. He is constantly urged to intellectual effort. He is thus prepared to take his place among other men in the affairs of life and to exer cise an influence in his community. Many a man in public life to-day obtained his training in the lodge hall.

All of the great beneficiary societies both by their work and their ritual inculcate moral truth. The rituals of some of the societies are not only beautiful in form and expression, but noble in the principles which they impress. They teach faith in God, duty to the moral law, fraternity toward man, and patriotism. They make a constant appeal to the best in man and set before him the loftiest ideal of manhood. They exert a moral force the influence of which cannot be measured.

In the exercise of practical fraternity they are drawing men closer together, developing the finer qualities of the mind and heart, breaking down the barriers of selfishness, widening man's horizon and helping to make certain the realization of Christ's conception of the universal brotherhood of man. The fraternal beneficiary society is a great agency in the development of man. Its possibilities are unlimited. We need to recognize more fully the indirect benefits which it confers and give wider scope to their influence. This is a field which ought to appeal to men of fraternal spirit, who are desirous and willing to be of use in the education and development of young men.—(*Extracts from an address by Rev. C. A. Lippincott, Chaplain, National Fraternal Press Association.*)

FRATERNITY

WALLACE K. THAYER

All honor and glory to the good Father Upchurch, the founder of Fraternalism! It was in the year 1868, only thirty-six years ago, in the little town of Meadville, Pa., that he gathered together the first little band of mechanics and artisans for the purpose of helping each other and protecting their homes in the event of sickness and of death.

He saw about him his fellow laborers living in squalor and want, dying in poverty, their widows and children becoming public charges. In the prime of life,—in the twinkling of an eye—the husband and father would be taken off by disease or accident, and the widow and children left starving.

There was then in this land no organiation for mutual helpfulness. No organization by which men bound themselves together in fraternity and love to meet with each other and extend the good hand of fellowship while living, and to care for each other's families in case of death or sickness or sudden disaster. All praise to the man who conceived the idea of such a union!

The first efforts at organization were crude enough. Members were received at whatever age, in whatever physical condition, each to pay the same quota in case of the death of a fellow member.

The idea, once conceived, spread over the world and carried with it the blessings of fraternalism everywhere, until now sixty million dollars are disbursed every year by fraternal orders, and one out of every three families in this broad land contains beneficiaries of the magnificent system.

Like all the great imperishable works of nature, the evolution has been slow and noiseless. Not with guns and drums, or with the blaze and blare of marching regiments; not like the spread of a great conflagration, nor a convulsion of nature, but like a slow, imperceptible, noiseless growth of earth's vegetation, has this work of love extended until the bare rocks of individualism and selfishness are covered and beautified by this voluntary co-operative system based on love and mutual helpfulness.

When the history of the great movements of the age has been truly written there will not be so much space given to the stupendous movements of contending armies in the field, or to the glittering politics of the state, which by their glamour and their fury fasten and hold out attention. The really great movements of the time are hidden and subtle.

Who notices the springing plant and grain and vegetable and tree? It is the thunder-bolt and earthquake that attract, but the great good to man comes from the silent workshop of nature, not from her cataclysms. The great movements of the common people,—as the rise of Puritanism and Methodism and universal education— the democratic movements—not the movements of kings or nobles or armies or politicians—give the character and the spirit of progress to the age. With all their demagogery and chicanery and tyranny and jugglery and manipulation, the great movements by which the people are now being uplifted—the common people, the workers —are organized labor and fraternalism.

Here and here only are the great masses banded together for unselfish purpose, for mutual help and uplifting, and he is indeed narrow who rivets his eye on the jobbery and corruption and blackmail and tyranny which must accompany all great institutions, especially when democratic in nature, and loses sight of what organized labor and fraternalism have done for the common workmen. It is because fraternalism is an institution of the common people, built by their own hands and not passed down to them from above, that we are so impressed by its grandeur. Here is another great democratic movement, a fit off-spring of the great democratic movement which gave us political independence in 1776, and is giving us industrial independence in the face of the tyranny of trusts and monopolies. By fraternalism we secure independence from state charity and private charity. We desire independence from pauperism.

In this age of combination for selfish purpose it is well that men are also combining together for unselfish purpose. When the plutocrat and the politician are joining hands against the people, it is well that the people are also joining hands against their oppressors. It is not class that is arrayed against class; it is not the upper classes against the masses. Fortunately the combination, which threatens American industry and American freedom, is the mere handful of multi-millionaires and vulgar political bosses united together to obtain unjust and unfair privileges and advantages.

The extortions of monopoly are founded on the special privileges wrenched from the government. In this comparatively small group, preying on the people, manipulating and watering stocks on Wall Street, and lobbying

with legislatures and common councils, are the presidents
and chief officers of the old-line insurance companies.
The moneys paid in by the policy holders are used by
them to speculate with and to influence legislatures. In
that small group of "high financiers," so called, which
controls more than half of the trusts of America, which
runs our railroads, and our oil and coal monopolies, is
numbered more than one of the trusted presidents of our
banks, trust companies, and insurance companies. It is
the money of the common people that they are using to
affect the stock market.

It is against this small group that the American peo-
ple is making war. We are not arraying class against
class, but we are arraying the American people against
this heartless criminal plutocracy. Everyone interested
in fraternal organizations recognizes the influence of
this small group when he asks for simple justice from
state legislature or insurance department. Behind the
legislature and the insurance department are the old-line
insurance companies and their allies. Yet despite the
money and power of this group, fraternalism has grown
until now it embraces within its two hundred orders,
more members than all the old-line insurance companies
have together.

Because fraternalism springs from ourselves, and not
from this privileged class; because it is of the people and
by the people, it is sure to be for the people. Our laws
and our treasuries are of our own making and are within
our own grasp and reach. We control them for ourselves;
they are not controlled by a privileged class who manipu-
lates them for their own benefit. A fraternal order is a
government of the people and for the people and by the
people. The referendum can be used, and is used, freely
and powerfully. Our officers are our responsible servants
employed by us and responsible to us.

Within ten years past the crude efforts of the founders of our orders have been perfected, until now we have the benefit of their grand humanitarian ideas, protected by all the safeguards which science and experience have evolved. Chief among these are a table of rates, carefully graded according to age, and sufficiently high to create a reserve fund to protect the order in its old age. For we are founded not for a day or a year, but for all time. The death rate now when we are young is low but it is sure to increase as we grow older, yet as we grow older we are less able to meet the increased cost of insurance. How shall we overcome the difficulty? Plainly by paying now, in our infancy, into the treasury a sufficient fund, not merely to pay the cost of insurance for the average man now, but the cost of insurance for the man through all time. To the mortality tables and to the actuaries we are indebted for carefully establishing the tables from statistics extending over a long period of time and a vast number of instances, and upon these tables we have based our rates. Fraternal insurance has become a science. The work of such federations as the National Fraternal Congress has lifted up from non sustaining brotherhoods, sure to perish, to brotherhoods which are self-supporting, and are bound to be self-supporting through all time.

It is a popular fallacy that fraternal orders are not safe-guarded by law. State legislation has brought them within its scope. Our orders are under its watchful eye as much as are the old line insurance companies. Our treasuries and our reserve funds are carefully guarded by statute. The character of our investments and our expenditures is rigorously scrutinized. The time has come when our treasuries are far safer, because more completely within our own handling, than the treasuries of the old-line insurance companies.

LARGER FRATERNALISM

M. L. CAMPBELL

The effect of public opinion, for good or for ill, will always be with us. That there is to a great extent, and especially among the better educated and business people of every community, a strong prejudice against lodge insurance, an unwillingness to recognize its strength, its manifold blessings to mankind and its perpetuity, cannot be successfully disputed. It is true that many men and a few women, embraced within the class here referred to, have been induced to partake of the insurance benefits afforded by these societies. They have not in any sense joined heart and hand in this great cause for the elevation and the betterment of mankind. They have never been truly initiated in spirit nor converted to the underlying principles of co-operative protection. They have hardly received a glimpse of the fruits of fraternity because their contributions have been solely in coin. Some of these people have gone through the forms of initiation and have consented to contribute to the mortuary fund because they wish to extend their acquaintance, because they have been urged to join by those who patronize them in a commercial way and for various reasons with which we are all familiar. Frequently their applications are given with the express stipulation that they shall not be required to attend the meetings. If they have occasion to admit that they are members of a fraternal society it is coupled with an excuse, or with an apology.

Even those who are in sympathy with the true purpose and objects of these societies and who give unstintingly of their time to make them a success, are to some extent depressed and have their faith arrested by the

expressions of doubt, predictions of failure and depre-
ciating remarks of the wise ones who have never felt the
warmth of the fraternal spirit and who have not recog-
nized the economy of co-operation in the business of life
insurance. Thus we suffer from lapses, not only of those
who were simply paying members, but also of those who
have at times been faithful workers and believers in the
fraternal cause.

Nor is this all. The adverse influence thus created,
augmented by unfriendly public opinion formed by those
who have ever been on the outside, seriously retards the
most zealous and well directed efforts.

While there will always remain a few exceptional
cases that will not yield to proper treatment, the great
majority of mankind may, by worthy examples and by a
continued, united course of fraternal instruction, be
counted with the active, working supporters of the fra-
ternal cause. It rests with us to devise ways and means
of establishing in the minds of intelligent people gen-
erally, an abiding faith in the ultimate stability of bene-
ficiary societies and a warm recognition of the fraternal
benefits that flow therefrom.

Herein lies a wide field for active and almost impera-
tive work for the fraternal press and fraternal lecturer.
To what extent, if any, it would be profitable for the
societies to unite in an undertaking of furnishing a series
of articles on fraternal subjects for some of the leading
periodicals of the country, is worthy of more than pass-
ing thought. One who is a free and easy writer, who is
thoroughly informed in regard to the origin, growth,
progress and accomplishments of fraternal societies, and
who can place the facts in a pleasing, yet convincing
style, could gain a reception for such work from many
of the best magazines.

The time may come, if it is not already here, when the

fraternal societies can unite in having public speakers of recognized ability, truly in sympathy with the cause, lecture at the different universities and colleges and in the principal cities throughout the country in behalf of the co-operative system of life protection. Better, by far, have its principles expounded by a fraternalist who has the courage of his convictions than by an employee or officer of an old line company. A lecturer employed by one society alone may be thought to have a pardonable bias in favor of his particular society, that will somewhat color the facts. Those not of his favorite society may take his statements with more or less doubt. But would this be so if the lecturer was fettered to no individual society, but represented in all its grandeur and strength the great principles of fraternal co-operative life protection?

What fraternalism needs is publicity. Any legitimate means of placing before the people the magnitude of its proportions, the beneficence of its aims, the correctness of its underlying principles, the necessity for the welfare of the whole people of the work that it is doing, is a necessary part of our system of propagation and advancement. Reference is made to what may be called general fraternal advertisement, such as will impress upon the people of the United States the merits of fraternalism in its larger aspect.

But, if it may seem that these and other methods that might be mentioned of moulding a healthy public opinion are too visionary and distant to be effectively applied at the present time, we can turn to something shorn of expense and having the merit of being nearer home.

First, let it be understood that to accomplish the best and most enduring results there must be a union of all fraternal interests, that for the time, entirely obscures friendly rivalry and petty jealousies of competing societies. As the inherent strength of each society must largely depend upon the loyalty of its members, so the welfare of all societies must more and more, as the years go by, be supported by a favorable public opinion of the fraternal system, correctly judged from the fruit it bears.

As one method for furthering one of the objects for which we are organized, and, likewise, a means not only of giving to the operations of fraternalism a larger publicity, but also to promote harmony among the many societies that, as a whole, constitute fraternalism, it is suggested that a union memorial day be established. The union memorial day should represent national fraternalism. By joint action of this body and the National Fraternal Congress a beautiful and impressive union memorial service could be written, adopted by the governing bodies of each affiliated society and, through them, recommended to their local organizations. On the day set apart for this branch of our work, all the members of all the societies in each city and village throughout the length and breadth of our land, should gather in some public hall and fittingly observe the day in commemoration and honor of those brothers and sisters who have gone before us. When the weather would permit a parade could be formed and a march made to the cemetery where the prescribed services could be conducted and the graves of departed members decorated with flowers and with some *emblem distinctly representing fraternity* in its larger sense. The written services should be supplemented by an appropriate address or oration. Reference could also be made to the material benefits to the people in each particular place, of those provident co-operative associations. For this purpose a statement should be prepared giving in the aggregate the contributions and assessments by all the deceased members of all the societies represented in the place from the date of their respective organizations there and the total amount of money paid to their beneficiaries.

The very magnitude of a gathering of this character under one roof, and of a mammoth parade of all the mem bers of all societies, the impressive memorial service with its ritualistic work, music, the orations and the decorating of the graves would to an accentuated degree demonstrate to the good citizens that fraternalism is a living, united force working as a unit in all essentials for the welfare of the people. Such union gatherings would strengthen weak-hearted members and cement the tie that should bind us into one common brotherhood, and draw to us in a great measure the respect of those who live around about us. It would tend to cultivate true fraternity among the fraternities and cause each participant to cherish a feeling of pride and honor in being identified with such a general movement for the common good of others.

Only the active members acquire the true fraternal spirit. Any movement that will attract to our meetings a larger number of members who will become real participants in the hardships and partakers of the joys incident to the voyage in the fraternal ship, will be of incalculable value to the fraternal cause. Men who labor shoulder to shoulder in any large field of disinterested endeavors to help themselves and others in the struggle for existence have for each other a closer regard than mere friendship, and the tie that binds them even death cannot sever.

Public demonstrations like the due observance of a union fraternal memorial day may largely assist in awak_ ening passive members to active participation in the work to the manifest gain of practical fraternity. On the days following the union gatherings every newspaper in the land would account with glowing words the onward march of fraternalism and commend the unselfish spirit with which those who labor in its ranks are actuated. At this time the public eye would be quick to see and the public ear attentive to hear the economical, co-operative principles underlying the business methods of these societies and the cause of this wonderful fellowship. Herein would lie an opportunity, never to be slighted, to expound through the press of the entire land the basic principles of co-operative life protection, its benefits to the state, to the municipalities and to the individuals. Indelible impressions will thus be made that will be invaluable to us during all these years to come.

SELFISHNESS

H. S. HUDSON

Two thousand years ago the first great Fraternalist was crucified upon the Cross of Calvary, but not until he had disseminated everywhere the doctrine, "Do unto others as you would that they should do unto you." And friends, no matter what our conception of religion may be, no matter what our belief as to the infallibility or inspiration of the Testament, we know that the divine spirit of the man Christ, crucified upon the Cross, has lived and touched the heart of every man that has bled upon the cross of human suffering; and to-night we, who stand here as exponents of progressive fraternalism, know that the essence of our doctrine lies in the practical application to the needs of our present day civilization, of the teachings of the lowly Nazarene, who bore the cross upon the far off hills of Galilee.

Sometimes we find a man who says, "I can be a fraternalist without belonging to a Fraternity." You and I know better. We recognize in that declaration the doctrine of isolation; the doctrine of the miser and the hermit; the doctrine that dwarfs and belittles every noble human impulse; the doctrine that fails to find any sympathetic respond in any normal human breast. I say that it is the doctrine of selfishness, not the doctrine of living, pulsing, throbbing human hearts. In our time, God never made anything greater than a human being—nothing greater than the people and, friends, whenever we sit idly by and see a human body, or a human soul perish for want of sustenance, we are all accessories to a national crime. The greatest curse hovering over the American people to-day is individual and national selfishness. Individual selfishness that does not hold itself responsible for the welfare of those they bring into the world. National selfishness—that makes it possible for a Standard Oil syndicate, and an Alms House to both exist under the same starry banner of the free.

Individual selfishness—forever reaching out and grasping and holding unto itself the substantial things of life without regard to the rights or comforts of others. National selfishness which builds navies and equips armies, while human beings exist from day to day upon scarce enough to keep the body warm while the soul starves. World-wide selfishness which permitted Napoleon to make widows and orphans, and to push from his side with the cold hand of ambition the only woman who ever loved him—that permitted the Cæsars to rule upon the banks of the Tiber, that allowed Nero to fiddle while a city burned. Aye, world-wide selfishness, that left Egypt a few pyramids upon the banks of the river Nile— that permitted Russia to send thousands of half-hearted soldiers to the far East to die before the sun-kissed banner of Japan. Have we no remedy for all this? Is there no star of Hope for those who bend their backs to the burden?

O, dear friends, if we could stand to-night upon some high eminence and witness the thousands of fraternalists marching by in solid phalanx, I could show you a force more potent to-day for the protection of the American fireside than all the armies and navies created since they fired upon New England's shores the shot heard 'round the world. And yet, to-night our alms houses, jails and hospitals cover the heads of thousands of victims of individual and national selfishness. Are we responsible? Think of it! Individual want and suffering in nearly every city throughout our broad land! Private greed eating at the vitals of the honest and the hard working! Everywhere individual selfishness grasping for self and personal gain! And a national selfishness that builds laws for the rich and alms houses for the poor! That clothes alien races and alien peoples with the mantle of liberty, while our own flesh and blood lacks the garments that keep the body warm and the soul pure.

Am I my brother's keeper? Does it seem possible to you, who sit here in comparative comfort, that out across the green fields, and the rolling prairies, waving with grain, kissed by God's sunlight and dew—over the mountains with their tons of precious metals—beyond the babbling brooks, the roaring rivers—there are cities teeming with the poor—the ignorant—the lawless—some living in fear of starvation and others, by some untoward circumstance, living in fear of the prison or the almshouse? We are not pessimists, but sometimes does it not seem to you that the Almighty dollar so obscures the sunlight for some men, that they fail to see the wife and child sitting in the shadow? That the greed of gold sometimes gilds our conscience, so that we forget that there is more sunshine in the flash of a human glance than in the glitter of a golden dollar? Let us all resolve here to-night to no longer be bound by the chains of individual or national selfishness.

CARDINAL FACTS AND PRINCIPLES

(From THE FRATERNAL MONITOR.)

The pronouncement has gone forth that the people desire protection rather than investment and speculation; that, left to themselves, they would choose this form of insurance; that other forms have been shown to be deceptive, expensive and not in harmony with the basic principles upon which the entire insurance proposition rests.

These general facts being self-evident, is it not in order that the fraternal societies send forth propaganda after propaganda emphasizing their accomplishments in the past along these lines and giving information as to their propositions for the future and the manner in which they purpose to perform them? Should there not be widespread education showing that the principles inculcated by the fraternal system are those having nothing in common with speculation? A general recognition of this fact and principle cannot but widely increase the scope and multiply many fold the usefulness of the fraternal system.

What is needed now above all things else is the enunciation of cardinal facts and principles. The fraternal system is essentially a protective one. It owes its origin to the demand for the protection it affords and to the opportunities it presents in the way of bringing the people together in closer social relationship. Its field is a vast one and there is no occasion for it to be misled by the specious representations of those who are ever seeking after false idols. Confined religiously to the purposes for which it was formed, it has a field which it will take many generations to fully occupy and, even after it has attained this end, its best thought and attention will be ever needed to guide it along safe channels.

LET US NOT EXPECT TOO MUCH

Those who feel inclined to temporize with the elements of safety and permanence are growing less in numbers each year. The light of experience has not been obscured of late by leading fraternal exponents. Rather, they have so turned it on and trimmed it that its penetrating rays are disclosing weakness and error wherever they have existed. These are being dealt with in no uncertain manner. Hardly a month passes but that one hears of one or more organizations which have taken action in the way of building permanently.

This leads to the observation that one should not expect too much. Why should a fraternalist demand that the protection he carries be furnished him at less than cost? He expects that the amount of his certificate will be forthcoming at his death without discount in any form. It is but a simple business proposition that he must provide his share of this certificate as such share is set forth by known and authenticated mortality tables.

We pay taxes for the support of the government that protects us, and the government collects from us on the equivalent of what we may term the assessment plan. It makes its levies in proportion to estimated expenses just the same as a fraternal institution should make its levies in proportion to its estimated disbursements. Who would have the assurance to ask, or expect, the government to conduct its affairs on an inadequate basis? Who would expect it to meet its obligations in any manner other than that of collecting their full equivalents? Yet a great many who carry fraternal insurance expect the societies to do this and some of them are loud in their protests and denunciations when their expectations are not realized.

SUBSTANTIAL PROGRESS MADE

THE MONITOR has been criticised in some quarters for being too insistent as regards sufficiency in rates and for not presenting to the public the many blessings and advantages afforded through the fraternal system. It is believed that such criticism is not verified by facts. Not an issue of THE MONITOR goes forth without containing page after page showing the beneficent accomplishments of the system. Each issue contains a list of losses paid by American societies. These verge on the billion dollar mark and exceed this when the societies paying benefits for sickness only are included. Indeed, it is with unalloyed satisfaction that the achievements of the system and its individual exponents are set forth and their substantial progress chronicled.

It has been well observed that one truth should not be emphasized unduly at the expense of another; that in this way exaggerations occur and real conditions become obscured. The truth as to the accomplishments and progress of the societies in the past may well rest on a basis distinctly its own. It, however, should not be improvised unduly as a basis for future operation. This has its problems and conditions to meet. Past conditions may not at all times prevail. There is an ever-changing order of things and the society best panoplied to conform to these is the one which builds on authenticated lines and which, while making all possible provision for the future, retains that elasticity in its context which permits it to adapt itself to actual conditions as they may develop.

The field of fraternal operation is steadily unfolding· and enlarging. What would have been deemed proper provision for the future in the early days of fraternalism would not now be tolerated. It is realized that the societies have won for themselves an important position having to do with interests of a great and far-reaching nature and it is, therefore, expected that they make full provision for the responsibilities they have assumed. The time is past when temporizing is permissible. The fraternal system has reached man's estate and must give and take as such.

VAST INTERESTS TO BE CARED FOR

On many occasions THE MONITOR has referred to the proportions to which the fraternal system has attained. During 1905 its exponents had an income of $88,263,411. Their disbursements were $76,678,424. This evidences that approximately $12,000,000 were added to the fund laid aside for future liabilities, in addition to meeting those incurred during the year. There were 913,856 members admitted, involving insurance protection of $885,203,000. In other words, nearly 1,000,000 people with approximately five millions of dependents took out additional protection in the stupendous total of nearly one billion dollars. This, bear in mind, but covers the members and insurance written during 1905. The total membership of the societies the first of this year aggregated 5,536,683 which, assuming that there are five dependents for each certificate-holder, shows that twenty-five millions of people are dependent upon the fraternal system for protection against the vicissitudes of the unknown and unknowable future. The grand total of insurance in force the first of this year was $6,836,045,-000.

When it is considered that the vast totals set forth above are for protection solely, a general idea of the magnitude of the system can be formed. Indeed, the totals are so large and so bewildering that their full meaning can hardly be grasped by any of us. They set forth the accomplishments of a system but a little over a third of a century old and which is going forward at a steadily accelerated rate. Its progress cannot but increase as the plans and purposes of the societies become better known by the people and as the fact becomes impressed upon them that proper provision has been made to meet the vast trusts reposed to the exponents of the system.

All in all, have we not occasion to take pride in the past and to refer to the present trend of thought in the way of making full and proper provision for obligations assumed as an index for continuous and successful future operation? While we may not rest our cause on what has been accomplished, we may refer to this with satisfaction and we may use it as giving assurance that future problems will be met and solved just as courageously and effectually as have past ones.

On the other hand, we should not lull ourselves into a sense of fancied security or abate in the least in our efforts for better and greater accomplishments. The institution or system which realizes that progressive effort is essential to continued vigor and progress is the one which most easily throws off the trammels of undesirable environments. We, therefore, should examine ourselves and our institutions carefully at all times and we should not be afraid to discuss openly and frankly whatever problems may arise in the onward progress of the system.

THE PRIVILEGES AND DUTIES OF MEMBERS

W. T. WALLACE

There is no fraternal way of paying a financial debt, save dollar for dollar. The desire to make a distinction between the words insurance and protection, by maintaining that a fraternal society can do the business of insuring selected lives for less than the mortality cost on which commercial companies build up their premiums, provided the tables of mortality are the same, has long since proved fallacious.

Leaving out all so-called speculative and investment forms of commercial insurance, we may define life insurance to be a promised compensation to one's survivors in the event of death. The promised compensation is to protect the survivors against penury and want until they can readjust themselves to changed conditions. To do this kind of business, certain laws and ratios must be understood in selecting risks and making rates.

All fraternal societies have agreed with all commercial insurance companies by employing competent examiners to pass upon the fitne s of those who apply for protection or insurance, and it seems to be the only point in which they have acted in unison during the past thirty-five years. Had the fraternal societies done just one more essential thing, they would have based rates and assessments upon some known table of mortality.

Prejudice prevented going that far. It may be asserted that some rates promulgated by a few leading associations were based upon mortality experience, yet the fact that assessments so based were not called for until deaths actually occurred, and subsequent assessments were not collected until death claims had exhausted the surplus of previous assessments, shows how little of thought or investigation was given to mortality table ratios, even though the original distribution of relative cost for various ages may have been based upon something of a mathematical character. Fraternal desire cannot change the laws of mortality—therefore, all basic cost for term or whole life insurance must be the same, whether conducted fraternally or commercially.

It is just at this point that differentiation begins. Insurance companies do business for profit. After those who are employed to conduct the business of commercial insurance have received their compensation, and the statute laws governing commercial insurance have been complied with, then, in times past, the overpayments were returned to the policyholders of a mutual company, and were called dividends. The tendency of every business where men trade, barter, deal or communicate with each other on a basis of money profit, is to enrich one class at the expense of the other. A sort of "survival of the fittest"—and the fittest is the one favored with a better knowledge of conditions and facts which are more accurate than those possessed by the less favored other class who, by reason of environment, education or disinclination do not, or cannot secure their equal share. If a man's profit in business is some other man's loss, or what some subsequent purchaser must pay in advance of a previous cost or purchase price, then it becomes a question of how much more one may love money rather than the rights and needs of his fellows, when you estimate the measure of his success in life.

While life insurance is a business for profit, to those who worship money and usurp power, regardless of the fiduciary interests entrusted to them, acting just without the shadow of the criminal code, and recognizing none of the unwritten laws of honesty or morality, to say nothing of that golden rule of conduct now two thousand years old—then it becomes a question whether men cannot associate in the solution of the problem of life insurance by eliminating, in a large measure, the blighting influences of greed and gain. Fraternal associations do this when they collect a cost, based upon a correct mortality experience, while they keep the element of expense in a separate fund—in no manner connected with their mortality account. Furthermore, their system of lodges, courts, senates or councils tends to make their associations social, friendly, intimate and fraternal, where the members become united in bonds of a closer fellowship than any commercial insurance company ever contemplated or provided for.

A member who may be enrolled with such a society, who never attends the meetings of his subordinate body, but pays all dues and assessments to continue his certificate in force, knows nothing about the mutual interests and needs of his brotherhood. He is not fraternal in any sense of that term. He is only using an association to secure an insurance that would cost him very much more in a commercial company, where he must, in addition to protection cost, contribute to men whose paramount interest is personal gain. All occupations attain early perfection in proportion to their power to attract men for profit and gain. Commercial insurance has thus perfected its system—first, in honorable trusteeship, then in unlawful graft. Managers have succeeded in divorcing themselves from the interests of their policyholders, persuading them, by new forms of contracts, to permit the retention of their large overpayments, under the guise of larger returns, in order that the self-elected directors might enrich themselves by the illicit handling of enormous trust funds, for which they account only to themselves.

Fraternal management of a commercial insurance business has been discouraged by men able to pay for large amounts of insurance on the assumption that lodge management indicates something unstable, or intended for men in humble walks of life,—a class distinction. Commercial insurance for the rich and well to do—fraternal insurance for the poor and uninformed. Many a man of wealth has fraternal insurance on his life, because he secured it when he could not afford to buy the higher priced commodity and may still continue it because it seems cheap. Yet the idea of any sentiment of fraternity may never have prompted him to take any interest in his order.

Is there any difference in the motive which prompts the payment of a dollar, as the business end of a proposition, either to a commercial insurance company or a fraternal society for life insurance? There is none which can be expressed in definite terms. In commercial insurance you have done everything that is expected of you. In a fraternal society, you have done but half your duty. The other half is your fraternal contribution—not of money, but of time, talents and influence. If these three essentials have not been contributed, you have been sailing under false colors.

Does Christianity consist of the payment of pew-rent? Is patriotism measured by the payment of customs duties? Are you a good citizen because of the taxes you pay? Pew-rents, duties and taxes are the mediums through which we "render unto Cæsar the things that are Cæsar's," but we have not rendered unto Divinity that which we owe to our neighbor. It is in this latter clause of the injunction where we fail.

If courts of law find that we organize under the bonds of fraternity to secure cheap insurance, then indeed may we fear being classed under the laws governing such business. It is not enough that we shall claim to do more than insure, we must show by our acts and records that

we are fraternal. "By their works ye shall know them."
Many of our judges do belong to fraternal associations,
who have themselves never done more than pay Cæsar's
tribute. Are they competent to judge concerning matters
beyond their experience? This very question has recently
been exemplified by one within the judicial circles of the
Commonwealth.

Fraternal societies call their members brothers, be-
cause their relations are intimate and social. In a com-
mercial insurance company they are called policyholders,
because their only privileges are to pay and wait. Those
who manage, direct or solicit in the various departments
of the companies may have nothing at stake other than
their salaries, beyond which their solicitation never
extends. The first requisite of their position is not the
carrying of an insurance policy in the company which
they represent; in whose care and keeping they must
place some of their own funds, and upon whose manage-
ment depends the safety of an insurance which they carry
for those at home. In the fraternities this very require-
ment is the initial step to position, honor or compensa-
tion.

It cannot be charged against these associations that
members will not avail themselves of this intimate knowl-
edge of management and affairs. Rather, should the
careless, unthinking make-up of general humanity be
charged with such weakness? The present management
by self-elected directors and trustees of the largest com-
mercial life insurance corporations does not permit of
any intimate knowledge of the actual details of control.
The lumping of millions of dollars under the head of
general expenses, legal charges and various other forms
of expenditure, as found in annual reports, gives no
information such as is desired and should be insisted upon
for the enlightenment of the policyholders, as well as the

safety of enormous financial interests covering the entire world.

, The investigation now in progress must inevitably lead to a betterment of existing conditions. If those who are insured in commercial companies will not themselves give some intelligent attention to their own interest, then the state or general government must be employed to give closer supervision thereto. Such a conclusion applies equally to commercial and fraternal organizations. If exact business requirements are not enacted by the latter in their mutual co-operative works and their opportunities to familiarize themselves with their condition, are not made use of in greater measure than in the past, then the great majority of their listless and unfraternal mem bership will impose upon themselves a supervision that will be inclined to treat fraternal protection just as it does commercial insurance, because we fail to impress others with any very material difference, save that of dollars and dimes.

TRUE FRATERNITY

EMMA B. MANCHESTER

"The Brotherhood of Man!" When these words were spoken—when man called man brother, liberty came into the world and Fraternity was born. When all men were declared equal, fraternity was exemplified in its fullest, broadest sense, and to-day history records nothing more beautiful, more inspiring, than the untiring efforts, through all the changes of the centuries, of those men and women who have labored to lift the human race out of ignorance and vice into a higher and nobler existence and unite them in "The Bond of Brotherhood."

Fraternity is one of the fairest flowers found in all the gardens of the earth, for the true definition of fraternity contains some of the rarest jewels of the English language, and the fragrance of this beautiful flower throws about it the sunshine of friendship and the dewdrops of charity and love, protecting the living, soothing the dying, holding in fond remembrance the dead and assisting with tender care the loved ones left behind. Love, friendship and helpfulness are the offsprings of that happy environment where men and women clasp hands in fraternal greeting and help each other to live useful and happy lives.

Fraternity is the grandest principle of these great organizations of ours; the one on which they are founded, but, alas! the one too often lost sight of in the conducting of their business affairs. We are too prone to allow our American idea of "business first" to interfere with the performance of our duty towards our fellow member. The smile of welcome to those who come; the kindly word of greeting to the stranger; the little message of good cheer to those who travel in shaded paths; the "Godspeed" to "those who run;" the right hand of fellowship to those who deserve our aid, even though it means an act of self-denial on our own part; all this is a part of the law of fraternal life.

If we are unmindful of the cry of charity; if we extend not the hand of brotherly or sisterly love; if we pause not to listen to the voice of those in distress; then, indeed, do we fail to exemplify in our lives even the first principles of fraternalism, for true fraternity never turns a deaf ear to the cry of the needy; never is blind to the wants of the deserving, and its strong, firm hand is ever ready to raise the fallen, to aid the distressed and to uplift the race.

No man or woman can wrap their cloak around them and live for themselves alone. The God of humanity inspired within us something grander and nobler than self, and in a little while you and I will look upon pages hallowed and beautified by our fraternal deeds while here on earth; or blotted and soiled by our neglect of the plainest duties assigned us.

The hand of fraternalism is stronger and mightier to-day than ever before. This is pre-eminently the age of fraternity, and surely within the borders of this great land we honor and love there is need of the encouragement, the assistance and the kindness which fraternity stands ready to offer. May the star of fraternity ascend higher and higher until all God's children stand under the light of its wonderful radiance; one brotherhood, that of man; one fatherhood, that of God.

True fraternity is mercy when it encounters the guilty; compassion when it stoops to lift the fallen; self-denial when it faces the needy; and tenderness when it mingles with the bereaved.

True fraternity is love. Love for the unfortunate; love of doing good for others; love for all mankind.

True fraternity is of God, for "God is love."

THE RELATION OF THE FRATERNAL ORDER TO SOCIAL MOVEMENTS*

Mr. President, Ladies and Gentlemen of the Conference:

It was with great pleasure I accepted the very kind and cordial invitation of Dr. Frankel, the Chairman of your Committee on Social Insurance, to open on behalf

---

* C. H. Robinson, Secretary-Treasurer of the Associated Fraternities of America, before the New York State Conference of Charities and Corrections, November 18, 1909.

of the fraternal beneficiary associations of the country, this discussion upon the very entertaining and instructive paper of my friend Dr. Brodsky, which we have all heard with so much interest and pleasure.

The name of your Association, "The New York State Conference of Charities and Corrections," the topics for special research and consideration, as indicated by the names of your standing committees; as well as the high character of your members, suggest that your organization is altruistic beyond that of any other state association with similar purposes. In short, this Conference itself has become noted as one of the great social move ments of this altruistic age.

The Care of Children; the Co-ordination of Legislation, in matters of social importance; the Care and Relief of the Poor in their Homes; the problems of Social Life Insurance; Public Health, including the prevention and cure of Tuberculosis; each and all these are of great importance to the people of this country in all walks and conditions of life.

It is not surprising that in these momentous social movements, the Empire State, which as early as the Knickerbocker *regime* was the first to establish free public schools, and which has always maintained a leading position in the education of the masses, should be a leader in other altruistic movements. I may be allowed to hope that in this, as it has long been said in politics, "As goes New York, so goes the Union."

For something over ten years it has been my pleasure, as well as my daily business, to study social insurance from the inside, and especially that branch of it represented by the fraternal orders, or fraternal benefit societies. This study has not been confined to their present condition in America, nor to the immense sums collected and disbursed by them yearly and since their inception, a little over thirty years ago in America; although the latter thought alone, might well occupy the attention of humanitarians, since it appears from "Statistics of Fraternal Societies" for 1909, that on December 31, 1908, the 115 societies reporting to that publication had 6,322,508 benefit members in the United States and Canada. These are organized into 102,625 lodges or subordinate branches. The total income for these 115 societies for the preceding year had been $102,599,213, of which $86,447,249 had been disbursed as benefits, and managing expenses, while the remaining $66,151,964 had been invested as reserve or emergency funds to insure the performance of their contracts at maturity.

These reporting societies constitute, in fact, scarcely one-half of the associations, fraternal in character, now in operation in this country. The grand total of their disbursements, however, since the date of organization has been $1,163,853,443, most of which has been paid to widows and orphans.

Your conference has a standing committee on the care of children; think, for a moment, what would have been the fate of some millions of children had these disburse ments not been made on the death of their fathers or natural protectors.

In England, the Friendly Societies, having similar objects, like forms of government and obligations, and corresponding benefits, have been in active operation for more than a century, indeed, some of them for several hundreds of years. Their disbursements for similar benevolent purposes have been simply beyond calculation, and only to be represented by a long row of figures, which might puzzle most of us to even point off in groups of three and read from the left, without hesitation.

It is of this branch of social insurance that the excel lent paper of Dr. Brodsky treats for the most part, and

I wish in behalf of the fraternal benefit societies of the United States and Canada, which I represent to-day, to express my appreciation of the care and research on the part of the writer which the paper exhibits; for the favorable manner in which he has presented the societies, and for the pleasing and intelligent manner in which he has treated the subject.

But, while for the most part, I agree with the writer of the paper under discussion, and will not for a moment criticise it—it is much too good for criticism—there are a few matters which I deem it my duty, as a fraternal representative, to make a little clearer, if I can.

The general tone of the paper, while favorable to fraternal orders as a whole, it seems to me suggests too much in the way of immediate action along the lines of business principles, which all must admit, must be ultimately reached. It fails to take fully into consideration the fact that such societies are an evolution, a growth, and that their inception was under conditions differing wholly from those now facing them. Minerva may have sprung fully armed from the head of Jove, but that was in the days of the gods. In human affairs the mills grind more slowly. The wireless telegraph did not immediately send out its mysterious flashes when Morse touched the magic key; nor were the telephone and nickle theatre, if you please, immediately in evidence. "Rome was not built in a day," nor should we expect a business development of a most perfect kind, from a purely fraternal organiza tion in a single generation.

The first fraternal benefit society in this country was organized less than half a century ago, and by a blacksmith. "He builded wiser than he knew," for he had no intention of bringing into the world a great protective system which has since been developed from his happy thought, of a labor union, such as was afterwards attempted in the organization known as "The Knights of Labor." He knew that many of the organizations of laboring men in Europe and especially in England had funeral benefits as a part of their plans, so Father Upchurch and his co-workers provided that on the death of a member each of the survivors should pay one dollar into a common fund to be paid to the family of the deceased; and this contribution was alike for all, regardless of age or occupation, and at the first, without medical examination of the applicant for membership. It was purely fraternal, and from such small beginning has the great system of fraternal insurance in this country been developed. The idea was attractive; it cost nothing to obtain members—the lodges did that without compensation. The order grew so rapidly that for many years the influx of new blood seemed, in the absence of knowledge of the effect of mortality laws, to preclude the idea of future trouble, and there were few lapses, the lodges, again, attending to that branch of the work.

These societies were then, originally, not business organizations founded upon actuarial rules; indeed, they could not at that time have been so founded. There were no reliable mortality tables upon which they could have based rates for such protection as they designed to furnish, or if there were, the contributions deduced from such tables would have been so large that the very class for which they were intended and to whose prosperity, both morally and financially, they have so largely contributed, would have been barred from membership. At that time the capitalized companies had no very definite system of rates or settled plane of operation. Tontine schemes were promoted by them; the contributions of lapsed policy holders were confiscated to enhance their profits; promissory notes were accepted to the extent of one-half the annual premium, and it was represented to the insured that his dividends would surely cancel his note. The capitalized companies were going to pieces like pitchers broken at the fountain, and the general public had little confidence in either the stability of the institu tions themselves or the integrity of their managers; indeed, nothing about them seemed sure, except that the cost was so high that protection for the family of the wage-earner was prohibited.

Under such conditions, the fraternal benefit societies came into existence in this country, and under these conditions, no other plans than those originally adopted by them could have been possible or successful.

Later the more interested, and perhaps the more intelligent of their members had their attention attracted toward the laws of mortality and it was suggested that as a member of fifty had twice as many chances of dying as one of twenty, he should, even from a fraternal point of view, pay a larger contribution to the mortality fund. As this idea grew the contributions assumed a graduation according to age, and for a similar reason, medical examinations, not required at the very first, were added; but still no table of mortality was assumed as a basis for contributions, extra assessments being relied upon to supply any defect.

At length one of the oldest societies finding itself with seventeen assessments within twelve months and a number of losses still unprovided for, figured that if they had twenty-one assessments in a year all the deaths would have been provided for, and a surplus would remain. They then multiplied the rate at each age by twenty-one and divided the product by twelve, and called this result a new rate table. I grant this was not a complete remedy for the disease, but it *was* progress; and since that time, the same society deduced from its own experience of some thirty years, a table of rates, which, if actuarial figures are reliable, is the most scientific of any so far constructed.

Under the auspices of the fraternal organizations and at the expense of their members, a table of mortality which will show the actual experience of from five to ten millions of exposed lives, is now in the process of construction by actuaries of national, indeed, of international reputation, and this for the sole purpose of enabling the societies to have a reliable basis for the contributions required, not only in general mortality, but by sex and occupation as well, and these will include experience in regard to accident and sickness disabilities. Is not this progress? But all these things cannot be done in a year.

It may be admitted that most, if not all these orders started out with no considerable knowledge on the part of their promoters of the science of life insurance or the laws of mortality; but, as I have attempted to show, this was at the time unavoidable; it may be conceded that the early societies placed fraternity above business; but had they not done so they would never have existed at all, and their magnificent record of billions paid to widows and orphans would never have been made. It must be acknowledged that they made grave mistakes and that their organizations could not long have been continued upon the original plans. Let me suggest, however, that the managing officers of these societies are not wanting in intelligence; among them may be found many of the most intelligent, and indeed, most brilliant men of the country. A few years ago I had occasion to look into this matter and I found that some hundreds of Senators and Congressmen held benefit certificates in these orders, and in a number of the states the majority of the members of the legislatures were members in good standing in fraternal benefit societies. The managers are educated, and the members are fast becoming educated to the necessity for rates adequate to pay promised benefits. There is now scarcely a society with ten years or more experience that has not been taking stock of its condition, actuaries of reputation have been employed to tabulate their experience and compute tables of contribution upon which the society may be perpetuated. More than twenty-five of them have, within the past few years, materially increased their rates, and is this not progress?

The trouble is that the American people want to build a house over night, as they do out in my home, Chicago. The cry, "On to Richmond," which nearly ruined the cause of the Union, at the beginning of the Civil War, is being raised in regard to fraternal societies. Insurance Commissioners and some legislators seem to want Chicago building methods applied to these societies—these small independent republics—compelling them to do at once, under the stimulus of drastic laws, what similar societies, the parents of our own, in England, have been more than half a century in even approaching.

If the law-making bodies of this country will kindly allow those societies to work out their own salvation, it will be done in a shorter time and with much less ultimate loss to beneficiaries than if it is attempted by means of drastic legislation.

The best definition of a fraternal benefit society with which I am acquainted is that found in the laws for the government and control of these societies in most of the States, viz: "Any corporation, society, order, or voluntary corporation without capital stock, organized and carried on for the mutual benefit of its members and their beneficiaries, and not for profit, and having a lodge system with ritualistic form of work and a representative form of government; and which shall make provision for the payment of death benefits, is hereby declared to be a Fraternal Beneficiary Association."

From its earliest inception, the fraternal order has

been one of artificial kinship—a sworn brotherhood. The ancient "wed" or solemn oath of brotherhood exacted by the guilds and earliest benefit societies, has given place to the modern obligation; the free and easy lodge meetings at public-houses, to tell stories, sing songs and drink unlimited quantities of beer, have been supplanted by the modern lodge wherein the members freely participate in discussions upon matters pertaining to the conduct of the business of both the local and supreme bodies of the orders. Not infrequently also they have discussions upon subjects of national importance, and papers or lectures by the members themselves or by professional entertainers. The lodge business is conducted upon rules laid down by the best authority on Parliamentary usage, and, in short, the lodge has become a night school of debate and parliamentary instruction, including information in civil government. It is rarely you will find an active lodge member of any order who is not able to express himself clearly and even logically in a public assembly upon any subject with which he is at all familiar.

The necessity for laying aside a part of his wages to meet his periodical dues inculcates in the wage-earner a habit of saving which finally results in savings bank deposits, the purchase of a home upon the installment plan, investment in loan and building stock, or some other form for small savings.

When we consider that there are now in this country about 7,000,000 members of these fraternal orders, this habit of small savings and investments must have a tremendous effect upon financial conditions.

The fraternal system also inculcates a feeling of independence. The member, during his productive years, sets aside a small portion of his earnings for the protection of his family or for his own old age, that neither may be dependent upon charity. His self-respect is built up and he holds up his head among his fellow men with the consciousness that he has provided for his family by his own exertions.

One of the social movements in which this Conference is taking a great and commendable interest, is the fight against that great scourge of the human race, Tuberculosis. In this fight these fraternal orders are also taking an active part. Nearly all of the societies publish official journals, some of them being excellent family magazines. These go every month to more than six millions of readers. Nearly every one of these publications, for more than a year past, has been runing a department of Public Health, under the management of medical men of high standing in the profession. These disseminate information for the prevention and cure of consumption and other infectious diseases, in a systematic manner and with an influence which no mere circularizing can attain. The Associated Fraternities of America, composed of delegates from fifty of these societies, has a standing committee on Contagious, Infectious and Hereditary diseases, and another on Public Health, whose reports and papers read at the annual meetings and published in the *Proceedings* are educational in a high degree.

The National Fraternal Congress, another organization composed also of about fifty societies, is in no sense behind the Associated Fraternities in this war on the Great White Plague. It also has bureaus and committees investigating the subject, and the papers of the N. F. C. societies are equally pushing the campaign of education.

Not content with educational methods, a number of fraternal orders have already established Consumptive Camps or sanatoriums of the most approved and modern kind for the treatment of members or members' families, when affected with consumption, and a number of others are engaged in raising the ways and means to provide similar institutions for the treatment and cure of their afflicted members. Still others have homes for aged and indigent members and for orphan children of members; also sanatoriums and hospitals for the treatment of those suffering from other diseases.

There is scarcely a city of any considerable size in the country in which local lodges of the various orders do not provide free beds and free treatment for their members.

Among the orders of a fraternal character which already have sanatoria in active operation, may be mentioned the Royal League, one of the first to move in this direction. Its institution is at Black Mountain near Asheville, North Carolina, and has been in operation about three years, with remarkable success in the cure of this dread disease. The Knights of Pythias, who have an institution for the treatment of members having consumption, at Las Vegas, New Mexico; the International Typographical Union, whose home and hospital at Colorado Springs have been in operation for a number of years.

Among those arranging for the opening of such sanatoria in the near future are the Brotherhood of American Yeomen; the Order of Eagles; Improved Order of Red Men; Royal Arcanum; Workmens Circle; Knights of Columbus; Foresters of America; Junior Order of United American Mechanics; the Photo-Engravers Union; International Printing and Pressmen, and the Boot and Shoe Workers Union.

Among the sanatoria already in active operation, is that of the Modern Woodmen of America, opened for patients the first of January last at Colorado Springs, Colorado. It is conspicuous because of the fact that the society has more than a million of members, and because it was made possible by the voluntary contributions of the members, which in a few months prior to the opening amounted to $65,198. With this and some money borrowed for the purpose, the committee in charge purchased a ranch of some 1,400 acres with ranch house and other buildings; built a reservoir and pipe line for a water supply; erected a dining hall, kitchen, laboratory, dormitories for nurses, offices for superintendent, tent-houses for employees, bought twenty-four cows and horses and farm implements, built cottages for the physicians in charge and their families, and sixty tent-houses or colony tents for patients. At the last Head Camp it was voted that each of the million members should pay in addition to his regular dues, ten cents annually toward the support of the Tuberculosis Camp. From the very opening day it has been filled to its capacity, and has now 118 patients. The capacity will be rapidly enlarged, as in a letter received from the President of the society a few days ago, he informed me that over one hundred of the local Camps have agreed to contribute $250 each, the cost of a tent-house, and these will be erected at once. But four patients have died during the ten months, and these were in an incurable stage of the disease when received. Of the seventy-six patients discharged since the opening, nearly all had increased in weight and general health, while a large percentage seemed to be entirely cured.

The money for the founding and maintenance of these sanatoria is not taken from the mortality, emergency, or other funds of the orders, but is raised by voluntary contributions for the purpose, usually by the members paying a few cents per month extra, at their option.

Like the societies themselves, none of these sanatoriums are operated for profit, but board and treatment are furnished at actual cost; in some, without any charge at all to the patient, and in numerous instances which have come under my personal observation, local lodges are paying the entire expenses of afflicted members who are not financially able to take the treatment otherwise.

Both the Associated Fraternities and the National Fraternal Congress are taking active measures to secure the establishment by Congress of a National Department of Public Health, with a Cabinet official in charge, and have appointed committees to co-operate with other organizations seeking the same end.

Both these associations sent delegates to the International Congress on Tuberculosis held at Washington, D. C., last fall, and their committees have made exhaustive and highly educational reports which have been given wide publication.

In conclusion let me say, that it is not alone the cheapness of the insurance furnished; it is not simply the right to treatment in a hospital or sanatorium if overtaken by disease or old age; it is not merely the protection furnished at cost for the family, nor is it all of these influences combined which have induced some seven millions of our fellow citizens to connect themselves with and maintain their membership in one or more of these societies. There is something more. Partly it is the adhesive power of organization; partly the influence of the solemn obligation of mutual aid and assistance, but above all, it is the indefinable power of a spirit of brotherly love which they inculcate and encourage; the mutual help in times of trouble and distress they practice; the hearty sympathy when a brother is overtaken by misfortune or adversity which goes with the membership; the silent tear mingled with our own at the graves of loved ones; it is all these and other manifestations of the fraternal spirit, in addition to expected material benefits, which have contributed to the growth and maintenance of these societies.

'Tis the honest grip of comradeship,
 Makes a fellow take heart again;
'Tis the word of cheer, from a friend sincere
 Makes him feel life's not in vain.
When the way is dark, and the luckless bark
 Is drifting from safety's strand,
Why, God bless the man, or the woman, who can
 Hold to us a helping hand.

When you're out of luck, and you're out of pluck
 And the fight don't seem worth while;
What will give you heart, to do your part?
 Why, a hand clasp and a smile.
So, when all is black, and we've lost the track
 In a world we cannot understand,
Then, God bless the friend, who is there to lend
 A smile and a helping hand.

HUMAN SYMPATHY*

What makes it possible for the dissemination of fraternalism? I see down the busy street a little white hearse with white horses. Back of it are two or three carriages and, as they move down with the little white coffin in the hearse, the street car man stops the clanging of his bell, the newsboy the crying of his wares, and the busy man pauses for the moment and looks up in wonder and surprise. The old bum with the marks of dissipation upon his face comes trembling out of the hell-hole of iniquity and raises his hat, and a tear steals down his face as he thinks of the way he knelt at his mother's knee and learned his evening prayers long ago.

The hearse passes on. This child was not a relative of any of these people, and they know not who it was, but

---

*Extracts from the address of the Hon. J. C. ROOT.

there is the feeling of human sympathy that arises and reaches through their hearts, and they feel a bond of sympathy for that good mother and father who have lost the little child being borne to its last home.

It is that feeling of human sympathy that occurs to all of us that made it possible to create the fraternal orders. The hearse passes on to the last resting place of the little child, and the street car driver clangs his bell, the newsboy cries his wares; the business man hurries on in his career, and the old drunkard is perhaps prevented for that day at least from imbibing that which will destroy soul and body for all time. This is the human sympathy that makes it possible to build up a great fraternity like this.

THE MYSTIC SPRING

You have heard the legend of the old man who walked up the mountain side in quest of the place where he heard there was a mystic spring. By imbibing of the sparkling waters of this spring he could be restored to youth again. The old man climbed feebly up the mountain side, stopping often to regain his wasting strength—decrepit, feeble and sad.

Finally he beholds the mystic spring, but over it hovers an angel. There is the silver cup. He seizes it eagerly and is about to dip up of the sparkling water and drink thereof that he may be made a youth again, when the angel speaks: "Have you considered that if you imbibe of this liquid you will be a youth and shall have forgotten all that has passed before?"

"What!" says the old man. "Will I have forgotten the good old mother who taught me to do what is right, and will I have lost all recollection of the good father who admonished me and told me to be a manly man, and that good wife who was the dearest person on earth?" (and the dearest person on earth to us is our little wife) "and those little children who clambered around my knees; shall I have forgotten them?"

And the Angel answered, "Yes, all, as if they had never existed, but you will be a youth again, and have a new life before you."

The old man hesitated, then threw down the cup, and said "No! No!" and clambered down the mountain side more feeble than when he ascended. Finally, as he reached the foot of the mountain he fell by the wayside and his spirit took its flight. There was a smile on his face as if he saw in the great beyond those he loved best.

* ⊦ *

THE SPOKEN WORD

I remember distinctly going away from home a few months ago, and on my return I missed a young man I frequently had seen on the street cars, and I said "What has become of him?" and the reply was "Didn't you know he was dead?" and I said, "No." The party said "Yes, he is dead, and left two little children, and his wife is clerking in the Boston Store. They had no relatives to assist them." I felt that I had been convicted. There I had been passing up and down in those street cars for months, frequently talking to that young man, and I had not spoken of insurance to him. A feeling of sadness steals over me unconsciously when I think of such incidents as that, and of the great good we might be able to do if we would speak a good word.

On another occasion I met a young man on the railroad train, and he was a stranger to me, and he said to me, "What business are you engaged in?" I told him I was in the fraternal insurance business, and I said, "Have you any insurance?" and he replied, "No." I said, "The first man to die in the organization I represent was a boy nineteen years old, and left his mother money which kept her from becoming an inmate of the poor house." He

said, "I have no wife." I said, "Have you a mother?"
He replied, "Yes." And I said "Have you a father?"
He replied "No, sir." Then I asked him "How did he
leave the mother?" He says, "With a little home and a
mortgage on it." I said, "Are you working?" He said,
"Yes," and he was earning nine or ten dollars a week—
something like that. I said, "Boy, you don't appreciate
your mother. You ought to sit down and think of the
care and anxiety of that mother when you came to earth,
and picture the agony of that mother when some accident
befell you—you tumbled from a tree, or fell in the water,
or were laid low with disease, and think how it brought
premature age to the mother, and perhaps silvered her
hair with gray, and the first thing you do go back and join
some fraternal order, and take a two-thousand dollar cer-
tificate for her benefit," and he promised he would do so,
and he took it in an organization in which I am interested.

A few months afterward the office boy came and said,
"There is a lady wants to see you," and I said, "Trot her
in," and a lady came to the door, a woman about forty-
five years old, neatly and plainly dressed, and she opened
the door and said, "Is this Mr. Root?" and I said, "Yes,
Ma'am," and she said, "I want to kiss you."

Well, boys, I made up my mind I would meet her half
way, anyhow. I said, "Why do you want to kiss me?"
and she said, "You met my boy on the railroad train, and
advised him to take out fraternal life insurance, and he
took it out and, although he was a husky, healthy, active
young man, it was only a few months when he came home
with a hectic flush on his cheeks, and his eyes an unnatu-
ral glare, and footsteps dragging, and said, "Mother, I
am sick, and my head aches," and I summoned a physi-
cian, and pneumonia had attacked him, and he was delir-
ious for days, but during a coherent moment he said,
"Mother, bring me the paper," and I could not under-

stand what it was he wanted at first, and he said, "The insurance paper," and I brought the policy or certificate, and he said, "Read it, Mother; is it payable to you?" and I said "Yes," and he said, "Mother, keep that; I have done the best I could for you. I feel I am not going to get well, and I want you to take this and pay the mortgage, and this will be a reminder of how I have loved you, and I want you to promise me that you will go to Omaha and see Mr. Root, and kiss him, and thank him for what he has done for me." Here are two pictures before you, and what a blessing it is to inspire a man to protect his family, and what a feeling of sorrow we have if we know we have neglected it! * * *

THE FRATERNAL PART

Some deputies are so darned anxious to get their commissions that they do not think about the fraternal part. I heard once of a colored man who went fishing. He had a young boy with him, and they got to a very deep place, where the boy fell into the water. The old darkey could not swim a stroke.

The good minister was coming down the roadway, and he noticed the boy go down and come up the first time, and he saw the old darkey tumble in and grab the boy, and he caught hold of a log, or something, and they finally got out. The minister said "What a noble soul you are, to risk your life for that boy! Is he your son?" "No," the darkey said. Then the minister said, "It was one of the grandest exhibitions of human sympathy I ever saw. You did it because you loved your fellow man, didn't you?" The darkey replied, "O, la, Massa, no! It wasn't that. He had all the bait."

I notice sometimes our inspiration comes from selfishness. I do not wish to reflect upon the deputy. Of all the people to whom you are indebted, you are the most indebted to the deputy. He is the man who takes rebuffs, and gets invited to get out of the office or be kicked out occasionally. And if the deputy be a lady, the other lady she solicits may stick up her nose and say, "I don't like you people, anyhow." The ladies ought not to think that way.

I do not think that there is a woman in the house to-day but who would be perfectly willing to have her husband have a sufficient amount of money to warrant him in asking another woman to share his lot, just as good as she is, if she should happen to pass away prema turely. I do not think there is a man but who thinks he ought to carry all the fraternal life insurance he possibly can so his wife will be independent, and when left alone will not be obliged to take the first rascal comes along to get some one to support her, but can say, "No, sir; I have my life insurance, and I don't have to."

COMMUNING WITH NATURE

A few months ago it was my pleasure to meet your good physician in the mountain districts, and a friend of mine, Professor Hawley, invited us to go up the mountain the next morning, so I said "Doc, will you go?" He said, "Will a duck swim? Of course, I will go."

The next morning we started, and as we went up by the brooks and listened to the rippling water coming down over the stones and rocks, and looked about on the won-ders of Nature, and looked beyond and saw the mountain tops, and the magnificent foliage, and observed the grandeur of it all, we could not help but believe that we were nearer to Nature's God.

Upon reaching the top of the mountain we camped, and the next morning we got up, and Professor Hawley says, "Come, look out and see the wonderful sights," and we looked, and there we beheld the most gorgeous scene mortal man ever saw. There was old Aurora, with all her grandeur, and with the glistening silver, and color of gold, and the ruby, and the rose, and the red and amber, and all the beautiful colors possible planted about the old rising Sun in the east, and from it and around it was a grand halo as beautiful as might surround the heads of Angels, and springing, and sparkling and radiating from it were great and beautiful points.

Then he said, "Look to the West," and we looked, and beheld where the cottages had been the night before that they had all disappeared, and we could see but a great bank or cloud of steam or fog, glistening and glittering, and as the heat of the sun became apparent the waves seemed to rise in blankets and pass off to the right and left, and finally disappeared, and my friend, Professor Hawley, handed me the glass and said, "What do you see?" and I looked down and saw the little homes at the foothills of the mountains, and he asked, "What do you see?" I replied, "That is the little home we all love." There may be a vacant chair, giving a tinge of melancholy to the scene, but there is concentrated all the love and affection of the human heart, and you and I, and every member of these fraternal organizations are seeking to preserve and protect that little home.

THE STRENGTH OF FRATERNALISM

(From THE FRATERNAL MONITOR.)

Those timid mortals who are ever constrained to rush to cover at the first rumor of discontent or disaster are to be commiserated more than censured. It has been said that "a coward dies a thousand deaths—a brave man dies but once." Is this not true in the practical affairs of life? Are not those of a timid, nervous or excitable temperament ever creating troubles and difficulties which

exist mainly in imagination? Are they not the real
fomenters of the strife and agitation prevalent in times
of public stress, or when general propositions and sys-
tems are in process of reconstruction or readjustment
to meet the higher and broader plane of things made
desirable by past operation or future probabilities?

Speaking to the subject of the agitation in old-line
insurance on account of the disclosures that have been
made, and with reference to fraternalism by reason of the
imperative necessity of readjusting to a basis made neces-
sary by past experience—combining the difficulties of
more or less magnitude which beset these two great
exponents of insurance operation, even though the fra-
ternal societies but aim to confine their efforts to making
provision for dependents in the event of death and for
disabilities during life—may it not be observed that both
of these systems will overcome the evils evidenced and,
in consequence, more fully perform the purposes for
which they have been formed than they have done in the
past?

THE SANE AND LOGICAL COURSE

With reference to the fraternal societies which have
had to advance their rates to a basis made mandatory by
actual experience, is not the correction of error the
only sane and logical course that can be pursued to make
sure that the future be shorn of the terrors which attach
to faulty and temporary operation? From this view-
point, are not the members of the societies to be con
gratulated over this fixed determination on the part of
those to whom the conduct of their institutions has been
entrusted to make their protection sure, safe, and endur-
ing?

A GOOD STORY IN ILLUSTRATION

As illustrating the absurdity of flying off at a tangent
when apparent evils arise, the story told of the sea cap-

tain, when he was solicited to connect himself with an insurance institution, possesses force. After attempting to evade the importunities of the solicitor, he finally observed that he would shut off further discussion by expressing his opinions frankly.

"I have been reading the newspapers and know for myself that none of these insurance organizations are seaworthy. I'll not trust my shipment to a tub that will go to the bottom before she makes port."

The captain fancied that he had effectually disposed of the solicitor. The latter strolled up and down the stern of the boat and watched some of the men at work with the pump. A large stream of water fell over the side of the vessel with a splash. As if suddenly struck with an idea, the solicitor turned quickly and started toward the gang-plank. The captain noticed his haste and called out, "Where are you going?"

"Why are those men pumping back there?" the solicitor asked.

"There is a little leak just aft the coal-bunkers and some water has come in," explained the captain.

"Just as I feared," shouted the solicitor, as he made a dash for the shore and safety.

"What's the matter with you?" bawled the captain. "Stop! What's your rush?"

"Rush! The ship's sinking, is it not?" the solicitor asked with great alarm.

"I don't know what kind of a silly joke you are trying to work with me, but you know as well as I know that there is no danger."

"Is it any sillier than your sober statement to me that you were not going to embark in the insurance ship because it's going to sink? If you will listen to me I can show you in less than ten minutes that, with all the noise and splash now heard, there is nothing wrong with the

ship itself. The hull is sound and nothing more than a
few seams have been sprung, in spite of the many stren-
uous storms she has passed through."

Does not the above story forcefully illustrate the atti-
tude of those who fancy that they see danger and disaster
to fraternalism, because of the temporary flurry in some
quarters due to past error and a misconception of the
real cost of the obligations assumed? Has not the fra-
ternal system passed through too many storms, emerging
in safety, to be questioned now, when the central and
sole purpose of those who are giving it their best thought
is to simply make it more sea-worthy and better panoplied
to perform the purposes for which it was created?

Why should anyone anticipate danger in discussing
propositions and conditions freely and openly? Was the
sea-captain afraid to say that a leak had been discovered
and that his men were repairing it? Rather, his sur-
prise that anyone should have fancied real danger to have
existed by reason of this condition, shows in most force-
ful terms the absurdity of such an idea.

AS TO DEMAGOGUES

THE MONITOR does not fear that anyone is placing in
the mouth of agitators and demagogues arguments that
they can use to their individual advantage when refer-
ence to actual conditions is made. Indeed, a policy of
temporizing or concealment would give them far greater
opportunity to ply their contemptible trade in the way
of leading people to believe that their vaporings and
imaginings have a foundation other than that of their
own distorted and perverted visions.

The fraternal craft is stauncher, stronger and more
sea-worthy to-day than it has ever been in its entire his-
tory. Its past record presents an irrefutable argument
against those who would impede its progress by misrepre-
sentation or the picturing of evils which do not exist. A

decade or more ago there was far greater opportunity for pointing to the dangers awaiting fraternalism in the future than there is to-day. The societies were then lulled into a sense of fancied security by reason of their abnormal growth, and their abnormally low death rate. Then, rather than now, was the occasion for misgivings.

During the past five or six years the societies awakened to a realizing sense that the contracts they furnish, to possess permanent value, must have a definite and tangible basis upon which to rest. They then began their campaign of education. The results have exceeded the most sanguine expectations of fraternal exponents. During this comparatively short period the societies having the largest memberships have revamped their affairs to conform to normal experience and operation, while new organizations have had impressed upon them the importance of making such provision from the very outstart.

Are not the above evidences of safe and tangible progress sufficient to encourage all true fraternalists and to cause them to rejoice in the results which have been encompassed? Do they not afford an earnest that the future is safe in the hands of such institutions? When the managements are alive to their duties and responsibilities, when they are duly impressed with the import ance of care and conservatism, when they realize that modern methods must be employed to meet modern conditions—when these elements are held to the fore as paramount to all others, it follows that the societies have emerged from the conditions surrounding early and primitive environment and have properly taken their places among the standard, orthodox and enduring institutions of the land.

EXTINCTION OF THE IMPROVIDENT

In a lecture on "A Step in the Ascent of Man," recently delivered by Granville Lowther, of North Yakima, Wash., it was said that only among the more advanced races of men the breadwinner makes provision for the productive period of his life and for his loved ones in the event of his death. The lower races have no such plan.

It was observed that nature has decreed that either animals or men who do not provide for emergencies tend to extinction. Mr. Lowther referred to the cold winters when thousands of animals that made no provision for food died of hunger. Famines among the poor and improvident are common. The nations that do not accumulate property are non-progressive and become "hewers of wood and drawers of water" to those that do.

The day of individualism has in a measure passed and the day of collectivism has come. In so far as such collectivism means the organization of persons whose interests are mutual, it is an unqualified benefit.

Selfish motives may have impelled the organization of all of our institutions. It cannot be denied that an element of selfishness runs through all of them. Organizations of whatsoever nature are, however, no more selfish as organizations than are the individuals who compose them. Again, it has been said that members are no more selfish after joining an organization than before.

Speaking on the subject of the selfish motives back of individual action, Mr. Lowther thus interestingly said:

In fact the tendency of organic life is to unselfishness rather than to selfishness. The nearest approach in Nature to absolute selfishness is unicellular life. This form of life does not even have to co-operate with any other individual to perpetuate itself; but multiplies by division. The multicellular life in which there are combinations of cells each and every one performing some office, yet all organized into a body, is a higher form than the unicellular. Take for instance the tree. The cells that compose the roots drink in the moisture and chemicals from the soil, while the cells that form the top or leaves, breathe the air and are as lungs to the human body. The trunk is a kind of commercial highway for the exchange of commodities gathered from earth and air. So in society, the individualistic life is the most selfish life. Groups, organizations, combinations of men, compel the learning of lessons in human rights, claims, privileges, principles of justice and sympathies which could never· be learned alone. Any particular organization of men with mutual interests, will work for the good of the organization, and that broadens both mind and heart in so far at least as the organization is concerned. The individuals of a corporation will desire the good of the corporation. The individuals of a Farmers' Alliance will desire the good of the Alliance. They learn that whatever is for the good of the body as a whole, is for the good of each and every member composing that body. Therefore, organizations of men, of whatever kind, mark a step in the progress of the race as distinguished from purely individualistic life. It is a step which prepares for that broader view of the universal brotherhood of man, when each will work for all, and all for each. A step which progressively helps us to realize that "no man liveth to himself and no man dieth to himself." In other words, it leads us out of the mere selfishness into that altruistic feeling which is necessary to the harmony and peace of mankind.

* * *

When I was twenty-two years old, I married a lovely girl of twenty. At the marriage altar, I promised to "love her, honor her, comfort and keep her in sickness and in health, and forsaking all others, keep me only unto her so long as we both should live." I had a little property but invested in a boom and when the boom collapsed I lost it. I was living on a salary and needing all that salary for expenses. But we concluded to economize, work a little harder and take out a life insurance policy for protection in case I should fail and the salary be cut off. We did so and carried it a few years, when one cold winter I took down with pneumonia. The doctor came one morning and seemed troubled. I read the signs and saw he thought it was doubtful if I recovered. I called my wife to my bedside and said, "I see the doctor thinks I may not recover. I think I will, but in case I do not, that life insurance policy will buy you a little home and help you educate the children." She planted a great big kiss upon my lips and said, "You will not leave us; but in any event we will be comfortable." Now do you know, I would not have given the pleasure of one hour of feeling that my wife and children were financially provided for, for all that I ever paid on that policy. I could not have bought a farm, I never had money enough at one time. I could not have protected my family by making a first payment on a farm; for in case of death my creditor would have taken the farm for the deferred payments and left my family homeless. Life insurance is the only form of investment I know anything about that will pay the full amount purchased, on a small payment, if you should die the next day after the purchase. I do not disparage other forms of investment. I believe in the effort to acquire a home; but if I were a young man starting in life I would first of all begin paying on some form of life insurance policy and keep it up. Then I would marry some lovely girl, strive to make a home and make that home my heaven on earth. But I would consider it cruel to leave the one I loved most, unprotected in case of my death.

INTERNATIONAL FRATERNALISM*

The same general principles govern insurance everywhere, and the experience of all countries is of interest to each. The great object we all have in view is to pro vide a reasonably safe—absolutely safe would be better— insurance, at a cost within the reach of the greatest number of the people. Enfolded in this object, is the social, moral and industrial amelioration of the toilers—the bone and sinew of a country. Here we have a wide and deep laid foundation, and in building upon it we touch many points of international interest. It need not·be empha-

---

*Extracts from the address of the Hon. Alexander Fraser, president of the Canadian Fraternal Association, before the National Fraternal Congress.

sized here that from the international point of view, the security of the investment made by the brother ranks as the feature first in importance.

In the early stages of Friendly Societies imperfect ideas as to adequate rates and other burning questions of our day prevailed as a matter of course. Times and conditions change and with them Fraternal Insurance should keep pace. At the present time there remains no doubt whatever, speaking broadly, what an adequate rate is and what it is not. Experience, the great Tribune, has spoken. It was neither the United States, nor Great Britain, nor Canada, that solved these questions singly and alone. All three have had a share in working out from their own experience, the problems necessarily involved in developing their systems on business lines, and few things are more interesting or instructive than a comparative study of the mutual advantages of international fraternalism from this point of view.

We are a small country, lying on your northern borders. Naturally we learn of you in commerce, in laws, and in the business of life. The responsibility of your example it is well to bring home to you occasionally. On the other hand, we are bound to Great Britain by the strong ties of blood and political connection. The sentiment that enters into our own growing nationhood attracts us to her people, her institutions and laws. We learn from her *con amore*. It should be the aim of fraternalism that we three, at least, should agree to learn from each other *con amore*. To respect each other as brethren in the bonds of fraternal unity should be regarded by us as a duty. To be moved by a common impulse in carrying out some of the great interests of humanity intrusted to us is something worth striving after, with all earnestness, and it seems to me there are two sources to which we may look for help to its attainment. First, and I invert the order purposely, to the searchlight of truth, which will show to ourselves and to the world the true condition of our affairs. Brethren, turn it on. Fear not the glorious sunshine from the blue sky, it will warm, vivify and nourish. Under the benign rays of actuarial truth a society will bear the tan of honest health on its face. It will grow and flourish. Rather fear the certain danger lurking under the covering cloud. Concealment, deceit, dishonor, death! Be candid with your members, nay, be courageous with them. After the battle will come your reward. No society should be allowed by this Congress—and the power is inherent in this great body, for it can speak to the State— to do unsound business.

A fraternal or friendly society is here to do good, not evil. Its business is not to exploit profits nor to encourage quackery, but to protect the home and family, and it is your prerogative, as a great controlling influence, to say "Yes" to the right, and "No" to the wrong.

As a second source, I look to an intelligent familiarity with each other's work that will relate our common interests and form an invincible bond of mutual defence and defiance. There should be a diffusion of fraternal ideas and of fraternal experience and work through the press— lay journals and special bulletins—to an extent not now accomplished. Our people mingle freely with each other. The United States opens her doors freely to men of British birth. Canada attracts people from both these countries. They come with the ideas about fraternalism which they found in the land of their birth, and a fraternal clearing house would bring the divergent notions into practical harmony, producing united strength instead of divergent weaknesses. The people must be reached.

We have copied you. Indeed, we have drawn largely upon our neighbors, but small though we be we have some things to show you. Three of these I shall briefly mention—the legislative restrictions we have placed on doubtful fraternal insurance, the question whether the lodge or local court has outgrown its usefulness, and the attention we pay to home life. These I present with our compliments. Canadian legislation does not aim at restricting the volume of fraternal insurance effected, but at regulating so as to safeguard it. By gradual steps our laws have been amended until our societies have been brought within the purview of State inspection. Obvious reforms have been forced from within and a public opinion formed that will not tolerate retrogression, but insists on further advance. The effect of our laws is to prevent schism in our societies, for a minority would not obtain legal recognition as a rival body unless on the basis of adequate rates. A lively interest is taken in insurance legislation by all our provinces and our Federal Parliament. The fact is that in Canada, as in the United States, Fraternal Insurance has become too large a popular interest to go unheeded by the State as a whole. Our laws are friendly and are enacted only after a careful consideration of the issues involved.

Has the time come when the original idea of the lodge as the local agent, the business-getter, of the society, has become obsolete? Does the society as a whole receive the best possible return in written up business from the large amount of money expended from lodge dues in the maintenance of lodges? We have asked ourselves this question in Canada. Our answer is not yet forthcoming. In Canada we recognize the home as the cornerstone and copestone of fraternalism. We have gone to Britain rather than to the United States for this ideal. We encourage home life, and the good pure womanhood and manhood that spring from domestic virtues. No people can acquire a character of equal quality from any other

source. We regard the mother especially. We like to
think of the babe at her breast drinking from Nature's
well-spring, pure and undefiled, a divine draught, having
no hurtful bacteria, and with that draught the tenderest
affection on earth—a mother's love for her child. O,
woman, how thoughtlessly generous is thy heart! With
what light prodigality canst thou throw away half thine
empire for a sucking-bottle! The health of the home,
the habits of the inmates engage our attention, and
though much remains to be done in this special line, the
results already obtained are highly satisfactory.

OF DEEP INTEREST TO THE PEOPLE

The government has made provision for the gathering
of statistics relating to injuries incident to industrial pur-
suits. Its purpose in doing this has not been to merely
gratify the curiosity of statisticians. Its aim is not simply
to provide figures and useless compilations to be entombed
in annual reports which are not generally read and under-
stood by the people. Rather, the purpose is to awaken
the people to the fact that there is a deep problem involved
in this subject and that it is worthy of the consideration
of everybody. It is of more than usual interest to society
and the people at large.

An employee injured in pursuing his occupation means
to the average person simply a single man forced to a
few weeks of enforced idleness. Again, it may mean the
support of a family incapacitated from earning wages for
the remainder of his life. If the latter is the case, or if
the employee is killed, in many cases society becomes
burdened with a helpless family to be supported while
the employer who reaped the profit of that laborer's work
gets another man and goes on without interruption.

The statistics showing the appalling accidents in industrial activities suggest that every possible safeguard should be thrown about conditions of labor so that the risk to life and limb is reduced to the lowest possible percentage. An appreciation of this is growing. The result is evidenced in the laws which have been enforced with more or less rigor providing for factory inspection.

Another consideration—indeed, it is the paramount one— has not yet received the attention it deserves. This is whether the employee, who does well if he receives enough to feed, clothe and educate his family, shall be forced to bear the burden of the risk of the occupation in which he is engaged, or whether this shall be borne jointly by him and the one who profits from the laborer's production. This is a broad question and its proper solution in all probability lies in the distant future. There is no time like the present, however, in which to agitate it.

Some employers, when an injured employee brings action against them, make haste to settle for a pitifully small sum. Others on general principles throw such cases into the courts, trusting to the ingenuity of their lawyers to get them off entirely. At best the injured employee has but a poor chance and, in many cases, if his capacity to work is destroyed, he and his family must face a bitter future.

Much of the misery thus occasioned may be avoided if one during his productive years secures protection against the hazards to which he is exposed. While he may not be able to assure an indefinite competence to his dependents in the event of his death, he can make provision which will tide them over current needs and assist them materially in outlining a course of life which will mean that they can at least remain together and have the necessities of existence.

In the opinion of THE MONITOR, the financial and

social benefits accruing through fraternal operation more fully meet the needs of the wage-earner than does any system of compulsory insurance whereby the employer and the employee are jointly liable for the hazards assumed. The ideas of progress, of thrift and of an improved order of things which are inculcated in the fraternal institution bear fruit which in time place the member and his dependents above the need of immediate assistance in the event of misfortune. They go further than this. They provide substantial sums by which the existing order of things is perpetuated and they otherwise fit one for the degree of citizenship which has as its central purpose the minimizing of the unknown hazards of the future.

Our industrial conditions as they exist at present are not infrequently a menace to order and prosperity. There is such strife between interests which fancy their purposes to be opposed to each other, that this not infrequently assumes menacing proportions. The fraternal system inculcates ideas looking to the recognition of the equities of others and demanding a similar attitude toward individual equities. The well-being and behoof of those occupying what may be termed the middle walks of life are vitally interwoven with the prosperity and continued expansion of fraternalism.

SOME PROBLEMS *

HON. E. E. RITTENHOUSE

I am glad of this opportunity to assure you that I am in most hearty accord with the purposes of this Congress, and to express my admiration for the energy and courage

---

* Extracts from the address of the Hon. E. E. RITTENHOUSE, former Insurance Commissioner of Colorado, before the 1908 session of the National Fraternal Congress.

with which you have taken up this difficult problem of adequate rates.

Every fair-minded man who knows anything about the principles of life insurance, knows that in demanding adequate rates, you are absolutely right; and that to ignore the necessity for this advancement or to unnecessarily delay it is little short of a crime.

Fraternal insurance, guarded by reserves based upon safe mortality tables, is the ideal life insurance, because of the social benefits and of the very low cost of management and of placing the business on the books.

Of course, it is not news to you to hear that a year ago the expenses of management of one hundred and twenty-two legal reserve companies averaged $9.20 for $1,000 of insurance in force, while for the same period the management expenses of five hundred and ninety fraternal societies averaged but $1.86 for $1,000 of insurance in force; but it is a very significant statement. This means that the fraternal officers have managed five times as many organizations as the old-line officers at one-fifth the cost.

The extraordinary popularity of this form of life insurance has long since demonstrated that there is a splendid field for it in this country. As soon as adequate reserves are laid by fraternal societies, fraternal insurance becomes an absolutely fixed and permanent institution in this country, to endure as long as the nation itself.

The old-line companies have a field of their own, but, when you have succeeded in procuring adequate reserves for all fraternal societies, and can give absolute protection at the minimum cost, those who are furnishing it at the maximum cost will have to take any unpleasant consequences that may ensue. However, there will be plenty of room for both systems.

Fraternal societies having a true representative form of government are wholly mutual, while old-line mutual companies are only partly mutual, because they are without this full representative government. Fraternal insurance should be absolutely free from all investment and speculative features of any kind. It should be just what you are trying here to make it,—pure insurance at actual cost. For these and other reasons fraternal insurance is in a separate and distinct class from the old-line companies, and this must be considered in framing legislation relating to fraternal societies, although the establishing of proper reserve funds is just as essential in one form as in the other.

The mass of our people know little or nothing about the scientific side of insurance, and it seems a mighty slow job to educate them in this direction; but, it is possible to make our public men and legislature understand the necessity for adequate rates, and for placing fraternal insurance societies under the supervision of Insurance Departments, in order that irregular practice and fraudulent schemes operated in the name of fraternal insurance may be eliminated, and that the public and the legitimate societies may be protected against such concerns. If all fraternal leaders would insist on adequate rates, the rank and file would soon join in, and the reform would come speedily.

Experience has clearly demonstrated that the pocket-reserve plan cannot survive. The hole in the dough-nut contains mighty little nutriment, and if we eat the dough-nut and undertake to lay aside the hole as a reserve food supply, we are going to do some very light eating when we are old.

The fraternal certificates outstanding outnumber the entire population of the eleven states and territories from the Rocky Mountains to the Pacific Coast, with Kansas and Nebraska thrown in. These certificate holders are to a very large extent wage-earners and people of moderate means; they are entitled to the fullest possible protection that both you and the law can give.

Now in these, and many other things, relating to the present situation, the problem is to put this necessary reform into effect with the least possible annoyance and injury to the societies and the certificate holders.

I appreciate fully the difficulties that are in the way, but difficult problems are being solved every day, and you will solve this one. It is easy to drift. It requires no constructive genius to idly ride with the current, regardless of where it carries us. Any scrub can do any easy thing, but it takes energy and brains to do the difficult things in this world. You have the energy, the courage and the brains to surmount the obstacles in the way of perfect fraternal insurance and I am sure you will win.

WHAT BECOMES OF THE FAMILIES?

(From THE FRATERNAL MONITOR.)

Appeals to the breadwinner to provide for his dependents are daily becoming more pronounced and insistent. At all hands the question arises, "what will become of us if our sources of existence cease?" Pathetic, indeed, are such appeals. They come from those whom we have sworn to cherish and protect. They come from those who brighten the home, who make living more than a mere existence and who inspire us to nobler and better deeds. Shall we fail to respond to such appeals?

From time immemorial the cry, "Am I my brother's keeper?" has been echoed and re-echoed. It has been insistent and it has refused to down at the bidding of those who would live for themselves and the present only. It gains in force as the years roll on. It is pressing for solution more earnestly to-day than ever before.

Our modes of living are daily becoming more complex. There are conditions to be met now which were not in evidence but a few years ago. These involve the manner in which one may provide most surely for to-day, to-morrow and the future. Lost ground is difficult to regain. One must be alive both to his responsibilities and his opportunities. If he neglects either, untoward results will arise.

The history of the average man abounds in regrets for opportunities lost and for duties unperformed. Were we all to perform our share in the world's work, the future would be fraught with nothing but happiness and glorious promise. We, however, pursue a narrow and temporizing course and for this reason notes of warning and admonitions of duty are necessary to arouse in us that latent spirit which has as its central purpose the doing of the right thing at the right time.

A BIT OF HISTORY

Far more pleasing is it to commend than it is to admonish. Yet, those on the watchtowers of the protection of the home would be derelict in their duty were they not to emphasize on all occasions possible the importance of the interests which are treated so lightly. There is nothing higher or more ennobling than the preservation of home and home interests. Yet these are sadly neglected by those to whom they mean so much. One would resent in most positive terms an insult to any member of his household. He, however, permits such household to face the uncertainties of the future with all of their appalling possibilities in a manner which should put the veriest self-seeker to shame.

As evidencing what becomes of the family in the event of the death of its provider, a few figures may be convincing. Some time ago an examination was made of the estates of deceased persons of the cities of New York, Allegheny, Pittsburg, Toledo, Albany, Schenectady, Providence and Troy. These showed that out of the estates of 43,337 deceased persons only 1,955 left estates valued at over $5,000.

Is not this a suggestive commentary on the business success, thrift and foresight of the average man? Does it not show that the vast majority of us fail to "make good" in life's struggles? Does it not show that we start off in the full blush of early manhood, with high resolves and ambitious purposes, and that in the final analysis we are worsted? Does it not show that times of prosperity are times when provision should be made for adverse conditions which are bound to arise soon or late in the lives of the majority of us? Does it not bring home in a manner that should be impossible of misunderstanding the imperative need of providing for those whom we have sworn to cherish, foster and protect?

A SMALL PERCENTAGE

The above figures show that less than five men in one hundred in the cities named conducted their business successfully or kept the money they had made or saved; or had built up protection for their dependents by insurance in a sum sufficient to yield so small an income on a five per cent. basis as $250 a year or less than $5 a week. Are not these figures suggestive? Do they not show that the majority of our dreams are Utopian? Do they not emphasize the fact that when one acts individually and for himself he finds but a frail reed upon which to lean in times of stress and adversity?

It is not easy to build up a successful business. It is even harder to keep money than it is to make it. The fraternal certificate of protection is, however, within the reach of the great majority of men, for the reason that it is paid for by small instalments, on a methodical basis and is beyond the reach of happenings that threaten the business or investments of the individual.

These are pertinent truths. They become more apparent as the years roll on. If they are not appreciated the chances are that the one so failing to profit from the experiences of others will leave his dependents on a basis yielding far less than the figures given above showing what five per cent. of those who succeeded left for their dependents. The remaining ninety-five per cent. comprise that vast army of those who left less than this sum and, in the majority of cases, left a deficiency rather than a balance.

FROM A BUSINESS VIEWPOINT

What would one think of the man who makes no provision for the future of his business? Who allows nothing for depreciation? Who creates no sinking fund against bonds to become due? Who fails to consider the replacement of old machinery by new and improved patterns? Who carries no insurance on his plant?

The individual, in conection with his family, is in just the same position. His life and health are its business capital. These of necessity depreciate as the years roll on. Not infrequently his services are replaced by younger and more vigorous persons. This is equivalent to the replacement of old machinery by new and improved patterns.

If no provision is made for such contingencies the results are comparable to the man who is shortsighted in business. The credit of such a man is limited in the business world. He is regarded as one who does not appreciate his responsibilities and the logical trend of business operation. Confidence in him becomes a steadily diminishing factor.

The income of a man establishes his financial value to his own family. His life is more uncertain than any commercial plant. He gropes along carelessly and allows those dependent upon him to reap the reward of his own neglect and improvidence.

Is it not manifestly the duty of every one to consider this subject in a commercial as well as in a sentimental way? Shall we as a people continue to pile up responsibilities and obligations without creating a sinking fund with which to meet them in the event of our death? These are questions vitally interwoven with general economic conditions. They affect the family—affect the nation. If they are provided for the nation is secure. If they are not a legacy of improvidence and penury is left, and history shows that these bring in their wake crime, chaos and general confusion.

FRATERNALISM'S OPPORTUNITY

We are at the threshhold of a great awakening as to social conditions. From all directions comes the cry that we are not living up to our opportunites; that the many sow while the few reap; that there must me a banding together of the people for social and moral benefit.

For upwards of a third of a century the fraternal system has been preaching the gospel of co-operation and protection. From a crude beginning it has grown to large proportions and enduring strength. The makeshift expedients in evidence during the early years of its operation have been eliminated. It to-day stands for permanence and a higher order of operation.

The fraternal society goes further in the care of its members than does the insurance company in providing for its policyholders. It meets its financial obligations according to their terms and, in addition, it cultivates and strengthens those social and fraternal ties whose value cannot be estimated in a financial way. It encourages brother to sustain brother, to do that which will prepare those connected with it for their increased opportunities and responsibilities. It lends a helping hand when adversity comes and it cheers the stricken and discouraged by words of comfort and helpfulness. The insurance company's obligation ceases when it has paid the amount stipulated. It has no interest beyond this.

Is not the fraternal system to-day in harmony with that for which men and women are most earnestly striving? Is not its purpose in the way of bringing about an Universal Brotherhood—one to which all lovers of humanity may subscribe? Are not its achievements such that those who are striving for better things may investigate and study with profit to themselves and the interests for which they are working?

A DUTY

The duty of both fraternal leaders and those who are in the ranks lies in the direction of striving for harmony more earnestly than ever before. Disorganized effort never produced desirable results. Rather, it but serves the purpose of delay and of defeating the ends to be reached only by unity of effort and harmony of purpose.

There are to-day over seven millions of persons marshalled under the broad banners of fraternalism. This mighty force would be impervious to any attack, were it to present an united and aggressive front to interests which may endeavor to impede its progress. Yet, one not infrequently witnesses the unseemly spectacle of this great and glorious system supinely begging for the right to exist and carry out its own destinies according to the ideas of those who have reposed their interests to its keeping.

The only danger the fraternal system has to fear is disorganization in its own ranks. This is a canker of deadly qualities. Its blighting effects have been felt in more than one institution. It is the very antithesis of harmony and union. It has nothing in common with fraternal plans and purposes.

The system should close its ranks against such forces. The care of the family should be its shibboleth. The protection of dependents should rank among its central and underlying purposes. The promotion of the social and moral welfare of its members—this should be kept ever in view. With such purposes as the dominating ones, fraternalism cannot but become a most potent factor in solving the great social problems which are now pressing so earnestly for solution.

COUNTERFEIT LOVE

WILLIAM T. STANDEN

There are men so entirely consumed by their own selfish conceit, that the practical benefits of the system of life insurance appeal in vain to them, while to others the same benefits appeal with irresistible logical force and effect. The deniers of the duty of life insurance are so utterly contemptible that to waste our time and energy on the possible thankless task of their conversion, would seem to be very unprofitable work; but the needs and requirements of their helpless families constantly stand as an incentive to us to once more try to convict the negligent ones of the enormity of their offense.

However eloquent the appeal may be, many will persistently turn a deaf ear to it. The persuasive tongue of an angel would in vain strive to break down the stolid indifference of some of these men. The sublime rhetoric of a voice from the very heavens would be wasted upon those who will not open their hearts to receive the conviction of duty, to which many so gracefully and so spontaneously yield passive obedience.

Trite, homely, common-place and common-sense arguments such as we use, are sufficient to convince many of the error of their neglect; but our hearts sink within us as we remember the almost superhuman task of evangelization before us. That we do not shrink from that task in abject dismay, is surely a potent argument in favor of the assumption that we honestly believe in our work and are sure of its unequaled practical utility. That we persist in the thankless task, shows that our conviction of the wonderful benefit achieved to the human race by life insurance, is built upon some solid and enduring foundation of absolute and indisputable fact.

Mere declamation and hot invective, may not count for very much in this work; but there are some unfortunately, who can only be brought to a realizing sense of their indifference, by forcible pen sketches of their mental, moral and characteristic infirmities. When they see themselves unmasked by the powerful searchlight which robs them of their artificial coverings, and leaves them in all the unlovely nakedness of their moral deformity, some at least who are not entirely callous to shame will leave the pathway of indifference and tread the brighter and better path of conscientious adherence to manifest duty.

However much we may be restrained by the desire to charitably judge the faults and the errors both of commission and omission in others, we gain nothing by a failure to paint them in their true colors, and may expect no profit from the reticence which withholds their social and family crime from the public lash,—for the neglect to insure the life of the breadwinner of a family is both a social and a family crime, of no mean degree.

What is the man who rejects the benefits which life insurance offers to him, and to his wife and little ones, but a contemptible example of the lowest and least excusable form of the vice of selfishness? To say that such a man loves his wife and children, is to proclaim an unmistakable falsehood. That sentiment which such a man dignifies by the holy name of love, is but a transparent parody of the genuine article—not love of his wife and babies, but love of himself, self-love of the most unworthy kind, because it inevitably involves others in evils which can only grow out of the persistence in reprehensible sentiments the very antithesis of true domestic love.

We envy not the condition of mind of the man to whom the beneficent principles of life insurance appeal in vain. We know him to be short-sighted, ignorant in the strictest sense of the term, and devoid of the domestic affection which nature implants even in the breasts of the beasts of prey, over whom he cannot truly claim precedence in the quality of moral perceptiveness. We know that if a last lingering remnant of controlling conscience is left to him, it must lash him with fearful pertinacity; and that if he still possesses any quality akin to the moral sensibility which controls better men than himself, he must perforce smother it ruthlessly in order to escape the penalty of continual and painful self-condemnation.

Such a man can never appreciate the true meaning of the title "husband." He can have no conception of the human or divine duty of fatherhood, if his helpless children in vain appeal to him to spread a mantle of protection over them to shield them from the biting blasts of coming adversity. Even the beasts of the field are controlled by a higher and more sublime sense of duty than actuates him.

Morally and socially such a man should be an outcast,.

if his neglect be wilful, premeditated, and persisted in when the necessary conditions that environ a life insurance contract are within his power to comply with. Such a man can only regard his wife and children as the playthings of the passing hour, and he can conceive of no duty that binds him to provide for them a shelter from the fiercest storms of life, which may assail them when he himself is no longer present to give them even the most feeble help or assistance. Dare such an one desecrate all that is good and true, by calling his vacillating sentiments of fancied affection, by the glorious name of "Love?"

THE CO-OPERATION OF MEN

HON. W. A. NORTHCOTT

The characteristic of this age is the co-operation of men for the benefit of the many. In the older civilizations the great force of organization was for the benefit of the few. History tells us that way back across the centuries nations had splendid armies and navies; they had arts and sciences; letters and wealth, kings and palaces, but all this perished from the face of the earth.

These older civilizations were built from the top instead of from the bottom. They forgot the people. A few were strong and rich and powerful, but the manv were slaves. A splendid army and navy can not make a nation great, its true greatness must come from the number of happy homes throughout the land. It is not so desirable that the one man be a giant, but that the many may be strong; not that a few may be learned from the great universities, but in the diffusion of knowledge among the children of the people from the little school houses on the hills and in the valleys. Not that great wealth is accumulated in the hands of a few, but that the means of livelihood and comfort are given to the many, and that every working man may have three square meals a day, and be able to clothe and feed his little children and send them to school. Greatness in a nation does not come through the absolute power of a monarch, but in the distribution of sovereignty among a free and intelligent people.

Over the gateway of the twentieth century is written the word "Organization." Shall this great force be used for the benefit of the many or for the benefit of the few?

The force of organization made Alexander the master of the world. With his organized phalanxes Caesar crushed the war-like Gaul. Through the genius of organization Napoleon made "the boundaries of kingdoms to oscillate upon the map." By the force of organization the captains of industry in America have accumulated fortunes greater than that of Croesus of old and have made themselves masters of the world's commerce and of the destinies of labor.

But now comes the spirit of co-operation and more than a million of men join hands in the federation of labor to demand and obtain a fair share of profits in the partnership with capital. In this day thousands of building and loan associations and savings banks make homes and a competence possible for the working people. Under the inspiration of this spirit of co-operation the fraternal beneficiary societies have enrolled six millions of people and have paid to the widows and orphans more than one billion of dollars. The co-operation of ninety million free people makes possible the American Republic.

Since "Father" Upchurch founded the Ancient Order of United Workmen in October, 1868, more than ten mil-

lion free men of this great republic have enrolled them
selves under this great white banner of fraternal insur
ance. During that period more than one and a half bil-
lion dollars have been paid to the beneficiaries of deceased
members. This vast army has wiped the tears from the
cheek of the widow, it has clothed little children and sent
them to school, it has taken mortgages from homes, it
has made desolate places glad, it has given a cup of cold
water to the thirsty, fed the hungry and clothed the
naked. The great good done by this splendid army can
never be told in words. These deeds shine out like the
bright stars on the dark mantle of night.

And then shall Fraternal Insurance die? Shall this
vast army pass into oblivion? Shall the failure to join
good business principles with the principles of charity
cause the death of this splendid system of the co-opera-
tion of men?

This question of adequate rates cannot be dodged or
side-stepped; it is a mathematical question and all the fir-
ing of guns and the beating of drums and the marching
with splendid banners, behind glorious music will not
save the fraternal system unless with it is combined cor-
rect business principles.

The Co-Operation of Men is a great force in the
world's affairs and finds its greatest exemplification in
these insurance societies that have the lodge feature.
They minimize the expense account; they add to the
insurance feature the great feature of brotherly love;
They join with the business proposition the proposition
of lifting the fallen and burying the dead. May the great
principle of the co-operation of men be so exemplified
in our societies that business and fraternalism shall go
hand in hand.

PUBLIC INSTALLATION*

Worshipful Masters and Brethren—Ladies and Gentlemen:

This day presents to our eyes an unusual, if not altogether an unprecedented spectacle. Clothed with the regalia and instruments of our calling, we, whose doors are ordinarily guarded by the drawn sword of the Tyler, and whose business is conducted beneath an impenetrable veil of secrecy, have left the sacred privacy of our Lodge. We have unbarred our doors, and have come up hither to perform our Masonic work, and to keep our festal day. We have drawn aside the curtain that others may see a glimmering of that Light whose meridian splendor it is our high privilege to enjoy.

It can not be, but such a movement upon our part, will attract attention and excite enquiry. We, ourselves, have invited the scrutiny of the public, and can not, if we would avoid their questioning. Who are these and what mean they by this service? Why have they left the usual avocations of their business to clothe themselves with these strange symbols, and to perform this mysterious work? What is this day more than others, and what especial interest have these in it?—The State has proclaimed no feast—they are not keeping a Christian fast— it is no political gathering, and no scholastic assemblage. They are not here in their capacity as citizens, nor in obedience to their spiritual rulers. Here we see men of every rank and calling—of every faith and party, meeting in harmony, as though bound by some mysterious tie

---

*Address of the Rev. GEORGE F. CUSHMAN delivered in June, 1855, before Fulton Lodge, F. & A. M., at Cahaba, Alabama.

which has carried them beyond the influence of human passion. The noise of political strife is hushed, and the bitterness of the theological hatred is for the moment assuaged. Every creed has here its representative, every party its adherents, sitting side by side in friendliness. Were they Brethren indeed the bond of union could not be stronger—the clasped hand and speaking eye tell of a mutual affection as fervent as it is real. Here the distinctions of society are done away. All are alike rich, and alike poor—there is no least and no greatest.—No worldly honor gives pre-eminence, and no title is recognized but that of moral worth. They meet all upon the same Level and part all upon the same Square. They walk between the same Parallels and are circumscribed by the same Circle. Again it is asked who are they and how is it that in this discordant age they have been able to bring Light out of darkness and order out of confusion.

Such Worshipful Masters and Brethren, are some of the enquiries and thoughts which our appearance this day must necessarily suggest.—We do not propose wholly to answer them—we are not competent even were it lawful. We can but say to the enquirers what was said to us. Come and see. But we may nevertheless to some extent raise the curtain that divides us from the world. We may say whence we are and whither we go. We may speak freely of the genius and aims of Masonry, though we may not unfold the means by which those aims are effected. We may enlarge upon our ancient claims to the respect and love of men, and upon those cardinal principles of morality and virtue, which, upon either hand are our pillars of Wisdom, Strength and Beauty. We may expose to the gaze of all men, that Masonic Ladder reaching from earth to heaven, by the help of whose rounds we trust at last to be able to reach the Grand Lodge above. We may speak of the Temple of Solomon

—of its beauty and magnificence—of its splendor and purity—the fitting type of that other Temple which all Free and Accepted Masons are to erect in their hearts for the in-dwelling of the Spirit of that God whose existence we all acknowledge, and whose majesty we adore. We may tell the world that Masonry is a fountain of Relief to the poor, of Charity to the distressed, and of Truth to all—that the prayer of the widow and the orphan, and the blessing of him that was ready to perish, have ever been our rich inheritance. We may say that while we feel the woes of all men and as far as we can alleviate them, Brother is still the readiest passport to our hearts. It dissipates all doubt and indifference, and enkindles in our breast the warmest love, and we neither may nor dare—whatever his name or lineage turn him if in adversity unrelieved away, nor refuse to wish him God speed if prosperity crowns his labors. It is no small part of the Mason's mission as far as man may to restore brotherhood upon earth, and to strengthen those fraternal ties which should bind man to man and fellow to fellow. The two great commandments sum up with admirable brevity our duty—the love of God and the love of our neighbor.

If it be asked when we received this mission, we are neither ashamed nor afraid to confess that we do not know. The origin of our Institution is lost in the antiquity of time. Age after age, and generation after generation, we trace our existence back far beyond any written records. Where these altogether fail, we still refer to the unbroken line of our traditions sacredly preserved. Not the New World still flourishing with the vigor of youth—not Europe exhibiting signs of advancing age saw our birth; but in the very cradle of our race was the place of our nativity, and we bear even date with the infancy of the world. That great epoch of humanity the christian era is not the startling epoch to the Mason.

Before the dawn of that day, Masonic Light had arisen in the East. Through the ancient and modern times of christianity amid the hidden systems of an idolatrous age, we carefully trace our way not to the origin but to the more perfect organization of our craft at the building of King Solomon's Temple. How long before that event we had lived and flourished, it were more curious than profitable to enquire. The necessities of man gave us our first being in our operative character, and the Mason and the Architect may boast, a common parentage. Even in the days of our first Grand Master, the venerable frosts of antiquity lay thick upon the brow of Masonry, and it had all the signs of age but its infirmities. The lapse of time, change of place and circumstances brought no decay, but like the Eagle from time to time it renewed its youth and gathered strength by progress. The Acacia sprang ever in its footsteps to be the emblem of its immortality. Empires rose and fell—thrones crumbled and decayed—dynasties were changed or expired, but Masonry still survived. Upon the pyramids of Egypt the date of whose construction no written record remains to tell amid the ruins of Balbaec and Palmyra, and upon the exhumed monuments of cities which have been buried beneath the accumulated dust of more than twenty centuries, the modern Mason reads with wondering awe his symbolic language. To Nineveh and Tyre—to the Holy City and the banks of the fruitful Nile, we can look back as the cherished homes of our ancient art. In the classic land of Greece—amid the vine clad hills and sunny fields of Italy—while Pompei and Herculaneum were still the pride of men, the cloudy canopy covered the East, the West and the South. Later still, St. John the Baptist, whose festival we now commemorate, and St. John the Evangelist, were selected as the christian patrons of an Institution—older than Christianity itself. With no fal-

tering step we have advanced from that day to this. We
have outlived the persecutions of Emperors and the blind
fury of Republics—we have survived the ignorance and
prejudices of men. No height of prosperity has been able
to destroy us—the hottest fires of adversity have only
served to purify the dross from the sterling ore. In the
dawn of our Era we still wrought our work, in the Dark
Ages our Light shone upon a benighted world, and we
can boast to-day of greater numbers and of a more
extended sphere than when in our virgin prime, the
Widow's son presided over the construction of the first
great Temple of the Universal Architect.

We may also claim an universality as wide as our
antiquity is venerable. There is no land where the
Masonic carpet has not been spread and no clime where
reverence for the Widow's son has not been inspired. In
the luxurious palaces and cloud-capped towers of the gor-
geous East—amid the rising cities of the West, the sound
of the Mason's gavel is heard. No barrier has been able
to impede our progress or stay our onward march. We
have crossed the wide Ocean—have followed the course
of rivers—have ascended the mountain-height and taken
up our abode in the loneliest valley. Continents have
felt our presence—the remotest island of the remotest
sea has responded to our brotherly salutation. We have
traversed the frozen regions of the North—we have
braved the heat and pestilence of the South. We have
made the sea-board our home, and have penetrated far
into the interior of all lands. From pole to pole our influ-
ence extends—the range of our empire knows no rising
and no setting sun. Civilization and refinement speak
our language—the savage and the barbarian acknowledge
the strength of the mystic tie. By the quiet hearth-stone
—in the busy mart and upon the ensanguined battlefield,
the sign is recognized and obeyed. They who are broth-

ers in peace can not be made enemies in war. The Mason carries about him an universal passport, and may claim in reality what the ancient Roman arrogated to himself but did not enjoy—to be a cosmopolite—a citizen of the world. By the power of the pass and token, he may travel without fear upon the shores of Jud or in the realms of far Cathay, or still prouder trophy of our power, he may roam our remote Western forests secure of a welcome not only to the homes but to the hearts of Brethren.

And we are not only thus extended into all lands, but in all lands we are one and the same. Long centuries ago it was the fond dream of the diplomatist and statesman, to establish one language for the nations of the earth—to be the language of courts. The Mason has alone been able to realize the dream which surpassed their skill and power. No Babel exists within the walls of his Lodge, and the confusion of tongues is done away. Greek and Barbarian, Jew and Gentile there make use of the same signs, and speak the same shibboleth. He alone has been able to obtain that union of sentiment which leads to harmony of action—he alone has been able to banish strife and discord from the scene of his labor and his joys. We speak with one voice, because we speak from the abundance of the heart.

Look at the great country of which we are citizens— its divided interests and conflicting parties raging ever like the waves of a tumultous sea. Though we share a common heritage and speak a common language, we are not at peace one with another. Faction raises its triumphant head and the madness of fanaticism sways the hour. When we meet in grand council in our Legislative halls, it is no longer to exchange fraternal sentiments and to provide for common interests but wrangle and debate—to attempt encroachments and to resist. The solemn sanctions of law—the guaranties of the Constitution and the obligations of official oaths, are wilfully disregarded or lightly explained away. Sectional strife and party selfishness are taking the place of an enlarged patriotism, and it can not be concealed that the folly and degeneracy of the sons are putting in peril that union which the Fathers founded by their wisdom and hallowed by their prayers. Dark clouds hang around the present—the patriot can augur no good from the history of the past, and the future is ominous with dread and fear. Fanaticism and folly are blind and reasonless, and will never voluntarily loose their deadly fangs, and there is—there can be no hope save in their destruction or our own. When we are compelled to exchange the patriot and statesman for the bigot and fanatic, it needs neither seer nor prophet to tell us what the end will be, unless some means can be devised to stay the progress of the plague. Its strong foundations will be undermined—its mighty pillars thrown down—the key-stone be loosed from the arch, and the great Temple of the Republic be buried in its own ruins.

If we turn to the religious world, we find a want of union no less to be deplored. Its own quarrels and divisions have drawn so largely upon its time and energies, that if it had the will it has not had the power to harmonize the interests of warring States. Alas, that we must say so christianity—not that which descended from above and is first pure and then peaceable, but christianity as it is developed in the Northern section of our land, has not been able to restrain from her own councils the reckless spirit of fanaticism which is doing so much to mar our happiness. We find christian societies as well as political parties sitting in judgment upon their neighbors—issuing their thundering bulls of excommunication, and like the over-righteous Pharisees of old uttering their *"procul! O! procul! este profani."* Religion is the favorite cloak of fanaticism in which it delights to walk forth in appearance, an Angel of light, but in reality filled with malice, hatred and all uncharitableness. It steals the very livery of heaven to serve the devil in. Thus disguised, it has crept slily amid the denominations of our land—those bonds of union in the judgment of our great Southern Statesman stronger than any political compact could be—and has pursued its noiseless and unsuspected way until at length it has leavened the whole mass. Now it is stronger than they with whom in its weakness it found a shelter, and with unblushing effrontery it throws off its disguise and claims to rule or ruin. It requires all to adopt its prejudices and imitate its follies—to lie upon its bed and to swear by its Gods upon peril of its determined vengeance. To such demands there is, there can be but one answer to be made, and christianity like the State has its North and its South. The strong cords to which the Statesman turned as his last hope, are proving to be like Samson's green withes, without strength or influence.

Under such circumstances, we may with pardonable pride, turn to Masonry and recognize her genius and her power. There is the two-fold cord that is strong, and the three-fold cord that is not easily broken. Her craftsmen every where pursue their appointed task in quietness and peace. Political strife can not enter her guarded doors—fanaticism can not raise its discordant voice at her altars. The questions that have shaken this government to its foundation, the questions that have forever sundered those who worship the same God and hold the same faith, have never been mooted in her councils. She exists in strength in the North—her Lodges rise upon the fertile Savannahs, and beneath the orange groves of the South, and no rivalry has ever sprang between them except as to who should best perform their Masonic work. Even in Massachusetts, once mother and nurse to patriots and statesmen, but now the hot-bed of misrule, and unreason the Southern slaveholder when cut off from christian altars, and in attempt tabooed from society, can stand upon the floor of every Mason's Lodge with his equals and his peers—yea with his Brethren. Far aloof from all disturbing questions with Compass and Level, Plumb-line and Square, the Craftsman plies his work. He fears no extraneous influence, and the Master's caution to take heed upon what he enters he applies as well to the subject of his thought and words as to himself. Whatever differences of opinion upon politics, upon religion, and upon questions of morality may exist elsewhere, none can be tolerated here. The silence that waited upon the construction of the first Temple, so that not so much as the sound of a hammer was heard, was the fitting symbol of that peace and harmony which in all ages attends upon the Mason's handiwork.

But it will be asked whence is it that Masonry derives its power.—Its antiquity—its universality, and its unity are alike remarkable.—Other organizations are limited in duration and extent. They spring up and die by reason of the strife and discord that are generated in their birth. The obvious answer is that Masonry retains its power because it is true to its own genius and principles. It has a mission to perform, and it turns neither to the right hand nor to the left, but studies to be quiet and to do its own business. This is *the secret—the great secret* of its success and favor with men. To every person seeking admission to its Light, it is asked what comest thou hither to do, and he is taught to reply, to learn to subdue my passions and improve myself in the sacred arts and mysteries of ancient Free Masonry. This is our only aim—

to subdue our passions—to act upon the square—to keep
the tongue of a good report, and practice charity.

We do not claim—we never have claimed for
Masonry any divine origin. It is not christianity—it is
not even a substitute for it. It is not the church. We do
not expect it to do the work of the church.—That hails
from heaven—we confess to an earthly derivation. He
is no true Mason who attempts to set up so unwarrant-
able a claim. While yet in the darkness of ignorance,
every candidate for Masonic honors upon bended knee,
is brought into actual contact with the word of God.
That is our Magna Charta, and is ever open upon our
altars. Thence we draw light and knowledge—thence
we receive our rules of thought and action. While we
recognize the Scriptures as our Grand Constitution, we
can not rightly be accused of claiming that Masonry is
either christianity or a substitute for it. We never have
given to the Ahiman Reson a co-ordinate rank with the
word of God. Our principles would men act upon them,
have a meliorating not a *saving* influence.

But while we do not claim any equality with, we may
rightly say that Masonry is a handmaid and adjunct to
christianity. It draws its principles from the same store-
house, and its lessons of morality are taught from the
same book. It has so far as it goes the same objects in
view, to subdue our passions, enlighten our reason and
elevate our moral nature. It addresses itself to the intel-
lect, the affections and the heart of men. Recognizing
his two-fold nature, its impressive and instructive lessons
are taught by solemn charges which speak to the under-
standing and by meaning symbols for the senses. Under
each of those mystic characters graven upon the Mason's
chart, there is a hidden and significant language which
affects all his relations to his fellows and to his God.
Where the uninitiated see an unmeaning sign, he reads

of Faith, Hope and Charity. He carries about with him the badges of the cardinal virtues that he may the better learn to cherish in his heart and practice in his life the duties of Fortitude, Prudence and Justice. He not only hears but he sees exemplified before him, Brotherly Love, Relief and Truth. He works in Patience to rest in Hope. These lessons and such as these—the great tenets of his profession are impressed upon his mind in every possible way. He reads them in the Ancient Constitutions and the word of God—in the open symbol and the secret sign, in the cordial grip and word. He is thus instructed in his duties to his God and to himself—in his duties as a citizen and as a neighbor—in his capacity as a Father, a Son and a Brother. In all the possible relations of life he is taught to square his actions by the unerring word of God and by the laws of morality and virtue.

If then, Brethren of Fulton and Halo Lodges, such are the characteristics and aims of our Institutions, a great weight of responsibility rests upon us. We have come to the Masonic Light and must walk as becomes it. We are now living in a critical period of our history. The fires of persecution have rolled away, and the greater dangers of prosperity press upon us. Everywhere we are rapidly increasing in numbers and influence—too rapidly we fear for our own best interests.—With the utmost caution that can be used it can not be but that some will find entrance among us who are not of us, and whose inconsistent lives will bring scandal upon our Order and disgrace upon themselves. It is the history of all organizations human and divine. If such be our misfortune we must make the tenets of our profession our rule and guide, and unceasingly use the gavel if so be the rough may become a perfect Ashler. Bear patiently with the infirmities of the weak. By kindness, by forbearance, by long suffering, by love correct if possible his faults.

Accept the offering of his sorrow and restore him again and again to the forfeited place in your affections—

> Think gently of the erring,
>   Oh, do not thou forget,
> However darkly stained by sin,
>   He is thy BROTHER yet.
> Heir of the self-same heritage,
>   Child of the self-same God,
> He hath but stumbled in the path,
>   Thou hast a weakness trod.

But if in the end he proves incorrigible and wilful— if there is no hope of his walking within compass—if he is obdurate and will not be circumscribed, then however painful it may be, there is still a duty to be done. While we bear with the weakness of all, we can tolerate the vices of none. We must exscind without mercy the wilfully corrupt member lest the deadly gangrene pervade and destroy the whole system.

Brethren of our Order, we should learn wisdom and caution by the lessons of experience. By our love for this venerable institution by our zeal for the sacred cause of morality and virtue—by the solemn obligations which we have taken upon us—by our duty to our Craft, to society and to ourselves, let us tyle well our doors. While we command the approaches to our courts, we shall be held responsible if the cowan and the eaves-dropper gain access to our sanctuary, or if any but the meritorious and deserving are rewarded with that badge which, when worthily worn is "more ancient than the Golden Fleece or Roman Eagle, and more honorable than the Star or Garter." May the Brethren of the Mystic Tie wherever dispersed, never fall into the grievous error of measuring their prosperity by their numbers, nor ever forget that he alone is the true Mason, Free and Accepted, who walks at home and abroad within the Lodge and out of it by the Rule and Square.

And now, though we have detained you long, we may not close without a word to the gentle Spirits who have this day graced us with their presence and gladdened us with their smiles. With your quick perceptions you will have already seen, ladies, in the course of our remarks, the reason, and the only reason why, by our ancient laws, our doors are barred to you, to whom our hearts are ever open as the day. It proceeds from no want of respect and deference for that sex which may well be called the natural guardian of morality and virtue. Masonry is a stern system of checks and restraints which we can not bring ourselves to believe, need to be applied to you "the precious porcelain of humanity," in order to subdue passion or teach you charity. Charity like purity, is one of the instincts of your nature, which you exercise and share in common with the Angels. A chivalrous deference to woman is peculiarly a Masonic virtue, and he is alike degenerate as a Son and as a Mason, whose bosom it does not animate, and whose conduct it does not rule. Look around you, and you will find that the elected representatives of your hearts—your fathers and husbands—your lovers and brothers are here, and though you seek not to join us, we, as in duty bound, will ever pray to join you and be received by you not upon one only, but upon all the points of a perfect Fellowship.

THE ASSESSMENT CLAUSE

The assessment clause in fraternal contracts has been the theme of many a profound discourse on the part of those who lie awake nights to evolve reasons why the fraternal system is not to be looked upon with favor by those who desire to ascertain in advance the limits of the obligations they are assuming. Its uncertainties have been pictured in most vivid colors. Members are liable for anything they may be called upon to pay. A most questionable undertaking has been entered into and no one can forecast its outcome.

As a matter of fact, the assessment or safety clause is the strongest feature in the context of fraternalism. It ensures that obligations entered into will be carried to a successful issue. Its central purpose is that of requiring that each member pay his proper share of the liabilities he brings to an organization. No reasonable person can object to this. It is the basis upon which enduring operation of whatsoever nature rests. It may be termed to be the court of last resort which provides for the integrity of contracts and makes provision for their performance.

The original basis of fraternalism embodied the idea that payments from members be called as needed. These payments were termed assessments, and they were called at infrequent intervals to provide the funds with which they discharge obligations. Such calls were made for only such amounts as were needed. Of necessity there was not that uniformity which now characterizes fraternal operation. Some years the cost might be extremely low. During other years, by reason of heavier death rates, they might be increased. The sole purpose was that of discharging current liabilities and no provision was made for the future.

In the development of the work it was found to be both more convenient and more businesslike to forecast in a general way the obligations to be met and to make provision for these at stated times. Thus the practice of monthly collections came into vogue. This was a decided improvement over the previous order of things. It permitted the members to compute the calls which would be made upon them and to make provision for these. It was a step in the right direction. It served the purpose of educating the members to an appreciation of the fact that there was an ascertainable basis upon which to predicate rates and that this should be considered.

Time wrought still further changes. While the societies were able to create what are known as emergency funds, in addition to meeting current obligations, they were brought to a realizing sense that the cost of protection increases with the attained ages of the members on whose lives it is carried. They were impressed with the fact that mortality tables were the only safe ones upon which to gauge future experience and thus the transformation to the present order of things began. To-day mortality tables are considered the only safe standards upon which to predicate the future. Operation is measured according to these and, as a result, what has been termed confusion in some quarters is neither more nor less than a transition from a lower to a higher standard of operation.

The safety clause has been retained and it to-day is one of the strongest features of any fraternal society. It is an earnest that, if unforeseen conditions arise, such organization has that elasticity in its context which will permit it to meet such conditions by making provision for them as needs may require. In other words, it means that technical insolvency is not that menace in fraternalism that it is in insurance companies not possessing it. History shows that many of the insurance companies which have been forced out of existence could have saved themselves had their organization permitted them to assess their policyholders a comparatively small sum to meet technical deficiencies.

The equivalent of the assessment clause in fraternal societies exists in the majority of other forms of securities. The land owner has to pay taxes and assessments for current needs and for extraordinary improvements. Despite this the average man is not loth to be a real estate owner. He appreciates that such taxes or improvements maintain or add to the value of that which he possesses and he, therefore, sees that his obligations are met. The owner of stock in banks or other financial institutions knows that his liability is not limited to his holdings. There may be an assessment if occasion requires. Why is it the fraternal society is criticised for possessing this assessment clause, when other forms of operation advertise it as a source of strength?

THE MONITOR'S attention was recently called to a section of the bylaws of a prominent insurance company which reads as follows: "All policies of insurance which shall be made by the said corporation in pursuance of this act, shall be made on such terms and conditions and for such periods of time, and confined to such persons, as shall be 'from time to time ordered and prescribed by the bylaws, rules and regulations of said corporation; and if at any time it shall so happen that there shall be just claims on the corporation for losses sustained to a greater amount than they have funds on hand to discharge for the time being, shall with all convenient expedition proceed to assess such deficiency in a ratable proportion on the members of the association, or their lawful representatives according to the amount of each member's insurance," etc.

The company in question has never assessed its policyholders. It is not believed that it ever will. The reproduction of this power to assess, if necessary, is not given for the purpose of criticism. Rather, it sets forth the fact that, unless liability is specifically limited, the inherent right to make up deficiencies among those who created them is reserved. This is an element of strength. It is not one of weakness. Right-thinking persons will admit its desirability.

So it is with the fraternal contract. A society whose rates are on an adequate basis is no more likely to assess its members, in addition to their regular payments, than is the company whose provision in this direction is referred to above. The reservation, however, is a most valuable one and should not be surrendered to meet the criticism of any one. It means that, if untoward conditions arise temporarily, an institution has the ability to meet them. It means that the integrity of contracts is maintained. It means that actual cost is the final arbiter of all things and that it is the part of unwisdom for any institution to burn its bridges so that it may be forced by the stress of events into a condition of technical insolvency which might otherwise be avoided.

FRATERNAL INSURANCE

GEN. J. T. YATES

An all-wise Providence seems to rule the destinies of man, and from the dawn of intelligence some several thousand years ago up to the present time the events of history are recorded facts and from them we see the guiding hand of this divine Providence that prepares for and meets the necessities of mankind from time to time.

As the world grows older and the population grows larger, the necessities of man increase and Providence provides for the various needs. It may be the telegraph, the telephone or the electric motor, the steam engine, the automobile or the aeroplane, and so in our day the desire of the laboring man, the artisan and mechanic is to own his own home and the opportunity to do so is greater now than at any time before in the history of the world, and it seems that the Divine Providence has provided for that necessity. Nearly every man's ambition is to become a property owner and never before were so many homes owned by the poorer class of people than at the present time.

Akin to the desire to own a home is the desire to protect the home; protect it not only by fire insurance but also with life insurance; to provide in the event of the death of the head of the family, an income for the loved ones left behind. Old-line insurance companies provide protection for the rich, but not for the poorer class of people on account of its high cost, but to provide for this necessity Fraternal Insurance has sprung into existence and is filling that want in a manner that nothing else will ever be able to do. It may not measure up to the science of insurance according to the old-line insurance actuaries, but it is paying its losses promptly and its continued success is assured and as time goes on it will improve to meet any necessities.

The progress of Fraternal Insurance has been marked by the change from the passing around the hat for a contribution of a dollar apiece from the membership to a graded rate according to age and occupation. Its improvement will not be based on the experience of the old-line companies, but on its own experience which will prove to be an entirely different proposition. It has come forward to fill a deep-felt want of the masses of the people and is a great agency through which a charitable God bestows his benevolences, upon that class of people who need it most, the widows and the orphans.

MENTAL WELL-WISHING*

This old world is being rapidly regenerated and made not unlike what heaven was formerly pictured as being. Startling as have been the innovations in the arts, sciences and inventions, they have been no more so than the changes which have been brought about in the conduct of humanity one toward another. True there is yet all too much selfishness and antagonism, but, thanks to the growing spirit of Fraternalism, the age of well-wishing is with us, and it is curing most of the ills to which humanity has for countless ages been subjected.

Instead of antagonism, there is a reaching out of one mind to help and strengthen another, with the result that Fraternalism has made a great band of co-operation and mutual help around the world.

A great cult has been built up in recent years by asserting that disease and sin have no existence. That probably isn't true, although the belief persisted in has undoubtedly calmed many troubled minds and eradicated many ills which were the direct result of worry and nervousness. Fraternalism offers the true panacea for the ills of humanity, and it is but carrying out the injunctions of the Master when He said· "Bear ye one another's burdens."

If it is possible—and it is—to send a message around the world in an instant through the instrumentality of wireless telegraphy, why should it be thought strange when it is asserted that the very fact that more than 7,000,000 of loyal Fraternalists are wishing each other well in itself does more to let the sunlight into hitherto darkened lives and drive out the gloom than anything

---

*E. N. Haag, in the F. M. C. Recorder, Philadelphia.

which has heretofore been conceived of by the human
brain. Indeed, as has been stated, it is a Divine injunc-
tion.

It is a fact that one angry, jealous, ill-wishing mind
in a community can, and often does, bring unhappiness,
if not also disease and misfortune, to many others. It
acts like poison. They killed witches in the old days, in
order to get rid of this evil influence. They didn't know
just what it was that was doing the harm, but it existed
nevertheless. The "evil eye" was but another manifes-
tation of this bad influence.

The very fact, therefore, as has been stated, that a
great wave of well-wishing is set in motion by the Fra-
ternalists, has in itself provided a remedy for most of the
human ills. It has brightened up the faces of the masses
and raised their heads toward the blue sky from the
downcast and downtrodden look and pathway which too
many formerly thought could not be avoided in this
world.

We are just beginning to realize the possibilities.
Many Fraternalists see the result, but are unconscious of
the cause. They admire the flower, but forget that the
rain and sunshine contributed to and are combined in its
beauty. We believe the day is rapidly coming when there
will be a great awakening in this respect; when people
will seek the well-wishing wave of mental healing put
forth by the united Fraternalists as they now go to san-
itariums and health resorts or seek to find relief for bodily
and mental ills in the healing properties of medicine.

A NECESSARY PROVISION

The public is awakening to the important part insurance in its various adaptations plays in its everyday affairs. More and more is it coming to be recognized as a necessary provision against the uncertainties of the future. While the sentimental considerations which move people to make provision for their dependents are not losing their force, these are taking a more practical turn and are but evidencing that sentiment of itself possesses but little value financially. It must be coupled with deeds which show that protestations in this way are supported by more than idle words.

A promising development in this form of economics is in the line of education. Colleges and universities and the Young Men's Christian Associations are providing courses of lectures calculated to inform people on the principles and needs of insurance protection. This will in time produce most wholesome results. It involves a wider interest in the fundamental principles upon which this proposition rests. It causes the people to think and plan in harmony with them. It awakens heads of families and others to a realization of their responsibilities and their duties.

An unfortunate situation exists in this connection with reference to the fraternal system. The old-line system has not been slow in grasping the opportunities which have been placed before them. They have provided these universities and colleges and associations with speakers whose duty it is to emphasize sound doctrines and to enunciate fundamental principles. Naturally, these being disciples of a given system, their views are largely molded by the cause of which they are exponents. They, in consequence, are not over-zealous in the way of according to the fraternal system the full meed of credit to which it is entitled.

THE MONITOR believes that fraternal leaders are short-sighted in this direction. It believes that it is highly important for them to see that the cause with which they are identified is granted a full and complete hearing. Fraternalism is based upon principles as enduring and as beneficent as are those of any other system. Its exponents need not feel called upon to explain or apologize for their temerity in insisting that it is one of the most potent factors to-day in making provision for the future of the dependents of those who have reposed their interests to its keeping.

The public affords the field from which the societies recruit their members. Such field should be cultivated painstakingly. No opportunity to enrich it should be ignored. No point of vantage in the way of shedding light on the plans and accomplishments of the system should be overlooked. As much care should be taken in this direction as in any other from which results are expected. If this is not done, it follows that in time a feeling of indifference and possible antagonism may be developed—a condition to be most earnestly guarded against.

Neglect brings in its wake results of a cumulative nature just as effectively as does earnest and intelligent effort bring that in which it is enlisted to a successful issue. If opportunities to show that the fraternal system is a growing and enduring one are not embraced; if its opponents are permitted to assume that they are the only ones worth while in this direction; if public thought is so molded that it looks upon fraternal societies as temporary and temporizing expedients—it is repeated, if such ends are permitted to be accomplished, an unfortunate situation will have developed for the fraternal system.

For this reason, if for no other, fraternal exponents. should be alive to their opportunities and should insist that they have an equal opportunity to present their cause for the consideration of those who are now and who may hereafter be interested in this subject.

We should build for a broader and greater fraternalism. Too long have we been reviewing the defects of early operation. These may be found in any system or any undertaking. They seem to be a necessary part of early and pioneer work. Time works many changes and it solves many problems. There is danger, during a period of transition, of going too far. In one's endeavor to correct error or abuse, it is possible that the pendulum swing too far and that unnecessary conditions be exacted. It is possible that a system or an institution be built along such rigid lines that it does not possess that flexibility so necessary to meet the ever-changing conditions which present themselves.

Fraternal exponents should eschew provincialism in the conduct of the affairs entrusted to them. They should build on broad lines. They should endeavor to see that the seedtime is just as properly cared for as is the harvest. If this is not done the latter will not be satisfactory. The seedtime to-day is in the way of acquainting the public with what fraternalism has done and can do. The same avenues for publicity which are open to the companies are within the reach of the societies. They should see that the educational institutions of the land be made familiar with the principles of fraternalism when presented on the basis of adequate rates. They are losing an important vantage point when they permit the insurance companies to become the sole possessors of this. field.

THE FRATERNAL SIDE OF LABOR UNIONS

An interesting article recently appeared in the St. Louis *Times*. It was a communication from Mr. Henry M. Hyde and it emphasizes the value of the fraternal feature in organized effort.

Mr. Hyde expresses the opinion that it will doubtless surprise many people, who think of labor unions as organizations existing solely for the purpose of forcing higher wages from reluctant employers, to learn that a large part of the energy and funds of almost every body of organized workingmen is devoted to various forms of friendly aid and mutual protection. In the aggregate they have paid out hundreds of millions of dollars as death, sick and out-of-work benefits to their members.

They take care of their fellow craftsmen who have been injured at work; they maintain employment bureaus which serve a most useful purpose as clearing houses between employers and men; some of them have established sanatoria where members who are ill may be treated at the general expense; they have provided pensions for those who have been permanently disabled by accident, and in some cases they have built great homes for old and decrepit members of their societies.

They have exerted, and now exert, a constantly growing influence in forcing through Congress and more or less reluctant or indifferent State legislatures, laws which look to the greater protection of their members from unavoidable risks in their work and which will give to the workmen a stronger standing in the courts. In almost every State, and also in Congress, it is a part of the duty of the regular legislative committees of labor unions to study carefully all bills introduced and to oppose those which will in any way make harder the lot of their members.

In practically all cases two striking and important things are to be noticed. In the first place, the stronger the fraternal feeling among its members the more powerful is the union as a factor in determining wages and hours of labor. In the second place, the more powerful the union the slower and more reluctant is it to begin a strike. It is the fraternal feature of mutual aid and helpfulness which binds the members of the union into a solid mass and which tends to attract to it practically all the workers in a given field.

It is further said that it is precisely such a solid and harmonious union which is in the best position to get what it wants in the matter of wages, etc., without resorting to hostile measures. This truth is being widely recognized by labor leaders. The general tendency is constantly to make more of the mutual benefits and privileges which are already a part of the work of all of the important bodies of organized labor.

It will be even more surprising to the casual public to learn that many of the older and stronger unions of the present day were originally formed purely as societies for mutual aid and protection among workmen in the same craft without any idea of taking part in negotiations with employers. This is fairly well illustrated by the huge and powerful brotherhoods which to-day practically control the situation on almost all the railroads of this country.

THE SPECULATIVE TEMPLE*

Another year has fled. Another wave is spent upon the shore of time. Another link is added to the long chain of years that reach beyond the flood. A year teeming with mighty events, and destined to shape the future of unborn millions, for weal or for woe. A year, whose history when written, will chronicle the convulsion and dismemberment of a great nation—the destruction of one of the fairest temples ever erected to Liberty and dedicated to Freedom—the erection of another, which Phoenix-like, sprung from a portion of its ruins, more just in its proportions, more severe in its beauty, and better adapted to secure the priceless liberties of those it was designed to shelter and protect. The record will tell too, that its perpetuity has been sealed by the holy rite of baptism in patriot and fraternal blood.

It is through such a year we have passed. It is through such events we still are passing; and although as *Freemasons,* and *here,* we will not enter upon any political discussion, yet we cannot, we dare not ignore the startling circumstances by which we are surrounded, or neglect to inquire in what manner, and to what extent, they are calculated to affect our mystic brotherhood. Leaving this high duty, however, to those to whom it properly belongs, we confine ourselves to the less important, but more pleasing task alloted us.

In the very first hour of our masonic career, we were taught the beautiful and salutary lesson, that no man should ever enter upon any great and important undertaking, without first invoking the blessing of the Deity.

---

*Address of John A. Lodor of Montgomery, Alabama, December 31, 1861.

This lesson commends itself to us as eminently right and proper. It enjoins a duty upon us we all recognize. It is the homage due from the creature to his Creator, and implies the corresponding truth, that He whose blessing is invoked *before* the commencement of any great enterprise, is also entitled to thanks *after* its performance. Recognizing these duties, it becomes particularly appropriate for us to return thanks to the Great Architect of the Universe, for the manifold blessings and comforts we have enjoyed during the year now past and gone. We thank Him that we have been spared, when so many have fallen like autumn leaves around us. We thank Him for the abundance we have enjoyed and shared with others, when so many around us were destitute and in want. We thank Him for the privilege of again assembling together in the capacity of a Grand Lodge, and of communing once more around the altar of our mystic temple. We thank Him that while our political sky has been covered with dark and lurid clouds, our beloved country convulsed and rent in twain, the soil of our native land bathed in fraternal blood, our masonic firmament has been calm, cloudless and serene, its pure atmosphere untainted by any fitful gust of passion, prejudice or fanaticism. We thank Him that while our national temple has crumbled to pieces before our eyes, and its constituent parts resolved into their original elements, our masonic temple still stands supported by Wisdom, Strength and Beauty, with its foundations unshaken, its symmetry perfect, and the sweet incense of gratitude yet ascends from our altar to Him in whom we put our trust.

The age we live in is progressive. The people among whom we dwell are utilitarian. They rush through life with reckless haste, chafing at the tardiness of railroad speed, and craving still greater rapidity for the electric telegraph. They pause but a moment in their career, to apply the practical test, *cui bono*, to everything under the sun, and unhesitatingly reject all that does not promise an immediate and lucrative recompense. Education, business, pleasure, preparation for usefulness and happiness, are all made subservient to the spirit of haste and the spirit of mammon. The slow, methodical and provident habits of our fathers are scoffed at with mockery and jest, while the impetuosity of Jehu commands unqualified approbation.

Such, in a word, is our age and our people, and such in the main, are their characteristics. There are some, however, who yet find time to step aside from the hurried duties and pleasures of active life, and enter our mystic temple, and learn with profit the lessons inculcated there.

On the wings of imagination they pass back through the long vista of departed years, until they reach that classic, nay, that holy land, immortalized in story and in song, in sacred and profane history. With path illumined by the sacred and historic page, they revel amid scenes of surpassing beauty and thrilling association, in which the gorgeous pictures of the Arabian Nights are equaled, and the brilliant vagaries of the opium eater are excelled. With Moses, from Mount Pisgah, they view the promised land overflowing with milk and honey —in the dim distance they behold the blue waves of Galilee, while upon the mountain tops the cedars of Lebanon rear their lofty summits high in the heavens.

They pause upon the brow of Mount Moriah to contemplate the magnificent temple there erected by King Solomon to the living God, and dedicated to His holy name. Its rare and matchless beauty—its massive and elaborate proportions—its faultless symmetry—its rich and costly material—its finished workmanship, all combine to give it more the appearance of being the handiwork of the Supreme Architect of the Universe than of human hands. Around and around it they wander, now advancing, now receding, they pause to scrutinize its most minute details from foundation to turret stone. Each separate part undergoes the severest criticism, and a fault or blemish is in vain sought for by the critic's eye. Its vaults and its arches—its gates and its porch—its massive brazen pillars, with its chapiters of lily, net and pomegranate work—its flight of winding stairs—its mosaic pavement with its tesselated border—its ground floor, middle chamber and sanctum sanctorum—its altar and ·its oracle—its cherubim with extended wings—its walls and ceiling of burnished gold—its folding doors with cherubim, palm trees and flowers, carved thereon—its windows, spires and domes—its outer courts, its inclosures and its walls, all pass before the scrutinizing gaze, and still, not an imperfection can be discovered. Separately or together, in parts or as a whole, in material or in workmanship, the investigation only discloses its surpassing beauty—its matchless perfection. Admiration gives place to wonder, and wonder to awe, as the conviction sinks deep in the heart, that *this* is indeed none other than the house of God.

The temple site is notable. High upon a mountain top, it commands an extensive range of vision over the lovely land of Judea, whose praise has been so often and so well sung by the bards of the Bible. From afar Mount Moriah was seen towering in the heavens, surmounted by the temple glittering in its effulgent splendor, a venerated landmark for the pilgrim Israelites, who periodically repaired from Dan to Beersheba, to celebrate the imposing ceremonies of their religion upon its hallowed summit. Upon its sides were groves of stately palms and fragrant bowers, where bloomed the peerless rose of

Sharon, while by Siloam's shady rill blossoms the lily of the valley. Here it was that Abraham erected an altar, and was about to offer his only son, a sacrifice upon it, typical of that other sacrifice afterward made upon it, the sublimest spectacle ever beheld by man, the crucifixion of the Son of God. Here too, it was, that David, the poet King of Israel, lived, died, and was buried. Here it was that Solomon dazzled the world with his wisdom, and left a name to be honored as long as time shall last. Jerusalem and the temple were the special objects of love, we had almost said idolatry of the Jews. The first was their holy city, the latter their house of God. As was the sepulchre to the Christian, the tomb of the prophet to the Moslemite, even so was the temple to the Jew.

The appointments of the temple were in perfect con sonance with its magnificence. A multitude of Levites of high and low degree were constantly engaged in its ministrations. The more than regal splendor of the high priest arrayed in his sacerdotal robes, the stately and imposing character of their forms and ceremonies, the inflexible rigor with which they were observed, the beautiful order and harmony with which the services of the temple were conducted, the number, variety and costliness of the holy vessels, the scrupulous care everywhere apparent, the habitual and universal reverence manifested by the Jews, all combine to command our admiration.

Viewing thus this magnificent edifice, remembering the beauty of its site, and the hallowed associations connected with it, we involuntarily pause to run a parallel between the Jews and ourselves; to compare their temple with ours, and thus to estimate the reverence each felt and manifested for the living God. Involuntary as is the act, the effect is most startling. In vain we cast our eyes around in search of a visible temple. In vain we look amid our piles of wood and stone, of marble and granite, for one whose form, or size, or beauty, will allow us, with all our partiality, to compare with that on Mount Moriah. So far, then, the evidence of love and devotion is with the Jews, and to them we must award the meed of praise. We attempt, however, to excuse ourselves for our omission, by the plea that we have no site on which to build, no quarries of stone, nồ forests of timber, no treasures of gold, silver, or precious stones, no hewers of wood or bearers of burdens, no craftsmen, or cunning workmen, with which to perform this arduous labor, no means with which to procure them, and therefore, we can erect no temple to our God, and make no dedication of it to His holy name. This is the natural, and almost involuntary excuse, and yet, like most pretexts set up for omitted or neglected duty, it is wholly insufficient; nay more, it is untrue. We have the site on which to build, higher and holier than Mount Moriah, in a lovelier clime than that of Judea, beneath a softer sky than that of Palestine. We have materials inexhaustible in quantity, and treasures of untold value. We have architects of wondrous skill. We have all the means at our command, and we should use them. We can erect a temple more spacious and magnificent than that of Solomon—one that time cannot effect, that barbarous force shall never destroy, that shall endure forever.

He whose voice we recognize in the whirlwind and the storm, in the gentle breeze that rustles the leaves above us, as well as in the muttering of the ocean wave, and pealing of the distant thunder, He hath said, in the great light that shines upon every altar, GIVE ME THY HEART. It was *there* we were first prepared to be masons, and *there,* in the human heart, with its atmosphere of love, its wealth of passion and feeling, its pure and lofty aspirations, its yearnings after immortality, beneath the sky of a terrestrial Paradise, we can erect a temple to our God, and dedicate it to His holy name.

As freemasonry was originally operative, but is now speculative in its character, even so, the temple we can build is not a visible one, composed of wood or stone, but is a spiritual, a speculative one—one composed of beautiful thoughts and acts, and adorned with still more beautiful virtues. A temple whose foundation is laid in Time, and whose superstructure continues in eternity; its base the purest morality; its elements the happy combination of all the virtues that adorn human nature; its loftiest pinnacle that unfeigned piety, so beautifully represented in Hiram, the widow's son.

Speculative as is freemasonry, and we love it for its speculative character, for its speaking emblems, and significant symbols, which open so wide the doors of thought, we yet hope it is not too speculative. We fondly trust we have not mistaken the boundless wealth of the human heart, or over estimated its capacity for earth or heaven, for time or for eternity. The whole range of science, literature and art, furnishes us no subject of study more interesting, more varied, or more beautiful than the heart, and yet, strange as it may appear, there is scarcely a subject we study less, or of which we know so little. We hardly pause to consider the wonderful precision and regularity with which its physical functions are performed, and still, sleeping or waking, in youth, manhood and age, it throbs and palpitates in cadence with the march of time, and only ceases to beat when the icy hand of death is laid upon it. We fail to comprehend that it has an empire and a ruler of its own, a ruler who often wields the sceptre with despotic sway, and by fostering the good, and curbing the evil passions, disciplines his realm into beautiful order, regularity and happiness, or who by casting loose the rein, gives unrestrained license to a horde of evil passions, and permits them, like an irruption of Goths and Vandals, to ravage, lay waste and destroy his fair dominions. We fail to realize the power of the passions, whose home is in the heart of man. Unseen, it may be, but still with resistless force, they drive us onward through the years of life. The heart, however, has its elysian fields, its sunny places, its shady groves, as well as its rugged rocks and unfathomable recesses. It has its springs of sweet and bitter water, its fountains of love as well as hatred, its fragrant flowers and luscious fruits, as well as its deadly upas tree; its fruitful fields, as well as its arid desert.

Like an æolian harp, it vibrates and responds to every breath of feeling and of passion. Subservient to a well regulated mind, its thousand strings are attuned to perfect harmony, and responsive to the power of friendship, love and truth, of sympathy, charity and gratitude, its low, sweet notes are heard, lingering like an angel's whisper on the ear, and anon swelling with delicious cadence into an anthem of praise, vibrating in other hearts, and ascending the electric scale of thought, through the realms of space, to the very throne of Omnipotence. When, however, unbridled passion rules the hour, and the fierce blast of the tempest and the storm is spent upon it, it responds only in discordant notes— fitful notes, in which are mingled the harsh voices of anger, envy and hatred; the wail of sorrow, the sharp cry of pain, the howl of agony, and the fearful shriek of despair.

As fire and water are useful servants, but wretched masters, even so are the passions to man. They are the motive power that propel him onward; the engine on the railroad of life. Subdued, their capacity for good is preserved, and their power for evil is divested. Thus regulated, we have at our command the power to press

onward and upward to high and noble ends, the power
to fulfill the destiny for which we were created.

The human heart may be compared to a rich garden.
There we find in abundance the sweetest fruits, most
fragrant flowers, and rarest exotics. With care and
labor, we can develop its wealth, and beauty and fra-
grance; without them, we shall have neither. They may
exist, it is true, but their growth will be checked and
stunted, their necessary nourishment be absorbed by nox-
ious weeds, which grow rapidly and luxuriantly in its
rich soil. These require neither care nor attention. They
flourish best by neglect; but as they grow and flourish
the sweetness of the fruit and the fragrance of the flower
diminish, and finally become extinct. As the permitted
growth of such weeds in a garden is injurious, if not fatal
to it, even so is the kindred growth in the heart of man.
They transform the purity and sweetness of Eden into
the barrenness and desolation of the desert.

Again, the human heart may be compared to a huge
folio, in which Truth writes the story of our lives, and
Memory photographs its every event. From the cradle
to the grave, not an incident is omitted; and in its suc-
cession of pictures not a shade of false coloring can be
found. As we turn over its pages, we pause, fascinated
by the sweet images representing our childhood, and our
childhood's home; the loved ones then around us, the
dear friends of our youth, our pleasures and sports,
our hopes and fears, our thoughts and feelings, all are
there—there, too, is the future of youth, bright with the
gilding of hope, and rich with the decorations of fancy.
As we again turn over its pages, how changed the pic-
ture! The boy is transformed into the man, with all the
man's associations, duties and responsibilities. We see
him eagerly engaged in the race of life, pursuing his fav-
orite phantom, wealth, pleasure, fame, or whatever it

may be. We note, too, that the pictures have lost that dreamy indistinctness characteristizing those of childhood, and acquired clear, bold, and decided lines. The color is deeper, and more solid, the general expression more harsh and unattractive. Still further onward, are pictures of a still more sombre hue. The bright coloring is almost gone; the decorations of fancy, no longer visible; the faces and forms of youthful friends are few and far between; the flowers faded; the leaves sere and yellow. The man, now old, leans heavily upon his staff, and his bent form and silvery locks tell their own story. Many and varied as are the pictures, the subject is still the same, and they form the panorama of human life. Truth has written the narrative impartially, and Memory illustrated it well. Chequered are its scenes as the mosaic pavement, and so changed from first to last we scarce can realize the fact that the venerable patriarchs who move so slowly and feebly before us were once young and happy children.

And yet again, the human heart is like the ocean, deep, boundless and illimitable. Its surface is another

Glorious mirror, where the Almighty's form
Glasses itself in tempests.

Moved by virtue, by high, pure principle, its waves softly undulate and with a gentle swell ebb and flow upon the beach of time. Beneath that surface are the coral caves, the Peri's home, where the gems of the sea are gathered together, and around them are the hidden reefs and rocks, like walls for their protection. Calm, placid and beautiful, as is the ocean at times, we yet know there is danger beneath its treacherous bosom—that the maelstrom has drawn many an unwary mariner within its vortex, and engulfed him in its unfathomable abyss— that the whirlwind's wrath, and the tempest's fury have marred its beauty, lashed its waves to madness, and gathered its waters into mighty, seething billows, which rolled on with resistless violence, making many a shipwreck upon its reefs and rocks. How sublime the ocean in its placid state! how terrible in its tempestuous wrath!

As is the ocean, so is the human heart. It has its glassy surface, its boundless extent, its hidden treasures, its gentle ebb and flow, and alas! it has its maelstrom, in which thousands of the unwary have been swallowed. Evil passions to it are the whirlwind's power that lashes its waves to frenzy, and makes shipwreck of temporal and eternal happiness upon its hidden rocks and reefs.

And still again, the human heart is like a mine of untold wealth. Deep within its recesses are vast beds and quarries of stone, strata upon strata, of every texture and quality. Here and there, are veins of glittering ore, surpassing in value the far famed gold of Ophir or of California. Here, too, may be found priceless gems, more brilliant and beautiful than the diamonds, rubies, emeralds and sapphires of any regal diadem. These beds of rock and stone are our ashlars in their native quarries; the ashlars we must bring to light, and make perfect by the tools of the fellow craft, as fitting stones for our speculative temple. Its priceless gems are the Cardinal Virtues; bright planets amid a galaxy of glittering stars; jewels of thought and action, which, if we but polish with the lapidary's care, are more brilliant and more beautiful, more, far more valuable, than the far famed Kohinoor, and all its kindred gems. It is with these we propose to ornament our speculative temple, and adorn and beautify it, with all that is costly and rare in the spiritual world.

The form, size, and character of our speculative temple, each of us must determine for himself. It may be massive and grand as Doric art; beautiful as Corinthian taste, or light, airy and elastic as the spider's web. Each of us is his own architect and builder. Each of us must select his own materials; fashion them for use, and use them; must place a keystone in the highest arch; a spire on the loftiest pinnacle; and sooner or later, must look fairly and squarely at the sum total of his own labor, and calculate its true value as our speculative temple, erected to God, and dedicated to His holy name.

No apprentice's zeal or fellow craft's skill is sufficient here. It requires all the master's knowledge and ability. His great trestle board lies open upon our altar, and from its speaking pages he may gather WISDOM from on high, to guide him in his glorious undertaking; STRENGTH commensurate with his task, to support him—strength to labor and endure, to persevere unto the end. With these, and the liberal arts and sciences at his command; with industry, skill, and the experience of cunning workmen, surely his speculative temple will rise in all the splendor of artistic BEAUTY, and be "a thing of joy forever."

The erection of our speculative temple is a matter of vital importance. However faithfully and zealously we may labor; however skillful and expert we may be in the use of our tools and implements, we must not forget that it requires the more consummate wisdom, and greater experience of the master builder. It is not the work of an hour, a day, or a year; it requires time, patience and perseverance, perhaps for years, to build it. The Jewish temple required an army of workmen, who were engaged seven years in its erection. Physiologists tell us, our physical temple is periodically reconstructed in the same length of time. With us, the time necessary to form *a fixed and permanent character*—the character we bear through life, among our fellow men—the character we must bear through the countless ages of eternity—that is the time occupied in the erection of our speculative tem ple. Indeed and in truth, human character is our tem-

ple. We may disguise it as we will; we may evade a
scrutiny of it; but *our character* as *it is,* with its faults
and blemishes, its weaknesses and infirmities, its vices
and its stains, together with its redeeming traits, its better
parts, is our speculative temple. Again we repeat, it is
for each of us to look well upon it—to weigh it, and real-
ize its just value.

If the proposition heretofore made be true, that we
can erect a temple more spacious and magnificent than
that of Solomon; if it be further true, that human char-
acter is that temple, then it follows necessarily that it
should be pure, spotless, and irreproachable; combining
the innocence of childhood and the wisdom of age; that
it should approximate perfection as near as the frailties
of human nature will allow. We know that perfection
on earth has never been attained; that the wisest as well
as the best of men have erred; and yet, with an abiding
faith in Him in whom we put our trust—before whose
altar we bend the knee; whose name we never mention,
but with that reverential awe due from a creature to his
Creator; and whose aid we implore in all our laudable
undertakings, we should make the effort to attain it.
Our speculative temple should ascend in all the glittering
splendor of Friendship, Morality, and Brotherly Love,
and shine, not with meteor glare, but bright, steady,
planetary light, winning the reverence and love of every
beholder by its elegance, its purity, and its worth. Like
the exemplar temple on Mount Moriah, it should be pre-
served as a hallowed shrine, and guarded with the same
vigilant care. It should be our pearl of price, set round
with walls and inclosures, even as was the Jewish tem-
ple, and the impure, the vicious, the guilty and profane,
be banished from even its outer courts. A faithful sen-
tinel should be placed at every gate, a watchman on

every wall, and the first approach of the cowan and eaves-
dropper be promptly met and resisted.

With the erection of our temple, but half our duty is
performed. It must be dedicated and set apart for its
appropriate use. And here how widely we differ in the
dedication of *our* temple. No holy day is set apart; no
gathering of the multitude; no army assembles with
gleaming spears and waving banners; no horsemen and
chariots of war; no beating drums, or pealing of artil-
lery; no pomp and ceremony; no sacrifice of oxen and of
sheep; no burnt offering; no meat offering; no peace
offering; no feasting or revelry solemnizes the occasion;
but in silence, it may be in solitude, in deep humility, in
all our sinfulness and unworthiness, with penitence and
prayer, we humbly dedicate our heart, our spiritual, our
speculative temple, to the Great Jehovah, King of Kings,
and Lord of Lords. It thus becomes a consecrated place,
requiring only a high priest to minister at its altar, and
perform its solemn ceremonies.

The selection of our high priest is a matter of the
gravest importance. We have no tribe of Levi, from
which the choice can be made, but we have a greater
than the Levite, in Emmanuel, the Prince of Peace, the
great I AM, to whom we dedicate our temple; to whom,
and whom alone, in his triune character of Prophet,
Priest and King, we bend the knee, and render the hom-
age of our heart of hearts. With the Omnipotent for our
high priest; with Faith, and Hope, and Charity, together
with all the bright virtues that dignify and ennoble
human character, as its lesser ministers, we may rest
assured, if we are but true to ourselves, the service of
our speculative temple will be no less beautiful than
pure; no less pure than holy.

Our speculative temple erected, and at least nominally
dedicated to the living God, it may not be an unprofita-

ble lesson to learn at whose altar we in truth are worshipping. "Know thyself," was the injunction of a heathen philosopher, given as the most difficult duty for man to perform; and yet, it is no less than this we must do, to realize the just value of our temple, and the identity of our altar. We have an aid, however, in Truth, who holding her mirror before us, bids us examine for ourselves. She strips off the flimsy coverings with which we have deluded ourselves; shows us that our foundation is laid on sand; indicates the faulty materials; points out its want of symmetry and beauty; and exposes the almost utter worthlessness of our speculative temple; then entering the edifice, she remorsely presses home upon us the humiliating fact that we have hushed the still small voice of conscience; displaced the faithful tiler from our temple door, and tolerated impostors at our altars; impostors who have assumed the sacerdotal robes and place of our great High Priest, and desecrated our speculative temple, by offering sacrifices to Moloch, Mammon and Baal, or it may be, to Venus or Bacchus. Impostors

> Who stole the livery of the court of Heaven,
> To serve the Devil in.

If such should be the result of self-investigation; if our Faith be weak and wavering; our Hope faint and feeble; our Charity palsied; our Brotherly Love cold and formal; if no Relief be extended to the suffering and distressed; no word of sympathy poured like balm on wounded hearts; if Truth be not the principle on which we act; if Temperance be but a license to commit irregularities and excesses; if Prudence characterize not our lives and actions; if we have not Fortitude to bear the adversities incident to human life; if Justice has been tutored to kick the beam in our favor, and never against us, we may be satisfied the foundation of our speculative temple is not well laid; our corner stone not well formed, true and trusty; that our ashlars were unwisely selected and negligently prepared; our edifice unskillfully erected; our jewels tarnished and lustreless. Then may we be likened unto the foolish man which built his house upon the sand; and the rain descended, and the floods came, and the winds blew, and beat upon that house, and it fell; and great was the fall of it.

And here, perhaps, it is proper we should advert to an error that prevails in reference to the object and aim of Freemasonry. By many it is considered as synonymous with Christianity, and then utterly condemned for failing to come up to that high standard of excellence. Christianity, however, is of divine, while Masonry is of human origin. Christianity is a matter pertaining to Eternity as well as Time, while Masonry is a thing of Time only. The moral teachings of both are the same. The one as applicable to Time *and* Eternity; the other as applicable to Time alone. As the hour is merged in the day, and the day in the year, even so is time lost and blended in eternity, although an integral portion of it. Within its appropriate sphere, Masonry is an invaluable adjunct to Christianity. The panoply of Christianity is broad enough to cover every mason on earth; that of Masonry, though a broad one, merely places its votaries in that position, where by advancing a few steps, they pass from the Altar to the Cross. The duties of the one end with the grave; of the other, a preparation here, for the endless cycle beyond it. It was well said "that the best mason makes the best christian, and the best christian makes the best mason."

Masonry is characterized by its universality, and yet the *individuality* of every mason is still preserved. In the church, the lodge, and other kindred bodies, the individual too often acts as though he had no character; as though by membership he had surrendered it, and retained only an undivided interest, a portion of its general character. He acts as though it was not incumbent upon him to maintain and preserve the high purity of character of the body to which he belongs. Every individual *has* a distinct character of his own, and yet it is *an integral* part of the universal character. Every mason should assiduously labor to preserve his own individuality; should give plain, clear and unmistakable marks of his own separate existence; should make his own ˋ

Footprints on the sands of time;

should *act* as though the universal character was exemplified and illustrated by his own; should *feel* as if all the responsibility rested upon himself alone, and thus, and thus only, will its exalted character be sustained. It is no excuse for one, that another fails to do his duty. It is no excuse, even though all others fail to do so. Sodom was destroyed because ten righteous men were not found in it. There the individual was merged in the general character—character so stained by iniquity as to excite the wrath of the Almighty in a manner so terrible as to be a warning forever.

No man should ever be allowed to enter our fraternity *in search of character;* on the contrary, he should bring character to its support. It is not mere familiarity with the minutiæ of masonic language and ceremonies that forms masonic character. That is but the drapery with which it is clad; the casket in which the jewel is set. That character is *the habit of life;* the same everywhere; at home and abroad; in the lodge, and in the world. It is evidenced by the fountains that gush forth from the heart, pure, sparkling and free; by the fraternal love, that glows like a live coal upon the altar; by the attentive ear, ever open to the cry of distress; by the fraternal hand extended to succor and to save; by the instructive tongue that promptly utters words of wisdom, sympathy and caution. The true mason strives to fulfill his duties to his God, his neighbor and himself, not with, but without ostentation. It is thus our speculative temple should rise, like its beautiful exemplar on Mount Moriah, where

> No hammers fell, no ponderous axes rung;
> Like some tall palm, the mystic fabric sprung.

It is these, and such as these, who bring and give character to a Lodge. It is these, and such as these, who are the perfect ashlars in our temple. It is these, and such as these, who have erected a speculative temple, in all the splendor of spiritual beauty, in their hearts, more spacious and magnificent than that of Solomon, and dedicated it to the living God. A temple that time cannot affect—that barbarous force shall never destroy—that shall endure forever.

High as we have attempted to raise the standard of Freemasonry, we trust it is not too high. We fondly hope there are many who have attained the full stature of Masonic manhood—we trust there are many such within the precincts of this Grand Lodge, many, who with a modesty equal to that of the violet, would blush to have their merit known. If my honored and revered friend and brother, the M. W. Grand Master,* he at whose command, long years ago, we first beheld the rays of masonic light, and at whose feet we sat, even as did the student at the feet of Gamaliel, was absent, we might say much of his merit as a neighbor, a friend, a man, and a mason. We would that we could add, as a christian, but as he is present, it would be indelicate to

*M. W. WM. H. NORRIS.

say anything in his praise, and we have nothing else to say.

Here we might appropriately close, hoping, trusting and believing the foundation of our speculative temple is laid upon the "Rock of Ages"—with its superstructure faultlessly symmetrical, and radiant with beauty—its materials incorruptible, and its ministrations marked by simplicity, fervor, and devotion; but we cannot resist the temptation to trace the parallel yet a little further.

Josephus informs us, the destruction of Jerusalem and its celebrated temple was preceded by many events, so remarkable in their character, the narrative seems almost fabulous. He tells us, that at the feast of Pentecost, as the priests were entering the inner courts of the temple, to perform their usual ceremonies, the earth was felt to quake—a mighty noise was heard, and the voices, as of a multitude, saying LET US DEPART HENCE! LET US DEPART HENCE!

He also tells us, that at a time when the city was surrounded by peace and prosperity—when no dark cloud appeared to threaten approaching danger, one Jesus, the son of Ananus, as with a prophetic foreboding, of the awful, impending fate of the holy city, began of a sudden to cry aloud, "A voice from the east, a voice from the west, a voice from the four winds, a voice against Jerusalem and the holy house, a voice against the bridegrooms and the brides, and a voice against this whole people!" By day and night, at the temple, in the city, through its streets and lanes, and upon its walls, he ever uttered his mournful refrain. When taken before the Roman procurator as a disturber of the peace, and scourged until his very bones lay bare, his only answer was, "Woe, woe to Jerusalem!" Dismissed as a madman, absorbed in his own gloomy anticipations, and insensible alike to the kindness of those who cared for, and the cruelty of those who maltreated him, he continued to wander around, ever chanting his melancholy song. At length, when more than seven years had passed since first his warning voice was raised, when peace had departed, and prosperity given place to the horrors of war—when Roman legions environed the city, and the engines of war hurled missiles of destruction against its ramparts, he still stood upon the wall, and uttered for the last time his melancholy prediction, "Woe, woe to the city again, to the people, and to the holy house!" then pausing a moment, he added, as though conscious of his own impending death, "Woe, woe to myself!" Scarcely were the words uttered, when he was killed by a stone from one of the Roman engines. His mission was ended. His allotted task performed. Through long years of derision, mockery and abuse, his warning voice was raised like that of the Grecian Cassandra, only to be disregarded. Like the dying swan, his sweetest note was his last, for when uttered, his troubled spirit was at rest.

Let the skeptic sneer, and the scoffer rail—let them deride the idea, if they will, that

> Coming events cast their shadows before;

we still prefer to indulge in the pleasing delusion, if indeed it be one, that the voices thus heard by the priests were the voices of the guardian angels of the temple, consulting together ere they plumed themselves for their lofty flight, and abandoned the magnifcent temple, so soon to be laid in ashes, and which had been erected in happier days, under brighter auspices, by King Solomon, and dedicated to the living God.

Shall we, my brethren, when our priests retire to the inner courts of our speculative temple, shall we hear the fluttering of angel wings—the murmuring of angel voices, deliberating ere they abandon it forever? Shall we be insensible to the symbols and emblems by which we are ever surrounded? Shall the anointed priest from the altar, and the beloved dead from the grave, utter no note of warning in our ear? Shall we be heedless and indifferent, as were the Jews to the voice of Jesus, the son of Ananus? Forbid it! oh, forbid it, Supreme Grand Master! We know but too well, our physical temple, like its prototype on Mount Moriah, will soon be laid in dust and ashes; but still we would not have our guardian angels depart and leave us to our fate. We would have them ever present, infusing spiritual life, and light, and hope within us, that we may be enabled to discard the dim light of reason, or religion of nature, which teaches us that man dies as the beast, and at his death there is no more of him—as well as that other creed, which inculcates the idea of the resurrection of the soul, but not of the body; and firmly relying on the merits of the Lion of the tribe of Judah, espouse that beautiful faith which teaches the immortality of the body as well as the soul. With such hopes as these, such faith as this, surely our speculative temple, like Elijah of old, may be transplanted from this vale of tears, to the New Jerusalem, that beautiful City of God, not made with hands, eternal in the heavens.

LIFE'S EVERYDAY AFFAIRS.

The public is awakening to the important part insurance in its various - adaptations plays in its everyday affairs. More and more is it coming to be recognized as a necessary provision against the uncertainties of the future. While the sentimental considerations which move people to make provision for their dependents are not losing their force, these are taking a more practical turn and are but evidencing that sentiment of itself possesses but little value financially. It must be coupled with deeds which show that protestations in this way are supported by more than idle words.

A promising development in this form of economics is in the line of education. Colleges and universities and the Young Men's Christian Associations are providing courses of lectures calculated to inform people on the principles and needs of insurance protection. This will in time produce most wholesome results. It involves a wider interest in the fundamental principles upon which this proposition rests. It causes the people to think and plan in harmony with them. It awakens heads of families and others to a realization of their responsibilities and their duties.

An unfortunate situation exists in this connection with reference to the fraternal system. The old line interests have not been slow in grasping the opportunities which have been placed before them. They have provided these universities and colleges and associations with speakers whose duty it is to emphasize sound doctrines and to enunciate fundamental principles. Naturally, these being disciples of a given system, their views are largely molded by the cause of which they are exponents. They, in con-

sequence, are not over-zealous in the way of according
to the fraternal system the full meed of credit to which it
is entitled.

It is believed that fraternal leaders are short-sighted
in this direction. It is believed that it is highly important
for them to see that the cause with which they are identi-
fied is granted a full and complete hearing. Fraternalism
is based upon principles as enduring and as beneficent
as are those of any other system. Its exponents need
not feel called upon to explain or apologize for their
temerity in insisting that it is one of the most potent
factors to-day in making provision for the future of the
dependents of those who have reposed their interests to
its keeping.

The public affords the field from which the societies
recruit their members. Such field should be cultivated
painstakingly. No opportunity to enrich it should be
ignored. No point of vantage in the way of shedding
light on the plans and accomplishments of the system
should be overlooked. As much care should be taken in
this ·direction as in any other from which results are
expected. If this is not done, it follows that in time a
feeling of indifference and possible antagonism may be
developed—a condition to be most earnestly guarded
against.

Neglect brings in its wake results of a cumulative
nature just as effectively as does earnest and intelligent
effort bring that in which it is enlisted to a successful
issue. If opportunities to show that the fraternal system
is a growing and enduring one are not embraced; if its
opponents are permitted to assume that they are the only
ones worth while in this direction; if public thought is
so molded that it looks upon fraternal societies as tem-
porary and temporizing expedients—it is repeated, if
such ends are permitted to be accomplished, an unfortun-

ate situation will have developed for the fraternal system. For this reason, if for no other, fraternal exponents should be alive to their opportunities and should insist that they have an equal opportunity to present their cause for the consideration of those who are now and who may hereafter be interested in this subject.

We should build for a broader and greater fraternalism. Too long have we been reviewing the defects of early operation. These may be found in any system or any undertaking. They seem to be a necessary part of early and pioneer work. Time works many changes and it solves many problems. There is danger, during a period of transition, of going too far. In one's endeavor to correct error or abuse, it is possible that the pendulum swing too far and that unnecessary conditions be exacted. It is possible that a system or an institution be built along such rigid lines that it does not possess that flexibility so necessary to meet the ever-changing conditions which present themselves.

Fraternal exponents should eschew provincialism in the conduct of the affairs entrusted to them. They should build on broad lines. They should endeavor to see that the seedtime is just as properly cared for as is the harvest. If this is not done the latter will not be satisfactory. The seedtime to-day is in the way of acquainting the public with what fraternalism has done and can do. The same avenues for publicity which are open to the companies are within the reach of the societies. They should see that the educational institutions of the land be made familiar with the principles of fraternalism when presented on the basis of adequate rates. They are losing an important vantage point when they permit the insurance companies to become the sole possessors of this field.

TOWARD A HIGHER STANDARD

It is a fixed rule of nature that everything must have a small beginning. Man himself, the greatest of all crea tions, exemplifies this fact. Left to himself at his entrance upon life he would speedily perish; without the minis- trations of gentle, loving hands he could offer but feeble resistance to the rude shocks which attend every phase of his development; without assistance and encouragement in later years he would fall an easy victim to the snares and pitfalls which lie in wait for him. In brief, man by himself is a picture of perfect helplessness. It is by com- ing in contact with others, by seeing their attainments, and by cultivating the spirit of emulation, to be at least an equal with them, that he makes progress and attains a higher social, moral and financial altitude.

And so it is with the institutions of human creation. A spring cannot rise higher than its source; an institu- tion cannot reflect greater purposes than are in the minds of those conducting it. There must ever be a community of interests and a harmonious blending of these for mutual aggrandizement and to attain praiseworthy ends.

In no channel are the salutary ends encompassed by united, joint action better exemplified than in the con- text of fraternalism. The keystone in this great human arch is progress. Man is not satisfied with his present environments. He is a social creature, and he wants to come in contact with his fellow man on a plane from which spring mutual sympathies and interests. Hence the society and the lodgeroom. He realizes that the future is fraught with great uncertainty. He wants to make provision for this. He cannot do it alone, as he has no assurance that he will live to see the consumma- tion of his efforts. Hence an amplification of the lodge whereby the many come to the rescue of the few who are distressed. The bond of fraternal union is thus cemented and all are benefited alike.

The foregoing is a most crude exposition of fraternal effort. It was made so advisedly. It is but in keeping with our remarks at the outstart, to the effect that everything, including man himself, has a small and humble beginning. It is within the memory of many fraternalists now at life's zenith when practical fraternalism first took root on American soil. We have seen it sprout, burst the clod and enter upon a most uncertain future. The ills incident to its childhood have been many and perplexing. It did not have the light of experience to guide it. Rather, it had to blaze its own way, and it had to ever contend with avowed hostility from without and false prophets from within. Only its inherent vitality saved it from premature death and decay.

Fraternalism to-day may be said to have attained its majority. It has reached that point in its history from which it can study its past with profit and contemplate the future with complacency. It no longer has to give an excuse for its existence. It has earned for itself through its benefactions a reputation that is world-wide. It has enshrined itself in the memories of hundreds of thousands of widows and orphans, whose burdens it has mitigated and whose hunger it has relieved. It is to-day the hope and mainstay of millions more. Every week it is disbursing fully a million dollars to the bereaved and fatherless. It has gathered and strewn the incomprehensible sum of one thousand millions of dollars since its inception—and, as has been said, it has but attained its majority.

Reader, can you see any points of comparison between the birth, development and growth of mankind and that of fraternalism? We have no difficulty in seeing many.

And, as man has steadily evoluted toward a higher stand-
ard, so will our beloved cause. The same elements which
induce progress in one will produce like results in the
other. The same elements of evil and decay have to be
guarded against. They go hand in hand. Both may be
improved, it will be admitted, but thus far nothing super-
ior has made its appearance.

THE FRATERNAL RESPONSE

The onward march of fraternalism is at once the pride
of those associated with it and the marvel of those who
view it from afar. Owing its origin to a demand for pro-
tection that would protect without being burdensome, it
naturally sought its adherents among those in the hum-
bler walks of life—those who realized the need of a help
ing hand and an encouraging word when the finger of
Providence rested heavily upon them and those who had
entrusted their future to them. It appealed to a respon-
sive chord in the human heart. Its high aims and
unswerving purposes ever stood between it and the shafts
of hostile forces, and thus its early mistakes—mistakes
which might have been fatal to systems of frailer mold
and less enduring vitality—merely dropped from it as
growths having nothing in common with it, while the
body politic grew and expanded with that world conquer-
ing power which brooks neither restraint nor retrogres-
sion.

Could one compare the system of to-day with that of
ten years ago, without knowing anything as to the leaven
of evolution which has been working ceaselessly and tire-
lessly, he would be amazed at the strides which have been
taken. He would be at a loss to understand how such a
transformation could take place short of an actual revolu-

tion. He would be constrained to inquire, in what manner can a system of such vast and far-reaching interests adapt itself so closely to the actual needs of its wide constituency?

A review of the progress of this country discloses equally as surprising results. But a few years ago the Monroe Doctrine was the unwritten law of the land. We were adjured to avoid all entangling alliances, to remain at home, live and die separate and removed from the rest of the world. This was a most beautiful theory, but it lacked one vital factor—progress. It failed to realize that destiny, fixed and inscrutable, crushes opposition before it as relentlessly as does the Car of Juggernaut; that we may theorize and contrive as we will, there is a fixed rule in the order of creation, and that when the time comes for this to assert itself all objections disappear; that America, despite its oft-expressed wishes to the contrary, has become a world-power and hereafter must accept her share of the benefits and perils brought to view on the international chess-board.

And so it is with fraternalism. Its opponents declare it to have been crude, unscientific and inequitable. It responded by remedying the defects which have been found in its context. They have urged objections against it, some of which possessed force, while others could be traced directly as the vaporings arising from avowed hostility. Valid objections have been received thoughtfully and good has resulted from their consideration. The good has been separated from the dross—and this process is one which is going steadily on and, beyond peradventure, will continue so long as the system is under the direction of man. So long as he continues striving toward the light it is safe. When he thinks he has attained perfection it will be in most imminent peril.

Fraternalists could not, were they so inclined, evade the great responsibilities which have been thrust upon them. Their marvelous success in the past has made their cause a world-power. They must meet the issue. Like our country itself, the haven fraternalism affords makes it the Mecca toward which those who wish to better their position are looking. It would be cowardly to evade the issue. It would be suicidal to shrink from the beckoning finger of Destiny. The orders must continue the onward march they have mapped out. They must extend the helping hand to those now not within the confines of the fold. They must proceed cautiously and withal firmly. Past successes must not intoxicate them; future problems must not dishearten them.

CHANGE A SIGN OF PROGRESS

Many folks are so constituted as to oppose all changes instinctively, and such folks usually call themselves con servatives. But proper changes are a sign, and also a condition, of progress. The constitution of these United States was at the time of its adoption probably the highest expression of political wisdom which the world had known—yet in the brief space of our national existence it has been amended no less than fifteen times. Why? Because either our national charter must be amended, or it would become our national straight-jacket. The particular changes which time and experience might make necessary could not be foreseen, but the probable need of change could be, and so the constitution—our fundamental, organic law—was made elastic, and contained provisions for its own amendment. Likewise the organic law of the fraternal system provides for change, and the means is a referendum or popular vote. Now, the standard is to be advanced, for time and experience have shown the imperfections, have shown, too, that they must be remedied, and reflection will develop the proper remedy to apply. You can help in this work, or you can hinder, but you cannot prevent it. With you or without you the system will move on. It is "kismet"—fate.

As to the officers, to whom will be entrusted *ex officio* the devising of the remedy in each particular case, you should trust them and loyally uphold their hands. When they tell you that your order needs more money, and how much more to be able to carry out its contracts—yours among the rest—you may make up your mind that it is true. They have at least as much loyalty to the order as you have yourself, as great an interest in its permanence and success; their official position and its responsibilities give them a better knowledge and a keener appreciation of the subject. These men are not frauds. On the contrary, in honesty and courage and brains they are easily the peers of any body of insurance men in the world. In most cases they are the successors of men who started wrong, the inheritors of a system whose imperfections most of them were quick to recognize, but imperfections which, in the absence of concerted action, it has always been beyond their power to cure.

WOMEN IN THE WORLD'S WORK *

A modern writer has said that "the advancement of a nation is measured by the place it accords to its women" and again "history shows that no nation can enslave its women, but it ensures its own barbarism." Every nation

---

*Address delivered by Miss Emma E. Bower before the National Fraternal Congress at its 1908 session.

owes much to its women, and the student of history clearly perceives that the advancement of a nation is marked by the progress of its women.

To attempt to speak within the limits of this paper of all women who have contributed to the world's work would be to undertake an impossible task. To even mention all the women who have done so much to help in the betterment of our own land would take us far beyond the time assigned us, but we will endeavor to sketch briefly something of the work that is being done to-day by the women of America, and let me say in the beginning, that in speaking of the women who are helping in the public life of the world's work, we do not wish for one moment to be understood as inferring that they are the only women who contribute to the work of the world. There is no nobler work in life than that that is being done every day, quietly, unostentatiously, willingly, by the great army of privates in the service, the mothers, wives and sisters of mankind who are "serving well the world" without expectation or desire for public recognition, "the home-makers" of life without whom life would not very long exist. They have always been, they will ever be, the heart of the nation, the keeper of the light that guides the weary mariner home. They need no longer feel that there is never for their sex any other vocation in life, for the day has long gone by when there were only two alternatives open to the mass of womankind, marriage (which meant usually domestic service) or domestic service without marriage. It is a far cry from the freedom of women in this day and age with its diversities of occupation and its diversity of opportunities, to that dark past when they were only the burden bearers and yet a cynic might say that they were never more the burden bearers than to-day. But it is burden bearing with a difference or interpretation. It is as much of a difference as the contrast between the work of a bondsman and a free man. "Bobby Burns," the "poet of the people," has sung of "the blessed privilege of being independent," and that privilege is just as dear to the heart of every true woman as it is to the heart of every true man.

There has never been a time since the world began when women have not had a part in its history, from the Garden of Eden (which most certainly had a woman in it) down to the time when the only perfect man born of woman lived and wrought His matchless work upon this sin-stained and selfish world, and the truest of His followers were women. Men were His professed disciples, but men also betrayed Him. No woman's voice, thank God, was lifted against Him in His hour of trial. She was the last at the cross and first at the sepulchre, and His church to this day is most largely maintained by her self-sacrifice and labor.

History could not well have been written and her name omitted, for from the beginning of time, it has been pretty generally conceded that a woman is usually at the bottom of most things. It is gratifying to reflect that in this enlightened age she is also frequently at the top as well and often in the middle.

Time when the phrase "woman's sphere" meant that she was to be confined within the four walls of what was too often not a "home" in the true sense of the word and that beyond its confines she was not to go. Her "sphere" meant a round of cooking, mending, scrubbing and other (so called) "feminine employments." Her "sphere" is still round, but is larger around than it used to be and it has an outside to it. We like the word "sphere" It means a perfect symmetrical "whole" and when a woman's influence and woman's work shall have reached their climax, we shall hear no more of woman's sphere than we shall hear of woman's rights or any other out worn phrases of man's inventive brain. There will be no competition between the sexes, as there never should have been. Women are rapidly proving that they were not created to be either man's inferior or his superior, but his equal. When "equal rights" shall have superseded "woman's rights" there will be no "taxation without representation," therefore no tyranny and no slavery of white or black.

Why it is to a woman now, that the title of the "First citizen of Chicago" is applied? And when recently at the great child labor convention held in the city of Cincinnati, Jane Addams entered Music Hall, where a gathering of more than twenty thousand people were assembled to listen to Senator Beveridge and other eminent speakers, she got an ovation from the audience (equally composed of men and women) not accorded to any other speaker on the platform, and why? Because she was a woman? No, but because of her work. It is not without cause that this quiet and unassuming woman, who has devoted her brilliant talents to the betterment of mankind, is called the "first citizen of Chicago," although she has not a vote to cast at a presidential (or any other) election.

Let us recall the names of a few of the women who have helped in the world's work in our own century and in our own land, those whose names have gathered world wide fame and lustre, not because they were women, but because in spite of being disfranchised citizens, they yet did a great work for public welfare and for every name I mention there are three score more who have helped in the ranks of the army of which their sister-women were officers. Shining as stars in the dark night of the history of slavery and the Civil War are the names of Lucretia Mott, Clara Barton, Lydia Maria Child, Dorothea Dix, Marie Chapman, Sophia C. Hoffman and hundreds of others whose lives were as truly given to their country's service as ever was that of any man who wore the blue and fought in the front of battle.

In the world of letters, Margaret Fuller, D. Ossoli, Harriet Beecher Stowe, Julia Ward Howe, Catharine M. Sedgwick, Adeline S. Whitney, Louise M. Alcott, Elizabeth Stuart Phelps, are but few of the older writers, and we all know those of the present day, the magic of whose pen has helped us through the drudgery of life.

Our women poets, the Cary sisters, Lucy Larcom, Celia Thaxter, Elizabeth Akers Allen, Charlotte Stetson, and that inspired modern prophetess of the New Thought, Ella Wheeler Wilcox, who shall say that the measure of their help to weary hearts can ever be gauged in words?

In the field of science which (as some writer has said) "knows no sex," the names of women shine with equal radiance. At the head of the list perhaps stands the name of Maria Mitchell, whose contributions to the cause of science are too well known to need comment. Elizabeth Aggasiz, Antoinette Brown Blackwell, Grace Anna Lewis, these are but a few of the women who have made their mark in the scientific world, and contributed to the history of the century. If we shall go abroad and speak of Madam Curie, the discoverer of radium; Miss Herschell, the great astronomer, and other gifted women who have helped their fathers, husbands or brothers to add to the store of human knowledge, our list would be too long to enumerate. Miss Dorothea Klumpe, the famous California astronomer who was the first woman to gain a degree of doctor of mathematics in France, has a special building of her own in the Great Observatory Garden of Paris. One of her duties is to photograph the stars in that section of the heavens known as the Paris belt. For this purpose she makes frequent balloon ascensions.

In the world of art are Harriet Hosmer, May Alcott, Emily Sartin and others. On the lecture platform, Mary A. Livermore, Anna F. Dickinson, Abby Kelley Foster; among women reformers, Elizabeth Cady Stanton, Lucy Stone, Susan B. Anthony, Francis Dora Gage, Frances Willard. These are but a few of the American women who have given their lives and their talents to the advancement of the world's work, the cause of women's emancipation and the abolition of all forms of slavery.

In the educational world, the names of Elizabeth Pea body, Catherine Beecher, Mary Lyon, Lucinda Hinsdale Stone (the mother of Woman's Clubs in Michigan and the first woman in that state to advocate co-education) come to us all as household words. Besides these the great army of women teachers, women deans of universities and colleges and women writers on educational subjects are literally "too numerous to mention."

In the business world women are as much of a necessity in these days as men and are about as numerous.

True, we have no women at the head of great corporations or trusts and it is to be hoped we never shall have, but such women as Rebecca Motte, Susanna Wright, Emily Ringler, Hetty Green, Helen Gould and many others have proven their ability to conduct their large business affairs as capably as any man.

The question has been sneeringly asked in the past— Did a woman ever invent anything? Can a woman invent? Let us see. The cotton gin, the invention of which revolutionized the industries of the world was due to a woman, Mrs. Green, although the patent was taken out in the name of Eli Whitney. One of the earliest mowing machines was invented by a woman and patented by a man. At the Centennial Exhibition there were gathered in the woman's pavilion hundreds of useful articles invented by women, but patented by men. The largest foundry in the city of Troy run to manufacture horse shoes and turning out one every three seconds, owes the invention of the machine which does the work, to a woman. The first large establishment in the country for the manufacture of buttons was due to a woman's brain, although run by a man. A woman invented the self-fastening button, also the satchel buttoned paper bag. A New Jersey woman invented the attachment to a mowing machine whereby the knives are thrown out of position when the driver leaves his seat, thus lessening the liability of accident. Elevators, lubricating felt for car wheels, (a most important invention), volcanic furnaces for smelting ore, steamer screws, machinery for cotton factories, wood sawing machines, musical instruments, syllable type, submarine telescopes, looms capable of doing the work of three ordinary looms are among the various inventions of women of this country which have been patented and exhibited as the work of man. Most of the designs for carpets, oil cloths, calicos and wall paper are woman's work, also designs for embossing of paper, monograms, etc. Women have invented sewing machines, (patented and sold by men) and almost every kind of household appliance. They are printers, sculptors, taxidermists, engravers, architects, designers and there is almost no profession of the present day which has not its women exponents, all doing good work in their chosen field. There are lawyers, physicians, dentists, preachers, missionaries, settlement workers and bankers. In Washington Arcade, Detroit, there is a woman's bank run entirely by women. There are no women prize fighters, jockeys, professional executioners, no women football professionalists, etc., etc. No women in Wall Street causing panics for which the world suffers.

Not long ago I read of a woman being arrested and fined for wearing "jumpers" in the discharge of her duties as a bricklayer. Why it should be any more indecent to wear jumpers than to wear tights upon the vaudeville stage, or at public exhibitions of any sort, the judge who imposed the fine did not say, but the ways of the law (so called) are like the ways of Providence, "mysterious and past finding out."

Out in New England, women with brains and artistic tastes have taken the hideous rag carpet of olden times and evolved from it the most beautiful and softly colored rugs and portieres. Some one asked one of the great painters of the world what he mixed his colors with and he replied "with brains." Women of to-day are mixing their work along all lines "with brains" and the result is a raising of the standard of all kinds of work.

Two of the greatest religious movements of the present age have women at their head, namely Christian Science with Mrs. Mary Baker Eddy, and the famous Theosophical Settlement at Point Loma, California, with Mrs. Katherine G. Tingley, one of the most remarkable women of the age.

A woman, Mrs. Cynthia Westover Alden of New York, is the founder of the wonderful International Sunshine Society which has a membership of nearly 40,000 with branches in every part of the world from the United States to Japan and Spain. It is a society incorporated under the laws of the State of New York, thoroughly organized, possesses a constitution (of iron), by-laws and all the paraphernalia of modern organization, yet without an inch of red tape in its make-up and absolutely free of any taint of selfishness or politics. Mrs. Alden also invented a street cleaning machine which was adopted and used in the city of New York while she was commissioner of street cleaning and Inspector of Immigration.

Women are printers, historians, librarians, travelers, agriculturists, light-house keepers, burnishers of gold and silver, electro platers and bronzers, watchcase makers, (and some of the finest parts of the best watches are made by women).

Time was when women kept house indoors, now they keep house in the whole out-of-doors. Witness the wonderful work in the cause of civic reform which has been done by such women as Rev. Caroline Bartlett Crane of Kalamazoo and Mrs. Belle M. Perry of Charlotte, Michigan. The latter is a full partner in the firm of Perry & Perry, printers and publishers; is an authority on nature study and bird lore and is devoting part of her extremely busy life to the propagation of the gospel of bird study and consequently of forestry, (for the two go hand in hand).

Women are colonists. We wish we had time to tell you of the wonderful work being done by Miss Maggie J. Walz of Calumet, who, coming to this country 25 years ago, poor and friendless, with only $7.00 in her pocket and not a word of the English language in her vocabulary, is now the owner of the only Finnish newspaper published in the world by a woman, and one of the two published at all. Miss Walz owns a $40,000 brick block in Calumet, mining stock, real estate, and an island given her by the United States Government as recognition of her services to her country people and to this her adopted land. She is one of the most remarkable women in this or any other country and is one of the truest philanthropists of the age, for she helps people to help themselves and her whole life is given to good works.

Women are authorities on political matters, even though they may be only law students (in this country at least) of the subject. Mrs. Jennie C. Law Hardy, formerly of Australia and New Zealand, now of Tecumseh, Michigan, is so thoroughly versed in political science, having studied it in all parts of the world, as to be a veritable mine of information on the subject. She was a member of the Senate in Australia, for in that wonderful country women hold- any position to which their brains give them access.

It was recently through the efforts of Mrs. Pauline Steinem of Toledo, Ohio, as the head of the City Federation of Women's Clubs, that the Juvenile Court law was established in that city. A law beyond the power of words to describe the good it does. Mrs. Sarah Platt Decker of Denver, Colorado, did a remarkable work as the president of the National Federation of Women's Clubs. She is a power for good in Denver.

Until a few years ago there was one field of man's work from which women appeared to be shut out, namely secret societies and fraternal orders. But it is not so to-day. Women are as necessary and as important a part of this most valuable department of the world's work as they are in other walks of life, and I think you will admit that the management of their branch of the fraternal orders is just as well conducted as that of their brothers. The women's societies of the Fraternal Orders are to the working woman what the woman's club is to her sister of the leisure class. Here she gets her first lessons in parliamentary law, and let me say right here that the way in which the sessions of one of our Orders is conducted compares most favorably with that of any other woman's (or man's) organization. Here the working woman comes for relaxation from the drudgery of domestic life, for it is drudgery as much as ever is that of the "man with the hoe." Here she finds her level among her own sex and her development in social and business life through the agency of the "lodge" is often truly remarkable. Here perhaps she is all the more willingly spared by members of the household circle because her life represents something of money value through the insurance clause in her membership and she feels the deeper and truer interest because her membership means protection from the sting of poverty to her loved ones in the event of her death. Here, too, the best instincts of her nature find development in her enlargement of environment and sympathy. The finest tribute we ever heard paid to the worth and value of the Beneficiary Societies was by a minister in his own church. He was not a member of any Order, "did not believe in secret societies," yet this is what he said: "If those who profess and call themselves Christians were as faithful to their obligations as are the members of the Fraternal Orders, I would not find the members of these organiations at the bedside of the sick and dying when the members of my congregation (who should have been there) were conspicuous by their absence."

Yes, women in this day have their place in all classes and all departments of the world's work. The time has gone by when a man brought before a magistrate and asked to give an account of his reasons for beating his wife on the occasion of a public holiday, could artlessly reply, "It's a poor 'art your Honor as never rejoices" and felt perfectly justified in celebrating the Queen's birthday by beating his own property. The world is moving beyond the period of the squaw, the crippled Chinese women and the inmates of a Turkish or Egyptian Harem.

Are women less womanly to-day because of their advancement in the scale of civilization? Is a well balanced, well poised, resourceful and cultured woman less womanly because she is that type and not another? For after all, the measure of a woman's worth is the measure of her womanliness. We leave you to answer the question.

The day of woman's degradation in every form is well nigh past and she is no longer even a stock joke of the ever hungry newspaper writer. The time-worn, moth-eaten chestnuts of the mother-in-law, the old maid and the mouse story have been long ago buried in oblivion. No one who studies the trend of events of the present time can doubt that woman's influence is one of the greatest factors in the history of to-day and that it is an influence for good. Who can deny, who cares enough for the subject to ask, "What she has done to help in the World's Work?"

THE WALL OF MISDIRECTED EFFORT

It is believed that there could be no more opportune time than the present for the earnest and aggressive fraternal worker. Never before were the needs of the people so great for protection as they now are. Never before were the purposes and fundamental principles of insurance better understood and, therefore, much talk, explanation and persuasion that formerly had to be done is not now only unnecessary but really worse than useless.

While work is the main essential to success, this is useless if not directed properly. Mere activity without any definite purpose and without due provision for obtaining the ends sought, will accomplish but little. Many a mistaken worker fancies he is doing great things because he is busy early and late. "See what an effort I am making," he says. "Surely, something must be forthcoming soon in the way of results."

The writer concurs in the idea that something will be forthcoming as a result of work, if this is properly directed, but mere blind effort, without any preparation or provision, will never enable anyone to retire on the results of previous effort. It requires thinking, planning and a line of action carefully thought out to bring things to pass. By all means work hard. One cannot succeed without it. Yet, when working physically, one's mind should be working also, and this should direct the physical part in a manner that will cause the latter to put forth its efforts where they will accomplish something.

Who has not heard the sad story of the "prisoner of the Chateau d'If?" This prisoner was walled up in an underground dungeon, and for twenty years he worked at a tunnel through which he hoped to escape to fresh air and the companionship of men. His only digging implements were his hands and feet. Every inch and foot of his progress caused him months of painful effort and nerve-destroying watchfulness against discovery.

After twenty years of such effort he brought up against a wall of granite. He found that everything before him was impenetrable stone. Crazed by the failure of his efforts he dashed out his brains against the rock, while those who found him said that, if he had turned slightly to one side with a tunnel half so long, he would have had easy access to the seacoast, which would have assured his escape.

Here is an illustration of one who worked with superhuman will and persistence. It was no fault of his that his energy had been misdirected. He simply worked blindly; fate was against him; he ran against a wall that he could not surmount and failure was his lot.

Are there not fraternalists to-day running up against the wall of misdirected effort? Are they not trying to overcome and thwart natural laws, rather than line up with them and work in harmony with them? Were they to exert but a tithe of the energy they expend, and were this properly applied, results would be forthcoming beyond their most cherished dreams and expectations. They, however, are blinded by their own preconceived theories and notions and, unless they come to a realizing sense that they can only succeed when they are working in harmony with nature's laws, it follows that failure will be their lot just so surely as day follows night.

We should draw a moral from the illustration referred to. We should see that, while we work unceasingly, we so fortify ourselves with the best implements and tools available that many of the difficulties we encounter can be readily overcome. We should familiarize ourselves with conditions and with a knowledge of the general principles upon which our structure rests. Knowing these, we should conform to them and should build in harmony with them.

THE INSPIRATION OF FRATERNAL CO-OPER ATIVE EFFORT

F. W. STEVENS

Every great movement must have some unselfish inspiration behind it to make it ultimately successful. True, there may be some selfish motives upon the part of individuals, but the work itself—in order to command the attention of the people—must appeal as something for the "greatest good for the greatest number." The inspiration, then, of the great co-operative work of the fraternal beneficiary society is the fact that it meant the financial and social uplift of the masses. It has taken the children of poor but respectable parents out of the gutter and given them even a better opportunity to compete with the world than their parents had before them.

Several generations of a family may have been only able to live from hand to mouth, yet by reason of the fact that one of such family has had the forethought to take out a little protection for the benefit of his wife and children, the child of the youngest generation is placed in a superior position financially, and if he is capable of grasping the opportunity he rises in the world, and thereafter that same family is placed upon a different level in relation to the community. There is inspiration in the very thought of what a membership in a fraternal society may do, not only for the immediate family but for future generations.

A working man was responsible for the present beneficiary system, and every fraternalist is familiar with the life and work of John Upchurch and how he builded for the future when his idea was only immediate relief for his fellow working men in the little town of Meadville, Pa. "Father Upchurch" started this great effort with a dollar, and now, within half a century, it has collected and paid out without profit over one billion dollars. It is not the thought of just the immediate relief of this billion dollars, paid out during a period of years, but the thought of the influence it has had in turning the course of lives for good that, without it, might have made paths to the poor houses and criminal institutions of the country

Just think of what irrigation has done for arid lands of different States. So, in like manner, has this great co-operative work irrigated the lives of thousands and caused them to look up and thank their Creator that they had an opportunity of leading and living happy and useful lives. If there is inspiration in the turning of streams and water courses so that vegetation shall spring up in place of barren wastes, is there not greater inspiration in the thought that many lives have been turned into new channels where they have been not only an aid and benefit to their immediate friends but to the community as well?

The value of the fraternal beneficiary society cannot be measured, however, entirely by the dollar and cent

basis. The fact that a goodly percentage of the member-
ship of these societies has come from the mercantile estab-
lishments and the professions has made the lodge room a
place where those of different callings could touch elbows
and learn something in detail of each other's struggles
with the stern realities of life and get a glimpse of con-
ditions from the other fellow's view point. Thoughts are
here exchanged by men from different walks in life, and
thus prejudice is disarmed and instead a mutual helpful-
ness encouraged that results in reforms in social condi-
tions that benefit the weak and make the strong more con-
siderate. In other words, there is a leveling of ideas and
opinions, and when there is a return to the home, the
workshop, the store and the office, a thought of the other
fellow is taken along, and as a result the sentiment of
the community is moulded for good. Isn't there an inspi-
ration in contemplating the great influence of this thought
exchange, brought about through the lodge system?

And now as to the part of the organizer and deputy in
this far-reaching co-operative undertaking. He has been
the pioneer in the work. It has been his business to get
men together, to link one man's ability with another, so
that they could accomplish collectively, for the benefit of
all, what they could not make possible individually.
Others have followed him in the finishing of the struc-
ture, but he has made the great building possible by rea-
son of his having laid a sure foundation. There must be
a thought of satisfaction come over a man who looks upon
a large building that has stood for a number of years
when he realizes that that building stands by reason of
his having put in a safe and sound foundation. So it
should be with the organizer and deputy when he sees
the growth and influence of this lodge and that society
which he was instrumental in starting. Many others
may have joined, but the same old name and the same old

number is there that was given when he called the charter membership together. Possibly he has been in the field for a number of years, and outside of a fairly good living, he has nothing financially to show as a result of his work. But "he has fought the good fight" of co-operative building, and the blessings of his efforts have gone forth in innumerable ways. Isn't there an inspiration to the deputy when he thinks on these things and contemplates the society's structure and its influence in the community?

The spirit of commercialism has possibly advanced in these societies as the volume of their business has advanced, but the influence of the fraternal thought that prompted them can never be lost sight of. There may be a selfish thought in one desiring to look after his own instead of that of the community, when he secures some protection for his family, but it is more than overbalanced by his willingness to help contribute his part to the support of the co-operative effort in behalf of his fraternal brothers. It will be the inspiration of what has been done in the years gone by, as well as what is now being done with still greater co-operative force, that will always keep the fraternal thought uppermost. The accumulation of funds made necessary by a change in business methods need not and should not cause any turning down of the old fraternal spirit, but rather it should be an inspiration again that will "thank God and take courage" in the accomplishment of greater things by reason of a greater power in numbers and money.

"A thousand eyes has the night,
   And the day but one,
But the light of a bright light goes out
   With the setting of the sun.

A thousand thoughts has the mind,
   And the heart but one,

But the light of a bright life goes out
When love is done.

A thousand promises has the world,
 And the lodge but one,
But the life of an unselfish aim goes out
 When fraternity is done."

THE UNPARDONABLE SIN *

What a portentous reckoning confronts a man as his last hour on this mundane sphere approaches. As Iris sits upon his pillow with the beautifully decorated but keen blade ready to sever the thread which binds the soul to its earthly tenement, which racked with pain and enfeebled by disease is no longer a fitting abode for its celestial occupant, what thoughts must fill the mind! How rapidly it reviews its earthly career. How boldly stands out, terrible and awful, the shortcomings of life, its selfish indulgences, its failures in lines of duty, brevity of provision for the family and absence of due love for his fellow man!

The impenetrable mist-curtain rises. What a sight! As a panorama two worlds open to his wondering eyes. He is at the point where the great earthly highway forks, one branch to the left and downward leading to Pluto's fearful realm; the other to the right and upward where the Great Author of the universe holds sway in his celestial abode. The eye instinctively turning to the right and upward is charmed and entranced by the sight. A paradisical highway of light so brilliant, yet soft and soothing, filled with ethereal chariots attached to angels so sylphic, so sweet, so beautiful in face and form, are escorting to

---

*The above is taken from a fraternal address delivered by Hon. John Sullivan, of Kansas City, Mo., at that place.

their heavenly home the accepted from the broad worldly highway below. Upward through the blue empyrean, near the orb of night, by beaming asteroids, through the milky way, unobstructed by the Great Bear, the little dipper, aerolite or meteor, passing that god of day, and through Elysian fields entering the great heavenly Kingdom. Peri in countless numbers, of such entrancing hues, filling all the way. The elysium of supernal bliss, light and glory greets the eye, with choirs of angels singing from the great high throne, clusters of fairies and elfs so bright and bewitching everywhere; nymphs and dryads so fascinating gracing woods traversed by limpid streams so cool and refreshing, lakes and bays of water of crystal clearness, bottoms covered with shells and coral of rainbow hues, and sands of diamond transparency, all presided over by Amphitrite, Galatea and Thetis, with their neried and naiad attendants in countless numbers, all yielding obeisance to glorious Neptune, who never allows angry wave nor discordant gale to mar the serenity of archangel-directed pleasure crafts. Avenues lined with magnolias in constant bloom, paved and curbed with pearl, magnificent mansions of onyx with ruby and sapphire trimmings, all avenues concentrating at the great white throne. There was Honesty avenue, Temperance avenue, Church-going avenue, Charity avenue, and hundreds of other avenues whose residents were located per the particular excellencies possessed in the world below, but thricely wide and encircling the great throne was "Provision for Family avenue," upon which daily promenaded all the heavenly hosts specially directed by the seraphim and cherubim of the realm. Silvery chimes so soothing, so enchanting, incense so pleasing to the senses, is as the air, fountains of nectar and ambrosia; at every corner, roses, carnations, orchids and violets in rich profusion at right and left. A paragon of perfection, the transcendent, super-excellent masterpiece beyond fancy's grandest dream.

A discordance distracts attention to the left and below. 'Tis Pluto's domain in active operation. The plaintive cries from Erebus are near at hand. The fumes from Avernus are awful. The fires of Tartarus can be seen belching forth. The nauseous stench from the steam of Styx is death-dealing; the lamentations from the banks of Cocytus are heart-rending. And beyond Tophet with its burning brimstone everlasting fire with its bottomless pit, is hellish and infernal.

Two messengers approach him, one dark as night, the other light as day. Follow, says each. At the parting of the roads are two courts, the one to the right white, of marble, pure and transcendently bright and inviting, presided over by St. Peter with ministering angels as court attendants. To the left a black foreboding building of black lava, sulphurous smoke emitting upon the judge's seat Rhadamanthus, Aecus and Minos as advisors, with Satan as marshal. Beelzebub, prosecuting attorney, Belial as court crier, Lucifer as clerk.

"John Smith, of the earth, number 110,506,844," cries Rhadamanthus. "Read his record," orders St. Peter.

Clerk reads: "He worshiped the true and only God. He kept the Sabbath day holy. He ever honored father and mother. He never killed. He never committed adultery. He never stole. He never bore false witness. He never coveted his neighbor's wife."

"I don't want him!" exclaimed Satan.

"Wait," cried Rhadamanthus.

Clerk:—"He has left a wife and four children unprovided for. He has been repeatedly solicited to join a fraternal insurance order for protection to his family in case of death, but refused to forsake his tobacco pouch, the expense of which would easily have offset the cost of such protection. The mother and children have moved into a basement flat and are trying to take in washing. Last night they went to bed supperless. This morning the little boy stole a loaf of bread at the grocery and is now at the police station. The mother is in hysterics on a cot at the police station where she went to intercede for her boy."

"I don't want him," said St. Peter. "I want all mortals to understand that provision for the family which my earthly disciples through these fraternal insurance orders has put within reach of the most indigent is first in the catagory of my requirements, violation of which I shall not tolerate in the slightest degree. It is the unpardonable sin."

"I don't want him either!" exclaimed Rhadamanthus "but he is a gem of a specimen for the pit of Alcheron. Belzebub, stop briefly at Erebus. Let him lament deeply at Cocytus. Dip him into the stagnant pool of Styx good and long. Then keep him a month in the sulphur-brimstone-petroleum room in the lower pit of Tartarus presided over by Hecate whose sex he has so greatly wronged, before letting him associate at all with even the forever and forever offenders."

One look upward to the celestial realm, one exclamation, "I intended to join the order, only procrastinated," and the fires in Sheol flashed up and out black and sulphurous, and there was wild commotion and great noise as the start downward was made.

THE MARKET VALUE OF OPTIMISM

· The world has had a surfeit of those sad, lugubrious souls who have developed the habit of bewailing the decadence of things; who picture the future in the lens of their own perverted visions; who have their gaze fixed on the hole in the doughnut instead of the doughnut itself. These form a bar sinister to progress and the natural and proper upbuilding of those things having as their central purpose the betterment of man and his surroundings.

Upbuilding is to-day the keynote in every line of endeavor. Those arrayed in its behalf are well entitled to a proud position among those called human benefactors. They shed light in dark places. They hold forth the things to be accomplished by progressive and upbuilding methods. Accomplishment is their shibboleth. They both plan and do. They are the ones who are responsible for, and to be credited with, the progressive results which have come to such a successful and desirable fruition during the past few years. They are the ones who make life worth living and who afford both hope and opportunity to those who are really desirous of bettering their condition and of doing something worth while during their comparatively brief span of life.

It was Elbert Hubbard who said: "Look out, not in; look up, not down. Lend a hand." This admonition has inspired many to redoubled effort. It has transformed doubters to doers. It has enunciated a line of effort to which we all should endeavor to conform. It stands for that which means greater accomplishments, higher and nobler aspirations and generally a purpose and an aim in life.

A BAD HABIT

The fraternal system, as the reader well knows, has

been undergoing radical changes during the past decade. These have been of an upbuilding and progressive nature. They have involved the abandonment of many theories and preconceived notions. They have been in the way of progress and of making ample and proper provision for the future. Indeed, such changes should have incited to aggressive effort on the part of those affected. Instead of this a class of faultfinders and self-exploiters has been developed. These have either arrayed themselves in the pathway of progress, or they have insisted that they have discovered a way and that this is the only way entitled to the consideration and adoption of those entitled to be recognized as orthodox fraternalists.

The great difficulty with some loyal and well-meaning fraternalists is that they are so committed to their own interests, or their own ideas, that they are unable to admit that there are others equally as earnest and loyal who may differ with them and yet remain honest and have at heart the best interests of the system. These are directly in the pathway of proper fraternal development.

The system is greater and more important than any individual or any institution. Its interests are so broad and far-reaching—they comprise so many phases of proper development and adaptation—that no one person or system can hope to name the point beyond which they may not safely go.

We are all but imperfect exponents of a great and growing cause. We should realize this fact and attempt to widen the horizon of our views. If we do not, soon we will be ranked among those who have been weighed in the balance of progressive effort and who have been found signally lacking in those things vital both to the future of the system, and the societies operating under it. We will not be regarded as of sufficient ability and breadth of view to conform to the upward and onward trend of events.

THE ECONOMY OF THINGS

There could have been no extension or adaptation of the fraternal principle such as the last decade has witnessed without the zeal, the industry and the persevering activity of those who have at heart the best interests of fraternalism along enduring lines. The service which has been rendered the individual and the State in the past is evidence that the future has many responsibilities to be met and solved. These cannot be brought to a successful issue without zeal and activity. There must be earnestness. This must be along proper lines. We must not look backward, nor must we dwell unduly upon the errors which we are to-day trying to eliminate from fraternal work.

We should see to it that fraternalism is represented by the integrity and efficiency of those who bear its banners aloft. We should not be unduly sanguine, nor should we lose force by threshing over things which have been passed. Rather, we should set our faces resolutely toward the standards which have been proclaimed as necessary for the permanence and the integrity of the fraternal system and the meeting of every pledge and obligation assumed.

Surely, the best interests of fraternalism should be very carefully considered by those to whom positions of trust and responsibility have been committed. If they are allowed to take a step backward,—if they are permitted to be considered from the viewpoint of interests other than those of the general system—it follows that disorganized effort will be in evidence and that real progress will be delayed.

OPTIMISM LEADS TO SUCCESS

There is no armour so effective in the fight for better things than is an optimism founded upon truth. Well has it been said that "a warrior encased in this armour from head to heel is invincible and at the beginning of the contest may count upon victory."

All the powers of such an individual or institution are immediately at command. There is no lagging of any one of them. Hope, bright with expectations and warm with intense desire, has been described as the lifeblood that runs through all, and they are bound together in a union of strength, by an unswerving faith which acknowledges no insuperable barrier and hesitates not to remove all obstructions which may stand in the way of desired accomplishments.

The world is full of those struggling along the beaten paths, bowing their shoulders to heavy loads, stumbling over rough places and often ready to succumb when the thorns pierce deeply. When the one imbued with optimism joins such a throng, his cheering voice is at once heard and new life runs through the fainting multitude. Hope dawns and they call to him to lead them in the new and better path.

We all know that there is no new and better road. There, however, is a better way of traveling if one takes hope and optimism as companions. These lead as does the needle to the magnet.

OPTIMISM'S MARKET VALUE

Who can measure the market value of optimism? Indeed, who can limit the possibilities of this quality? It scoffs at difficulties. It derides the possibility of failure. It ever points on to greater and better things. It is the light which shines when darkness threatens. It points the way to success and it leads on.

To-morrows are always the products of yesterdays. This is on the principle that seedtime must necessarily precede harvest. Yesterday was the sowing. To-morrow will be the harvest. If the right seed is sown the harvest can be trusted. Nature, our great Teacher, in all Her works proves this. "As a man soweth, so shall he reap," is well recognized as an abstract theory. We should transform this into a definite and actual fact. The reaping may not always be just at the time or in the way planned. The harvest, however, is always the best suited to the garners of the sower.

OUR PRESENT DUTY

Our present duty is in the way of building for greater and better things. We should look forward to this with confidence. We know that our system has accomplished things almost beyond human comprehension. It is practically in its infancy to-day and under proper, vigorous and earnest direction the future can be made even more progressive than has been in the past.

There should be a truce to petty bickerings and captious faultfindings. These have nothing in common with the principles of our system. They rank among the greatest errors and evils which have crept into it. They very properly belong to that order of things against which we all, as true fraternalists, have so resolutely set our faces. They produce nothing of value to any one. They are the sources of much evil and many disappointments.

All forms of operation have been undergoing changes the past few years. This very condition is an evidence that they are progressive and vigorous. Were they otherwise they would not have manifested in their context that restless desire to plan and work for greater and better things. Such a spirit of emulation is evidence of vigor and vitality.

We all should come to a realizing sense of the market value of optimism. This is the quality which transforms failures into successes—which brings things to pass.

FRATERNALISM AND WHAT IT MEANS TO THE PEOPLE

C. ARCH WILLIAMS

Fraternalism! What a beautiful word! So full of poetry and rhythm, so suggestive of all that it means. Upon pronouncing it one hears in its musical syllables the joy of all the thousands of widows who have been saved from the awful pangs of poverty, the happy laughter of the great army of children who have been rescued from the grinding slavery of ignorance, and when we see this beautiful word in print and contemplate with pleasure its compactness and completeness, it suggests a beautiful pic ture of the thousands of young men who are leading lives of usefulness in the rich valley of friendship, who, but for the inspiration and help of fraternalism, would be wasting their lives upon the barren rocks of selfishness or over- come with despair in the dreary desert of loneliness.

When you ask a man to join an order and he tells you he is too busy, that he has no time for such things, tell him that fraternalism is a work for men, not a play- thing for boys. Tell him that in your request, opportu- nity is knocking at his door, one which no man of sense can afford to ignore.

It is well to urge upon him his duty to protect his fam- ily so that upon his sudden removal from health and life, they shall not be left in want, but strive harder to show him that fraternalism is something greater than mere life insurance; show him that insurance is only one of the practical adjuncts of this modern movement, and that the principles of fraternalism enter into and influence every line of business and every profession.

Corporations are fraternal in principle. Their purpose is co-operation, mutual help. We should not confuse them with trusts and monopolies, which represent the abuse of fraternal principles, which represent the dominating selfishness of some men.

This abuse and selfishness has had its day, but like all wrong, it must give way and retreat before the advancing hosts of truth and right.

And so, to-day, we in this country are entering the fraternal era, in which the various manufacturers are organizing, in which the captains of industry and commerce now organizing their respective competitors into associations for mutual helpfulness, realizing that the old, selfish, cut-throat methods must be put aside.

The various professional men are organizing in order to help each other and that as compact, harmonious bodies they may benefit the people.

Religious denominations are working more in harmony with each passing day and the several states of our Union are striving, through Congress, or by uniform state laws, to work for the common good of all the people.

All of these things, my brothers, are the result and practical evidence of the increasing influence of the ever lasting principles of fraternalism, and the man who fails to recognize that this is true, when you call them to his attention, is wilfully and shamefully blind to the signs of our time and his own best interests.

The immediate business before you is to increase the membership of your Council. That is one of the many details of this great organization, and just as the practical details must be looked after in a large commercial business, so must they be cared for in this order.

But you can do our order no greater honor, nor render more valuable service to the cause which this order represents, than by opening the eyes of any man you know, whether he joins this or any other order, and whether he needs the insurance or not, to the dawn of this fraternal era.

Our society has worked and is now working for the alleviation of the poor, the needy and the sick and distressed, and has been and is promulgating the beneficent principles of fraternalism for the betterment of all the people, whether they are rich or poor in this world's goods.

But we cannot point with pride to a large membership, if, in securing it, we have harmed or even traduced a sister fraternity. And in this connection, it is a pleasure to say that men cannot belong to this order very long before they became imbued with the spirit of true fraternalism, which means kindliness to all men and all associations of men, and especially toward those associations which are working in common with us for the benefit and betterment of all the people in America.

And so, I say to you, my fellow laborers in this great fraternal work, aim high, let your ideals be such as to inspire you to zealous and persistent work in this great cause; disdain to hold to any petty idea of its purpose and achievements. Make it your business to fraternally refute the disparaging statements of those men who speak without knowing whereof they speak, concerning fraternal societies. You can nobly serve our order and your fellowmen without procuring the application of a mocker or a skeptic, if you can only start him in the path which leads to fraternal light.

The American people are beginning to realize that liberty and selfishness are not synonymous. The citizens of our Republic are coming to see clearly that the progress and prosperity of the individual depend upon the progress and prosperity of all the people.

Individual liberty is a barren privilege if it excludes consideration for others. The only liberty that counts for anything is that which all citizens possess and enjoy in common. Upon this and its continuance, the future of our country depends.

Fraternalism is not a mere modern invention, tacked on to our social system. It is an outgrowth of liberty itself, made possible and necessary by the evolution of social conditions in this country.

Our population has rapidly multiplied during the past century. Our resources have increased at a remarkable rate. The intricacies and interdependence of our business affairs have increased so amazingly that as a matter of necessity all of our people are concerned in every part of it.

But they are not concerned in order to limit the benefits of any individual or class, if honestly obtained. The people are concerned in order that every man may be accorded the privilege of co-operating and that his dividends shall only be limited by his own ability and energy.

The people of this nation are of right entitled to share in the pride which we take in the vast amount of business transacted annually in and by our own country. But to share fully in that pride, one must feel that he has had a part in that business and has received his just share of its-profits.

This condition is sure to be realized. The principles of liberty are too sound to be smothered by selfishness. The greatest good for the greatest number is so firmly grounded in our Republic that corporate greed can never tear it out. In every section of our country to-day this rule of action is being displayed in large and brilliant letters. Let no man mistake its meaning. The American people never will destroy property or property rights to avenge the privations imposed upon the many by the greed and selfishness of the few. But the people are determined to regulate the use of all privileges granted by them to individuals to the end that all persons holding such privileges shall benefit themselves by benefiting and not by oppressing the people.

The people of this country do not desire and never will attempt to run the business of any individual or corporate body, but are insisting more strenuously every day that no business shall be conducted by any person or persons so as to oppress the people.

And all this has come to pass not because of the business acumen of a few men, but as a natural outgrowth of our changing social conditions. It is the practical manifestation of fraternalism in all of our affairs, in business, in professions, in religion, politics and statesmanship. It is a part of our national life. It reaches down to the very foundations of our Republic, and up and out through every phase of American life. It rings true at every point of contact and is drawing every line of thought and action on the part of our people to its control.

One of the chief stumbling blocks in the way of speedily realizing for all the people the maximum benefits which would flow from a general recognition and application of fraternalism, is the reluctance of the average man in his chase after dollars, to give attention to anything which does not fall within, what he terms, business.

Fraternalism has grown very quietly, but constantly, and only so far as some phase of it has affected any line of business, has it been recognized by many of those in that line, and then, usually, without their analyzing or understanding it.

Men are prone to coldly treat anything in business which even seems to savor of sentiment. The word fraternalism strikes many business men as one having no relation to the commercial vocabulary, and they therefore consider it wholly outside of their business sphere and something to occupy their leisure hours only, if at all.

This being so, men have been slow to realize the advent of this fraternal era. Many of them have been and now are advocating fraternal principles in their business without thinking for a moment that the methods of business they urge bear any relation whatever to fraternal societies.

Men of this class have looked upon fraternal societies as camping grounds for the wage-earners, as commendable and beneficent institutions, but of no great interest to men of affairs. But one by one they are seeing a new light, and when once they do see it, such men are just as earnest advocates and energetic workers in the field of fraternalism as any wage-earner who looks upon it as the sole protection for his family.

OPPORTUNITY FOR FRATERNALS*

The great American game is money-making. Just the other day a celebrated English financier said we were getting rich ten times as fast as the English were. We read in the newspapers that baseball is the national game, and we have only been able by the greatest care to keep Thanksgiving day out of the hands of the football game. But the all-absorbing game that nearly every one tries at some time or other to play, is money-making. We

---

*Written by the Hon. Charles B. Landis for *The Chariot*.

knock each other down playing that, more often than playing baseball or football, or other rough games. Why we play it so roughly is hard to explain. No great money-maker can tell you why he wants to make money, except as it is in baseball; you want the runs for the fun of making them, and to get more than the other side. The great English game is said to be hunting, and the game of the French is dressing, but money-making is our pleasure as well as our business.

Down on Indian creek when we were boys and the property of the country had not yet passed into corporate ownership and control, it was not thought creditable to drive a hard bargain with a relative or friend. Much of what we call the "good old times" was due in that community to the friendliness which we seem to lack in these later and more prosperous days. No explanation of why members of the same family should cling together and treat each other generously is necessary. As the English are fond of saying, "Blood is thicker than water," and because it is, the world will never leave off reproaching Jacob for taking advantage of his brother Esau, and for his sharp practice in getting the birthright for himself. They were brothers and that fact makes defense impossible. It was thought almost as mean to be exacting, and bargain shrewdly with your neighbor. The farmers' boys in a particular neighborhood went to school together, grew up together, and without by-laws or constitution established brotherly relations among themselves. The emulation was, who shall get the most head-marks or spell the other boys down. But of competition, as in the present day sense, there was none. When the boys became owners of farms, either in the old neighborhood, or farther west, the feelings of interest and friendship still held. Many a man down "on his luck" has made a new start in life because he and Jim

Jones, the banker, went to the same little red school-house; and many a great statesman's first successful dash in politics was because the boys in the old neighborhood, and scattered over the surrounding counties remembered the fishing trips, squirrel hunting, and spelling schools they attended together; and this appeals to the best in us. It would be a reproach to human nature if it were otherwise. President Hadley of Yale places the beginning of a successful politician in college. In my opinion there is a lesson that is taken much earlier. It was given down on the pike in the country, and up town with the boys.

How to extend and foster this neighborhood friendship and brotherhood is the question. The time ought to come when it will mean as much to the world at large as it did once in the country neighborhood or village. George Ade makes two girls lifelong friends because they ate olives out of the same bottle at the girls' school. We cannot all get thus acquainted, but it is a fair inquiry to ask what industrial organization and what corporate forms of business best take these old relationships into account, then to insist that in the long run the game of business shall be played, if not in brotherly fashion, at least fair.

More than half the trouble with the modern corporation is that it is impersonal. It feels free to treat men as though there was no such thing as friendship, and as though, commercially, they were strangers. Not that the men who are in the offices of these corporations are not friendly—when you meet them. But as officers of the corporation they become remote, are shut in from approach of the average men, and are apparently impervious to public criticism. They are still friends, but as officials they are compelled to settle questions and treat folks from the one standpoint of dividends. If old Commodore Vanderbilt really never said "the public be d—d," you could not make the public believe otherwise. In the head of a corporation is often centered more power than any one of a dozen monarchs now reigning in Europe, by hereditary right actually possess. There is an unrest about corporations, not because they have decreased cost of living, and increased the wages of those who work for them, but because they do not, as now controlled, engage the individual and neighborly interest of the men who must live by them and with them. Human nature will not easily suppress itself, and in a conflict between a series of corporations in which the rank and file have no part and the nation of which the rank and file are a part, it is not difficult to pick the final winner.

This same feeling, deep down, is the principal trouble with what we call the old line life insurance companies. We all know that they are sound and with comparatively few exceptions economically and honorably conducted. But they somehow shade off into purely business corporations. They have no place for sentiment, or sympathy. In the nature of the case there must be hard and fast rules for the medical examiners, skillful putting of phrases in the insurance contract, hard bargains to keep up the interest rates, quick-witted manipulations to get in on the ground floor in large stock and bond transactions, and finally the president of the compay to whom we have committed our savings for years is as remote from us as Albert Edward VII or Wilhelm II, and possessed of fully as much power.

Somehow we must satisfy this instinct, deep and ineradicable for fellowship, friendship and personal co-operation. The political party is very much superior to the corporation, for it keeps close to the folks, and must do so if it is to hold the public confidence and be entrusted with power to administer the government. A "boss" can get out of touch with the people. Like Jethro Bass in Comiston, before he can become a boss he must get himself elected "selectman." Then he can sit in the throne room at the Pelican and make and unmake measures, and cause vacancies and fill offices only so long as he "keeps in touch" with his constituents. If he is to become a leader and not a "boss," a final force for good, and initiate progressive policies he must maintain somehow the brotherly relationship which he once held with the boys in the country and the town. That is Roosevelt's power. He was president, but before that and while that, every one of us seemed to know him. If we had been born on his street when he was a youngster we feel that we should have known him, played marbles and ball with him and "scrapped" with him. Had we gone to his college we should have been proud of him because he became president, and though we were neither born in New York nor went to Harvard we feel he is our kind of a man. He does not seem far away from us like the head of the Oil Trust, the Steel Trust, or the British Empire.

The fraternal insurance company ought to find it easy to keep up this sense of fellowship and this oneness with the people and communities where it operates. It ought to follow and must follow sound financial plans, look carefully after experience and mortality tables, and not be afraid to turn down a poor risk; but with all this in mind, it seems to me that great opportunity rests in their chance to give to men that social and fraternal fellowship—to help men meet men, and co-operate with them, not only for the protection of their families' after death, but for heartening and helping each other in life.

A prominent member of one of the great fraternal organizations once said in my hearing, "We have a straight business proposition." I wonder whether that is the best way to commend his case. Let us see what it means. When men deal with men not connected to them by any natural or fraternal tie each naturally does the best for himself that he can. That is business pure and simple. It is what makes the game of money making more brutal than football under the old rules. Let me cite an instance: L. D. Brandeis has pointed out that in fifteen years the Massachusetts Industrial Insurance Companies have received sixty-three million dollars, paid back twenty-three millions, have accumulated a surplus of ten millions, so that one-half of what has been paid in, to say nothing of interest, has gone to pay the expenses and dividends to the stockholders. This is business, but it seems to me we want less business and more brotherhood. We need more of the old feeling that it is wrong to drive a hard bargain with our old friends and neighbors; that it is exceedingly discreditable to take 20 per cent. and get all we can. The man who would have taken such profits from his neighbors or friends as the Massachusetts Industrial Companies have taken would have been compelled to move. The old Indiana farming communities would not have tolerated it. Plainly we need not only publicity but the old neighborhood restraints upon sharp business methods.

If the fraternal societies will help to restore and maintain this old friendly feeling which was the very basis of the first friendly societies out of which the Fraternal Beneficial Orders have come they will not only reap a harvest of appreciation, but attain a tremendous growth.

UNCLE DANL'S CONVERSION*

"Well, haow's things goin' with ye, Henry? Layin' by suthin' f'r a rainy day, be ye?"

"Not very much, uncle. I've tried to, but it's pretty hard work."

"Seems t' me I c'd save money on what you git as a sal'ry—tho' of course, I dunno jest what that is," and Uncle Dan'l paused a moment as if to give his nephew an opportunity to state the amount of his earnings.

Receiving no answer, however, he went on: "At your age, Henry, a dollar looked putty big t' me. When y'r Aunt Sarah an' me was married we didn't see a dollar in money comin' in every day, I tell ye. But we man aged t' save money out o' what we did have, so'st we never got into debt. If we couln't pay f'r things we went without 'em," and Uncle Dan'l nodded his gray head wisely.

"You had your own house and garden, uncle," said Henry. "And you kept a cow and pigs and chickens. You and Aunt Sarah were brought up on farms, and knew just how to make the most of what you raised. But in the city, where you must pay rent, and buy everything you eat—pay good prices, too, if you want it fit to use—what you have left over goes for fuel and for clothes and for insurance——"

"That's jest it," interrupted Uncle Dan'l. "I mistrusted ye'd got into some o' them plaguy catchpenny insurance schemes—jest robbery, I call 'em. Better save yer money an' put it in the bank, a good sight."

"I don't agree with you there, Uncle," said Henry,

*Written by Kate Woodward Noble, for the New England Order of Protection Journal.

firmly yet respectfully. "If I were to die and leave Bessie and the boy, I should have the satisfaction of feeling that she had something to fall back on. By and by we hope to be able to save something from my salary, but about all we can do now is to pay our way and our insurance. It's only about forty dollars a year for Bess and me, both together."

"You hain't ben gittin' that little creeter insured, too," broke in Aunt Sarah, who had been an interested listener "I sh'd think she'd git it into her head ye was waitin' f'r her t' die so'st ye c'd git the money."

"Bessie isn't so foolish, auntie," laughed Henry. "Of course she's insured in the same lodge that I am, and she's as anxious as I am that it should be kept up. Why, only think what it would mean if either of us were to be left with the boy, to have a fund of $2000 for his education."

Just then a neighbor came in and the discussion of insurance was dropped, and was not again resumed as Henry Powers left his uncle's home the following morning.

Uncle Dan'l and Aunt Sarah Powers were a typical New England couple, brought up in the old days of simple country living and staying on their farm in the outskirts of the village in their later years as they had in their youth. They had seen the march of modern improvement, but had not been in its path and contented themselves with the old ways that had served them in their youth; the old well, with its curb and bucket; the kitchen sink of wood, without a drain pipe; the wood stoves that must be frequently replenished; the corded bedsteads and other antiquated furniture, not old enough to be interesting because of its age, and not new enough to give the desirable amount of comfort. Henry was their favorite nephew, and his occasional visits to his aged relatives were bright spots in their otherwise monotonous lives, for they had no children of their own.

Uncle Dan'l's knowledge of insurance matters had been unfortunate. One of his neighbors, insured heavily in an old line company, had been taken ill with pneumonia. The time for payment of the premium slipped by unnoticed by the family in the anxiety and stress caused by the father's illness, and when the man died, the whole amount of insurance was lost to the survivors. The money would have made the widow and children comfortable until the children were grown, but the loss of it entailed upon them considerable privation. Another neighbor was insured in a fraternal organiation that held out dazzling prospects, but which, not being properly managed, went to pieces. The man was too old to secure insurance elsewhere, and what he had paid was lost so far as his family was concerned.

It was not strange, therefore, that he judged all insurance alike and firmly determined to have none of it. It seemed to him that Henry and his wife were pursuing a foolhardy policy, and his honest old heart ached for them as he thought it over. Aunt Sarah thought as he did, and many were the conversations the two held about it in the weeks that succeeded Henry's departure.

"I s'pose it looks all right t' them," said Uncle Dan'l on one of these occasions. "Them insurance men do talk dretful plausible—I've heerd 'em many a time. But I allers told 'em, 'No, sir, not f'r me.' I knowed too much about 'em 't take any risks. I managed t' scrape enough t' hev a home an' a leetle suthin' besides an' if one of us has t' go, t'other one of us won't hev t' want."

"Well, young folks allers think they know best," said Aunt Sarah. "Henry's a good boy, an' Bessie's a nice little woman, an' I hope t' massy both'll be spared a good many years yit. Maybe insurance nowadays is diff'rent fr'm what 'twas when you an' I knew 'about Will Stewart an' Mr. Welton."

"Let's hope so, anyhow, Sary."

One day Uncle Dan'l came home with a letter. "Sary! Sary!" he shouted, almost before he got inside the door. "What ye think I got f'r ye now?"

"W'y, Dan'l, how excited ye be! What is't? Not bad news, I hope?" as she caught sight of the letter which Uncle Dan'l was waiving at her.

"Bad news? Massy, no! It's a letter fr'm Henry. He wants us t' come down t' see him next week a-Thursday an' go t' some kind o' doin's Friday—I dunno jest what. This is what he says: 'I want you an' Aunt Sarah here Friday night to go to an entertainment with Bess an' me. Git somebody t' see t' the cat an' th' chickens an' stay over Sunday with us. Bess says she'll cry her eyes out if you say no, an' the boy says he wants you— or he would if he could talk.' Shall we go?"

"Guess you forget 'bout Thursday's bein' Thanksgivin' Day, didn't ye, Dan'l?" asked Aunt Sarah, with a smile. "I s'pose he means he wants us t' come t' Thankesgivin' with 'em an' stay over. Jest let me look o' that letter won't ye?"

Uncle Dan'l, with a muttered, "F'rgot 'twas Thanksgivin'," meekly handed over the letter and departed to the barn. Aunt Sarah read it more carefully than had her spouse and found that her surmise was correct. Bessie had written the invitation to the Thanksgiving feast, and Henry's note, which was all Uncle Dan'l had stopped to read, was a sort of supplement. When Uncle Dan'l came in, plans were talked over, and a note of acceptance dispatched by the next morning's mail.

Thanksgiving Day was spent at the home of Henry Powers in real old New England fashion—the morning church service, the afternoon dinner with the big turkey as the piece de resistance, in the preparation of which Aunt Sarah was allowed to assist to her heart's content, and the "visitin'" during the rest of the day. When questioned about Friday's mysterious "doin's" Henry only laughed and said, "You'll see," and Bessie was equally non-committal. Uncle Dan'l and Aunt Sarah were greatly mystified, but there was nothing to do but possess their souls in patience.

Friday night came at last. The baby boy, sound asleep in his crib, was left in the care of a trustworthy neighbor who had often come in to stay with him on similar occasions, and Henry and Bessie escorted their guests to the town hall, where a good-sized audience had already gathered. The men and women composing this audience were an intelligent, prosperous looking body of people, and all seemed greatly interested. The program of the evening opened with selections of music by a small, but excellent orchestra, followed by several recitations, all of which were greatly enjoyed by the old couple. There was a slight pause, then one of the fine looking men in a small group seated on the platform rose and came forward.

"If that ain't Mr. Dean, from the bank down t' Amosia, I'll miss my guess," whispered Uncle Dan'l excitedly. "He's one of the smartest an' coolheadedest business men I ever see! An' ain't that Jim Shore with him? Whatever be they goin' t' do?"

"They are officers of our insurance lodge," replied Henry, "that is, of the order the lodge belongs to. I want you to hear what they have to say about insurance."

There was no more time for conversation then, for the speaking begun. Uncle Dan'l had had business dealings from time to time with both these men. He knew their reputation for good judgment and for business probity, and would have taken the simple word of either in preference to the bond of many another man. Both were enthusiastic members of the society, holding high places in its executive bodies, both state and supreme, and as they told the story of what the order stood for, what it had done in the past, and what it was pledged to in the future, Uncle Dan'l listened with rapt attention. Other speakers followed, to whom he listened with almost equal interest. The presence of the men whose character he knew was, to him, a guarantee of the rest. By the time the speaking was ended he was thoroughly converted and, as was his wont under such circumstances, surrendered most graciously.

"Tell ye what, Henry," he said, as they walked homeward, "I've ben condemnin' all these years what I reely knew nothin' about. You keep up that insurance, whatever ye do. A lodge that'll look out f'r y'r payment when y'r sick, an' pays prompt when the time comes, is a mighty good thing f'r a workin' man. If I wa'n't too old I'd jine myself. I'm a-goin' t' talk t' two or three young fellers I know down home an' git 'em t' see 'bout startin' a lodge there. We'll help, won't we, Sary?"

To which Aunt Sarah heartily assented, and the conversion of the old couple was a source of great satisfaction to those who had brought it about.

FRATERNAL INSURANCE*

The distinguishing feature of these societies is that they are associations whose members are banded together through a spirit of charity or fraternity for mutual assistance and protection. They are wholly outside the line of ordinary life insurance companies, which deal in insurance for the general public on a business basis. Their membership is chiefly made up from those of limited means who are seeking insurance at the smallest outlay. Over one-fourth of the population of this country may be said to be directly or indirectly interested in these societies. A knowledge of their principles and of the character of the insurance which they offer is a matter which concerns every American citizen regardless of his interest in insurance as a profession.

Nearly all our existing fraternal societies have started within the past thirty or forty years, but they have a long line of predecessors extending back through centuries. Their proper understanding requires a glance at their historic relations. To the student of sociology as well as of economics a peculiar interest attaches both to their origin and history. As a race we are communal as well as social in our very instincts and in those instincts are the fundamental impulses that have developed all our political and social organizations.

* * * *

The fraternal society must be studied not as the mere artificial product of an advanced civilization, but as an organization whose roots and tendrils are implanted deep

---

*Extracts from a lecture delivered by Mr. Walter S. Nichols, editor of the *Insurance Monitor* and *Law Journal*, before the students of Yale University.

down in our common humanity. Civilized communities
have no monopoly in this spirit of fraternalism. It was
the active force at work in primitive days when the fam-
ily relationship grew into the patriarchal form of gov-
ernment and this in turn expanded into the tribal state.
As tribes solidified into nations this social evolution moved
along lines so familiar in the physical world. The homo-
geneous pursuits of the tribesman became the hetero-
geneous occupations of the civilized state. Each occu-
pation had its separate corps of workers, who banded
together in a society for their common interest and pro-
tection in the economic struggle which followed the
barter and trade between the groups. Thus was evolved
the early benevolent or fraternal societies that are met
with in so many of the nations of antiquity.

* * * *

As the power and influence of the Guilds declined
they were succeeded by the modern British Friendly
Societies, from which our own have been so largely pat-
terned. Members chiefly from the working classes united
for mutual aid in sickness and for funeral benefits,
through contributions to a common fund. They recog-
nized the distinctly insurance character of their work and
sought to frame scales of moneyed contributions which
would be adequate. But they knew little of the princi-
ples of insurance, and their frequent and disastrous fail-
ures at last attracted the attention of the British Parlia-
ment. Investigations by that body aided by leading Brit
ish actuaries disclosed the total inadequacy of their rates
and the mismanagement which characterized their affairs.
Attempted legal reforms were strongly resisted for a
while by the members, and it has required nearly a cen-
tury of legislation to place the friendly society system of
Great Britain on the comparatively sound basis where it
now rests. Under the existing laws in that country, such

societies are induced to register and to accumulate reserve funds and charge rates which, like those of ordinary life companies, will be adequate to meet their future obliga tions. When registered they are required to have expert valuations periodically made of their resources and liabilities and proper balance sheets published of their affairs. The knowledge of their condition thus furnished to their members and to the public is relied on to check mismanagement. The law makes no attempt at further interference.

The strength of the system in that country lies in the fraternal ties which bind the members to their societies. It was this which enabled reforms to be successfully introduced into many of them which, according to any commercial standard, were already bankrupt. The strength of the system in any country must depend on the fraternal character of the society in fact as well as in name. The chief weakness of the system lies in the temptation to divorce its two-fold functions of benevolence and insurance, to regard the society either as a mere insurance organization for business purposes, or else as a brotherhood whose ties are strong enough to outweigh any defects in its insurance methods. When the fraternal spirit among the members is wanting, its work, to be a success, must be carried on along the business lines which characterize the ordinary insurance office. Such a change has actually taken place on a magnificent scale in the more recent development of these societies. It was from the fraternal society both here and in Great Britain that industrial insurance was evolved. It was just fifty years ago that the managers of such a society in London conceived a plan for abandoning its fraternal features and furnishing insurance to the poor on a strictly business basis. This was the origin of the famous British Prudential Insurance Company, whose policies are now found in the home of almost every working man in that country. Such was the origin too some twenty years later of the Prudential Insurance Company of America, which started as a friendly society in New Jersey and whose policies along with those of its later competitors are to be found in millions of American homes.

*   *   *   *

The great aim of these societies is to furnish insurance at the least possible immediate outlay to their members, and to avoid the expenses incident to insurance as a business. Hence their paid officers and agents are as few as possible. The salaries needed for expert talent are usually wanting. The work is largely carried on through the members themselves and their lodge system. Their equipment for conducting the society as a financial business corporation is limited. Surplus in the sense of business profits is regarded as foreign to their character and the accumulation of funds beyond what is absolutely needed is discouraged as a temptation to extravagance as well as an additional tax on the members. Dividends of surplus profits to the members are not allowed. Any supposed excess of funds is met by reducing the assessment and any interest which a member might have in those funds is lost on his withdrawal. He has no right to claim a surrender value as in the ordinary company on giving up his certificate.

You note how in all these features the idea of fraternalism distinguishes these societies from ordinary life companies. They enter directly into the question of the proper remedies for their defects. The failure on the part of many officials and life insurance experts to properly appreciate them has been one of the difficulties in the way of reform. A premium rate adequate to the risk and a reserve adequate for future deficiencies in the life insurance sense would seem to be essentials if they are to furnish anything more than mere temporary or term insurance. But it does not follow that this rate must be computed on a table of mortality heavier than their own experience nor that it must be loaded with a margin for contingencies and expenses like that of the ordinary life companies. Nor does it follow that their reserve funds as in the case of ordinary companies should be in excess of their obvious needs. It would seem essential too that as in the case of our ordinary companies, official valua tions of their assets and liabilities and balance sheets of their accounts should be required. It does not follow, however, that the same measure of supervision and con trol over their affairs should be exercised by the state authorities, since they are not ordinary business corpora tions nor subject to commercial insolvency in the strict sense of the word. It is held by many that the functions of the state are ended when, as in Great Britain, such valuations and balance sheets are published, and the members are left with a knowledge of the facts to deal with their societies as they will. These are all contro verted questions on which I hesitate to express any decided opinion.

* * * *

The hardest task of all has been to educate the mem bers up to these needed reforms, which mean to them heavier assessments and an insurance more costly than was promised when they joined. The insurance officials of our various states and the best representative men of these societies themselves are now earnestly striving both through legislation and through the education of the membership to solve the difficult problem. The laws regarding these societies to-day are little else than mere rules for their organization and management. No pro visions for securing their permanent solvency are made as in the case of our ordinary life companies. In most of the states they are left to run their own course. Their members as a body are exceedingly jealous of attempts by legislation to increase the cost of the insurance which they offer or in any way to reduce their popularity or their freedom of action. Through the ballot box they stand ready by their numbers to defeat any attempted laws which they believe to be inspired by a spirit of . antagonism. Any attempted legislation for the regulation of these societies to be successful must be framed in a friendly attitude with a recognition of their rights as mutual clubs to regulate their own affairs within proper limits.

Now a few words in conclusion concerning the character of the insurance offered by these societies. In essential respects it is widely different from that furnished by our regular companies. In the first place it is strictly benevolent in its character and limited to the members and their dependents. It aims to relieve the necessities of these in a way more effectual than the random charitable assistance furnished by ancient associations. It needs for its success that the members should be bound by a spirit of real fraternity to their association, and not use their memberships as a mere cloak for ordinary insurance purposes. It needs that the members should be actively interested in the affairs of the society and should be ready to bear their share of the burdens in case of errors in its management. Their fraternal bonds are the chief substitute for the commercial security required of an ordinary business corporation.

To that large class in the community whose instincts and tastes lead them to seek insurance protection from such societies they aim to offer that protection at the smallest immediate cost. The work is done chiefly by the members. Expenses are reduced to a minimum. No dividends are provided for and the assessment rates are reduced to the lowest figures. These are the strong points urged by its advocates. Fraudulent claims too are less likely where the members take a personal interest and for that reason these societies, in theory at least, should be peculiarly adapted to deal with sick and accident risks where fraud is a special danger.

* * * *

Despite their defects these societies are doing a great and responsible work among those who prefer the form of protection which they offer. The communal spirit which created the ancient clubs of Rome and the guilds of more modern Europe has been strengthened by the antagonistic spirit of selfish individualism which characterizes our commercial age. Fraternal insurance should be dealt with as an evolution of these more primitive societies that is here to stay, backed by the votes, if need be, of the millions who support it; but calling as in Great Britain for beneficent laws and the intelligent co-operation of its membership to remedy its defects.

A REMEDY FOR POVERTY

REV. CHARLES G. PURDY

Who would not if he could do away with poverty? We have heard too much about money being the root of all evil. Not money, but the want of it has kept the world in tears and sorrow. The single tax might or might not have a favorable effect upon poverty, even if universally adopted. There are two sides to that question, and each side is so well defended that there is little likelihood that either will capitulate to the other for many years to come.

My plan of abolishing poverty by universal fraternal life insurance cannot be successfully opposed, and I do not believe that men of note can be found who will raise their voices against it. The means by which I propose to bring about universal insurance through the societies now existing may not meet with instant approval, but it must win out in the end, because it is based on sound reasoning and because it appeals to the most advanced socialistic thought of the times.

Probably no one realizes as he should the value of life insurance. The work it has performed in helping upward the human race is infinite and cannot be estimated by us at its true value. When we think of all the homes it has saved, the children it has educated, the sorrows it has helped to assuage, the burdens it has lightened, we cannot but believe that life insurance is one of the things of which modern civilization has most reason to be proud.

But if this can be said of life insurance as a whole, if this be true to some extent of that form of life insurance which is the product of a desire for gain only, what shall be said of that form of insurance represented by the fraternal societies? What shall we say of those fraternities which have paid out during the past forty-five years more than $1,000,000,000; not to the rich, not to those whose children would be educated any way, but to those who, had it not been for this form of insurance, would have been in many cases left without the means of proper living?

My first contention is that the salvation of this and all other advanced nations depends upon what is called, rightly or wrongly, the middle class. The very rich and indolent, given up to selfish pleasure, and the very poor and ignorant, satisfied to live in filth and rags, constitute but a small proportion of our population, either as to numbers or influence. Between the two comes the great army of workers, self-reliant and brave, and in this blessed country of ours, it represents 90 per cent. of the whole population. It embraces every profession, every trade and every kind of industry. Some of this class are well-to-do, more are barely able to make both ends meet, but all are workers, and all belong to the same great class. It is this class which maintains the fraternal societies.

My second contention is that some method must be found whereby this entire class can be induced to carry life insurance, and that when this is done it will constitute the longest step ever taken toward the abolition of poverty. One class of economists claims that poverty is due to an actual lack of money, while others say there is money enough, but it is not put into circulation. Both may be right to some extent. I only speak of it here in order to call your attention to the probable effects of universal insurance. As I have already said, the frater nal societies have paid out during the past forty-five years the enormous sum of over $1,000,000,000. Now I have no means at hand to show just what will be the amount paid out when practically all those who should be insured in these societies are thus insured, but certainly $1,000,000,000 or more would in this case be paid out every year. Just imagine if you can the effect upon the prosperity of this country by the distribution of such a sum of money among the class of people of which I am speaking. It would not be spent in the capitals of Europe, it would not be spent on fast horses or wine suppers. It would be used in completing the education of children, and paying for homes, and in a thousand ways which make a happy and prosperous people.

My next contention is that inasmuch as the great middle class of citizens constitutes the government, because they cast 90 per cent. of the votes, they should have government backing for their life insurance, not merely because they have the power to demand it, not because there is a dollar in it for any living person, and not even because the societies need it in order to succeed, for they will succeed anyway. We want our government back of these fraternities and every certificate they write, because until we get it, thousands of honest workingmen and women will die every year, and leave behind want as well as sorrow. We want government backing because life insurance is a necessity for the worker, and the fraternal societies offer the only means of obtaining it at a price within his reach. With such indorsement and supervision every honest man would seek membership in these societies. The selfish man could not say as now that commercial insurance is too expensive and the fraternal insurance not reliable, as an excuse for not protecting his family.

You may say that government backing is impossible. Not at all. When a company of wealthy men decided to build a railroad across the continent, did they do it with their own capital? No. In spite of the fact that they had or could get plenty of money, and expected to make the project add very much to their fortunes, in spite of the fact that it was a purely selfish affair, the only money they spent of their own was for printing the bonds. Then they went to Congress and said, "We want you to guarantee the interest on these bonds so we can sell them." Steamship lines are now being subsidized to the extent of millions, every cent of which will go to increase the wealth of those already rich, and although the class to which these men belong does not represent more than 5 per cent. of the people, Congress generally gives them what they want. Now, why should not the fraternal societies representing a class which embraces

90 per cent. of the people do something practical for themselves in a matter purely unselfish, a project in which no living person is to reap any profit, and which by no possibility can ever involve the country in the loss of a dollar?

We know that the fraternal societies have been misrepresented and we know that because of this misrepresentation they contain 'but a small percentage of those who should be enrolled among them. And this·abuse has come from such high and apparently respectable sources that even members of these societies pretend to see disaster ahead. I would recommend to all such a few facts. The fraternal form of life insurance is older than the commercial or so-called old-line. The history of these commercial companies practically dates back only about fifty years in this country, and during that time over 90 per cent. of all those incorporated have failed and gone out of business. And yet the few remaining have the effrontery to warn people against fraternal insurance and to claim that they only have solved the problem. In the light of history criticism of fraternal insurance comes with bad grace from these people. After fifty years of experiment they are as far as ever from a correct solution of the question. As a matter of fact, they have drifted away from real life insurance. Most of their policies represent a three-cornered speculation which is no more life insurance than betting on a horse race is business. I refer to that form of policy issued under a multitude of more or less attractive titles in which the seeker of insurance for his loved ones is told that he won't have to die to win. The man who invented that phrase and that form of policy was a born confidence operator.

The confidence man always works on the cupidity of his intended victim, and when an insurance company tells a man that insurance for his family can be made a source of profit to himself, he does the same thing. In this form of policy the beneficiary is always defrauded, inasmuch as the sum received is but a small fraction of the amount that should be received in return for the premiums paid. Permit me to illustrate this point: We will suppose a man finds that he can devote a given sum to life insurance for the protection of his family. This amount, if invested in straight life insurance, will give his beneficiaries $4,000 of protection. He meets an insurance agent, and not having very well defined ideas on the question, he is induced to invest his money in a policy of the "don't have to die to win" variety, giving his family the magnificent protection of $1,000. If he dies before the expiration of the period which this has to run his family receives this insignificant sum—not much more than enough to bury him. If he live out the period, he receives the thousand dollars, finds that he is then too old to get more insurance or that advancing years has made it difficult to pass a medical examination, and realizes too late that a life insurance policy should be solely in the interest of the beneficiary, and not for the policy-holder.

How can fraternal insurance be made universal? I take it for granted that you admit my contention that if the government guaranteed the payment of the certificates in every fraternal society whose record showed that it had and was maintaining a certain standard of excellence as shown by its death rate, etc., that these societies would soon embrace the bulk of all those who require insurance. It is a fact, no doubt, that what keeps most people from accepting fraternal insurance is the doubt in their minds of its permanency. If this doubt be entirely removed our point is gained. There is only one way in which to remove it, and that is a government guarantee back of every certificate. We must either adopt this plan, or the plan of the commercial companies of spending millions in advertising, and to do that we must greatly increase the cost of our insurance.

First, let this matter be called to the attention of the next Fraternal Congress for action. When that body has formed its plans so far as to decide what shall be demanded of our Congress, the real work begins. At every congressional election and at every state election let the candidates be asked to subscribe to the demands of the fraternities. If they refuse, they get no fraternal vote. This agitation alone will be of immense benefit. That we will finally protect ourselves by our votes I have not the least doubt, and five years should be sufficient time in which to bring about this result.

The century just closing will be spoken of through thousands of years to come as the "Age of Invention." In looking back it seems almost as though the world awoke for the first time with the dawn of the nineteenth century. And while the twentieth century cannot hope to equal the nineteenth in this respect, it has a grander and more glorious work to perform. The triumph of socialism and the universal recognition of the brotherhood of man are to be accomplished. And as the end of the eighteenth century saw the beginning of the tidal wave of invention which has made the nineteenth the most wonderful in history, so is the end of the nineteenth century watching with hope and joy the rise of socialism, which is to make the twentieth century the most glorious. Not dreamers, but practical men in every walk of life are helping on the good work. And life insurance for the worker, the pride and hope of our nation should be, and I believe will be, the first great triumph of socialism.

WHAT IS IT?

F. H. DUCKWITZ

What is it that bands together over five millions of people under the banners of fraternal co-operation? If there is nothing aside from the insurance adjunct—if there is nothing in addition to it—are we not wasting time and effort in the way of impressing upon the people at large the fact that we, as fraternal exponents, are endeavoring to exemplify the teachings of humanity, which are that we all must meet and unite upon a common platform?

The Hon. John Sullivan asks, "What is it that bands together millions of people under a given emblem?"

Is it its teachings, responding as such do to the cravings of the human soul and to its glorious work performed? In local bodies the social element in man's nature develops. The social instinct distinguishes in great degree the human species from the brute creation. The man who best manifests his love for his fellowman by finding happiness in healthful communing with his brothermen, is most far removed from the lower species, most nearly approaches the Creator's ideal of man, and in local bodies we go to study that greatest study given man—his fellowman.

There is much to be considered in the above extract. There is something more than the purely business prop osition and, in these days when our leaders feel con strained to consider only one phase of the general situa- tion, it is in order that attention be called to the real basis upon which the fraternal structure rests.

We may have our rates adequate, everything may be adjusted to conform to the nicest consideration of the actuary, and otherwise we may be said to so have revamped our affairs as to be enduring for all time. Yet, if we fail to keep in touch with our members, if we do not appreciate the elements of fraternal operation aside from those of a financial nature—it is repeated, if we do not consider these vital and underlying principles to fraternal operation, we will meet with absolute failure.

There is something more and beyond the financial benefits afforded; there is something in the way of fraternity and affinity in local bodies that is a most important and vital feature. If we eschew these, it means that we eliminate the central and important principle upon which the structure rests. For all intents and purposes we might as well be insurance companies pure and simple.

It is not believed that the fraternal system to-day is ready for a proposition of this nature. It is not believed that the ends attained in the past, comprising as they do a crown in the constellation of fraternal operation of most radiant qualities, will allow this to be obscured by purely mercenary or mathematical considerations.

The fraternal system has more to do than that of furnishing financial protection to the dependents of its members. It unites members having a central purpose and it affords a common platform upon which all can meet. This means not only the protection of dependents, but it means the advance of those who are associated together in the bonds of fraternal brotherhood. Just now the question as to adequacy in rates is the all-important one and it is not the purpose of the writer to detract from this in any way. However, in undertaking to attain these ends, we should not lose sight of the central and funda mental principles upon which the entire fraternal structure rests. Rather, we should so present our proposi tion that all elements bear their proper relation to each other and that in their entirety they present a system that stands not only for the protection of dependents, but for the mutual well being and behoof of members. If we consider these central and cardinal features, it is believed that many of the conditions now supposedly impossible of reconcilement will disappear or at least be alleviated by the bonds of fraternal union.

FRATERNAL LIFE INSURANCE *

This morning, in discussing assessment life insurance, it was brought out that assessmentism is a pathological phase of life insurance, by which it is meant that it was a mistaken system of life insurance, the course of which was predetermined by the character of the system itself. That course means dissolution, the only escape being a reform of method before the necessary result of the system has become realized. It will be recalled, as stated this morning, that all of these companies operated on what was known as the business assessment basis, with a few conspicuous exceptions, háve either failed or been reorganized upon the level premium plan into the old-line companies. The methods of these reorganizations would be interesting, and might properly form the subject of another lecture, but there is no occasion to discuss them to-day, nor have they a proper place in either of the two lectures proposed for to-day. It will be recalled that the few assessment societies which have so far held out without reorganization are either in a moribund condition, or the effects of error in plan have been temporarily offset by great economy of management, great care in the selection of risks and the accumulation of reserves albeit insufficient reserves.

We have a much more cheerful task before us this afternoon, for we shall be considering the course of the

---

*Extracts from the Address of Miles M. Dawson before the Wharton School of Finance and Commerce of the University of Pennsylvania.

same pathological phase of life insurance assessmentism, in a class of institutions, which have on the whole. been exemplary in the matter of economy of management, and also in the selection of risks, and which in addition have very great vitality on account of the strong fraternal sentiment that binds their members together and causes them to cling to the institution in solving its difficulties, instead of deserting it as soon as the danger signal goes up. I refer to the fraternal life insurance societies of the country.

*   *   *   *

The last ten years, and especially the last five years, have been years of readjustment of rates in the fraternal societies of the country, many of the most important of them having changed from incorrect and unsafe plans to more scientific methods. Had there not been anything to offset the natural effects of the incorrect plans, and had those societies possessed no greater vitality than the assessment companies the result would have been the passing out of existence of many of the fraternities. On the contrary, there have been but two or three important fraternities to decay and go out of existence, and in each case it was due to failure to act promptly rather than to the deficiencies of plan, which might easily have been remedied. Moreover, while ten years ago, these societies had in round numbers one-half of the total insurance in force, they have through the period of readjustment more than held their own absolutely, showing a good increase in membership each year, and the only effect of the readjustment has been that they have lost in relative position, having fallen perhaps from half the total to about one-third the total. Their popularity still remains undiminished and, the readjustment period passed, there appears to be no reason why they should not regain their relative position also.

Let us consider somewhat closely the nature of the fundamental error in the assessment plans. The first of these plans to be considered is that of equal rates without regard to age, which we may call the flat assessment plan. Under this, members admitted at the age of 20, 30, 40, 50 or 60 were all assessed the same amount toward the payment of death losses, although, according to one of the standard tables, at the age of 20, the risk of death calls for a payment of $7.80 per $1,000 or about 65 cents per month; at age 30, for $8.43 or about 70 cents per month; at age 40 for $9.79 or for about 82 cents per month; at age 50 for $13.78 or $1.15 per month, and at age 60, for $26.69 or $2.22 per month. It will be observed, therefore, that the older members would be assessed much less than their insurance actually cost and the younger members much more. That such a plan could have got started at all was due, therefore, to two circumstances outside of the historical conditions to which I adverted this morning; viz., that there was extreme economy of management which more than offset any additional cost to the younger members for the time and, second, that the fresh medical selection kept the total cost far below that indicated by the tables for several years, and as the societies grew very rapidly, in some cases for many years.

Evidently, however, the plan has within it the seeds of dissolution, for the members admitted grew older constantly, and this threw more and more burden upon two classes of members, viz.: Those who are still at the younger ages, and more especially those who are newly admitted at the younger ages. After a time, it could not but result in the refusal of young persons to come in and also the withdrawal of many of the younger members. Where there was great economy of management, however, so that the excess charged for mortality upon the younger members did not equal the difference between the expenses in the society and the high expenses in other companies, and where also, the mortality was kept at a low point by a large growth and fresh medical selection, the development of this difficulty was delayed for a long time, and many were deceived thereby.

Notwithstanding this, after a time the idea became prevalent among the patrons of fraternal societies, as well as elsewhere, that there ought to be graded rates for the various ages. There was great distrust at the time of actuaries by the members of fraternal societies and there was also great distrust of fraternal societies on the part of actuaries. The members believed actuaries to be false scientists, employed to bolster up the hated old-line business and actuaries, knowing that the assessment plan was fallacious and in the end ruinous, were wholly out of sympathy with the fraternal societies which employed such plans. Consequently, when the idea first became clear in the minds of the patrons of the societies, that there ought to be graded rates, they naturally turned to the mortality tables to help themselves, and they found their rates according to age, that is rates of mortality according to age. They believed a reserve to be an unnecessary thing and a "fifth wheel for a wagon," as they called it, and this view was somewhat confirmed by a book published by the late Mervin Taber, in which he divided a premium into what he called its "elements," viz.: Mortality, reserve and expenses. This division was meretricious and misleading in fact, being good for one year only, the division of the level premium into such elements changing with each year and after some years, the mortality charge actually exceeding the whole net premium, encroaching upon the accumulations of a reserve. But this was not made clear in the book.

Therefore, the next plan was what has been known

as "graded assessment," that is assessments graded according to ages at entry. Precisely as under the other plan, only enough was intended to be called to pay current losses, but now the assessments were made, for instance, 65 cents at age 20; 70 cents at age 30; 82 cents at age 40; $1.12 at age 50; $2.22 at age 60, or other varying rates, supposed to represent the mortality at the various ages. Once fixed, these rates were not intended to be changed; that is to say, a member who entered at 20 would pay at the same rate until he was 40, 50, 60, 70, 80, 90 or what ever age you please.

Supposing now that this rate was properly determined at the age of entry, it must be manifest that when a man was 20 years older, he will be subject to an average mortality rate at an age 20 years higher, and not to the rate at his original age. Let us assume, therefore, members admitted at 20, 30, 40, 50 and 60, for instance. The member at 30 pays but a small advance, about 5%, on the member at 20; the member at 40, shows an advance of about 25% on the member of 20. The member of 50 shows an advance of over 70% on the member at 20. The member at 60 an advance of over 200% on the member at 20. Now let us look at these same members 20 years later, and for the moment assume, that no new members are admitted, so that it is a mere question of distribution of cost between these members. The member admitted at 20 is now 40. In order to pay for his insurance at twelve assessments per year, the mortality being as per this table, should be paying 82 cents instead of 65 cents, or more than 25 per cent. additional. The member admitted at age 30 is now 50 and should be paying $1.12 or 60 per cent. more than before. The member admitted at 40 should now be paying $2.22, or 170 per cent. more than before. The member admitted at age 50 now 70, should be paying $5.17, or 360 per cent. more than before. The member at age 60, now 80, should be paying $12.04, or 442 per cent. more than before.

It, however, is not of absolutely the first importance that each of these should receive his insurance for twelve assessments of the same size as before. The important question to determine is whether the ratios of the payments which they are making at the outset to one another is a correct ratio now 20 years later, so that each of them is paying his fair proportion of the total cost. Twenty years before the member admitted at 20 and the member at 40 were paying in the proportion of 65 to 82 and that still remains their rate. In other words, the man at 40 was paying about 20 per cent. more than the man aged 20; each of them is now 20 years older and the cost to the member admitted at age 20 who is now 40, is 82 cents per month or 25 per cent. more; for the member admitted at age 40 who is now 60, $2.22 per month which is not 25 per cent. more, but is 170 per cent. more in round numbers. It, therefore, follows that this plan becomes correspondingly advantageous to the members as they become older and necessarily disadvantageous to the younger of them. Thus, for instance, the member admitted at age 60 is paying $2.22 instead of $12.04 or about five and one-half times as much. That is, he is getting five and one-half times the benefit, while the member at age 40, who is admitted at age 20 is only getting 25 per cent. additional benefit.

This would be bad enough for a society which admitted no new members and would be extremely unfair to the younger members. It would, however, soon work its own cure, either by the disease running its course and destroying the institution, or by a reformation of plan. The admission of new members, especially in large numbers, tends to divide the extra cost of the old members' insurance over their own payments among a larger num-

ber, but it is yet more unfair, because in effect it taxes
not merely upon the member at 40 who is admitted at 20
an unfair share of the mortality, out of all proportion to
the cost of his own protection, but it taxes also the newly
admitted members at age 20, the same proportion which
the other member pays at 40. After some years this
must necessarily be discontinued. The length of time
that it can continue depends upon the growth of mem-
bership, economy of management, excellence of fresh
medical selection and other things, but in the end it must
always spell nein, unless relinquished.

The fact that members who are admitted at 20, for
instance, do not continue to experience the death rate
proper to the age of 20 promptly, has not failed to be
noticed by the patrons of fraternities, and in consequence,
some years ago, a fraternal society was organized which
offered protection, the rate increasing as the member
grows older, but it was realized that this sort of insurance
would not be attractive if the plan were carried to its
conclusion and, therefore, it was provided that there
should be no increase after the member attained the age
of 60. The society created no reserve to take care of the
excess cost of protection to members beyond 60 over their
payments and, therefore, this plan when carried on long
enough to get a considerable membership beyond the age
of 60, also threw upon the younger members and upon
the new entrants, a large part of the burden of the cost of
the protection furnished to the older members. This plan
in its original form attracted a good many of the more
discerning and questioning patrons of fraternal insurance,
and it has been adopted by a few societies other than the
societies which originally introduced it, but it has not
become widely popular.

When the time finally came for reorganization, some
of the societies which by reason of comparatively poor

medical selection, slow growth or lack of economy, became victims of the defects of the system earliest, passed out of existence. Their fate served as a warning to others, and there began to be an active movement for adequate rates and sound plans. This movement has gone forward, until at the present time several of the most important fraternities have made changes in their plans looking toward financial strength and permanence. These changes for the most part consist in the adoption either of level rates correctly computed on a scientific basis, or of level term or increasing term rates during the working period of life, merged into level rates beginning at old age. The societies have employed, in connection with devising these plans, various actuaries, and have shown a commendable disposition to study their conditions thoroughly, and to adopt new rates which will, when shock to the organization has passed, put it upon a permanent and solid basis. They have approached the problem with courage and intelligence, and the work which they have accomplished within a few years has received the approval of all who are thoroughly acquainted with the nature of the problems before them, and has enlisted sympathy and co-operation on all sides. Moreover, they have notwithstanding, the somewhat radical changes which have sometimes been necessary held a large proportion of their old membership and in every case, as soon as the shock of the readjustment had been recovered from, they have again begun to increase their membership.

This favorable result is due to several things, among which may be mentioned the following: The vast amount of education of members which has gone forward in recent years. The loyalty and fidelity of both the officers and the members, and their willingness to make sacrifices for what they believe to be a great and worthy cause. The fact that these changes are brought about by the action of representative bodies, a larger majority of the members of which must perforce be convinced, before anything is done. The fact that the members of these representative bodies, having served the societies in various capacities for many years, have a thorough practical knowledge of the conditions and consequently have been able in most cases to suggest variations from the proposed program, which while not impairing the sound basis of the new rates, make them more acceptable to the membership. And the fact that economy of management goes a long way toward offsetting the strain upon the membership due both to the check in the new growth which takes place for a time and the consequent loss of the large advantage of fresh medical selection, and also to the introduction of reserve charges which are found necessary under practically all the plans proposed.

It would be beside the purpose to instruct you to-day in what may be called physiological life insurance, or the normal phase of it; and I shall not undertake to do it. But I must lay down a few elementary principles in order that you may understand the nature of the changes which these societies have been compelled to make in their readjustments. The methods of computing premiums, after you are furnished a mortality table fairly expressing the mortality to be expected, and also have determined upon a rate of interest, at which funds not immediately required will accumulate, will perhaps be explained to you later in this course. Suffice it to say at this point, that you only need to know how an actuary knows that a rate is computed correctly. This I will undertake to explain in as few words as possible.

Assume 100,000 members admitted at age of 20 and that they die precisely as per a certain mortality table. Let the rates be paid level for life or increasing for life, or increasing for a time and then level, theoretically it matters not which. In any event, if the rates have been correctly computed and the company has precisely the mortality called for by the table, and earns precisely the assumed rate of interest upon any funds that are not immediately required, the following will be the case, viz.:

Starting the first year with the premiums for that year, improving them at the assumed rate of interest to the end of the year, paying out of this fund the losses according to the table for the year, adding the premiums for the new year by survivors, improving at the same rate of interest up to the end of that year; paying the losses for that year; and repeating this process until the highest age in the table has been attained and passed; there should then remain precisely sufficient money to pay the claims of the last members to survive, and nothing left. This is the test of just and adequate rates, no matter whether the company be a fraternal society or an old-line company.

A variation has been offered from this of the following nature, viz.: That the discontinuances of members be taken into account, and no part of the reserve contributed by them be returned upon surrender. If this is admitted, it must necessarily be with great caution, because these discontinuances vary, it has been found, with ages, with years of insurance or membership and with calendar year, that is, according to whether you take the experience of one calendar year or another. Moreover, it is not believed that any society can permanently collect large reserve funds from its members, without accounting to them if misfortune overtakes them, by some sort of surrender value.

Two remarkable statements as to the part which an actuary should play in these readjustments have recently been made—one by a distinguished college professor and one by a man prominent in fraternal circles. The former ridicules the idea, that the subject can safely be dealt with by a representative body of laymen, and practically affirms that the actuary's word should be accepted without question, and that the formulation of sound plans should be left completely to him. The other has stated, that, on the other hand, the actuary should play the part of an attorney only, and should not make his own personal views felt at all in the matter, except in the form of special confidential advice to the leading officers as I understand his statements. From personal experience, I am able to say that both views seem to me to be wrong. The greatest possible advantages accrue to the society from a free interchange of views between the actuary, serving as a consultant of the society and the members of the representative body; such modifications being made as seem to the latter to be desirable, taking into account the peculiar conditions, subject always of course to explanations by the actuary as to the normal and necessary results of the modifications. Even in the most technical matters, it is found that the representatives, when once interested, easily get a firm grasp of the principles; their suggestions are frequently of the highest value and no actuary, working alone in the seclusion of his office, can possibly meet all the practical objections to a plan which he formulates, that will be raised in a representative body of this character. The best results, therefore, are likely to be obtained by the co-operation of the scientists and the members' own representatives, and it is my firm conviction also that the highest form of government is by an instructed common people.

I cannot close without paying my tribute of earnest admiration to the leaders of the fraternal societies and particularly to the members of these societies. They have everywhere arisen nobly to the duties before them and even when they have declined, in any considerable body, to acquiesce in the proposed changes it will be found upon examination that there are peculiar circumstances which excuse them and explain their action. The willingness to have plans introduced has been remarkable; objections have most frequently been to special features which bore more heavily upon members in one section than on members in another.

THE FRATERNAL SYSTEM *

The system of life insurance represented by fraternal benefit associations should not be confused with the so-called mutual companies which in times past have worked hardship and injustice upon their policyholders and whose operations have been such as to leave unfavorable impressions upon the minds of our courts.

The system of insurance or protection represented by fraternal benefit associations is distinctly the people's system intended to afford protection at the lowest cost, to be operated without profit to any one and to be managed and controlled through a democratic form of organization by the members themselves. Much misapprehension as to these associations exists in the minds of those who have not had occasion to trace the history of their origin and development and to familiarize themselves with the real purposes of these organizations and the methods through which their members seek to carry them out. The story is both interesting and instructive.

The English Friendly Society is a very ancient institution, but the modern fraternal benefit society or association, as known on the American continent to-day, is the

*Extracts from a brief submitted by Mr. George W. Miller in a case before the Supreme Court of New York.

development of the last forty years. A little over forty years ago a mechanic named Upchurch, living in a little village in Pennsylvania, conceived the idea of forming an association among his brethren for the purpose of affording in the way of benefits paid some protection to the families of its deceased members. He called a meeting of a number of his fellow workmen at his home and there laid the foundation for what became the Ancient Order of United Workmen, which is popularly known as the pioneer of these institutions in this country. The idea was to protect the families of wage-earners and men of moderate income, whose earning capacity as their families were growing up, would not permit them to carry insurance for any substantial amount in old-line life insurance companies; and these societies were organized with the idea of operating them at a cost of management which would be nominal compared with the cost of the expensive organizations of old-line companies, with the solicitation and extension of the order work to be done by the membership without compensation, to the end that insurance in substantial sums might be obtained at a cost within the reach of those who were to be protected by this system of insurance. The men who organized and who for years conducted these institutions were unskilled in the science of life insurance. They knew little if anything about mortality tables or the cost of protection, but thought that an institution was in a flourishing condition as long as it continued to have money enough in its treasury to meet its current obligations. At the beginning no heed was paid to age or physical conditions and every man in the organization contributed a like amount upon each call for funds, regardless of these considerations, but the man of strong and robust health would in the nature of things be expected to live, and the average run of such man would live much longer than the man whose

health was undermined by disease and whose constitution
was broken; and so, too, would the young man in the ordi-
nary current of events outlive by many years the old man,
thus requiring the young man and the strong man to pay
into the organization in the long run a much greater cost
for the same promised benefits than could be expected
to be paid by the man of broken health or the man whose
span of life was nearly run. The unfairness of this situa-
tion in time became apparent, and then began a system of
medical examinations which would raise the standard of
health of those who came into these organizations; and
it became apparent to their managers that there should
be a difference in the contributions made for the benefits
promised according to the age of the members, and tables
were formed regulating rates of contributions according
to ages, but in an arbitrary sort of way, without any
scientific accuracy and with little if any regard for the
question whether the institution as an institution, or rather
the members collectively, occupying on the one side the
position of the insurers, through the agency of the asso-
ciation formed, were collecting from the members as
individuals, occupying on the other side the position of
the insured, such sums of money as in the end would
enable them to carry out their promises and redeem their
obligations.

Added to the payment of death benefits and sometimes
funeral benefits were the social and fraternal features of
the lodge room affording opportunity for the exemplifi-
cation of the brotherhood of man. It was an attractive
system of protection, for the men who were the certificate
holders not only had a voice in the management of their
respective societies, but they were the real managers
through the representative form of government which
enabled them to legislate for and control the society or
association.

In the organization of these associations there was the supreme body, having general control of the entire membership, and then in the various states where the association did business a state body having charge of certain features of the work and working subject to the control of the supreme body; and then a step further removed were the local lodges, tents, councils, or courts, as they might be called, and the members of the organization held a membership in some one of these local bodies organized and scattered throughout the territory where the association under its charter was authorized to do business. At stated periods, as the laws provided, each one of these local bodies would elect its representative to its state body and that body would in turn elect its quota of representatives, based upon the membership in the state, to the supreme body, and that body meeting annually, biennially, triennially, etc., as the laws of the particular association might provide, would meet to receive the reports of its managing officers as to its condition, deliberate upon and consider the condition of the institution and its needs and necessities, legislate as wisdom and experience might dictate for the government and control of the whole organization, elect officers who were to manage the affairs of the society between the meetings of its supreme body and fix their salaries.

In fact in the early days when the membership was small, each lodge or local body sent its representative direct to the supreme body, but as the membership increased that created too large a body for effective work and the basis of representation was reduced from time to time as the membership continued to increase.

In these institutions there are no stockholders and no dividends are paid. They are not organized for profit and never have been, and the statutes of the various states of this Union, where laws providing for the organization of such associations have been enacted, in nearly every case prohibit the organization of such associations for profit, or, in other words, provide that they must be organized "not for profit," but for and carried on solely in the interest of the members.

There was in the early days the post-mortem plan of collecting assessments; that is, after death, and in some societies a call was made after each death and in some after a number of deaths, but in time experience demonstrated that a wiser method would be the so-called ante-mortem or the collection of assessments at stated periods of time in anticipation of the deaths expected and with the rapid growth of these associations the current collections exceeded the current claims for benefits, thus giving to an institution an apparent prosperity, and many, if not all, of the founders and early managers of them believed that a constant steady accession to membership was all that was needed to maintain them in a flourishing condition, even upon rates insufficient to produce the cost of the promised benefits.

Two things contributed to create this apparently prosperous condition. It has already been explained how in time there began the system of medical selection. By this way only the select lives of the community gained admission into these associations, so that the average health of the members at the start would be considerably above the average health of the community at large, and this had a tendency to decrease the death rate, and, hence, keep down the current maturing claims for benefits. In addition to this these associations began early to adopt age limitations, both maximum and minimum, as one of the tests of eligibility for membership. The maximum age ranged from about 45 to 51, sometimes a little higher. This resulted in a young membership, and these two elements combined produced a low death rate with its consequent effect upon the claims for benefits which the associations were called upon to meet, and thus they were enabled to run along for 10 to 20 years upon a table of rates wholly inadequate and yet apparently in a safe and flourishing condition; but insurance experts tell us that within a period of about five years the effect of medical selection as to those who have been in an association that long wears off and the average health of those members who have been in an association for that period of time, or longer, drops down to the average health of the general community, so that in time the beneficial effect of medical selection is somewhat decreased, although, of course, the association still enjoys the benefit of it as to new entrants during the early years of their membership.

In addition to this the advance of the members into the older ages, or the massing of the membership into the older ages, for in a matter of twenty years' time, say, the man of thirty has become the man of fifty; the man of forty, the man of sixty; the man of fifty, the man of seventy, and the association then begins to suffer from a death rate resulting from old age, and what old age carries with it to destroy life; and although an association may continue to enjoy a healthy growth in membership, it will not overcome, as will be hereafter demonstrated from the evidence, the increased death rate resulting from the massing of the members into the older ages. As time went on the managers of these associations, good men elected from the ranks of the membership, began to study these problems and to realize that there was such a thing as the cost of insurance or the cost of protection promised; that an insurance company or fraternal benefit association could not obligate itself to pay benefits for less than the cost of the promised protection or benefits, and continuing upon that basis, avoid insolvency and ruin any more than a merchant can sell goods at less than they cost him and avoid financial ruin. In these institutions there is no source of revenue except the money contributed by the members with such interest accumulation as the surplus on hand from time to time may earn. No endowments are made for their benefit and no speculations may be indulged in from which they may reap profits to replenish their treasuries. The members themselves, through their monthly contributions, must pay into the treasuries of these associations sufficient funds to enable them to redeem their promised benefits as they mature from time to time, and if the members are not doing this, if the rates of contribution are not sufficient to accomplish this result, no growth in membership can ever make up for the inadequacy in the rates, for the faster an association grows and the more promises to pay benefits are made, upon rates of contribution insufficient to enable the association to redeem such obligations, the worse the condition of the association becomes.

The managing officers and the members of the law making and governing bodies of these associations, beginning to realize and understand the necessity for sound insurance principles to be applied in the conduct and management of this system of insurance, if it was to be perpetuated, began to test the financial solvency of their institutions, by applying thereto standard tests used in making valuations, or, as the merchant would say, in taking stock in insurance companies or fraternal benefit associations, when it was discovered that all of these fraternal benefit associations, which had for a number of years been enjoying an apparently prosperous growth, increasing in membership, paying current claims as they matured and distributing their millions of money into the homes of their deceased members in the way of death benefits, and into the homes of their members in the way of disability benefits, were operating upon a basis that would eventually lead them to financial ruin. It was the popular system of insurance protection. It had been demonstrated that it was possible through this system of insurance to furnish protection to the man of moderate means at a much lower rate than he could obtain it in the old-line life insurance companies. Billions of dollars had been paid in benefits. Obligations in the way of promises to pay death and disability benefits running up into the billions were outstanding and the men and women who held certificates in these institutions and were depending upon them for their insurance protection on the American continent were numbered by the millions.

The cost of protection, in so far as the payment of death and disability benefits are concerned, as distinguished from the expense of management, is practically the same in one association as in another, and in fraternal benefit associations, as in old-line life insurance companies. While one association may for a period of years have a lower death rate than another, or some fraternal benefit association have a lower death rate than some old-line life insurance company, on the whole men and women die at a rate per thousand according to standard tables of mortality prepared from the tabulated experience of thousands and millions of lives, and the association or company which enjoys a lower death rate to-day than is to be expected, according to standard tables of mortality, must have a higher death rate to-morrow, for the members must die, and if the actual death rate for a period of time is below the expected, it is bound to be offset by a subsequent period when the death rate will be above the expected. It takes a dollar, therefore, to pay a dollar of insurance obligations in a fraternal as well as in an old-line life insurance company, and a fraternal benefit association can be operated upon a sound

and solvent basis just as surely as can an old-line life
insurance company, if the members of the fraternal asso-
ciation will pay into its treasury in their monthly con-
tributions sums sufficient in amount to enable the asso-
ciation to meet its promised obligations as they mature
from time to time. In other words, the difference between
the cost of insurance in a fraternal benefit association
operating upon an adequate table of rates and in an old-
line life insurance company lies not in the cost of paying
death and disability benefits, but in the expense of man-
agement.

In the conduct of an old-line life insurance company
high salaries are paid to managing officers; expensive
offices are conducted in various sections of the country
where the company has its business; applicants for insur-
ance are procured through an extensive agency or solicit-
ing force, to whom must be paid substantial commissions,
all of which, or a very substantial portion of which comes
from the pockets of the policyholders and is raised by
loading the premiums so as to make them include not
only the cost of the benefits promised as distinguished
from cost of management, but cost of management as
well.

To illustrate by figures taken from the report of the
commission on rates referred to hereafter, the average
cost per policy in four old-line companies in 1903 was
$24; with appellant it was $1.43. The average cost per
$1,000 based on business in force in the four companies
was $10 and with appellant $1.14. It cost them $35 for
each new policy written, as against $3.11 and $17 for each
$1,000 of new business as against $3.03 for appellant
(for 1907). (Fols. 1908-1909.)

We never knew of a policyholder explaining the bene
fits to be obtained from holding a policy in an old-line
life insurance company to his friend or nighbor and

attempting to get that friend or neighbor to become a policyholder as a friendly or neighborly act. The business of the old-line company is not procured that way; while in the fraternal benefit association the officers, with scarcely an exception, are paid moderate salaries—most of them low salaries—there is no expensive agency force in the field to be paid either high salaries or substantial commissions, for while these associations are permitted to some extent to employ deputies, it is within narrow limitations, and these limitations are placed upon them in most of the states by statutory provisions. The work of solicitation has been largely done by active, enthusiastic members who have at heart the welfare of the order to which they belong and who solicit the applications of their friends and neighbors into their local lodges, tents, councils or courts, as they may be called, with no other hope of reward than the satisfaction of having been responsible for bringing to the family of the applicant the protection which a certificate in one of these associations affords.

As the managers and members of these associations began to understand these matters and the necessity for placing their respective associations upon an adequate basis, there began a process of readjustment which has been going on now for a number of years, the purpose of which has been to take these institutions with their valuation deficiencies, and create in them a condition of financial solvency which will insure their perpetuity and enable them to redeem their promised obligations.

ORGANIZED EFFORT

I. I. BOAK

The fellow who shoots at random may hit the mark he desires to hit, but the chances are against it; in fact, the result of random efforts are accidents, whether they hit or miss. Here is a great truth in a few words, and will bear repeating. Let's put it this way: The chap who shoots a rabbit that he didn't aim at, shoots a rabbit by accident. If he misses a rabbit that he didn't aim at, he has missed a rabbit by accident; either accident is due to a lack of one great fundamental necessary to real success. The greatest of all great essentials in the make-up of beneficial progress is SYSTEM or ORGANIZATION.

Did you ever stop to think that no mortal ever saw anything since time began that could be recognized as successful but was due to some system? This is true of the workings of nature herself.

The trees and flowers do not bud in mid-winter to be ruthlessly destroyed by the biting frosts; the seasons come and go as they should come and go. It is just this that makes them seasons. Not only does nature provide things properly and beneficial to mankind, but the beast of the field is taught by the same teacher. That such teaching is not spasmodic or irregular is evidenced by the action of the squirrel, who lays by his winter's supply when that supply is available, and he learns by some mysterious means just what kind of a winter it is going to be, and regulates the amount of his supply accordingly; the beaver is taught to dig holes in the bank of the river to crawl in during the winter season, and he digs those holes in the fall and at no other time.

In short, all of the lower creation seem to learn some

system or correct method of self-preservation, man being the only exception. He ofttimes destroys his health, happiness or prospects by irregularities and dissipations; he seems to hope that, although such methods as he is daily practicing are always disastrous, the destructive forces may in some way be stayed in his case. The most ridiculous, or perchance the most awful, results of human energy are due to the misapplication of such energy. It takes as much muscular energy for a switchman to throw the switch the wrong way, killing or maiming his fellow mortals, as it does to throw it the right way and let the train proceed in safety as it should. The schemer who defrauds his fellow man and lives by crooked methods has to think and plan and operate his plans just as accurately as the upright citizen, who in some way returns value for every penny he gets in the world. Perhaps, however, the most that can be said against unorganized or unsystematic effort is that it results in failure; failure because of waste; waste because of a lack of tact to use pronounced talent. This is at least far more generally observed than viciousness—general because it takes in millions of men every year. It embraces thousands of business firms. Its sway reaches from the thrones of nations to the huts of the lowliest subjects in the realm. The individual side of it is constantly before us. Many a good farmer has been lost to the land, because of some fellow's determination to be a physician.

We could carry the illustration into all the walks of life, if time and space would permit, but wouldn't it be well to consider the subject from the standpoint of our fraternal system? Numerous instances have come to the notice of the general public, because of the breaking up and going out of business of orders and societies on account of the lack of well-directed effort. These failures are often attributed to almost any cause but the right one. Some say a lack of energy; others, lack of capital, and again, lack of confidence, etc. It is in order right here to point out the great truth that confidence has been responsible for much of the world's successes, and a lack of it has naturally caused failures galore. Now, remember, confidence is always inspired by some deep underlying principle. People do not put confidence in persons or projects without scrutinizing investigation. Therefore, it follows as a matter of certainty that a fraternal order which has grown and prospered and which has in its membership thoughtful men engaged in the various trades and vocations of life, and which has the confidence of its members, is built on proper lines, and its success can be attributed, first, to *confidence;* and second, to proper *organized effort,* which means that every member is exactly what he should be—an active, productive worker, thus bringing to the society the highest measure of prosperity.

Co-operation means organization, and as we approach perfection in organization, the more helpful and efficient is our scheme of co-operation. Organization is everything—from the highest form of government to the minutest detail of a successful life. No machine is complete until every piece is in place and moves in harmony with every other piece; no friction, no discord, no grating or grinding anywhere. This is ideal co-operation, and the nearer we can approach this ideal, the more effective and helpful will be our work.

SOUND INFORMATION *

I hardly know what you desire me to speak on this morning. It was suggested, I think, that I should say something about legislation. If you refer to the legislation of this session affecting fraternal societies, I am then in the position of the author who wrote a treatise on "Snakes in Ireland," beginning with the paragraph, "There are no snakes in Ireland." There was very little legislation this session, almost none, affecting friendly societies. You are interested in section 1 of the Act which went through. On any application to the Insurance Registrar for incorporation as a friendly society under sections 33 to 39 of this Act, the applicant shall be required to show to his satisfaction that there is real and substantial reason and necessity for the society proposed to be incorporated, and that the granting of the application would not be contrary to law or to the public interest.

Of course, you are aware that the policy of the Legislature was to prevent the further incorporation of life insurance societies in this Province. That was settled in 1890. The policy of the Legislature was to enable the existing societies to reform their financing where reform was necessary, as it generally was, and not to be interfered with by the competition of perhaps some irresponsible young societies that might at any time be started. The difficulty is largely a question of competition, and a young society can get along, if the lives are reasonably well selected, for ten or fifteen or even more years. The effect of incorporating new societies would be to bring

---

*Extracts from the address of the Hon. J. Howard Hunter, Registrar of Friendly Societies for Canada, before the Canadian Fraternal Association.

into competition with existing societies that were strug-
gling with the question of financial reform, competing
societies that had no sense of responsibility and no imme-
diate liabilities impending. That would have put the
existing societies at a very serious disadvantage, and in
fact reform would have been indefinitely postponed. That
policy has been adhered to. But the societies that were
here referred to are sick and funeral benefit societies.
There is a small class of societies giving small benefits
which can be incorporated under the Act, in connection
with large manufacturing establishments. We have sev-
eral of them in this city, but there has been a disposition
lately to apply under guise of that section for societies
that are really speculative in their character, or entirely
visionary, and it was thought wise to put a stopper on
such applications. The friendly societies of this coun-
try are not intended to be in any case speculative; they
are intended to be *bona fide,* and for the benefit of the
members.

I read with much interest the notices of your pro-
ceedings in the paper. I was very glad indeed to notice
that you had been favored with the attendance of the
President of the National Fraternal Congress on this
occasion. The proceedings of that body I have read with
a great deal of interest; they have been most instructive,
and ought to be in the hands of everyone interested in
the welfare of friendly societies.

I was struck with one or two facts mentioned in your
last proceedings. It was there said that the insurance
contracts on foot in societies forming that Congress
aggregated more than five and a half billions of dollars.
The amount is simply paralyzing, even to the imagination.
And numerous societies are not represented in that Con-
gress but are represented in another Congress which
is known I think as the Associated Fraternities. I also

noted in your proceedings that the annual payments of insurance moneys by the societies in the Congress stood at fifty-two and a half millions, for the year 1902, or over a million per week. Distributed among 25,000 homes. Also that during the previous ten years the societies forming that Congress had paid out over three hundred millions of dollars in benefits to the beneficiaries of 192,470 members.

The very magnitude of these operations makes it a duty of the Fraternal Congress to examine as to the stability of all. Such work is, of course, grand and imposing and magnificent. But the disturbing question is, will it stand? To that question the Fraternal Congress has addressed itself and examined especially as to what a minimum rate for a whole life insurance of $1,000 should be, the expense of management being excluded. In 1899 the Fraternal Congress compiled a mortality table and table of rates representing the minimum of safety.

In Ontario, of course, we have no such enormous sums in the form of liabilities, but still the amount is very, very large. So much so that it has often been the source of great anxiety. As you are perhaps aware, in 1896, having the same question present to my mind as the Fraternal Congress had in 1899, I computed the minimum table of rates, that is the minimum of safety, for a whole life insurance of $1,000. I took the experience of the Canada Life, a very carefully managed company, as you know, erring very often on the side of safety in the selection of lives. I thought that was the best that was known. The mortality in the Canada Life was considerably lower than the mortality shown in the tables that we know as the H. M. tables. Therefore, I took the mortality of the Canada Life for 46 years, from 1847 to 1893, as the basis of my calculation, and I reached the net rates of premiums for, of course, non-participating whole life policies, that you now find appended to the Ontario Insurance Act in appendix "A."

Naturally, I followed with a great deal of interest the proceedings of the National Fraternal Congress when they published their table, and I was very much gratified to find that their rates did not differ materially from the rates which I had arrived at. (Applause.) And in some cases were almost identical. That I think ought to satisfy every reasonable mind that the minimum of safety has been ascertained. And if that has been ascertained the duty of the societies is perfectly plain. That is of financial reform. I was glad to observe, by one of the morning papers, that your president had ·been calling your attention to this matter which overshadows every other matter that can possibly be brought before this association, the financial stability and solvency of societies.

Now the Fraternal Congress has been testing its own table by the actual mortality experienced by the societies forming the Congress during the year 1902. The actual mortality experienced was found to be 95.03 of the mortality shown by the table. What more striking verification could you have or could you desire of the accuracy of that table?

One of the largest societies in the country has rectified its rates. A large number of other societies are gradually rectifying their rates. There is a general movement, but I confess I would like to see greater rapidity in the movement. Some of the societies seem not to appreciate the extreme importance of the question. I was very glad to see that the Independent Order of Foresters had· made itself conspicuous in the question of the reform of its premium rates. The respected head of that institution and I have differed on many questions from time to time, but we do not differ at all on the question of reforming rates, and I was greatly gratified to find that he had shown so good an example to all the rest in the matter of dealing with an extremely difficult and perplexing question.

I fully appreciate your position in dealing with your people. These societies were started at a time when there was very little information available as to mortality, and what information there was, was in such a form as to be very unintelligible except to minds strictly mathematical. Having no guidance you were just in the same position as those great English societies; you went through the same phases, and I hope will reach the same result as those great English societies that have reformed their finances and have immensely gained, not only in numbers, but in public confidence and in financial strength.

Perhaps you are not aware, how that reform was brought about in England. The Manchester Unity in 1870 published a valuation of its policies, and the result was extremely damaging to the Manchester Unity. It showed that actuarially the society was insolvent. There was an explosion. The officers were blamed. The officers that afterwards were extolled for being so bold and manly in taking a difficult question in a firm way and dealing with it; but first they were very unpopular for making this disclosure. It created a tremendous sensation in England; so much so that a royal commission was issued the same year to inquire into the financial solvency of friendly societies. That commission sat for a number of years taking evidence, and the result was the Imperial Act of 1875, which requires a five years' valuation of the policies.

The two great English societies are not even now quite actuarially solvent, and they do not deny the fact. They say we are worth so many shillings in the pound and we are short so many shillings and pence in the pound, amounting in the aggregate to a large sum. That is the actuarial solvency. Of course, commercially they are solvent; that is to say, they pay all debts as they arise; but they are not satisfied with that; they say we must be actuarially solvent, and they have continually worked to that point, sometimes taking very strong measures with recalcitrants, cutting off lodges that did not comply, cutting off whole districts of lodges that did not comply. It is in that way that they have made the very radical reform that is so striking a feature of the English societies.

I have been reading with considerable interest papers that have appeared in THE FRATERNAL MONITOR, an excellent paper and an undoubted friend of fraternal societies. It cannot be doubted that it speaks in the true interest of the societies. It is anxious to see the same reformation accomplished here that has been accomplished in England. The great difficulty with us is how to get there. A leading correspondent or contributor to that paper is Mr. Barnard, an actuary, whose papers are always interesting and valuable. He suggests that you get there by turning the policies into term policies, and he argues very plausibly that the policy was in its origin a term policy. What would that mean? Nothing of that kind should be attempted without seeing where you are going. A term policy means a policy the premium of which would vary year by year, if not month by month. That you would have to pay the natural instead of the level premium. You call them dues, but that is only another phrase for premium, consideration for the insurance. The natural premium is a very fluctuating amount, as everyone will understand. A young man of 25 is a very different subject for insurance from a man of 75, and the difference in the premium is enormous.

Now, you have to deal with old men in converting your policies. If you were to convert your policies into term policies and charge at the attained age, for that would be the only sensible way of working it out, charge these men year by year the premium proper for that year of their life, you would have a very warm time. I have just made a few hasty calculations that perhaps may interest you. This is a subject that is considerably discussed in the United States just now, and in a modified form appears to be proposed by the Mutual Reserve, as a scheme of getting out of the difficulties arising from its older class of policies.

Now, taking the Canada Life experience, the natural premium for one year is at age 25 about $6.40 for $1,000 —just the term insurance, a year's insurance. At age 40 it would be about one and a half times that. At age 50 it would be two and two-fifths times that. At 55 it would be more than three times, at 60 nearly four and a half times, at 65 six and a half times, at 70 more than nine, and at 75 it would be about 15 times as much as at 25. Now, if you were to exact from your people who had reached 75 years of age a premium of 15 times $6.40, jumping it up in that kind of way, I think you would probably have a very serious time in your meetings. Therefore, I am afraid, although from a mathematical point of view Mr. Barnard is perfectly correct, you are just charging those people exactly for what you are giving them. It is a strictly logical bargain in one sense, but human nature is not logical. If we are waiting for human beings to be logical we will never do anything.

Now, besides the difficulty of dealing with policies in that sort of way, there is this further difficulty that that was not the real intention of the parties that entered into that contract. The parties really intended a whole life contract. In 1901 I explained to you the genesis of the societies and how it came about that things have taken their present form. Immediately after the American War there were an immense number of bubble companies formed on the old-line pattern. We often hear of friendly society bubbles, but our friends who talk so much about friendly society bubbles should remember that there were bubbles of the other kind, a great many of them, and they were bubbles of the other kind, a great many of them, proved a great sorrow to the public. A great number of such enterprises were started as joint stock life companies, and they ran their course very rapidly. When they failed, as immense numbers of them did, it was found that the alleged reserve, about which they had been boasting for years, was not there. It had disappeared. If it had ever been there it was wasted or stolen.

The re-action on the public mind was naturally very sharp, and Americans, with that quick intuitive action which is characteristic of the nation, started a new sort of organization, doing business in whole life insurance, taking a small amount per month. They said, "You will avoid the danger of these reserves being lost by keeping them in your own pocket; we will call on them whenever necessary by assessment, and you need not be in any nervous state of mind about the preservation of the reserves, for we are not going to have any large reserves, and we will call upon you whenever any money is necessary." Now, that addressed to a people who had just suffered so severely, gave an immense impetus to assessment life insurance in the United States.

The State of Massachusetts, in 1877, passed a law to facilitate the creation of these societies, and they went to the extreme limit of forbidding fixed premiums and reserves. Just think of the length to which they went in their insanity. Under that act Massachusetts, as you know, was filled with these assessment life insurance societies, which became the scandal of the United States and gave a black eye to fraternities, because many of them assumed the names of fraternities, and adopted the lodge feature, signs, pass-words, and everything else. It was part of the scheme. There was a perfect carnival among these societies for a short time in Massachusetts, and when they fell down, as, of course, they speedily did, they made a great public scandal and loss to the community. Then the tide set back again in favor of reserves. People said after all reserves are necessary, but the reserves must not be wasted or stolen. That is the moral that we should have drawn, instead of the moral that we did draw. Now, it was out of that time and out of that state of feeling that this present contract arose. It was intended to be a whole life contract. It was never intended to be a term contract.

A term contract is a new contract every time you pay a new premium, and you might impose new conditions. It is like a fire insurance contract; you may call it a renewal every three years, but it is in law a new contract. The company is not bound to renew, or if it does renew it may impose entirely new conditions and a new premium. On the other hand, the premium payer cannot force the company; he is not chargeable for any renewal premium, and he cannot tender and force upon the company the premium and demand a renewal of the contract. That is the position in which a term contract is. You make a contract for a specific time, and at the end of that time, unless you bind yourself to renew it on certain terms, both parties are at liberty to renew or not and on such conditions as they may agree upon. That was not the intention at all of the contracts in force in Ontario. It was an all-life contract under which the policy-holder on tendering the amount of the premium as the policy directs it to be paid, can force you to take that premium. It is not a new contract at all but a continuation of the old contract. Then over and above all that the Ontario Insurance Act provides as in all other cases that on tender of the premium you must take it and the contract must be continued. You can settle the premium by your by-laws, and friendly societies have the extraordinary power of changing the rates from time to time, which of course has proved their salvation in many cases. They can say, "We will continue your contract, but by our constitution and by-laws we have amended our table of rates, here is our table of rates, and you must tender the amount required by that table before we will continue your contract." But you cannot refuse to continue the contract on this tendering the proper premium.

HOMES FOR WORKMEN

The late issue of the Consular and Trade Reports refers to the movement in Austria-Hungary to enable the poorer people to secure better homes. It is explained that the question of providing suitable dwellings for the people has received considerable official attention and that the government is awakening to its responsibilities in this direction. The steps suggested for the relief of the people are of interest to us for the reason that they involve considerations of a similar nature here.

Particular attention has been given to ascertain both the mode of living and to establish regulations as to proper living. Those who have given the subject consideration insist that it is in order to reduce taxation on homes and to afford special advantages to those who are desirous of securing and paying for homes of their own.

Public authorities do not seem to be so considerate in this country. They exempt from taxation large enterprises, churches and charitable institutions. In other words, they shift the burdens of these to those who can but illy afford to bear them. No effort is made to reduce the taxation on the homes of those who have to struggle so hard to secure and maintain them for the proper housing and protection of their dependents.

Even the funds of fraternal societies are not exempt from the tax gatherer. These are in no wise an asset or a holding in the ordinary acceptation of the term. They are neither more nor less than sinking funds created for the liquidation of liabilities which are to mature in the future. They are not created for the profit or the advantage of any one. They are simply held in trust temporarily, and the societies which hold them at all times have liabilities of an unmatured nature which will more than offset them.

It is claimed that in this country the interests of the people are paramount to those of the classes. This being true, why should such scant attention be paid to them, and why should effort be so constantly put forth to reduce their holdings in the way of taxation and otherwise?

Much money has been spent in the way of organizing schemes and institutions for the relief of those who may find the burdens of life to bear down upon them with crushing force. If effort in this direction were centralized in the way of encouraging home building and in the way of encouraging proper hygienic and sanitary regulations far better ends would be served. Is not much of the so-called sympathy now extended to the public of a maudlin and sentimental nature? Is it not impractical? Does it not touch upon extreme cases rather than act as a preventive through which the existence of such cases may be made impossible?

THE WILL OF THE PEOPLE

Although it is somewhat early to even forecast the results of legislation in the several states affecting fraternal societies, the prevalent belief is that but little will be accomplished in this direction. The sessions of the legislatures are drawing to a close. In many of them the period for the admission of new measures has passed. In others proposed laws have been recommitted to the committees from which they came and, if they reappear for consideration, it is probable that material changes and modifications will have been made.

From many points of view such an outcome may not be regarded as wholly undesirable. We have been in the throes of a severe moral shakeup during the past few years. Violent passions have evidenced themselves at times. In some quarters these have supplanted that calm and comprehensive judgment so essential in the well ordered conduct of things. Under such conditions it is manifestly unwise to enact into a law that which is ruinous and revolutionary. It savors too much of the practice of punishing a child when under the control of anger. It alienates and embitters. It accomplishes no desirable purpose.

Legislative 'epidemics are comparable to infectious diseases. There is a degree of regularity in their appearance. We have forty-eight State legislatures and when these are in session the tubercle of doing something startling begins to evidence itself. A few rampant demagogues can cause it to multiply with amazing rapidity and in a short time it develops into a particular shape of legislation, starting in one state and sweeping over others like a "wave." Possibly, in the course of progress, there will be hospitals and sanatoria for the cure of those thus afflicted, but until this period arrives it is the duty of level minded persons to consider just as thoughtfully what they should not do as what they should do.

A DEPARTMENT OF CONCILIATION

There exists what is known as the "Association of International Conciliation." Its particular field is the consideration of world problems—those which confront the entire human race. Its mission involves profound changes not only in diplomacy but in popular thinking. Its contention is that many of the real and fancied differences existing between the nations of the world may be removed by a right and righteous solution of the first principles involved. It believes that the first step in this direction is that of affording practical aid in knowing and understanding one another.

The same relations which exist between nations may be said to exist between the several states of this country and the several counties into which they are sub-divided, and so continue down until they apply to the relations between neighbors. Indeed, one may apply them to our business and social affairs. The same methods which stand for success in the most far-reaching combination of capital or people are equally as essential in small combinations or individual effort.

A parallel of the differences which not infrequently arise between nations may be found in the lack of harmony which exists in fraternal operation to-day. That it is of a temporary nature and will soon blow over goes without the saying. It, however, is regrettable for the reason that it is a bar to progress and serves the purpose of arousing criticism and suspicions among those who look upon such antagonisms from a neutral standpoint. It is not beyond the range of probability that a "Department of Conciliation" might bring about desirable results in the fraternal field. If it is of value in world problems, why can it not be applied to those affecting more closely the every day affairs of life? Are not the differences among fraternal leaders those of judgment only? Are not all working for the selfsame end? Is not the barrier which separates them of a somewhat vague and intangible nature? Could it not be easily removed if there were a frank interchange of opinions and review of conditions in the spirit of conciliation?

THE FUTILITY OF ARGUMENT

As a rule arguments fail to convince. Rather, they serve the purpose of dividing those indulging in them into hostile camps. These are more interested in supporting their own side of the contention than they are in ascertaining the real truth. They not infrequently distort facts so as to make them almost unrecognizable. Arguments of this nature work more harm than good.

In the majority of questions of a general nature there does not seem to appear on the surface to be any reason why the proponents of 'one side should abandon their own contention or yield against their own interests to the arguments of the other side. The action of each party in yielding, or refusing to yield, to the arguments of the other appears to be entirely dependent upon its own will and pleasure. When self-interest—the desire to secure an advantage at the expense of others—is in evidence, the controversy becomes more and more hopeless. Unless abandoned, or unless there is a common ground on which all may meet, such antagonisms grow until they threaten the very life of the interests thus bandied about.

In national affairs the same situation is in evidence. There is such a bewildering array of apparently irreconcilable differences that he who insists that he is wholly right and all others are wholly wrong must eventually give up hope of accomplishing anything. Yet order is brought out of chaos by the nations yielding to certain conditions and shaping their conduct against their own apparent interests in obedience to the rules which are shown to be applicable.

THE MONITOR believes that such a course may well be adopted by those representatives of the fraternal system who seem to fancy that their own particular interests are paramount to those of the system itself. There is a standard by which action should be measured. There is a limit beyond which operation cannot safely go. There are conditions which may not measure up to such standards. In such event it is manifestly the part of wisdom to proceed with discretion. It is far better to yield apparent interests and shape conduct so as to accomplish that which is possible.

LAWS ALONE NOT SUFFICIENT

It is an error to fancy or assume that the sanction which secures obedience to the laws of the land consists only of the pains and penalties imposed by the law itself for its violation. There is a higher law which compels obedience. It is not written in the statutes nor is it interpreted by the courts. In its final analysis it is a law which makes and unmakes institutions as well as nations.

Public sentiment is at the root of all law. If public sentiment is back of the attempts to secure legislation with reference to fraternal operation they will succeed. If it is not, they will fail signally. Laws are capable of enforcement only so far as they are in harmony with the opinions of those on whom they are visited. As opinions change, old laws become obsolete and new standards force their way into the statute books. Laws passed, which are sometimes in advance of public opinion, ordinarily wait for their enforcement until the progress of opinion has reached recognition of their value. The force of law is in the public opinion which prescribes it.

It is believed that attempts to force fraternal legislation in advance of public opinion sustaining them will prove futile. Indeed, on the basis that the members of these societies control them just as much as do the people of the country control it, and decide what shall be the law and what shall not, it may be said to be a question of practical ethics as to how far attempts should go in the way of securing legislation, even though the need of this be admitted by those whose training and experience qualify them to speak with authority on the subject.

HARMONY IN THE RANKS

It is just as important that there be harmony in the ranks of an organization as it is that there be harmony among the organizations themselves. If this is not in evidence, the seeds of decay have begun to germinate. In time they will bear deadly fruit. But one thing awaits an organization in which dissensions and bickerings dominate all other considerations.

Deference to the will of the majority is the cardinal principle upon which co-operation of whatsoever nature rests. This means deference to public opinion. Well has it been said that such deference is shown in proportion to a people's advance in civilization.

It has been said that the nearest approach to defiance of popular will will be found among the most isolated and least civilized countries—those whose ignorance of the world prevents the effect of the world's opinion. Again, in every such country internal disorder, oppression and wretchedness marks the penalties which warn mankind that the laws established by civilization for the guidance of national conduct cannot be ignored with impunity.

The time is opportune for fraternal leaders of all shades of belief to come to a realizing sense that individual views possess value only to the extent that they can be impressed upon others through the means of persuasion and education. If they are repudiated they possess no value. If they are accepted they in time become a part of the principles and beliefs by which operation is measured and efficiency gauged.

There is another thing which fraternalists everywhere will do well to keep in mind. There should be a truce to calling attention to the past and the evils which have been uncovered. Such a course is utterly out of harmony with the spirit of the times and the trend of events. He who is ever bewailing the adverse conditions which surrounded him in the past is but illy prepared to meet the problems of the future. We should consider only the past for the information, it affords. The very spirit of progress is opposed to such reactionary practices.

Face front! should be the slogan. The wonderful accomplishments of the system should not be obscured by the dismal forebodings of prophets of evil. Fraternalism has accomplished much. There are even better things in store for it. Its leaders, however, should see to it that they are in harmony with those whose interests they represent. They should endeavor to merit the moral support and confidence of their members. They should learn a lesson from the nations themselves. The greatest and strongest government is the one which possesses the confidence and loyal support of its people. The strongest fraternal society is the one constructed along similar lines.

A BESETTING SIN

Indecision is a besetting sin of mankind. To it may be traced practically all of the disappointments visited upon us. We have opportunities but we fail to embrace them. We wait for a more convenient time. We fancy that something better may be presented to us later on.

The Louisville *Herald* has reproduced a "Legend of Lost Opportunities." It refers to those who, in all climes and all ages, call sadly and regretfully to mind the thousand golden opportunities forever lost. The unwisdom of their failure to make the most of conditions available is beautifully taught in the following Indian legend:

There was once a beautiful damsel upon whom one of the good genii wished to bestow a blessing. He led her to the edge of a large field of corn where he said to her:

"Daughter, in the field before us the ears of corn, in the hands of those who pluck them in faith, shall have talismanic virtues, and the virtue shall be in proportion to the size and beauty of the ear gathered. Thou shalt pass through the field once and pluck one ear. It must be taken as thou goest forward, and thou shalt not stop in thy path, nor shalt thou retrace a single step in quest of thine object. Select an ear full and fair and according to its size and beauty shall be its value to thee as a talisman.

The maiden thanked the good genii, and then set forward upon her quest.

As she advanced she saw many ears of corn, large, ripe and beautiful, such as calm judgment might have told her would possess virtues enough, but in her eagerness to grasp the very best she left these fair ears behind, hoping that she might find one still fairer. At length as the day was closing, she reached a part of the field where the stalks were shorter and thinner, and the ears were very small and shrivelled.

She now regretted the grand ears she had left behind and disdained to pick from the poor show around her, for here she found not an ear which bore perfect grain.

She went on, but alas! only to find the stalks more and more feeble and blighted, until in the end as the day was closing, and the night coming on, she found herself at the end of the field without having plucked an ear of any kind. No need that the genii should rebuke her for her folly. She saw it clearly when too late.

A FITTING APPLICATION

The indecision set forth in the above legend is in evidence in the everyday affairs of life. We are not satisfied with that which is available. We essay to attain the impossible and, in so doing, pass by opportunities which can readily be transformed into most desirable realities.

In fraternal affairs the untoward results of indecision have been repeatedly shown. A member becomes dissatisfied with the organization to which he has committed the protection of his dependents. He has misgivings as to its permanence. He has been told by some one that its future is fraught with uncertainty; that it cannot carry out its obligations and that he can change to another organization which will afford him that which is lacking in his own institution. He listens to his so-called friend or adviser and transforms his allegiance and his protection to another institution.

Is not his action to be compared with that set forth in the legend, where inordinate greed was manifested for that which was best? In the quest for this most desirable opportunities were passed by. As the end of the journey was approached it was found that the opportunities decreased both in size and number. Eventually they disappeared altogether.

So it is with the fraternalist who is ever changing from one organization to another. He is losing most desirable opportunities. He is subjecting his dependents to unnecessary hazards. His spirit of unrest—his desire to secure the very best of everything—has led him far afield. He eventually comes to a period in his life when the doors of opportunity are closed against him.

Far better would it be for such members to be content with that which they possess. If errors or weak points exist they, as constituent members of the organization, should put forth all their powers to remedy them. They should endeavor to co-operate with those whose central purpose it is to build up growing and enduring organizations. They should not shirk their duty by seeking something which they fancy or which they are told may be better. Distance lends enchantment and adds to the attractiveness of anything. The traditional pot of gold at the foot of the rainbow is a pertinent case in illustration.

PERFECTION IS AN IDEAL

While it should be our central purpose to keep ever in view high standards, we should not lose sight of current conditions. We have to take the world as it is—not as we wish it to be. We cannot expect to attain perfection. This is but a standard to keep us moving in the right direction.

There are those so constituted as to oppose change instinctively. These usually call themselves conservative. They fancy that adherence to given ideas or fixed forms of operation are evidence of consistency and of wisdom.

Change is a sign of progress. The individual or organization in a receptive state will be ever ready to discard the old for something better. There are changes needed in all forms of operation. These should be made frankly and with the knowledge that they will redound to the good of those affected. Those who stand in the pathway of progress may hinder it, but they cannot prevent it. Far better is it to co-operate and unite for a better order of things.

If an evil exists the remedy should be applied. With or without the individual, systems will go on. Those alive to their opportunities, and who would not share the fate indicated in the legend, should conform to the progressive order of things and seize upon those things that will advantage them.

TOWARD A HIGHER STANDARD

The marvelous progress made bv the fraternal system should be a source of satisfaction to every one identified with it. From a crude and inequitable basis it has grown into a mighty system. It numbers millions of members under its banners. It carries billions of protection for their dependents. Each year more than one hundred million dollars are disbursed to the dependents of members. The close of each year witnesses greater accumulation as an earnest that the future will be provided for.

It is a fixed rule of nature that everything must have a small beginning. Man himself, considered the greatest of all creations, exemplifies this fact. Left to himself at his entrance upon life, he would speedily perish. He needs the ministrations of gentle and loving hands. He is unable to withstand the rude shocks which will not impede his progress later on. He has to grow and expand with the years. He is strengthened by coming in contact with others, by seeing their attainments and by endeavoring to equal them.

So it is with all institutions created by man's hands or brain. There must ever be growth and development. There must ever be a community of interests and an union of these for mutual wellbeing and for the attainment of desirable ends.

HAS GROWN TO MAN'S ESTATE

Fraternalism to-day may be said to have attained its majority. It has grown to man's estate. It has reached that period in its history from which it can study its past with profit and contemplate the future with complacency. It no longer has to give an excuse for its existence. It has won for itself, through its benefactions, a recognition that is world-wide.

Fraternalism, through its accomplishments, has enshrined itself in the memories of hundreds and thousands of widows and orphans. It has mitigated their burdens. It has come to their assistance at a most opportune time. It has interposed its protecting folds between them and the future with which they, single-handed, might not have been able to contend. It to-day is the mainstay and hope of more than seven millions of members and over twenty millions of dependents.

Every week the fraternal system is disbursing fully eighty million dollars to the bereaved and fatherless. It has gathered and strewn the incomprehensible sum of $1,500,000,000 since its inception. As has been said, it has but reached man's estate. Its past accomplishments are small as compared with that which is to be done in the future.

FRATERNAL PROGRESS

Could one compare the system of to-day with that of ten years ago, without knowing anything as to the leaven of evolution which has been working ceaselessly and tirelessly, he would be amazed at the strides which have been taken. He would be unable to understand how such a transformation could take place short of actual revolution. He would be constrained to ask in what manner can a system of such vast and far-reaching proportions conform so closely to the actual needs of its wide membership?

But a few years ago fraternal opponents declared its proposition to have been crude, unscientific, inequitable and unstable. It responded by remedying the defects which were found to exist in its context. Such opponents then brought forth additional arguments against it. Some of these possessed force, while others were traceable directly to selfish purposes, and were discarded as the vaporings arising from avowed hostility.

Valid objections were received thoughtfully and good resulted from their consideration. The good was separated from the dross—and this process is to-day going on steadily and, beyond question, will continue so long as the system is under the direction of man. So long as he continues striving toward better things the system is safe.

When he thinks he has attained perfection it will be in most imminent peril.

The lesson to be drawn from the Indian legend is one we may consider and apply to the general affairs of our life. We should not pass by the opportunities of to-day in the hope that greater ones will appear to-morrow. We can only act in the present. We should so build that to-morrow's opportunities will be in the nature of results from to-day's action.

As fraternalists it is our duty to stand by the organizations with which we are connected. We should not try to evade our responsibilities. We should not seek shelter when signs of disturbance are in evidence. Rather, we should come to the front and by our effort and presence add to the confidence of those who are united with us in this great work. He who deserts or skulks in the rear when there is opposition at the front has been regarded from time immemorial as one unworthy of the confidence and assistance of his fellow men.

As a rule, fraternalists have stood by their system most loyally during the work of reconstruction. There are those who became frightened or who fancied that they could not continue to profit unduly at the expense of their associates. They withdrew and believed that their actions would cause consternation in fraternal ranks. The gaps thus occasioned were soon filled up and at the end of each year the system showed substantial increases.

To-day the cause stands for higher and better things than it did a decade ago. That it will continue to prosper and improve is a foregone conclusion. This is indicated by what has been done in the past. Fraternalists everywhere should bestir themselves in behalf of both their organizations and the system of which they are exponents. In so doing they advance their own interests and at the same time contribute to the protection of the dependents of others. The opportunities of to-day are practically without limit. The future depends upon the manner in which these are employed.

A FIXED SALARY BREEDS EXTRAVAGANCE

This is to be a disagreeable article, intended to make the young and old man working for a salary think seriously about himself.

If you talk to a man who has $15 a week salary, he will say to you:

"I can just manage to live on it—fairly well—but I can't save a cent. I see no hope ahead for the future."

The man with a salary of $100 a week will say, in exactly the same tones:

"I can just manage to live on it, and keep my family half decently—but I can't save a cent. I don't know what would become of my children if anything should happen to me."

And it is always the same story, no matter what the salary or the wages—the full amount is always spent, it is difficult to make ends meet, and there is nothing left over to show for long years of work.

To the man of small salary it may seem absurd to talk of the man with ten or twenty or thirty thousand dollars annual salary spending every cent and being always behindhand—yet that is what happens almost invariably.

This writer knows one individual with a salaried income about the same as that of the President of the United States—and that foolish person is always worrying about meeting bills, the same as the man with $10 or $15 a week.

The president of a great railroad, a man whom every

inhabitant in this country knows by name, drew an enormous salary for a great many years. Yet when his employer—a hundred-time millionaire—died, this salaried man, with more than $50,000 a year, had nothing to show for his years of work. He was an old man, and the sons of his late employer combined together to provide for him. He could tell a very good story of the extravagant habits that come of a fixed salary.

The purpose of this article is not to make the salaried man feel foolish, or merely to convince him that he is extravagant. Unless some useful suggestion were made, this page of white paper would be utterly wasted.

Let us consider, therefore, why it is that the salaried man, with a steady, regular income, is nearly always the man who has nothing saved up against a rainy day.

Why is it that the rich man in telling his life story nearly always describes some business venture, some enterprise that he went into on his own account, as the basis of his success and fortune?

In the first place, we do not appreciate that which comes without any especial effort. What we can do easily and regularly, we take as a matter of course.

The man working for himself, with the element of uncertainty in his work, is compelled to realize the possibilities of future difficulties. Constant change, fluctuations in profit keep him out of a rut and alive to actual conditions. The man with a salary simply looks upon that as a minimum. He arranges promptly to spend all of it, no matter what it may be. He knows that he will have it this week, and next week. He usually thinks that he ought to have a great deal more—sometimes he ought to, and sometimes he deceives himself.

If he had a house and sold it, if he even had a horse and wagon and sold them, he would look upon the purchase money as Capital. He would feel that he ought to keep that money, or at least some of it, for a future day.

But not one salaried man in a thousand realizes that as he draws his weekly salary he is selling himself, his youth, his strength and his future prospects on the instalment plan.

At the end of a week, when a man draws his salary, he has sold one week of his life, and one of the best weeks. It is strange that in a nation where a great majority of working men and women work for a salary, so few realize what the salary means. It means discounting the future, and selling yourself for weekly payments.

You are working for a salary, and so you spend it as it comes.

You have been doing this in the past, and despite an occasional feeble good resolution, you will continue doing it in the future.

Have you no lesson to learn from the experience of others?

Don't you know any poor old man who for years and years drew a good salary but saved none of it? Don't you know that we are all about alike, and that if you keep on as at present you will be in that old man's place?

Even when you look over the past and think of the total amount you have earned in the last five or ten or fifteen years, can you not see that it would have been possible without suffering for you to have saved such a sum as would make you feel independent now?

The difference between a man with $2,000 or $3,000 in cash saved and the man with nothing is the difference between independence and dependence, between weakness and strength.

We laugh at the old story about the man who gave up cigars or cocktails or some trifle, and with the money saved established independence.

But we ought not to laugh. The late George M. Pullman, talking one night to a number of men, including Marshall Field, John W. Doane and others, said to a very young man who was with them:

"When I was your age, I was doing fairly well and earning a pretty good salary. But I had my sleeping car in mind. I wanted to build the car, and I made up my mind that to succeed I must have some money. The cigars that I smoked cost five cents each. I gave them up, and gave up other things, too. The total didn't amount to much, but the habit was valuable."

The determination needed to make a young man give up his pleasures and small extravagances is the kind of determination that gives real success.

George M. Pullman possessed determination. He gave to this country a sleeping car system of inestimable value, besides making himself enormously rich. If he hadn't had the courage to save on a salary and to give up what most young men consider absolutely essential, the great Pullman sleeping car enterprise might have gone up into the air in the smoke of cheap cigars. Millions of men in the United States have had good ideas and taken them into the grave with them because they hadn't the determination to save the money necessary for carrying out an idea.

Millions of men have the capacity to go into business on their own account, to have a salary list of their own, instead of figuring on some one else's list—but they lack the ONE quality. They cannot resist the temptations which make the salaried man extravagant.

To the man traveling through this world of fierce competition money is like quinine to the explorer in an African fever swamp. The man who sells his life week by week and spends the money as it comes, is spending whatever chance he might have of independence.

The worst of it is that, besides making men extravagant, the salary system makes a great majority of them indifferent and careless. It kills imagination and special effort. It keeps a man in a rut and prevents his ever doing the best that is in him.

One word of urgent advice.

If, reading this, you should make up your mind to save, save on yourself.

Cut down your own expenditures. Cut off your useless pleasures and self-indulgences. Don't cut down on your family on your wife or children or on others, who have a right to look to you for support.

The average extravagant salaried man can easily reform and make the necessary change without affecting any one but himself. He need not economize at the expense of others.

Don't forget this. The mind that controls itself is made stronger through self-control. When you control yourself and limit yourself, you not only save money, but add to your own effectiveness.

Try it.

WHAT THE YEARS HAVE BROUGHT FORTH

HON. OLIN BRYAN

Fraternal protection is neither too new to be uncertain, nor too old to be in decadence. This, like wine, enriches with age. Only two score years of history. It seems as we look back that it represents forty centuries of accomplishments. Someone has said: "Opportunity is the command of God." Surely the projectors of these societies seized the right hour in human destiny, and caught the tide at the flood which led them on to fortune.

Out from the beginning, one with its little circle of timid, yet hopeful, souls, we have in a single generation

witnessed the marvelous extension until we number to-day
no less than two hundred and twenty-five different asso-
ciations, operating upon the same plan, all welded into a
distinctive and peculiar "system." From the group of
doubting Thomases only a half dozen dreamers, we have
seen the widening of the ripple to a living army of more
than five and one-half million. From the scant protection
of a few hundred dollars to the few homes, we now have
in force protection of more than nine and one-half billions
of dollars. The ledger accounts show a disbursement
already made of more than one and a half billions of dol-
lars. Now in the treasuries of the societies ninety mil-
lions, which is some guarantee for the maturing certifi-
cates of to-morrow. During the period of a half of a
life, measured by man's Biblical allotment, plus five, we
have the records to show an average contribution to
American homes of more than one hundred thousand dol-
lars a day. Already we can gaze upon the countenances
of our deeds of helpfulness with intense enthusiasm, for
these are "Like proud crags, high up, that wear the
morning ere it comes."

One of the heathen philosophers wrote: "I learned
that no man in God's wide earth is either willing or able
to help any other man." This, doubtless, was true far
back in the corridors of time. How vastly different
to-day. Individuality is not to be minimized. Every man
is peculiarly himself. There is in the weave and woof
of each man that which differentiates him from all other
men. But from these traits which mark men there is the
wholesome and inspiring revelation that all true lives
blend into some other lives, and that each correct life
helps many other lives. While it is true that, "Like snow,
which falls flake by flake, our petty, thoughtless acts,
regarded singly, may seem of little importance; yet,
accumulated, they form a power as resistless as the

avalanche"—it is equally true, that good and well-directed deeds may individually seem of little moment; yet, accumulated, they, too, form a force which for humanity's uplift is much more potent than the ingenuity of man can measure.

Through the spirit of sacrifice, and the aids which flow into our souls from other hearts, come our strongest currents. Men do not attain anything worth while of themselves. It is only in proportion as they give of their lives to others that they receive the sap of moral and soul strength which enlarges them into the trees of real beauty and grandeur which produce nourishing fruit in God's vineyard. The true philosophy of life underlies these fraternal beneficiary societies. They had their birth in the womb of man's necessity, and they are what they are because they have been mighty contributions to home and to man's betterment, individually and collectively.

They exist in an extensive and surer sense. Differ as we may, as to their future, we cannot fail to agree that, wisely or unwisely, men of every station of life, from the daily toiler to the capitalist of leisure, men of the trades, of the field, of the colleges, of the professions, men of ripening years, as also men at the foothills of life's mountain, in every state, in every community, in every church, as also outside of the church, believe in these associations. They have confidence in their workmanship and stability. In them they have as that which surged in the heart of Columbus, or fed, in the hours of deepest travail, the heart of Washington. More than eighty years ago, forty years before these societies came into existence, Daniel Webster said that "with America and in America a new era commences in human affairs." Distinguished then as was our country, by free representative governments, entire religious liberty, improved systems of national intercourse, a newly awakened and an unconquerable spirit of free inquiry and a diffusion of knowledge through every community before unheard of, he mentally reviewed these institutions, as he caught the sweep of vision, culminated in the thought: "America, America, our country, fellow-citizens, our own dear and native land, is inseparably connected, fast bound up, in fortune and by fate, with these great interests." Could his prophetic vision have swept down through four score years, and beheld as we now behold what these fraternal beneficial societies have done for man's strengthening, for home protection, for education, and for life's opportunities, to these would have been added, these associations as another distinctive American institution, which is as indestructible as our Government. That people have faith in these societies no sane man will dispute. But this is an exacting, a testing and a searching age. We do not care so much about the history of things or of men as we do about their present weight and value, and their future security. This is strictly a commercial age. The emphasis is on the dollar, and not the man. The Missouri mind is everywhere in evidence, "you will have to show me." Sentiment! Yes, it is a beautiful thing, but it does not alone answer the requirements. So let us get down to business, and measure up what we have in these societies, and see where we stand in the commercial mart of to-day. We understand that, fraternity, standing alone, will not pay our contracts of protection which mature to-morrow and the other to-morrows in extenso. Our business side, which provides the "ways and means," must take care of these.

Addressing ourselves to this, primarily, we notice the character of our contracts. Our contracts are more than a mere agreement between the individual member on the one side and a soulless corporation on the other. If such was the scope of our contracts, then the inherent security of every contract would be the ability, in dollars and cents, of the corporation to pay, upon the happening of the contingency. This is the old-line insurance contract. The fraternal protection contracts are much broader. The contracts are between the individual member, the corporation and every other member, who is an integral and component part of the whole body. To illustrate: A— a member of our Order has a contract with the Order, and with 77,563 other members, and each additional member extends the circle of the contractual relationship. True, this is not such a contract as A can, in law, enforce against the other members individually or collectively, independently and apart from the corporation itself, but the "moral quality" and the "fraternal compact" are powerful factors in this extensive contract. This has been clearly demonstrated. Many of the societies commenced business without scientific knowledge of any approximately correct standard of measure. Thirty years' experience, more or less, later furnished the data upon which a fair standard could be formed. This ascertained, a measurement was made, and as soon as it was known that the cost had been and was, too low for continued safety, a change in rates was made, and the membership, in a significantly large part, in each case responded loyally, and showed an intelligent appreciation for correct methods and plans of operation. All societies are not now on a correct table of rates, but the movement is in this direction, and has been for ten years past. Once the membership appreciates the necessity for an increase in rates to insure soundness and stability they will meet it as they have done, squarely and manfully. No man today quibbles about the price, if it is the right figure. What he wants to know is, is this the very best price for security, consistent with the underlying principle of every such society, "protection without profit?"

There can be no hard and fast table of rates for all societies. Every society ought in fairness and equity be permitted to make its own table, upon its own experience, provided it shows, and can show, that it is on the right side of the ledger account. No reasonable man expects these societies which only in these last few years have been able to get their rate bearings to swing out and make good for all actual shortage by a single stroke. It cannot be done without destruction. There is neither sound logic nor good sense in asking or attempting it. What we want, what we should have, and what alone should be exacted, is to so adjust the finances of every society as to insure headway, no matter how slow, if gradual and sure, towards certain mathematical ground. Upon this plan these societies can operate safely. They should be secure, sound and honest. They cannot be operated for profit—the crux of the test which differentiates these associations from old-line companies is in this. If there is profit, they are not within their definition. So that, no fixed table, as such, can meet the necessities of every society, without doing violence, unless it is for such societies as are unable to determine the correct rate from their own experience. These should have a minimum table. The intelligence and character of the membership of these fraternal orders is also the strongest guarantee of permanency. Ignorance is dangerous; education is a bulwark of security. This is an intensely intellectual age. Knowledge is not confined to any class. The public school system, the public press, and the lodge rooms furnish the best conceivable avenues for learning. These three sources reach men of every walk of life. Men are by instinct inherently fair and honest. This is incontrovertibly true with intelligent men. The rights of property, of liberty and of life are safe in the keeping of an average American jury. Rarely do you find twelve men, whether in our large cities, or the country districts, who are not capable to intelligently comprehend and grasp any facts submitted. The necessity is for a clear presentation. Venality is rare, and injustice the exception, and rare at that, throughout the land. Such being true, what have we to fear at the bar of public opinion? We are not only in the house of friends in any forum, court or assembly in America, but we are under the eyes of their protection. We have the best guarantee for the harmony and perpetuity of these societies in the straightforward, plain and unreserved dealings with the membership. They are all partners in the business. Every member has mutuality of interest with every other. Keep him fully informed, and bring home to him all information touching the business management of his Order. He wants knowledge. He is with every other member, if he has time to give any thought, a seeker after truth. This is the policy of these associations. Another security which we have is in the publicity given to the management. He who runs may read. Another evidence of great moment is the fidelity and honesty of the lodge officers. This insures confidence. Confidence is the cement and concrete of the structure. We have a less percentage of defalcations in fraternal orders, by a large ratio, than in any other business involving the handling of such sums of money. Surety companies acknowledge that the bonds of the officers of the societies is the best risk on the market. This is worthy of our thought, and means much in the life of these institutions. Then, again, these orders are monuments to high ideals and most progressive business management. They are abreast with the best known and most progressive methods for accuracy and clearness.

Another security, not to be despised, is their place in the hearts of the people. Only merit stands the real test. Shams, pretense and fraud go down before public opinion. The oak stands the hurricane, the house on the rocks the storm, the man of character survives the minds of adversity, and the collective body, through which char acter is reflected, comes out secure after the onslaught of abuse, unwarranted and unfair attack has gone to its hid ings. Fraternal protection has met the enemy, and to-day the enemy is ours.

"DEARER THAN THE BRIDE"

"To be or not to be—that is the question." And it usually is answered when a man decides whether he will marry or not. This assumes that his decision will stand. If it is negative, it is not likely to stand, however strong he may make it.

If a man does not take a wife, he "had as lief not be." This is on the assumption that he can get a woman to have him. If he can't, he had much liefer not be.

Queer world this if it were not for courting, wedding and home-making. Queer world if, mortals inspired by the example of the birds, June were not particularly the month for mating. Sad world if we could not have the memories of those hours in woodland bowers, by clear streams, in budding gardens—perhaps in front parlors. "All the world loves a lover."

But "how much the wife is dearer than the bride!" A fair percentage of men fail to fulfill the future they picture for themselves and their brides. Life is seldom what it seems. Yet but rarely does the wife exact the full mede of the lover's promise. To her it is enough that he does his best.

And when in later years he looks back upon that life and is honest about it, how much of the credit for what he has accomplished he finds due to her. Due to her patience, her wisdom, her foresight, her intuition, her gentleness, her guidance of their children, her sympathy with him in his effort, her hand to soothe, her word to encourage.

He may not be one of the kind to say much about it—"the lover lost in the husband;" but he feels it, and if he does not feel it in full before it is too late, he has to feel it then with a bitterness that nothing ever can mitigate. He may have given her candy, flowers, opera, automobiles, but none of that expressed it.

There is a debt he owes her. It cannot be measured. But it can be recognized. With all her work or all her planning, her only income is through her husband. Shall it be possible that that income may be cut off at any moment, leaving her with no reward for the past and the necessity of redoubling her work to gain merely subsistence? That is hardly the "square deal."

HORSES PRAYER FOR POLICE

By direction of Acting Police Commissioner Bugher there was posted to-day, in every stable where police horses are kept, a card bearing a copy of "The Prayer of a Horse." This is it:

To thee, my master, I offer my prayer: Feed me, water and care for me, and when the day's work is done, provide me with shelter, a clean, dry bed and a stall wide enough for me to lie down in comfort. Talk to me; your voice often means as much to me as the reins. Pet me sometimes, that I may serve you the more gladly and learn to love you.

Do not jerk the reins, and do not whip me when going up hill. Never strike, beat or kick me when *I* do not understand what you mean, but give me a chance to understand you. Watch me, and if *I* fail to do your bidding see if something is not wrong with my harness or feet.

Examine my teeth when *I* do not eat. I may have an ulcerated tooth, and that, you know, is very painful. Do not tie my head in an unnatural position or take away my best defense against flies and mosquitos by cutting off my tail.

And finally, oh, my master, when my useful strength is gone, do not turn me out to starve or freeze, or sell me to some cruel owner to be slowly tortured and starved to death; but do thou, my master, take my life in the kindest way and your God will reward you here and hereafter. You may not consider me irreverent if I ask this in the name of Him who was born in a stable. Amen .

The Acting Commissioner found the prayer in Pittsburg recently, and it struck him so forcibly that he obtained a copy and arranged to have it reproduced for the Police Department. He thinks it will serve to obtain better treatment of the horses by men who sometimes lose their tempers and abuse them.

THE DEPUTY SYSTEM

DR. R. J. BRODSKY

Complaints have been recently heard of certain "practices" arising out of the deputy system and which are disastrous to the very existence of the fraternal system. The increased rate of lapse the fraternal associations have shown for the last few years, the high number of short-term deaths they suffer from to-day, and the large expense fund they have to maintain—these were likewise blamed to the deputy system which was adopted by all fraternal beneficiary associations of some significance. One went even so far as to maintain that the deputy system transforms a fraternal association into a commercial institution or that deputy system is contradictory to the fundamental principles of fraternalism, and suggested as the practical remedy against all these evils the return to the old method of operation referring spe-

cifically to the old plan of obtaining new business. The
deputy system has been attacked and condemned indis-
criminately by fraternalists and insurance commissioners
and to the great rejoicing of the old-line companies whose
literary spellbinders untiringly heralded the approaching
end of the fraternal world.

The character of this article does not permit us to go
into the details of the entire controversy of merits and
faults of the deputy system. We shall, therefore, limit
ourselves in the following pages to the consideration of
the method by which the deputy system could be given a
fair trial.

It is an axiomatic truth that the value of an institution
has to be deduced from the function it performs. In
the case of the deputy system from the function the latter
performs within the fraternal beneficiary system. Once
having recognized the real nature of the deputy system,
it would be easy to ascertain the evils inherent to it and
to separate them from all those casual and unhealthy
growths which eat the fraternal organism and which have
their origin in some other source than the deputy system.

Now, what is the function of the deputy system in the
fraternal mechanism? To answer this question, we must
briefly examine the role and the place of the fraternal
beneficiary system itself within the various systems of
insurance in the United States.

The fraternal beneficiary system came into existence
as a protest against the high cost of insurance as sold by
the legal reserve companies. With the battle cry: "The
protection at cost," the fraternal beneficiary associa-
tions entered the field of insurance occupied heretofore
by the legal reserve companies and were met by the latter
with a feeling of hostility. A hard and continuous strug-
gle which lasts up to the present ensued, a struggle for
existence and supremacy. In the earlier phases of this

war the assessment and fraternal associations have been in the position of an attacking army and have, without great strain, forced the enemy to retreat. Later on, however, the situation changed. The old-line companies, having fortified themselves, carefully studied the plans and methods of operation of their enemies, building up a standing army of insurance agents, furnishing them with the newest and most effective weapons, and organizing a thorough information and press service. From defense they went then over to systematic attack. With the slogan of "co-operative humbug," "temporary vision" and "insolvency" of fraternalism on the lips, the thousand-headed army of insurance agents invaded millions of homes of American people. The volunteer army of fraternal workers, however enthusiastic they may have been, could not repulse the enemy. A member of a fraternal organization, desirous to win his friend for fraternal cause, was frequently overpowered by the fertility of thought and readiness of speech of an insurance agent trained in his particular trade. Yet the large and steady influx of new blood, the continuous growth of the fraternal association was the essential condition for the success and survival of the fraternal system. The fraternal association operating on the assessment plan, in order to preserve its superiority to the old-line company, had to keep down its "average age" and the mortality rate at the lowest possible degree and this could be done only by securing large numbers of young members. Then also the fraternal association, having expanded itself throughout the country, could not with equal efficiency watch the condition of its far removed branches and was in need of a special organ for their maintenance or revival. Finally, when the fraternal field became a combatting ground for hundreds of fraternal associations, the need for a special man thoroughly familiar with the plans

and rates of organization and willing to call on customers
with offerings became urgent. Thus, as a matter of natu-
ral process of evolution and growth of the fraternal sys-
tem or as a result of competition with old-line companies
or of mutual emulation, a condition arose within the fra-
ternal circles calling for the need of field workers. The
fraternal organization became complicated and made pos-
sible and even necessitated establishment of an indepen-
dent organ, the organizing department. It suggested
itself to the aggressive fraternal managers as an economic
proposition and was taken up. The experience justified
their expectations.

The fraternal deputy followed the steps of the insur-
ance agent and, being equally trained, but broader minded
and representing higher ideas, had an easy case. He
satisfactorily performed the function the society wanted
him to accomplish; he continually brought a number of
new and young members, organized new branches, filled
the decaying lodges with new spirit and assured the
numerical growth and perpetuity of the organization. Fra-
ternal associations, in having adopted the deputy system,
adapted themselves to the conditions governing every
modern business enterprise. They have read the signs
of the times and have been fully rewarded; they have been
successful and have prospered numerically. On the other
hand those fraternal associations which did not read the
signs of the times, and which entertained a hope of the-
automatical growth, through the membership itself, hav-
ing reached a certain age, have found themselves in a
state of dormancy. The large part of the membership of
such an organization being of advanced ages, a young
person could not easily be induced to join it. The old
member who has been called upon to do the soliciting
work gratuitously had neither time nor particular skill;
he failed in his attempt to rejuvenate the organization.

To strengthen our argument we could also bring into memory the project of Prime Minister Gladstone of giving insurance to workmen at cost through the gratuitous service of the Post Office. After forty years of operation the Post Office reported a business of 13,000 policies in force!

Having shown that the fraternal deputy in his function as solicitor is an indispensable part of every well administered fraternal machinery, few words may be said in regard to the evils which the deputy system incurs. They are most exclusively the high lapse rate which occurs as the result of overpersuasion from the solicitor. This evil can, however, be partially remedied by the increased helpfulness or an additional service the society would be willing to offer to the member. On the other hand, the increase of expenses in fraternal orders cannot be entirely charged against the deputy system. The increased cost of new business is not the result of the adoption of the deputy system, but is due to the existence of the "cheap-rate" organizations which make the business of soliciting to the deputy representing an "adequate rate" organization rather difficult and therefore expensive. In such a case the unfair competition makes it impossible for the "adequate rate" society to enlarge the size of the organization whereby a greater economy in current expenses could be achieved. But even granted that the expense fund was steadily increased by adoption and expansion of the deputy system, it cannot be denied that the equitable distribution of ages, the low mortality rate and saving in mortality cost brought about by the deputy force sufficiently correct the evil in question. Similarly, the increased number of short-term deaths has nothing to do with the deputy system. The deputy is hired to obtain a possible large quantity of new business; he gets it as it comes, and it is up to the medical depart ment to make a careful investigation of the quality of risks brought in. In the hands of the medical department the power is vested to accept or to reject them and upon it the responsibility should lay for the high rate or short-term deaths. To be sure, a deputy exercises some influence on the local physician, who is elected by the former. But this evil can be corrected by taking out the office of local physician from the jurisdiction of the deputy, by keeping it out of "politics" and subjecting it directly to the central medical department thus making this office an appointive one.

Summing up, it may be said,—that the deputy force is an inherent part of the fraternal system. It is an inevitable result of the competition between the fraternal associations and old-line companies as well as between the associations themselves. Some one must be there to carry the ideas of home protection to the general public. Some permanent machinery is needed for writing fraternal insurance. Like every institution, this machinery may be incomplete. It is, however, in evolution and is working in the line of continuation and perfection. The problem which confronts the fraternal manager, therefore, is not whether the deputy system should be abolished or the membership should be urged to do the soliciting work, but what is the most economical and efficient method of handling the deputy force.

SINGLENESS OF PURPOSE

HON. J. C. ROOT

A little seed planted in fertile ground. The planter watches eagerly for the tiny sprouts to appear above the surface. With delight he notices the bursting earth, the pale, colorless shoots peeping up; every day he observes the growth, the taking on of verdure color, the tiny branches springing out as if to balance and give symmetry to the mother-stem; the budding and blossoming, the shimmering leaves. In a few months a miniature tree stands before him which gradually develops until it becomes a majestic, wide-spreading, high ascending monarch, firmly rooted, able to resist the tempest and the storm. Its fruit falls into willing hands; its protecting shade is grateful; the soughing music of the gentle breeze playing upon its boughs as if a veritable harp; the roaring, rustling of the leaves of many trees in the forest and the pattering rain on the shields of green makes a picture so refreshing that we love to contemplate it.

The tree represents that which comes from a single thought put into action. The man who planted the seed had confidence in the outcome. In his mind's eye he saw the mighty tree, but no doubt he also counted well the possibilities of defeat, the dangers of frost, the incursion by animals seeking succulent herbage to devour, the mischievous boy who might cut down the little treelet, the crushing, mangling, destroying cart wheels that transports the logs, or wood or gathers the sap. Indeed almost countless dangers might be encountered in its reaching its maturity, but the planter stood on guard, he protected the sapling so well that success crowned the effort.

Every great enterprise must have a perfect inception, however humble may be its beginning. Singleness of purpose and untiring effort is almost certain to assure its growth, prosperity and success. Many men are social and financial failures because they scatter their efforts; have too many irons in the fire if you please. The Captains in the financial world, the giants in law, the most famous in medicine, the greatest inventors, the finest musicians, the most successful politicians, the most masterly railway managers, the shrewdest promoters, the leading merchants, the favorite authors, the influential editors, the leaders of men have all reached recognition by personal concentrated devotion to the end sought to be accomplished.

My experience justifies the assertion that a man who shirks his duty or who depends on others to do the work he plans while he dwadles away his time in pleasure seeking, or worse, will seldom succeed in his enterprise. Success demands personal effort and the magnetism of his enthusiasm. If he leads, his followers will learn his pace and be useful to him. If he is indifferent and unappreciative, his followers will lose courage and interest. A mob of men without a recognized leader can soon be dispersed.

Every great revolution in government, politics or religion has had its idol, some man has given it inception and evolved the principles which he has impressed forcibly upon everybody who would listen to him or read his declarations and denunciation of existing evils. Men and women have deluded thousands of people by incredible fallacies, through their persistent singleness of purpose. Cults of most ridiculous pretension have flourished and the promoter has been worshipped and enriched almost as effusively as the adoration of Saints, in the primitive ages. Thousands endured hardships and encountered dangers almost appalling to follow Brigham Young to his "Holy City" on the western "Jordan" and American

"Dead Sea." Thousands more are worshipping whom they deem the female personification of Deity whose printed book (copyrighted by the oracle), if read, is believed to cause miraculous cures which defy medicinal skill. Others are credulous of communication with the spirits of the dead and materializing of their forms in the dimly lighted seance while tambourines, bells and irridescent stars and hands float recklessly about in the gloom. Hundreds deceived and cajoled by "pipe-dreams" of "get rich quickly" schemes (and they are myriads), are coaxed and persuaded out of their hard-earned money to later on reap a harvest of disappointment.

Even the mystic realm of fraternity has been invaded by avaricious men, who have betrayed their trust, audaciously deceived their fraters and delivered them over to syndicates and combinations and appropriated to themselves all the surplus and reserve funds in the treasury or deposit vaults. Bankers have manipulated the funds of their depositors until spurred by the protests of their victims, they have been prosecuted and paid the penalty for violation of Federal laws.

So that singleness of purpose may accomplish great results of evil as well as good. Can anybody conceive of a more noble aspiration than the determination of a good man to make his family happy? What delight comes to one's soul when the woman of his choice says: "I will thee wed." How proudly he introduces his bride as "My wife" after the good minister has "made them one." What joy comes to his household when a "rosebud" of a little girl or a "carnation" of a "kid boy" is added. The sun seems brighter, the stars have a more merry twinkle to the happy father and the indulgent mother. The benediction of love illumines the home altar and woe to him who casts a shadow over it.

Every man cannot achieve wealth, position or become

a leader in a great undertaking. The majority of men are unable to accumulate wealth and leave their families independent when they are "called hence" without co-operating with others. This undeniable fact has caused the creation of fraternal societies. Some of these are for social purposes and in this respect are useful if they do not attract men away from their home life. The man who leaves his little wife to solitude or the perplexities of the proper care and entertainment of their children to spend all his leisure time at the club or social society, is selfish or perhaps thoughtless. The fraternal societies which have proven a National blessing are the Beneficiary Societies which only demand an occasional attendance of its members. Such societies generously bestow care in sickness and distress and when a member departs to that "bourne whence no traveller returns" the dependent beneficiaries receive a substantial sum of money to protect them from poverty and want.

In such societies there is, or should be, a concentrated effort of the members to accelerate growth and accumulate funds to meet all possible future contingencies. It is a labor of love. If a "master mind" will accept leadership and devote his time and talents to his work, its progress will be manifest but not unless his constituents will encourage and support him unselfishly. The uncertainty of life makes affiliation with such societies almost imperative. Daily we read of railway accidents with fearful mutilation and loss of life, terrible holocausts, steamship casualties, "Devil Wagons" violating speed limits through city streets, slaughtering self-absorbed pedestrians; mine explosions, the ravages of riots and wars, murders, epidemics and the numberless contingencies which destroy life.

While faith points to eternal life in the Great Beyond, and hope buoys us to expectation of longevity, it is a pleasing thought that our loved ones can be protected by the fostering care offered by the fraternal beneficiary societies. Not only this, but such societies are enlarging their scope of benevolence by erecting homes, sanitoria and hospitals for the care of the aged, the indigent and the fatherless.

With the advance of civilization, there comes increased safeguards to human life. Sanitation, inspection of food, better water supply, punishment of reckless drivers and engineers, suppression of incipient revolutions and prosecution of criminals.

Statisticians assure us that the actual, to the expected longevity of human life has increased during the last fifty years, but this is no assurance of individual experience. While many will attain a ripe old age, those exposed to contagion, accidents, cataclysms, the devastating storms, floods and extremes of heat and cold will continue to prematurely "fall by the wayside."

Much has yet to be accomplished in educational methods to inform the people of the lurking dangers to human life. It is a pleasing thought that men of great wealth are furnishing large sums of money to build and endow institutions to educate experts and investigate the physical conditions with a view to extirpate disease and prevent epidemics. The Heaven inspired inclination to do this, is a rift in the cloud of supreme selfishness, reflecting honor upon such philanthropists and thankfulness to Almighty God. In startling contrast these men stand radiant before the American people when compared with the men of great wealth who hand down their millions to their descendants, many of whom are degenerate spendthrifts and demoralizing elements of society.

In conclusion, I believe that the future is radiant with promise. The past victories of great minds encourage the rising generations to the loftiest aspirations and the most laudable ambition. It is natural for man to penetrate the unknown. The inventor laboriously toils to produce something that has taxed the less ingenious to build; the chemist, despite the noxious vapors and poisonous elements, experiments to produce something new, to relieve human distress or aid mechanical and scientific progress; the mechanic tries to improve industrial or transportation appliances; the statesman considers the wants of the people and safeguards for our National government; the electrician studies transmission of messages by voice or metal connections, the improvement of power and light and application of mysterious currents for physical ills; the railway magnates are designing and planning the best methods of employment of men and operating their roads; the author racks his brain to develop some new phase of human experience or a new poetic sentimental thrill; the musician listens to the birds, harkens to the sounds that emanate from many sources that he may compose a new anthem or a "jingle" to meet public favor; the philosopher and the historian studies the phenomena of thought and the ancient monuments, tablets and parchments to prove the utterances of sages or expose their fallacy; the theologian endeavors to peer beyond the vale that hides the mysterious and for evidence to dispel fanaticism; the doctor, the lawyer and in fact earnest men of every calling and profession are seeking to discover something that will increase their own usefulness and benefit their fellow men.

Ambition has no bounds; it is not chained, Prometheus-like to the rock of discouragement; its possibilities are boundless. It is laudable, but after all the highest aim of the ordinary man should be to live an honorable life, protect his dependents and do his best to prove himself an unselfish humanitarian.

AN ALLEGORY

CONTRIBUTED BY A LAY MEMBER

And it came to pass at the close of the day that the busy hum of wheels and artisans and trade seemed to die away, and I found myself on an eminence overlooking the affairs of men which involved the fate of nations and the world. The fierce strife for mastery; the bickerings and contentions among those who thought of self and self alone; the sufferings and privations of others who were as the nether stone in the affairs of life; the insistence with which each one forced his theories and views upon his fellows; the unselfishness of still others willing to offer up their lives and hearts' blood that freedom and justice might prevail—these unfolded as a panorama before me. And a new sight was given me to see the disembodied spirits ascend to the place of judgment hard by the gates of the Eternal City. And, as the gates of the city opened to the throng of them who were found worthy, I saw that no word or question was asked as to whether the soul was of any particular creed or form of opinion. All alike, if found worthy, were received.

And I marveled greatly, having been taught that there were certain orthodox and cardinal rules which were con ditions precedent both to success in this world and to acceptance in the Great Beyond. And I looked again from my eminence to throngs below so great that no man could number, many being bleeding, bruised, and broken. And as I looked down, behold! the clouds opened and multitudes were busily engaged in bearing precious ointment, cooling drinks and bandages and lints to staunch the blood, and they ministered to all alike with tender hands and loving hearts. And while I looked I saw multitudes in the valley and heard the voices of a few high in authority saying, "Behold, how evil and ignorance and loss doth abound where we are not." And as I pondered I saw an angel near by, to whom I said: "Canst tell me why the loud voice to the multitude dost so mislead the people?" And the angel said unto me: "They are low in the valley, my child! Only after long, weary climbing through adversity and vilification and sorrow shall they come up hither and see as thou dost see."

And a long way off I saw a great new country, the greatness whereof was more than words could tell, and the people thereof had but scant knowledge of brotherly love and co-operation. And again I saw coming down from the land of the blest a great company of those who believed in and taught the principles of co-operation and the Brotherhood of Man and, even while they taught, I saw still another great multitude and heard another loud voice saying: "Come now and see that what I have taught you, lo! these many years, is true. Can you not see for yourself now that these teachers of such impossible doctrines are as in ignorance and worse?" And many people cried, "Amen! Amen!" And as I looked down upon them and heard their clamor, I turned in sorrow and said to the angel: "Shall I not haste to undeceive the people?" With sadness, he said: "Having eyes, they see not, and having ears they hear not, neither do they understand. Only through the same sorrowful way that you came up, can they come up higher." And I marveled greatly.

The angel showest me a great lake wherein the floods were overwhelming the land insomuch that very great multitudes were buffeting with the waters to save themselves and their families and friends and, while they struggled, I saw a great ship, with many helping hands, go quickly and gladly to save them from their peril. And the name of that ship was Fraternity. And she sailed to where the waves were most overwhelming and where the most danger and the most want prevailed, and I saw vast hosts upon the shore bearing banners marked with the inscription, "Monopoly," and I heard a loud voice crying out to the multitudes: "Lo! these many years have I spent in teaching you that danger and evil prevail everywhere these fraternalists are found." And my heart burned within me and I besought the angel saying, "Suffer me, I pray thee, to speak to these great congregations that evil counsels prevail not." And he said, with sorrowful countenance: "They do not yet see. Mayhap through fire and flood and sorrow and pain they shall yet come up higher, that they shall see what you see."

And again he showed me another plain and still another great multitude. They bore banners innumerable and went forth to battle against the workers who wrought the good works of fraternalism. And the inscription upon their banners read: "There is but one manner in which provision both for the present and the future can be obtained, and that is to be afforded through us and us only." And yet louder voices I heard saying: "Away with them! Starve them! Did we not tell you how that evil and uncertainty prevailed where these people are?" And the people cried out yet the more, after the manner their priests had done for many years. "Away with them! Away with them! Let them starve!" And, behold! the face of the angel was turned white so that the brightness of the sun could not more lighten it, and he spread out his hands toward them, and said: "Oh, Jerusalem, Jerusalem! How oft would I have gathered you as a hen gathereth her brood, but you would not!"

And behold the angel said unto me, "It were fit to build a memorial for these who so shut Heaven's gate, and so narrow God's world, that many of the elect lack the bread that perisheth and hundreds of millions are shut out of eternal life. And it is meet that it be builded in a narrow city, on a narrow neck of land, between narrow strips of water, along narrow crooked streets whereon walk narrow men whose narrow thoughts are drawn out by skillful artifices to cover most of the universe. It is fitting that it be a narrow monument and the narrowness thereof, and the breadth thereof, and the depth thereof, and the transparency thereof, shall be equal."

And I was exceedingly sorrowful when I saw him begin to erect a narrow memorial to rest under the souls of those who not only lived for self alone, but who in divers other ways stood in the pathway of others who would fain participate in the blessings and bounties of this world. And it came to pass, while I sorrowed with a great sorrow, and while I thought what these things should mean, behold! I heard an angel say: "Go! pour out the vials of wrath!" And there were voices, and thunders, and lightnings and earthquakes, such as were never before. And the voice said, "Reward these even as they rewarded. Double unto them the cup that they filled to others. For unto them is their judgment come!"

And I besought the angel, saying, "Command thy servant, I pray thee, that I go to my city, and with scorching words and withering speech shall I rebuke them that they suffer not. I will hurl at them my words, and I will hurl at them thy words, and with great punishment will I punish them, and with a great contempt will I cover them." And while I gladly waited until the angel should joy at my words, he turned him about and wept and said: "Thou shalt go but only the words of the banner that I give thee shalt thou speak." Whereupon he took a banner of purple and wrote at the bottom thereof in words of silver, "Learning and Knowledge shall be in thy courts"; at which I waxed joyful and hasted to go, because this was the great pride of my people. "Wait," he said, and above he inscribed in bright letters of burnished fine gold, "HUMILITY! CHARITY! FRATERNITY!" at which I grieved and turned to go. "Stay yet," said the angel, "The zeal of thy house hath eaten thee up! Those who have scoffed at and derided thee, and that for which thou dost stand, have had their lesson. Behold one now for thee. The infinite bigness of thy head is equalled and balanced by the littleness and narrowness of thy soul, which is well deserving a place of honor among those on the memorial of nothingness."

And as I turned away with the banner toward my people, with haste and confusion of face, said he: "Do thou and thy people hereafter cease vain disputes and useless controversies. Hereafter let all dwell together with amity" And behold! mine head began to get smaller and smaller, and yet smaller, for mine heart was bleeding and broken and behold! my heart began to wax larger and larger until I realized that all the people of the world could dwell there in harmony and in the bonds of Fraternity—and the Lord gave me grace to understand the meaning of the angel as he said in a loud voice, "Now is the last become first, and the first has become last." · And, giving me a pen, he said: "For every uncharitable word thou hearest in private, do thou with this pen write two for me that shall be heard upon the housetops. No arm or voice lifted against thee shall prosper so long as thou cleavest to the banner I gave thee." And straightway he was carried by a great cloud up in the heavens out of my sight. May the words on that banner, "HUMILITY, CHARITY, FRATERNITY" and "Love One Another" ever ring in the ears of him who hath ears to hear!

THE UPLIFTING INFLUENCE OF FRATERNALISM *

I feel that it is good to be here to-day. It appeals to me as a happy and appropriate impulse that led our fraternal orders to establish headquarters at these fair grounds, where their members and friends may find rest and comfort, and it is equally as fitting that one of these fair days should be set apart for special observance as fraternal day, for as an important and a growing factor in our civilization, the fraternal society contributes much to the inspiration essential to the inauguration and success of such splendid and wholesome public enterprises as our State Fair.

I am asked to speak on the subject "Fraternal Orders." It is more important that I should be brief on this occasion than that I should do the subject full justice. It is a subject with which I have had much to do in the past several years. A national committee of Insurance Commissioners, of which I have the honor to be chairman, has had our fraternal insurance system under especial and exhaustive consideration with a view of bringing about such legislation in the various states as will materially aid in the solution of the problems which confront the system, for, like every individual as well as every other institution, the fraternal system has its perplexing questions calling for wise determination. It is in the recognition of difficulties and courageously dealing with them that we as individuals or institutions grow strong.

---

*Address of the Hon. Reau E. Folk, Insurance Commissioner of Tennessee, at the Tennessee State Fair.

FRATERNAL INSURANCE

It is not my intention to go into any technical discussion, but briefly stated, the great problem of fraternal insurance to-day is of placing rates of contribution upon an adequate scientific or experience basis, so that a society may be able to carry out its contracts without imposing harsh and burdensome assessments upon its members at advanced ages. In the efforts which the insurance commissioners of this country are making towards placing this great and beneficent institution upon a basis which will be a guarantee of its perpetuity, we have the hearty co-operation of a great majority of the leaders in the fraternal world, and the sympathy of the best fraternal insurance thought, and we have every confidence that the situation will be met at an earlier day by that wise character of statesmanship which, foreseeing difficulties in the future, provides means for obviating those difficulties before they become acute.

If I should be asked as to how came the fraternal order into being, my answer would be, that it came as a result of the development of a sense of mutuality between men; that it comes as a result of the divinely implanted instinct in the human breast to bear one another's burdens in the hour of need; that it comes as a consequence of the gregarious impulse of man, the impulse of companionship; that it comes as evidence of man's humanity to man. Back of the thing that is are the things that made it so. Back of this amiable and pleasant gathering to-day; back of the constitutional right we have as citizens to come together for any peaceable purpose, are the efforts and sacrifices of those who suffered that we might have this privilege. Back of the congregation in the church on the Sabbath day are a thousand battle fields dedicated to the cause of religious liberty, the right of each man to worship God as he sees fit. Back of the bal

lot, which sometimes I fear we hold too lightly, are six
thousand years of human thought and endeavor to give
men the right to govern themselves; and immediately
back of election franchise are the blood and heroism of
our revolutionary forefathers. Back of the rose is the
mystery of germination, the science of horticulture, the
sweat of the brow, the labor of hands. Back of our fra-
ternal system, back of every order represented here to-day
are the brotherhood of man and the development of inspi-
rations of fraternity in human hearts and minds to a prac- ·
tical basis.

MODERN EDUCATION

While the fraternal beneficiary society is an evolution
of modern times, yet we find its prototype in reading of
ancient days when men banded together for one purpose
or another, grew into the habit of organized relief to the
distressed and unfortunate of their number, and again
through the middle ages we find record of the co-opera-
tive guilds organized for mutual aid. Out of these guilds
grew the Friendly Society system of England, which has
flourished for more than a century and a half, wielding a
potential influence among the masses of Great Britain.

The American Fraternal Beneficiary Society is of
comparatively recent origin. It was in 1867 that Father
Upchurch founded the Ancient Order of United Work-
men, the pioneer American society. The fraternal insur-
ance idea found fertile soil in this land of free institu
tions. Its growth in these forty-three years has been
marvelous. There are to-day in the neighborhood of 600
fraternal societies in the United States and Canada,
counting those that are purely local in their nature. There
are about 150 orders'of comparative general operation.
These societies have in the neighborhood of eight million
members, so that on an average every fifth man one meets
is a fraternal society member. In Tennessee we have

thirty-nine orders with a combined membership of ninety-three thousand souls. These fraternal orders constitute an important co-ordinate branch of our social and economic life. They bear a most vital relation to our civilization and the development toward civilization's highest ideals. Not only do these orders provide mutual protec tion in case of death and distress, but they bring men together about noble standards of human conduct. Next to the home and the church the fraternal order wields the most potential and uplifting influence upon the destinies of our people, serving to promote healthy impulse and clean thought and action in all the relations of life. It helps to make good citizens. I venture to say no more worthy fraternal member ever came out of a lodge room without being a better citizen for having gone.

UPLIFTING INFLUENCE

Organized society has need of the strong uplifting influence of the fraternal order. Just as in the individual man there is a constant struggle between right and wrong, between truth and error, between good and evil, so is the combat between these same opposing forces ever being waged in civilization and the civil affairs of man. The forces of error are ever on the alert, ever organized, and eternal vigilance is the price of victory over them. In this conflict the influence of the fraternal order through its noble ideals of man's duty is a mighty factor on the side of truth. Before its teachings the red flag of anarchy must fall. It stands for peace as against turmoil; it stands for order against disorder; it stands for civic honor and for the law and the enforcement of the law, recognizing as a bulwark of our institution the wholesome respect for law and strict observance of it.

The fraternal order founded upon brotherhood may love the sinner while it hates the sin; it may be moved by compassion for the criminal all the while it abhors his crime.

A great American, who has passed into the beyond, is credited with saying: "I would rather than all else that it should be said of me when I am gone that I plucked the thorn and the thistle from the pathway of my fellow-man wherever I could and planted a flower wherever I found a flower would grow." That noble sentiment pulsates with the essence of true fraternalism, of true brotherhood.

I leave this beautiful thought, this fraternal impulse, with you to-day. He who aids his fellow and helps to smooth his pathway, lays hold upon the higher meaning of life and solves the mystery of happiness. The man who helps to make life worth while for his neighbor makes life worth while for himself. Then let us, following the exalted precepts of our fraternal orders, pluck the thistle of weakness and the thorn of despair from the path of our fellows wherever we can, and plant instead blossoms redolent of cheering words and helpful deeds. For we shall not pass this way again.

MODERN SANITATION*

I have selected the subject of modern sanitation to present to you to-day because it is one in which not only the medical profession, but the public are vitally interested.

As modern sanitation cannot properly be enforced without the active and earnest co-operation of the public it is not only fair but exceedingly important that the

---

*Address delivered by Dr. Alvah H. Doty, Health Officer of the Port of New York, at the fourth annual meeting of the Association of Life Insurance Presidents.

latter should be familiar with the advances which have been made in this science and its purposes at the present period.

In order to more fully understand this it is necessary to know something of the condition which existed in earlier times relative to the means which were taken to preserve the public health. Medical history even prior to the Christian era makes frequent references to the various methods which were in vogue at that time. It is of interest to know that through all ages cleanliness has been looked upon as a factor in the prevention of disease. This is specifically referred to in the Bible in connection with the Levitical laws. That cleanliness has stood the test of time is evident from the fact that to-day it forms an important part of the ground work of modern sanitation. Unfortunately other methods which were employed in earlier times for the protection of the public health were either farcical or worthless or too drastic for practical use and were employed simply because they were the fancies of those in charge of this work. They included the burning of magic powders, incantations, etc. While these conditions gradually gave way to more reasonable and practical measures, they still included methods which were of little or no value or were unjustifiable. Houses and their contents were burned and vessels were sunk at sea by official order to prevent the transmission of disease. This occurred even as late as the eighteenth century and furnished sufficient evidence of ignorance as to the real means by which infectious diseases are transmitted or rather the means which should be taken to prevent their extension. Cholera and bubonic plague from the East frequently visited Western Europe, and the ravages which they caused and the mortality which followed their appearance would appear almost incredible. The measures taken to prevent the extension of these diseases was of the order to which I have already referred.

While during the past century sanitary methods have steadily improved in value, it was not until about 1880 that sanitation was placed on a scientific basis and a new era in this important work was established. At this period Pasteur and Koch gave to the world the result of their bacteriological investigation, the value of which cannot be overestimated. They proved the germ origin of many of the infectious diseases and furnished a stimulus for further exhaustive bacteriological research in this direction. As a result we are now familiar with the specific organism, the cause of cholera, typhoid fever, diphtheria, bubonic plague, tuberculosis and other infectious diseases. A knowledge of these organisms, their habits and the methods by which they can be destroyed, places in our hands means which are quite sure to be successful in dealing with outbreaks of all infectious diseases, for it is reasonable to assume that the methods which are employed in dealing with those we know of will also be effective in dealing with diseases, the specific organisms of which have not yet been discovered.

The next important step in connection with this subject has been to determine the true means by which infectious diseases are transmitted from one person to another. So far as matters pertaining to the public health are concerned there is no belief which has been so generally accepted as the theory that infectious diseases are transmitted not only by the clothing and effects of the sick, but also by the clothing of those who are well, baggage, rags, cargoes of vessels, money, etc. In the past this has dominated all regulations, the object of which has been to prevent the transmission of infectious diseases. Inasmuch as this means of transmitting infection has been referred to in the earliest medical writings, it could not have been suggested by careful scientific investigation. It is known throughout the world as the fomites theory, and refers to various articles, which are supposed to transmit the germ of infectious diseases in their active state from one person to another. Curiously enough this theory is not supported by scientific proof. However, it is plausible and popular because it easily explains outbreaks, the origin of which are unknown. Practical sanitarians have slowly but surely secured indisputable evidence that it is fallacious and that infectious diseases are not transmitted by fomites except in very rare instances, but usually directly from one person to another, or by food and drink as in cholera and typhoid fever, and within the past few years we have obtained conclusive proof that insects constitute a potent factor in the transmission of infection. We are now also better acquainted with the fact that mild, irregular and unrecognized cases constitute one of the most common and dangerous factors in the transmission of infectious diseases and are responsible for many outbreaks the origin of which cannot be determined. Further than this, we have more recently learned that apparently well persons known as carriers may act as the medium of infection without presenting any evidence of the disease themselves. This presents a comparatively new and very important medium of infection.

In modern times probably no diseases have caused greater loss of life than malaria and yellow fever, particularly the former, because it may be found in all parts of the world. No more impressive evidence of the erroneous theories which have hitherto been accepted relative to the transmission of infectious diseases can be presented than in the cases of the diseases to which I have just referred. Malaria was formerly supposed to be contracted by poisonous emanations from swamps known as

miasma, and yellow fever was believed to be transmitted
by fomites in the shape of clothing, bedding, baggage and
numerous other articles. If the statement had been made
a decade ago that the clothing and effects of those suf-
fering from yellow fever were not a media of infection it
would have had but few if any supporters and would have
been regarded as an exceedingly dangerous theory to pre-
sent. To-day we know that malaria is not transmitted
by emanations from swamps or low lying districts, but
by specific organisms, and that the only part that swamps
play in the transmission of this disease is by furnishing
breeding places for the mosquito. Furthermore, yellow
fever is not transmitted by clothing, bedding or other
effects of the patients, or even by their discharges, all of
which are now known to be perfectly harmless, and that
both malaria and yellow fever are transmitted only by
certain varieties of the mosquito; in yellow fever it is the
stegomyia, and in malaria the anopheles. Bubonic plague
was also formerly believed to be transmitted by clothing,
etc.; now we know that it is transmitted chiefly by
infected rats through the medium of the fleas which infest
them. Evidence has also been presented to show that
fomites, except in some rare instance, takes no part in
the transmission of other diseases. No belief has indi-
rectly, at least, contributed more to the extension of
infectious disease than the fomites theory, for it has been
employed to explain outbreaks the origin of which can-
not promptly be determined, and has given those in charge
of public health work as well as others encouragement to
assume that diseases enter a community on some one's
clothing or effects. This to a certain extent relieves a
health official of the important duty of making an exhaus-
tive inspection to find out the true origin of the outbreak
—the most important duty of a public health officer.
When to this is added proper isolation of the cases,

besides thorough and scientific disinfection whenever it is required, there can be no outbreak of an infectious disease which cannot be brought under control, and under these methods the great loss of life that has followed their appearance in the past need never occur again. There is no doubt that if proper sanitary regulations could be enforced in sections of the East, which are regarded as the home of bubonic plague and cholera, these diseases would become an unimportant factor as a menace to the public health or would disappear from the earth. The relief this would extend to commerce and the traveling public in the way of protection and the absence of annoyance, detention and expenses of quarantine, etc., would be incalculable.

It is exceedingly important for the public to know that while the clothing and other material in direct contact with those actually sick with infectious disease may be regarded as a medium of infection, the effects of well persons, baggage, cargoes of vessels, rags, money, etc., transmit disease only in rare instances. As modern practical sanitation does not guarantee absolute protection, we are not justified in making health regulations to comply with rare instances, but must ascertain and deal promptly and effectively with the common or ordinary media of infection. It may be a comfort for you to know if you have been in proximity to a case of small-pox, or some other infectious case, the possibilities of transmitting the disease to your home or elsewhere through the medium of your clothing is exceedingly remote.

In making the above statement, I am not advancing a theory, but am giving the results of my own practical investigation regarding this subject, which I am quite sure is in accord with the belief of other practical sanitarians. The fact that a person who works among rags or those who are continuously in close contact with money occasionally contract an infectious disease is not scientific or reasonable proof that these articles are media of infection, because the people who deal with them are exposed to the same outside influences that others are, and may become infected in the ordinary way.

In a superficial investigation of this detail, which I am sorry to say usually occurs, this fact is not considered. A careful inquiry at banks or more particularly the Treasury Department in Washington will clearly show that those who are constantly handling and re-handling money, particularly that which is old, filthy and offensive and which is forwarded for destruction, are no more subject to infectious diseases than those who follow other vocations.

There is a well marked element of hysteria on the part of the public relative to the matter of personal infection, and many things are done which to the practical sanitarian are not only illogical, but absurd, and the public should know it. For instance, there is a very urgent call for the disinfection of money. From the standpoint of public health there is no justification for such action, besides no more farcical or unreasonable thing could occur than an attempt to carry out this treatment, even if it were necessary. Steam only could be used for the purpose, because no other agent could penetrate a mass of paper money; besides, when and where would this be done, and who would do it? It is true that the money in circulation is filthy and offensive and should be frequently withdrawn from circulation and the new bills substituted, but let us secure this in the proper way and not on the grounds that it is a common medium of infection; for it is not. Some people very reluctantly make use of strap hangers in public conveyances for fear of infection. Those who are timid in regard to these matters should know that while these articles may contain many bacteria or germs, they

are usually of a harmless character and are not patho
genic organisms or those which transmit disease. Furth
ermore, the same bacteria are constantly found on our
hands, clothing, etc., and it is also well to bear in mind
that infection is not lurking everywhere or on every
object, because this is not so.

I have mentioned the mosquito as the only medium of
infection in malaria and yellow fever. It is also respon-
sible for the transmission of other diseases and we also
know that other insects act as a medium of infection. The
extent of this is yet unknown, but there is but little doubt
that we are at the borderland of further important dis-
coveries in this direction.

So far as the mosquito is concerned the lesson which
the public must learn and act upon is that the extermina-
tion of this insect is not for the purpose of preventing the
annoyance which its bite inflicts, but to remove an active
and dangerous medium of infection. While practical
sanitarians are fully alive to the peril from this source,
the co-operation and the active interest of the public
have not yet been properly secured and the subject is
still occasionally viewed from a humorous standpoint.
The extermination of the mosquito is practical, and can
be successfully carried out. No more satisfactory proof
of this can be asked for than the results which have been
obtained in Cuba, Panama and elsewhere.

There are other means of general infection which are
very dangerous to the public health. Of these infected
water and milk are the most common and important. It
is largely by exposure to infected water on the part of
Mohammedans, who go to various sections in the East
to perform certain religious rites, that cholera is trans
mitted throughout the world. It is also an infected water
or milk supply which is commonly instrumental in trans-
mitting typhoid fever in certain communities.

Some time ago in visiting a Central American town I noticed that the chief sources of drinking water consisted of a large well on one of the principal highways from which water was constantly being drawn in pails and other receptacles. I expressed my surprise that in the presence of modern buildings that there should be a water supply of this primitive character and one which could be so easily infected. The official who accompanied me rather reluctantly explained that some time before the general government had appropriated quite a large sum of money for a modern water supply, but the inhabitants of the town had decided that they would prefer to have a new opera house instead, and the money was allowed to be transferred for this purpose. This may appear to you as rather a relic of the middle ages, but upon careful consideration you will find that practically this same condition exists in our own and other civilized countries throughout the world. Expensive and elaborate public buildings, speedways, parks, etc., which are as a rule available for the use or pleasure of only a portion of the population, are constantly being constructed; whereas, in the same place there exists a general water supply which is a disgrace to any civilized community. Public health officers know this to be true, but their efforts to secure sufficient appropriations for proper water supplies and for the purpose of carrying out other means for the preservation of the public health are either met with opposition or small and insufficient appropriations are made. Public parks are not nearly as valuable or as necessary for the general welfare as public baths. I do not mean baths where a fee is charged, or those which are unattractive or situated in a part of the town, improper for women and children to visit, but which are free of expense and attractively constructed and properly situated. The class of people in any community who in a general way are a menace to the public do not as a rule care to bathe. Public baths educate these people as to the value of cleanliness and indirectly aid in carrying out modern sanitation. I know of no greater monument for any one than the gift of a distinctly modern public bath.

Evidence of contaminated milk supplies are constantly before us, but it is not often that they are effectively dealt with. This would not be the case if the public demanded that proper action be taken in the matter.

In 1882 cholera apeared in Naples and extended with great rapidity and severity; one thousand deaths in twenty-four hours was of frequent occurrence. Recently another outbreak of this disease has appeared in the same place, but at no time during the epidemic, so far as the official reports indicate, were there more than twenty-five to thirty deaths in one day, and within six weeks after it began the outbreak was declared at an end. It is of interest to know what has worked this wonderful change, and the explanation is perfectly clear. First, Naples has within the past few years secured a proper water supply; second, during the last outbreak modern sanitary regulations have been carefully enforced. This is all there is to the story.

I have recently had under observation two vessels which departed from Naples, each having on board over one thousand steerage passengers. In both instances a case of cholera occurred within two days after departure. The cases were promptly suspected by the ship's surgeon, and were isolated and disinfection performed, but in neither instance, although the passengers were in close contact with each other during the voyage, did a secondary case of this disease occur. If this result can be secured on shipboard, it certainly can be obtained on shore.

In the well-known outbreak of typhus fever, which

occurred in Ireland during the famine of 1814, or there-
abouts, it is claimed that eight hundred thousand cases
occurred. One-third of the population of Dublin suc-
cumbed to it, and the outbreak lasted two or three years.
In the fall of 1892 this same disease appeared in New
York City, and had gained some headway in a thickly
populated tenement and lodging-house section of the city
before it was detected. As soon as it was discovered by
the Department of Health and active operations begun,
the disease was brought promptly under control. It
lasted only a few months, and the number of cases did
not exceed seven hundred, almost every patient being con-
fined to the tenement and lodging-house population.
Furthermore, during the fourteenth century bubonic
plague appeared in Europe under the name of the "black
death" and lasted about twenty years. It has been esti-
mated that during this reign of terror about one-fourth
of the population of Europe succumbed to the disease.
During the past ten or fifteen years plague has again
appeared in various places in Europe, and also in South
America, and later in the United States. In not one of
these instances did it make any serious progress, and
although it occurred in the Chinese quarter of San Fran-
cisco, there were but one hundred and fifty cases in two
years. I cite these instances simply to show you how
easy becomes the problem of protecting the public health
if modern sanitary regulations are in force.

I may say a word in regard to the subject of disinfec-
tion, of which there is considerable misunderstanding on
the part of the public. Knowledge of the true means by
which infectious diseases are transmitted and the rejec-
tion of the fomites theory has reduced disinfection to
within very narrow limits. This under ordinary condi-
tions is now confined to the treatment of discharges and
material in the sick apartment. Even here the disinfec-

tion of clothing is far less important than the destruction of the discharges of the patient, which in certain diseases is the chief if not the only source of infection. Contrary to the general opinion disinfection should be performed only under the direction of the physician or health official in order to secure the proper results. We are all familiar with the household disinfection, where saucers of carbolic acid are placed under the bed, small pieces of sulphur are burned in the room, or some textile fabric soaked in a so-called disinfectant is hung in the apartment. As a matter of fact these methods are absolutely worthless. Sulphur dioxide or formaldehyde gas produced in sufficient amounts to kill infectious organisms is not respirable in the human being; therefore a patient could not remain in the apartment undergoing treatment.

Prevention is the key-note of modern sanitation, and around and about it has been constructed the most formidable barriers against infectious disease. When proper sanitary methods are enforced there is no outbreak which cannot be successfully controlled. Alarmists and theorists do not willingly accept this, and often predict that the appearance of an infectious disease in a community where proper sanitary regulations are in operation will be followed by practically the same serious results as have occurred in the past. There is absolutely no substance or justification for such belief, and in this paper I have endeavored to prove it to you.

With these means at our command, a general infection through a water supply, for instance, either on land or at sea often justifies the criticism of those in charge of the public health wherever this may take place. The prevention of such an occurrence, the management of outbreaks of infectious disease, disinfection, vaccination, and other sanitary precautions must in order to be successful be placed in the hands of competent medical officers who are not only theoretically but practically familiar with the subject. Unfortunately the public do not demand this and in some communities the protection of the public health is either in the hands of laymen or medical officers who know but little of the practical side of the subject. Local health officers should in some manner be under the jurisdiction of a central body, preferably the State Board of Health, who shall pass upon their qualifications and exclude those who are not properly fitted for this work, for sooner or later these officers must face an infected water or milk supply, or an outbreak of infectious disease, or some other emergency of this character, and if they are not qualified to deal with it, not only will the community they preside over suffer, but other sections also. The unnecessary loss of life, the injury to commerce, etc., which almost invariably follow such a condition, fully justifies the expenditure of generous appropriations to prevent it.

It is imperative that each community shall have a proper water and milk supply, also equipment and means by which infectious diseases can be properly isolated and treated, and facilities for dealing with other matters relating to the public health. Unless soon brought under control outbreaks of infectious disease travel with great rapidity and severity where overcrowding, poverty, etc., exists. On shipboard infectious diseases are almost always found in the steerage. This indicates the necessity for preventing overcrowding when it is possible to do so, also to insure cleanliness, fresh air, etc.

When the time comes that the public shall take an active and determined interest in matters pertaining to the public health, then the value of modern sanitation will be fully realized.

TERSE FRATERNAL THOUGHTS

—Do not return kindness—just pass it along.

—Who ceaseth to be a friend never was a friend.

—To rule one's anger is well—to prevent it is better.

—Fraternal societies are dependent upon their members.

—The interests of all fraternalists run along parallel lines.

—Enthusiasm is a certain cure for all fraternal weaknesses.

—He who loves his home should make provision to preserve it.

—When you play, play hard. When you work don't play at all.

—The protection of a man's family is man's most sacred duty.

—Fraternalism cannot be perpetuated on an insurance basis alone.

—In dull times let the luxuries go, but keep the policy in force.

—The greatest successes come from persistent and steady effort.

—To any intelligent man life insurance is a necessity—not a luxury.

—Believe in your society and the system of which it is an exponent.

—There is all the difference in the world between a dream and a plan.

—A determined resolution which leads to work produces the best results.

—Loyalty to friends has been termed one of the most exalted of all virtues.

—The young man usually needs more protection than does the older man.

Bear this in mind: "Don't take yourself too seriously—no one else does."

—Sprinkle salt on the tail of every fraternal idea which comes your way.

—Loyalty to one's fraternity has been the keynote of every successful society.

—Make provision for the future. The rainy day is bound to arrive some time.

—Fraternalism has done more than charity to foster self-respect and thrift.

—Life insurance is an antidote for poverty, wretchedness, misery, and crime.

—Is not the percentage of successes greater in fraternalism than in other lines?

—Nothing is won without enthusiasm and hard work. They are seldom defeated.

—What's the use of following in footprints of others, when one can make his own?

—Every member should understand the foundation upon which fraternalism rests.

It has been pertinently observed that the fool friend is worse than the bitter enemy.

There is no power in the country strong enough to stop the progress of fraternalism.

—The test of the plan is its result; the wisdom of an act lies in the benefit accomplished.

—An authority has declared that nine out of ten widows have only the common necessities.

—The lodge and the home should be regarded as co-workers. The former protects the latter.

—The fraternal certificate is not for personal profit. It is for the benefit of dependents.

—Ask the man who says "I cannot afford it," if his family can afford to have him neglect it?

—It is the duty of every member to know fraternalism and the foundation upon which it rests.

—Fraternity is not an empty word. Yet we should at least practice as much as we talk about it.

—The permanence of the fraternal proposition is more certain to-day than ever before in its history. ·

—The inquiry of every fraternal management should be "How to improve our service to members."

—The increase in fraternal insurance has done much toward making the United States what it is to-day.

—All of the insurance companies and journals are very much interested in the "regulation of fraternals."

—The hope of the individual who wishes to provide protection for his dependents lies in the fraternal society.

—Have you ever considered that upwards of seven millions of people are banded together by fraternal ties?

—All lovers of home are desirous of its preservation. The home is the foundation of enduring government.

—Strive to be successful in whatever you undertake. Success covers a greater multitude of sins than charity.

—The fraternal spirit never weakens. Almost every hamlet has seen evidences of its existence and of its strength.

—Turn your waste moments into profit. Turning waste into profit is to-day giving employment to thousands of men.

—The income that outlives the man is the manner in which the proceeds of a fraternal certificate have been described.

—A minister once said: "My brother, your trouble is you live in Grumbler's Alley; why not move up in Hallelujah Row?"

—Your heirs may contest your will and scatter your estate, but your fraternal certificate will go to whom you intended it.

—Let us not attempt to accomplish the impossible. The practical affairs of life are enough to occupy the time of all of us.

—Fraternalism will soon become the protector of every American home, if the increase continues at the present rate.

—It is just as sensible to lapse savings bank deposits or real estate investments as it is to lapse a certificate of insurance.

—Uncertainty as to the outcome of one's finances is the greatest cause of worry. Adequate insurance is worry's foe.

—The fraternal system is to-day endeavoring to build squarely. Numbers alone do not make an organization strong.

—It is said there is a mortgage on every married man's life. This runs to his family and death may foreclose it at any time.

—Even the enemies of fraternal operation now admit that it can and does perform the purposes for which it was originated.

—Fraternal co-operation is the best way to advance one's interests through a union with others having the same object in view.

It has been well said that the man who dies uninsured and has left his family without protection has committed a social crime.

—The fraternal deputy must have confidence in the system and the institution he represents. Without confidence he cannot succeed.

—Neglect of the basic principles of fraternalism is responsible for practically all of the problems which have been presented for solution.

—Paw sez, "backbone keeps a fellow straight." Maw sez, "she keeps Paw straight." Resolved: Maw is the backbone of our family.

—The proper way to build up a lodge is not to try to pull down another one. The process of "twisting" has never brought good results.

—The age in which we live has often been characterized as a practical one. The results of the fraternal system are in line with the age.

—When one temporizes with the protection he is carrying for the benefit of his dependents, he is neither more nor less than tempting fate.

—The fraternal spirit should be shown to the new and strange members and to the visitors as well as to those who are ill and in trouble.

—It costs no more to pay an assessment promptly than it does to be in arrears and be protected only half of the time. Be prompt in your payments.

—You should be a firm believer in the principles of your order before attempting to persuade others that it is worthy of their consideration.

—Bill Arp has said with reference to insurance for one's dependents: "It is the next thing to getting religion. It is a confession of mortality."

Have you ever inquired as to the number of homes from which the fraternal certificate has lifted the mortgage? The totals would be interesting.

Viewed from any standpoint, there is nothing that will take the place of the fraternal certificate in developing independence, self-reliance and thrift.

—Life insurance is a plan which enables every provident man to apply the truest and most practical principle of practical benevolence in his home.

—The true cause of the non-success of some societies is the lack of co-operation on the part of the individual members. Each one has a duty to perform.

—It is the best course to settle all differences quietly. Too much publicity along this line has been harmful to old-line as well as fraternal insurance.

—We preserve youth by exercising our brains. A society preserves its youth and continuous progress by exercising those qualities vital to its existence.

—The fraternal system, its far-seeing exponents believe, will show better results during 1910 than during the previous year. This was a year of progress also.

—Nothing is so convincing as a man backed up by good argument. What better argument does one want than the certificate of the society he represents?

—More protection will be written this year than ever before. People in all lines recognize their need for protection. Fraternal deputies have great opportunities.

—Lack of success in a company or a society comes from one of two sources: Lack of co-operation or from unbusinesslike management and plan of operation.

—Right thinking men and women realize that they have a duty to perform toward their dependents. This is in the way of making provision for their future.

—Lapsation is a source of great expense as well as perplexity. It costs as much to care for and keep in line the army of lapses as it does to procure new members.

—The attention now given to national public health cannot but be reflected in the years to come. A vigorous, healthy population is our greatest national asset.

—Since their inception the fraternal societies have collected a vast mine of information which should be used to great advantage in the effort to promote public health.

—Discouragement is the acknowledgment of defeat. Are you willing to acknowledge that you have been defeated in any thing which has engaged your attention?

—Lord Roseberry has said: "Thrift is blessed, not merely because of the accumulation of substance, but because of the foundation and strengthening of character."

—The fraternal system to-day exercises a mighty influence in preventing pauperism. The societies have solved the difficult problem of giving aid without giving charity.

—The strength and endurance of fraternalism is more and more in evidence. The increasing space which is allowed to it in the old-line papers bears evidence of this fact.

—The man who has no accumulations but has money enough to pay the small premiums of a fraternal certificate should lose no time in making provision for his dependents.

—The great deeds of the world have been accomplished by steady, painstaking application coupled with unyielding persistence. Fraternalists should employ such methods.

—Insuring one's life for the benefit of others is the most unselfish act that one can perform. No selfish or thoughtless person will make this provision for his dependents.

—The one who particularly needs fraternal protection is the young man or woman who has a family of young children to support who would be left destitute in the event of death.

—Here is an excuse a father made for not taking out a certificate: "When my father died we were all quite young and had to get out and hustle. Let my family do the same."

—It has well been said that the world accepts one at his own estimate. If the fraternalist would have the public appreciate the dignity of his calling he must first appreciate it himself

—The poor man can be as independent as to the future welfare of his children as the rich man, provided he accepts the opportunities for protection afforded by fraternal societies.

—The obligations of a true fraternalist mean that each one is to help the other, not only in cases of distress and difficulty, but to use his best efforts to keep others out of trouble.

—The English Friendly Societies are good models for us to copy. They have gone through the same experiences and are regarded now in the same light as is the Bank of England.

—If a man wants to protect his wife and family against loss by his own death, he can do it at a small annual outlay which will hardly be missed, through the fraternal system of protection.

—Here is a strong argument against lapsation: "Each day shortens your allotted time on earth. Don't lapse and cause your family to have a harder battle with the perplexing problems of life."

—The persistence of the carpings of old-line insurance journals with reference to all of the fraternal organizations does them no good. Upbuilding is much more useful than destructive criticism.

—It would seem that the seven millions of people in this country who carry fraternal life insurance are sufficient from the viewpoint of numbers to prove the popularity of this form of protection.

—To become all that it is capable of becoming should be the aim of every fraternal society. If its management has not such an end in view it does not appreciate either its duties or its opportunities.

—Publicity is one of the necessities of fraternal growth. The member should teach his family the benefits of fraternalism and he should be an enthusiastic exponent of his society and of the system.

"The only direction in which a train will go without motive power is down hill—and at the bottom it will stop." Don't trust to momentum to keep your affairs in the vanguard of progress.

—The *Fraternal Brand* says: "The tear of sympathy is not borne of earth. It is a pearl from Heaven strung to the eyelash. It glitters there to tell the world that the soul is within and is keeping watch and ward."

—It has been estimated that the lapse rate is six per cent. lower among women than it is among men. This shows that women are more persistent members and take more interest in the fraternal part of the work.

—See that officers for the year upon which we have just entered are of that progressive kind which brings things to pass. Your prosperity for the coming year depends upon those whom you place in positions of trust.

—The proceeds of a fraternal certificate cannot be taken for the debts of a number. They belong to his dependents. This is one of the many ways in which the fraternal certificate is safer and better than an old line policy.

—The conscientious, steady "old reliable," who does his best every day, seldom making grandstand plays, but all the while plugging away and keeping up a good average, is the one who counts for the most in the long run.

—The promise of a fraternal society to pay a death benefit means more than mere words. In all of the reliable organizations that promise is well protected and will be kept, if the member conforms to the promises which he makes.

—An exchange thus admonishes its readers: "Let us make an earnest effort to live up to our obligations as brothers and sisters of our great fellowship and we will be better Christians, better neighbors and better men and women."

—In determining the value of your fraternal certificate employ the same principles that you would use in building up your business. Do not temporize with the future. Ascertain if the rates are sufficient for the benefits promised.

—When one considers the length of time fraternities have been in existence, the amount of good they have done and are doing every day, one does not wonder that they are a constant source of worry and anxiety to the "old line" contingent.

—"A fraternal society is, indeed, the poor man's bank. It secures the little home, the business against the event of death, and has been equal in hundreds and hundreds of cases to the task of opening up avenues of usefulness and self-support to the widow."

—Nearly every one has an opportunity to protect those dependent upon him. There is a period in the lives of practically all of us when we can present a clean bill of health. There is a point when all lives pass from the acceptable into the undesirable class.

—It has been estimated that ninety per cent. of the membership of the average fraternal society never secures a new member. This means that the burden of growth falls upon deputies and the remaining ten per cent. of members who work. Is this a proper average?

—Fraternal societies, both as a matter of business economy and philanthropy, should extend their activities more generally into the field of remedial and preventive measures having to do with public health. Such a course would meet with the approval of the public generally.

—Senator Robert L. Owen, of Oklahoma, says that there are three million people seriously ill all the time in the United States from preventable diseases, of whom one million are in working period of life. He estimates the financial loss from illness to be five hundred million dollars.

—A widow grinding her life away in toil, with hollow-eyed and hungry children, is indeed a fitting object for pity. How long would your savings last your family in the event of your death? You could not bear to see your family reduced to this condition. Life insurance is the solution.

—One hears much as to the progress made in the cure and prevention of disease. While advances have been made as regards sanitary conditions and environments the fact remains that death awaits us all. In time of youth we should prepare for age. We should prepare for our dependents.

—Here is something which will apply to those who defer their duty of protecting their dependents until a more convenient season: "A Harvard scientist tells us that the earth is sixty million years old. The attitude that some people have toward life insurance seems to show that they are confident of reaching that fine old age themselves."

—A Massachusetts paper contains the following: "An inter esting fact which is not generally known regarding this movement (savings insurance) is that some of the leaders are now in consultation with prominent school authorities, with a view to having instruction in thrift, savings and savings insurance included in public school arithmetic.

—The Rev. R. S. MacArthur says: "Next to a good hope for eternity is the comfort which comes to a man from knowing that he has made provision by life insurance for his old age and for the support of his family in the event of his own death. To do so seems to me a religious obligation—an obligation often as binding upon women as upon men."

—"The fraternalists number more males of voting age than there are in thirty-eight states and territories with the army and navy thrown in for good measure. They can muster an army greater than the combined war strength of Germany, France, Russia, Austria-Hungary, Italy, Great Britain, Japan and Turkey."—*Everybody's Magazine.*

—It is said that of all lands, in America the position of the wife is the best. There are degrees of "best" according to conditions. The wife is entitled to the best, not alone on the occasion when she promises to aid some man in sickness and in health, but also when the stress of life comes and especially when she may be left to meet that stress alone.

—There is a Chinese proverb which says: "Soldiers may not be needed for a hundred years, but cannot be dispensed with for a single day." China also carries out the same theory in regard to health. There, doctors are engaged by the year. They are paid to keep their patients in health. Their pay is reduced according to the number of visits they have to make to sick patients.

—It has been said that out of every nine applicants for insurance in this country one is permanently rejected. Every day brings one nearer the time when the securing of insurance protection becomes an impossibility. After one's health has been impaired he must carry alone the risk which organizations combined for mutual help are unwilling to assume. Is not this a great responsibility?

—Those who question the future of fraternalism do not appreciate the true import of development. The simple fact is that the fraternal system to-day is conforming to the needs of the people just as other interests are revamping their affairs and expanding. Change does not mean disaster. It but indicates that the greatest beneficence of all time—fraternalism—will accomplish more for the good of humanity in the future than ever before.

—One of the recent endorsements and tributes to fraternalism was given by Insurance Commissioner Button of Virginia. He said in part: "This department is heartily in sympathy with the better class of fraternal beneficiary societies in their desire to place themselves on a permanent and enduring basis. I believe the next generation will see a group of representative fraternal societies furnishing sound scientific insurance at a reasonable cost."

—The amount of insurance in the various large countries has been thus estimated: United States, about $21,000,000,000; Great Britain, $4,000,000,000; Germany, $1,400,000,000; France, $750,-000,000; Austria, $375,000,000; Scandinavia, $150,000,000; Switzerland, $144,000,000; Russia, $62,000,000. Some of the fraternal societies carry more protection on the lives of their members than is carried by the countries named above, with the exception of Great Britain.

—According to the *Pharmaceutical Era,* the daily average number of persons who are seriously ill is three million. On the assumption that there are three hundred working days in the year, nine hundred million working days are lost each year through illness. Computing the average daily wage at $1.75, the annual loss due to this cause is $1,575,000,000, and yet there are those who say that there is too much insurance protection carried by the people of this country.

—One hears much of the unfraternal spirit in evidence among members of the societies. When he considers the unfraternity there is on the outside of the societies, it is believed that he will find occasion to change his mind. It is true that practically all fraternalists are not living up to the full measure of their principles and usefulness. Yet they have started in the right direction and, if the spirit of fraternity is properly cultivated, they will reach the desired goal in time.

—Turkish justice is thus illustrated: A man, while repairing a roof, fell into the street upon a wealthy old man who was killed. The son of the victim caused the workman to be arrested. The magistrate gravely decreed that the workman should be placed exactly upon the spot where the old man had stood, and then said to the one clamoring for justice: "Now will you go on the roof of the house, fall down upon this man and kill him if you can." It is needless to say that the son declined to mete out justice of this nature.

—The soldiers of peace in this country are even more useful than are the soldiers of war. Likewise the hazards they incur for home and family are equally as great. Last year four thousand were slaughtered in mine disasters alone and seven thousand more were maimed for life. For every 270,000 tons of coal a life is made a sacrifice. Of every one thousand who went down into the gloomy depths of the coal mine five were killed. For the soldiers who die in peace there are no pensions. The fraternal certificate is that which makes provision for the future.

—In Germany the family doctor is no more—for the poorer classes at any rate. Compulsory insurance has driven him out. This defense of the family doctor has been made: "The passing of the family doctor is deplored because it is believed that his successor, a medical officer of the various insurance funds, may be

tempted on account of the very low scale of fees to render per-
functory and inadequate service. Again the insurance doctor does
not feel the stimulus of doing his best, nor the confidence of each
patient as well as of his family and friends, which encourages the
family doctor to put his best foot forward."

—This is the golden age of now. The banks are full of
the best money. The stores are full of the best of goods. The
homes are full of luxury. The shops are full of orders. Wages
are higher than in any country. Women have more avenues of
employment and better pay. She has more clubs; more protection;
more right to hold and deal in property. Husbands are doing
more to protect their wives and homes; life is more in earnest;
people take more interest in each other. It is a better world to
live in—more comforts, more luxuries, more friendship—reading
is better. Travel is solid comfort. Oh! it is a great thing just
to be living in an age like this, in a country like ours.

SOME ADMONITORY NOTES

The smile that is honest—won't come off.

—Self-complacency is a frost—it kills growth.

—Sometimes to unlearn what we have learned, is learning.

—Progress is a growth but it does not come through inaction.

—Men are born equal in endeavor—In all else, individuality rules.

—The deputy who can adapt himself to local conditions—wins.

"Practice the art of deciding what to do. The man who never comes to a point will never come to anything."

We all want to succeed but few of us are willing to pay the price.

—"Plan to-day, plug to-morrow and the profits will come of themselves."

—Work and stand by that to which you belong, it will then stand by you.

"The man with the initiative is the engine; the man without it the caboose."

—When one adds to the prosperity of his society he adds to the value of his certificate.

—Bear this in mind: "The achievement will never rise higher than the confidence."

—The accomplishment will never amount to any more than our belief and trust in its success.

—Opportunities are not the whims of chance. They are made by brains and not by good fortune.

—Set your aim high, but not beyond your opportunity, or ability, and be satisfied with nothing less.

—"Noah was six hundred years old before he knew how to build an ark—don't lose your grip."—*Hubbard.*

—The dreamer spends all day thinking of his difficulties. The worker spends his time trying to overcome them.

—"Blessed is the boy who wants a good thing and hustles for it."

—Persuasion plays a very important part in the destinies of men. Very few can be driven into any particular line of effort.

"Men who wait to be told what to do next are like loiterers in the park waiting for a policeman to suggest that they move on."

All the talking you can do will not go half as far as will a smile. Talking reaches the brain; but smiles go directly to the heart.

"No matter how patiently you may sit in the barnyard, the mooley cow won't back up to be milked. Same way with business."

—Everything makes way for the successful man, and men obtain success who are self-reliant, strong, bold and always on the job.

—All pessimists should be required to converse in the sign language only—and with their hands tied behind them—Be a Booster.

—The secret of success of fraternalism lies in its self-government, its social and moral tendencies, and its fair treatment to members.

—Believe in yourself and your future. Have confidence in that with which you are connected, and ever have a definite purpose in view.

—This paragraph will bear repeating: "The only difference between a rut and a grave is in the length and breadth. Don't get into the rut."

—Fraternalism is in a more flourishing and prosperous condition to-day than it ever has been. How much have you done this year for its welfare?

—Dr. Johnson has said that to improve the golden moments of opportunity and to catch the good that is within our reach is the great art of life.

—The person who is afraid of obstacles will not achieve any particular success. Results follow in the wake of the man who has iron in his blood.

—"Go out on the firing line and blaze away at something. Get busy and stay in the fight. The best marksman had to waste some powder in practice.

—James Allen said: "Men imagine that thought can be kept secret, but it cannot; it rapidly crystalizes into habit and habit solidifies into circumstances."

—There is but small chance for the one who can do a little of everything and not much of anything. Centralization is the keynote of success these days.

—Kaufman has said: "Progress is the result of elimination. Jump into the sieve. If you're big enough, you won't slip through—the little ones and the chaff will."

—The impractical theorist has had his day. The results are in evidence. The practical man is now straightening out the complications created by those who mistake theory for practice.

—Don't be afraid to take the initiative in any desirable line of effort. Remember that "men who exercise initiative are builders of the world—the majority of others are tenants and janitors."

—The man who spends his time sitting on nail kegs at the grocery store ranks as a producer along with the hen that sits on a door knob, except that the hen is honest in her intentions.

—One cannot advance alone. He must go forward with others. Neither can he stand still. He either goes forward or backward. Therefore, line up with those having similar objects and purposes and be an upbuilder.

—What is Difficulty? Only a word indicating the degree of strength requisite in accomplishing particular objects; a mere notice of necessity for exertion, a bugbear to children and fools; a stimulus to men.—*Samuel Warren.*

—When organizers realize that more results are forthcoming from a fair and frank presentation of their proposition than possibly can come from misrepresentation, they will be started on the road to permanent and enduring success.

—Here is something for the organizer to remember: When a man finds fear taking possession of him he needs to buckle on his armour, take a new grip on life, and go in the fulness of his strength against prospects he thinks will turn him down.

—Dig deeply and absorb fully, and you will get what is yours; then take a new hold on life; give the lion's tail another twist, and by that time you will be fully equal to the occasion, and be willing to wager that you can write more new business than any other man.

—Here is something worth thinking about: "The skyrocket is a brilliant thing as it soars upward. So is the career of a suc-cessful man. But the rocket's life is short and its sparks do not keep anybody warm. See that your career possesses more than sparks which die, or your family may find the end a cold one."

—There has been much discussion as to the difference between the employer and the employed. Really this difference is greater than is generally believed. The one sells his goods while the other sells the labor that makes the goods. The one deals in products while the other deals in time. Each sells something of value and each receives the prevailing price for it.

—When the conduct of men is designed to be influenced, PER-SUASION, kind, unassuming persuasion, should ever be adopted. It is an old and true maxim "That a drop of honey catches more flies than a gallon of gall." So with men. If you would win a man to your cause, first convince him that you are his sincere friend. Therein is a drop of honey that catches his heart, which, say what he will, is the great highroad to his reason, and which, when once gained, you will find but little trouble in convincing his judgment of the justice of your cause, if indeed that cause really be a just one. On the contrary, assume to dictate to his judgment, or to command his action, or to mark him as one to be shunned and despised, and he will retreat within himself, close all the avenues to his head and his heart, and though your cause be naked truth itself, and though you throw it with more than herculean force and precision, you shall be no more able to pierce him than to penetrate the hard shell of a tortoise with a rye straw. Such is man, and so must he be understood by those who would lead him, even to his own best interests.—*Abraham Lincoln.*

BENEFITS PAID SINCE ORGANIZATION.

Ancient Order of United Workmen.............	$ 178,000,000 00
Royal Arcanum	136,280,070 00
Knights of Honor	96,307,250 00
Societies out of business	89,672,848 00
Modern Woodmen of America	84,000,000 00
Knights of the Maccabees, Supreme Tent	38,569,669 00
Woodmen of the World.....................	36,000,000 00
National Union	30,217,281 00
Insurance Department, Knights of Pythias.....	31,198,131 00
Knights and Ladies of Honor................	30,031,150 00
Independent Order of Foresters.............	29,121,616 00
Catholic Mutual Benefit Association...........	22,482,348 00
Catholic Benevolent Legion	20,646,711 00
Locomotive Eng'rs Mut. Life and Acc. Ins. Assn.	19,570,789 00
Brotherhood of Railroad Trainmen............	19,253,436 00
National Protective Legion...................	17,885,842 00
Catholic Knights of America................	16,800,000 00
Improved Order of Heptasophs..............	16,792,652 00
Catholic Order of Foresters................	16,298,014 00
Knights of the Modern Maccabees...........	16,067,625 00
A. O. U. W. of Massachusetts..............	14,545,983 00
A. O. U. W. of Ontario.....................	13,689,507 00
Brotherhood of Loco. Firemen and Enginemen	12,504,745 00
Brotherhood of Locomotive Engineers........	12,500,000 00
Pacific Jurisdiction Woodmen of the World....	13,146,172 00
Brotherhood of Locomotive Firemen........	10,979,377 00
United Order of the Golden Cross...........	10,379,733 00
Order of Railway Conductors...............	8,817,567 00
United Order of Pilgrim Fathers.............	8,536,880 00
New England Order of Protection...........	7,694,614 00
Free Sons of Israel Independent Order........	7,565,000 00
Ladies Catholic Benevolent Association.......	7,799,984 00
Ladies of the Maccabees of the World.........	7,913,792 00
Royal League	7,389,411 00
Supreme Tribe of Ben-Hur..................	7,095,365 00
Knights and Ladies of Security..............	6,583,394 00
United Ancient Order Druids (America)......	6,483,182 00

Court of Honor ....
Canadian Order of Foresters.................
Royal Neighbors of America................
Protected Home Circle ....
Womens Catholic Order of Foresters.........
Ladies of the Modern Maccabees.............
Brotherhood of American Yeomen............
Brith Abraham Order ....
Modern Brotherhood of America............
Fraternal Mystic Circle ....
Catholic Mutual Benefit Association of Canada.
Knights of Columbus.......................
Assurance League of America...............
Order of Canadian Home Circles............
Fraternal Aid Association...................
A. O. U. W. of Oregon.....................
Expressmen's Mutual Benefit Association......
Societe des Artisans.......................
Massachusetts Catholic Order of Foresters.....
Polish National Alliance....................
Order of Sparta...........................
Degree of Honor A. O. U. W...............
Commonwealth Provident Association........
Sons of Benjamin Independent Order.........
Iowa Legion of Honor......................
Women of Woodcraft.......................
Canadian Order Chosen Friends.............
Legion of Honor of Missouri..................
United Commercial Travelers of America......
Shield of Honor ....
Fraternal Union of America................
Mystic Workers of the World..............
Loyal Americans of the Republic............
Odd Fellows Relief Association..............
Loyal Association ....
Canadian Royal Templars of Temperance......
American Insurance Union..................
Order of Columbian Knights................
Woodmen Circle ....
Fraternal Brotherhood ....
Ancient Order of Gleaners.................

Mutual Protective League..................
Junior Order, U. A. M......................
Catholic Knights and Ladies of America.......
Artisans Order Mutual Protection...........
Western Catholic Union....................
Order of Scottish Clans.....................
Order of Mutual Protection.................
Catholic Knights of Ohio...................
Brotherhood of America....................,   00
Roman Catholic Mutual Protective Society....
The Grand Fraternity ....
Telegraphers' Mutual Benefit Association......
Select Knights and Ladies..................
U. S. Letter Carriers Mutual Benefit Association
L' Union St. Joseph du Canada...............
North American Union ....
A. O. U. W. North Dakota................
Order of the Golden Seal...................
Catholic Relief and Beneficiary Association....
Royal Highlanders ....
Masonic Mutual Life Association............
Foresters of America ....
Sons and Daughters of Justice..............
Knights of Father Matthew..................
Legion of the Red Cross....................
Knights of St. John and Malta..............
Mutual Aid Society, German Lutheran Synod..
Empire State Degree of Honor..............
Alliance Nationale ....
Workmen's Benefit Association..............
Canadian Order Woodmen of the World......
United Order of Foresters..................
Equitable Fraternal Union..................
German Beneficial Union ....
United Artisans ....
American Benefit Society ....
Woodmen Accident Association............:..
People's Mutual Life Association and League..
Home Guards of America...................
Catholic Women's Benevolent Legion.........
The Loyal Guard ....

Loyal Mystic Legion of America..............
Association Canado Americaine...............
New Era Association ....
Royal Benefit Society.......................
Sons of Temperance.......................
United Benevolent Association...............
Yeomen of America ....
Modern Protective Association ....
National Benevolent Society ....
Triple Tie Benefit Association...............
Mutual Benefit and Aid Society...............
Modern Samaritans ....
Christian Burden Bearer's Association........
Catholic Knights of Illinois..................
Fraternal Reserve Life Association..........
Fraternal Champions ....
Modern American Fraternal Order...........
Mystic Toilers ....
Church Fraternal ....
Modern Order Prætorians ....
Bankers Union of the World ....
L'Union St. Jean-Baptiste d'Amerique........
Beavers Reserve Fund Fraternity...........
Degree of Honor ....
Highland Nobles ....
Union Fraternal League ....
Independent Scandinavian Workingmen's Assn.
Life and Annuity Association...............
American Catholic Union ....
Columbian Woodmen ....
Order of the Iroquois......................
American Patriots ....
Royal Fraternal Union ....
Workmen's Circle ....
North Star Benefit Association..............
Patricians, The ....
Home Fraternal League....................
Fraternal Bankers Reserve Society..........
Order of the Amaranth.....................
Red Men's Fraternal Accident Association....
Fraternal Reserve Association...............
International Congress ....

Homesteaders ....
Fraternal Benefit League ....
Keystone Guard ....
National Benevolent Legion ....,....
Daughters of Columbia ....
Order of the White Cross ....
Independent Order of Puritans ....
Pension Life Society ....
Catholic Women's Benevolent Legion ....
Occidental Mutual Benefit Association........
Modern National Reserve ....
Hibernian Life Insurance Association.........
Capitol Life Association ....
Catholic Ladies of Columbia ....
Fraternal Order of Connecticut ....
National Fraternal League ....
Heralds of Liberty ....
Ideal Reserve Life Association..............
Sons and Daughters of Protection...........
Aid Association for Lutherans ....
Fraternal Bankers of America...............
Gold Reserve Life Association....,.........
Lone Star Insurance Union ....
Eastern Star Benevolent Fund..............
Royal Achates ....
Woodmen's Modern Protective Association...
National Annuity Association ....
Vesta Circle ....
Fraternal Life and Accident Association......
National Mutual Relief Association..........
American Stars of Equity...................
Progressive Order of the West..............
Lincoln Annuity Union ....
Modern Workmen of the World..............
American Order of Scottish Clans............
United Aid of Sheboygan....................
Home Protection Association................
Home Defenders of America ....
Pioneer Life Association ....
Modern Romans ....
Family Protective Union ....
Family Hearth Society ....

Kinsmans Mystic Senate ....
Archaean Union ....
American Woodmen ....
Fraternal Order of Mountaineers.............
American Fraternal League ....
National Fraternal Union ....
National Protective Association ....
Mutual Benefit Association of America........
Progressive Fraternal Union ....
National Home Guard ....
Commoners of America ....
Ancient Order of Shepherds ....
Universal Friends of America ....
Farmers Life Insurance Association..........
Guild of the East ....
Home Watchmen of the World..............
Union Fraternal Association ....
Fraternity of Home Protectors..............
Wage Earners Protective Union ....

Total $1,306,903,158 00

SOCIETIES PAYING CLAIMS FOR SICKNESS

Ancient Order Foresters (England and America) $
Independent Order of Odd Fellows............
Foresters of America ....
Knights of Pythias ....
Ancient Order Hibernians ....
Red Men, Improved Order ....
Independent Order of Rechabites ....
American Mechanics, Junior Order...........
Order of Eagles ....
Sons of America, Patriotic Order of..........
American Mechanics ....
Benevolent and Protective Order Elks.........
Irish Catholic Benevolent Union..............
Daughters of Liberty.......................

Total .... $ 408,519,023 00
Grand Total $1,715,422,181 00

National Fraternal Congress Table of Mortality

Age	Number of Living	Number of Dying	Yearly Probability of Dying	Yearly	Yearly Cost Discounted at 4 per cent.	Expectation of Life	Average Duration of Life
20	100000	500	0050			45.6	49.7
21	99500	501	005			44.9	48.8
22	98999	502	005			44.1	47.9
23	98497	503	005 8			43.3	47.0
24	97994	505	005 5			42.5	46.1
25	97489	507	005 6			41.8	45.2
26	96982	510	005 7			41.0	44.3
27	96472	513	0053 6			40.2	43.4
28	95957	517	00538 7			39.4	42.5
29	95442	522	.0054693			38.6	41.6
30	94920	527	.0055520			37.8	40.7
31	94393	533	0056466			37.0	39.8
32	93860	540	.0057532			36.2	38.9
33	93320	548	.0058723			35.4	38.0
34	92772	557	.0060040			34.6	37.1
35	92215	567	.0061487			33.9	36.2
36	91648	578	.0063067			33.1	35.3
37	91070	591	0064895			32.3	34.4
38	90479	606				31.5	
39	89873	622				30.7	
40	89251	640				29.9	
41	88611	660				29.1	
42	87951	683				28.3	
43	87268	708				27.5	
44	86568	734				26.8	
45	85826	761				26.0	
46	85065	790				25.2	
47	84275	822				24.4	
48	83453	857				23.7	
49	82596	894					
50	81702	935					
51	80767	981					
52	79786	1029					
53	78757	1083			13.222		
54	77674	1140					
55	76534	1202					
56	75332	1270					
57	74062	1342					
58	72720	1418					
59	71302	1501					
60	69801	1588					
61	68213	1681					
62	66532	1778					
63	64754	1880					
64	62874	1985					

National Fraternal Congress Table of Mortality—Continued

Age	Number of Living	Number of Dying	Yearly Probability of Dying	Yearly Insurance Cost per $1000	Yearly Cost Discounted at 4 per cent.	Expectation of Life	
65	60889	2094	.0343904	34.390	33.067	11.8	
66	58795	2206	.0375202	37.520	36.077	11.2	
67	56589	2308	.0409620	40.962	39.387	10.7	
68	54271	2430	.0447753	44.775	43.053	10.1	
69	51841	2539	.0489767	48.977	47.093	9.5	
70	49302	2645	.0536489	53.649	51.586	9.0	
71	46657	2744	.0588122	58.812	56.550	8.5	
72	43913	2832	.0644912	64.491	62.011	8.0	
73	41081	2909	.0708113	70.811	68.087		
74	38172	2969	.0777795	77.789	74.788		
75	35203	3009	.0854957	85.476	82.198		
76	32194	3026	.0939927	93.993	90.377		
77	29168	3016	.1031010	103.401	99.424		
78	26152	2977	.1138345	113.835	109.457		
79	23175	2905	.1253506	125.351	120.520		
80	20270	2799	.1380858	138.086	132.775		
81	17471	2659	.1521951	152.195	146.341		
82	14812	2485	.1677694	167.769	161.316		
83	12327	2280	.1849599	184.960	177.846		
84	10047	2050	.2040410	204.041	196.193		
85	7997	1800	.2250844	225.084	216.427		
86	6197	1539	.2483460	248.346	238.794		
87	4658	1277	.2741520	274.152	263.608		
88	3381	1023	.3025732	302.573	290.935		
89	2358	788	.3341815	334.182	321.329		
90	1570	579	.3687898	368.790	354.606		
91	991	404	.4076690	407.669	391.989		
92	587	264	.4497445	449.745	432.447		
93	323	161	.4984520	498.452	479.281		
94	162	89	.5493827	549.383	528.253		
95	73	44	.6027397	602.740	579.557		
96	29	19	.6551724	655.172	629.973		
97	10	7	.7000000	700.000	673.077		
98	3	3	1.0000000	1000.000	961.538		

PRINCIPAL FRATERNAL OR SECRET SOCIETIES NOT FURNISHING INSURANCE AS A SPECIAL FEATURE

ANCIENT ORDER FREE AND ACCEPTED MASONS

The returns of the Grand Lodges of the United States and British America are given below: The Grand Lodges are in full affiliation with the English Grand Lodge, of which the Duke of Connaught is Grand Master, and the Grand Lodges of Ireland, Scotland, Cuba, Peru, South Australia, New South Wales, Victoria, and also with the Masonic bodies of Germany and Austria. They are not in affiliation and do not correspond with the Masons under the jurisdiction of the Grand Orient of France. However, they do affiliate with and recognize Masons under the jurisdiction of the Supreme Council. Freemasonry is under the ban of the Church in Spain, Italy and other Catholic countries. The membership, therefore, in these latter countries is small and scattered.

Total membership in United States and Canada. 1,309,697
Royal Arch Masons 266,919
Knights Templars 172,149
Colored Masonic Bodies 150,000
Nobles of the Mystic Shrine 138,000 2,036,765

The above figures give only members of the various Masonic bodies in the Western Hemisphere. The Ancient Accepted Scottish Rite Masons do not give their figures, although these comprise a membership of many thousands. The Sovereign Grand Consistory has had a continuous existence of one hundred years, with its Grand Orient at New York, where, under the protection of the Grand Orient of France, it was organized. It has fraternal relations throughout the confines of Freemasonry. The official address of the Supreme Council is No. 320 Temple Court, Beekman Street, New York.

The Sovereign Sanctuary of Ancient and Primitive Freemasonry is composed of Masons who have received the 95th degree of the Patriarch Grand Conservator of the Rite; it has jurisdiction over the continent of America. It was formerly instituted in the United States in 1856. The American body is in affiliation with the various Masonic powers of the world and has a regular exchange of representatives throughout the different countries. The Degrees of the Rite, which are ninety of instruction and seven official, are conferred in the subordinate bodies of the Rite thus: Fourth to 18th degree in a Chapter of Rose Croix; 19th to 42nd degree in a Senate of Hermatic Philosophers; 43rd to 90th degree in a Council of Sublime Masters of the Great Work.

The Ancient Arabic Order of the Nobles of the Mystic Shrine is not a regular Masonic body, but its membership is composed strictly of Masons who have reached the 32nd degree A. A. S. Rite or Knights Templars in good standing.

INDEPENDENT ORDER OF ODD FELLOWS

The membership of the Independent Order of Odd Fellows which comprises the Grand Lodges of Australasia, Germany, Denmark, Sweden, Switzerland and the Netherlands is 1,492,478

The American organization is not in affiliation with an English order entitled the Manchester Unity of Odd Fellows, and numbers 1,441,403

The first reported lodge was organized in England in 1745. The numerical standing of the order, excluding the

Manchester Unity of Odd Fellows is	1,441,403	
Manchester Unity	1,021,474	
Encampment Branch	216,225	
Rebekah Lodges (sisters)	395,898	
Rebekah Lodges (brothers)	208,033	
Chevaliers of the Patriarchs Militant	22,136	3,305,169

KNIGHTS OF PYTHIAS, SUPREME LODGE

Established, February, 1864.
Total membership, 703,804.
Membership of Insurance Branch, 74,006.
Representing insurance of $111,365,000.

ORDER OF GOOD TEMPLARS

This Order, based on total abstinence, is organized in nearly every State of the Union, England, Ireland, Scotland, Wales, Germany, Denmark, Sweden and Norway, Canada, West Indies, East, West, and South Africa, Australia, New Zealand, British India, Iceland, and other countries. Its next International Supreme Lodge will convene at Hamburg, Germany, June 6, 1911.

Membership	419,749	
Juvenile Branches	239,586	659,335

ORDER OF THE SONS OF TEMPERANCE

The National Division of North America was organized in the city of New York in 1842. In the course of its existence it has had nearly four million members on its rolls. Its present membership in North America is 34,879, of whom 13,537 are in the United States.

GRAND ARMY OF THE REPUBLIC

First post organized in 1866.
Total membership 220,600

IMPROVED ORDER OF RED MEN
Founded, 1763, Reorganized in 1834.
Membership 475,450

UNITED AMERICAN MECHANICS
Membership 31,850
National Councilor, SAMUEL A. CHARLES, Jersey City, N. J.
National Secretary, JOHN SERVER, Philadelphia, Pa.

WOMAN'S RELIEF CORPS
Auxiliary to the Grand Army of the Republic.
Membership 161,646

UNITED AMERICAN MECHANICS, JUNIOR ORDER OF
Founded, 1853.
Membership 201,897
National Councilor, H. L. W. TAYLOR, Newport, Tenn.;
National Secretary, M. M. WOODS, Philadelphia, Pa.

BENEVOLENT AND PROTECTIVE ORDER OF ELKS
Founded, 1868.
Members in United States 304,899
Exalted Ruler, J. U. SAMMI, Le Mars, Ia.; *Secretary,* FRED
C. ROBINSON, Dubuque, Ia.

SONS OF VETERANS, U. S. A.
Organized, 1879.
Composed of lineal descendants of honorably discharged
soldiers, sailors and marines of the late Civil War.
Membership 50,000

ANCIENT ORDER OF FORESTERS
Founded, 1745. Established in America, 1836.
The American Branch has a membership of........... 41,116
Total membership throughout the world............. 1,289,904

FORESTERS OF AMERICA
Founded, 1864.
Jurisdiction limited to the United States.
Membership 231,996

ANCIENT ORDER OF DRUIDS
Founded in England, 1781; in America, 1839.
Membership in America 30,340
Members elsewhere 90,000   120,340

ORDER OF EAGLES
Founded, 1898.
FRANK E. HERING, *President,* Kansas City, Mo.; CONRAD H.
MANN, Secretary, Kansas City, Mo.
Membership 312,847

ANCIENT ORDER OF HIBERNIANS
Founded, 1836.
National President, MATTHEW CUMMINGS, Boston, Mass.;
National Secretary, JAMES T. McGINNIS, Joliet, Ill.
Total members 250,000
Ladies Auxiliary 65,000   315,000

KNIGHTS OF MALTA, ANCIENT AND ILLUSTRIOUS ORDER
Founded in Jerusalem, 1048; in America, 1889.
Membership 30,000

KNIGHTS OF THE GOLDEN EAGLE
Founded, 1873.
Supreme Chief, Dr. E. F. LAKE, Denver, Col.; *Master of
Records,* A. C. LYTTLE, Philadelphia, Pa.
Membership 86,668
There is also a ladies' auxiliary society, known as the Ladies
of the Golden Eagle.

INDEPENDENT ORDER OF RECHABITES
Founded in England in 1835; in America, 1842.
Membership 491,000

YOUNG MEN'S INSTITUTE
Organized in San Francisco, March 4, 1883.
Membership 16,568
The object of the organization is to associate together Catholic men for their moral, social and intellectual improvement; for the establishment of libraries, reading rooms and gymnasiums.

POEMS

FRATERNAL LOVE

BY GEO. W. REED

Love is immortal. If but mortal, why
  Its failure evermore
To find in human language, words
  To give, from its vast store
Of beauty, sweetness, holiness,
  Its full expression? Naught
Of tongue, or pen, portrays the depths
  Of hearts with pure love fraught.

Love is immortal. Whereso'er it dwells
  In purity and power
Its boundlessness, its mystery,
  Unfolding hour by hour,—
Reveals its fountain infinite,
  Unfathomable, divine,
That yields to mortal life but drops
  From its o'erflowing wine.

If love were finite, would it strive
  Thro' all Life's changing years,
In helpless aspirations, 'midst
  Earth's wisdom, hopes and fears?
Its depth, is Immortality;
  Its pain, our lack of sight,
To learn its grand immensity,
  In Heaven's perpetual light.

Love's highest service, that earth knows,
  Is ours; to inspire—to seek
The best, that Love's clear-sightedness
  Can proffer to the weak,
The saddened, lonely, all, who need
  Pure fellowship, and power
T'regain lost Opportunity,
  While dark misfortunes lower.

Love is immortal. Shall our lives' best hours
  But mere existence prove,—
While wait divinest ministries
  Of pure fraternal love?
The love that broadens, day by day,
  Devoid of self's demand;
The love that bears Hope's wreckage safe
  To Joy's enchanted land.

Love that unfolds, and deepens, while
  Kind words, and noble deeds,
Lead up to light, and peace, and rest,
  Despite earth's tears and needs;
That glorifies grand gifts of life
  To Fraternizers of the worlds,
Where'er beneath the sun, and stars,
  Their banners are unfurled.

ON THE SHORTNESS OF HUMAN LIFE.

WASTELL (BORN ABOUT 1565.)

I.

Like as the damask rose you see,
Or like the blossom on the tree,
Or like the dainty flower of May,
Or like the morning to the day,
Or like the sun, or like the shade,
Or like the gourd which Jonah had
E'en such is man;—whose thread is spun
Drawn out and cut, and so is done,
Wither, the rose, the blossom blasts,
The flower fades, the morning hastes,
The sun doth set, the shadow flies,
The gourd consumes,

        and

          Man

            he

              dies!

II.

Like to the grass that's newly sprung,
Or like a tale that's new begun,
Or like the bird that's here to-day
Or like the pearled dew of May,
Or like an hour, or like a span
Or like the singing of a swan
E'en such is man;—who lives by breath,
Is here, now there, in life and death.
The grass decays, the tale is ended,
The bird is flown, the dew's ascended,
The hour is short, the span not long,
The swan's near death,

        Man's

            life

                is

                    done!

III.

Like to the bubble in the brook,
Or in a glass much like a look,
Or like the shuttle in the hand,
Or like the writing in the sand,
Or like a thought, or like a dream,
Or like the gliding of the stream,
E'en such is man;—who lives by breath
Is here, now there, in life and death.
The bubble's burst, the look's forgot,
The shuttle's flung, the writing's blot,
The thought is past, the dream is gone
The water glides,

        Man's

            life

                is

                    done!

LIFE

HENRY KING

Like to the falling of a star,
Or as the flights of eagles are,
Or like the fresh spring's gaudy hue,
Or silver drops of morning dew,
 Or like a wind that chafes the flood,
Or like a wind that shafes the flood,
Or bubbles which on water stood,—
Even such is man, whose borrowed light
Is straight called in, and paid to-night.
The wind blows out; the bubble dies;
The spring entombed in autumn lies;
The dew dries up; the star is shot;
The flight is past;
                    and
                        Man
                            forgot.

ABOU BEN ADHEM

Abou Ben Adhem (may his tribe increase!)
Awoke one night from a deep dream of peace,
And saw within the moonlight in his room,
Making it rich and like a lily in bloom,
An angel writing in a book of gold:
Exceeding peace had made Ben Adhem bold,
And to the presence in the room he said,
"What writest thou?" The vision raised its head,
And with a look made of all sweet accord,
Answered, "The names of those who love the Lord."
"And is mine one?" said Abou. "Nay, not so,"
Replied the angel. Abou spoke more low,
But cheerly still; and said, "I pray thee, then,
Write me as one that loves his fellowmen."

The angel wrote and vanished. The next night
It came again, with a great wakening light,
And showed the names whom love of God had blessed—
And lo! Ben Adhem's name led all the rest!
                                    —LEIGH HUNT.

THE BLUE OF THE INFINITE

O the breadth of the ocean is in this sky!
The clouds are its billows; and mountain high
They rise and they fall, and are inward pressed
Till more blue is revealed, like a place of rest.

From the mountainous shore are its billows rolled,
In thunderous surges, fold on fold,
Till high in the zenith, the depth of this sea,
The blue of the Infinite bends o'er thee.

It bends, till it touches thy Soul, and then
Thy heart beats quicker with love for men,
And thy hand is ready, thy thought is clear,
And something within breathes "God is near."

WHERE LOVE IS.

The wolf came along, and he sat by my door,
And he scratched and he howled with a terrible roar
That wakened the neighbors, but in spite of his din
He never was heard by the dwellers within;
For spite of his yowl, and in spite of his screech,
I sat there inside quite outside of his reach;
  For love was my guest,
  And a guest so fair
  That I didn't e'en hear
  Mr. Wolf out there!

The winter winds came with their withering blast,
And over the world an ice-mantle was cast.
The rivers froze up, and down by the sea
The rocks were a vision of bleak misery;
But never a chill entered in at my door,
And never a note of old Boreas's roar;
  For love was my guest,
  And a guest so warm
  That I cared not a jot
  For the trumpeting storm!

The mists hid the sun from the sight of the day,
And over the world was a shadow of gray.
All hushed was the song of the caroling lark,
And the earth lay chilled in the gathering dark;
But deep in my soul was no trace of the night,
For deep in my heart was a harvest of light;
    For love was my guest,
    And a guest so gay
    I saw but the flowers
    On the dark highway.

O love is a guest that will kill all care,
And Love is immune to all dark despair,
And Love is a cure for the lack of gold,
And Love is a screen from the winter's cold,
And Love is the source of a golden stream
That lightens the soul with a lustrous gleam
    Where Love is a guest
    There will come no fear,
    And the darkest ways
    Are the Roads to Cheer!   —BLAKENEY GREY.

HOLD THOU MY HANDS.

Hold Thou my hands!
  In grief and joy, in hope and fear,
  Lord, let me feel that Thou art near:
    Hold Thou my hands!

If e'er, by doubts
  Of Thy good Fatherhood depressed,
  I cannot find in Thee my rest,
    Hold Thou my hands!

Hold Thou my hands,—
  These passionate hands too quick to smite,
  These hands so eager for delight,
    Hold Thou my hands!

And when, at length,
  With darkened eyes and fingers cold,
  I seek some last loved hand to hold,
    Hold Thou my hands!   —WILLIAM CANTON.

KEEP AT IT

Hi Somers was the durndest cuss
  Fer catchin' fish—he sure was great!
He never used to make no fuss
  About the kind of pole er bait,
Er weather, neither; he'd jest say,
"I got to ketch a mess today."
  An' toward the creek you'd see him slide,
  A-whistlin' soft and walkin' wide.
I says one day to Hi, says I,
"How do you always ketch 'em, Hi?"
  He gave his bait another switch in,
  An' chucklin' says, "I jest keep fishin'."

Hi took to readin' law at night
  And pretty soon, the first we knowed,
He had a lawsuit, won his fight,
  An' was a lawyer! I'll be blowed!
He knowed more law than Squire McKnabe!
An', though he had no "gift of gab"
  To brag about, somehow he made
  A sober sort of talk that played
The mischief with the other side.
One day, when some one asked if Hi'd
  Explain how he got in condishin,
  He laughed an' said, "I jest kept fishin'."

Well, Hi is Gov-ner Somers, now;
  A big man round the state, you bet—
To me the same old Hi, somehow;
  The same old champeen fisher yet,
It wan't so much the bait er pole,
It wan't so much the fishin' hole,
  That won fer Hi his big success;
  'Twas jest his fishin' on, I guess;
A cheerful, stiddy, hopeful kind
Of keepin' at it—don't you mind?
  And that is why I can't help wishin'
  That more of us would jest keep fishin'.
              —ANONYMOUS.

THE FOUNTAIN

A living fountain sings
Within our souls, and flings
Its waters, vibrant with eternal life;
It gathers force each hour,
And flows with quiet power
In strength to those who stand amid the strife.

This fountain sweet and pure
That helps our souls endure,
Feeds flowers from out its overflowing brink;
We breathe it in the air,
This fluid fine and rare,
Its sparkling spray gives life to all who drink.

And in its springing tide
God lives, and shall abide
With man, till in that wondrous future dim
When earthly tests are past,
Man finds himself at last
Absorbed within the Source, at one with Him.

But till that glorious day,
'Tis man's to work away
As doth the fountain, fed by God's own life,—
To gather force each hour,
And flow with quiet power
In strength to those who stand amid the strife.

ARIEL.

GIFTS

"O World-God, give me Wealth!" the Egyptian cried.
　His prayer was granted. High as heaven behold
Palace and Pyramid; the brimming tide
　Of lavish Nile washed all his land with gold.
Armies of slaves toiled ant-wise at his feet,
　World-circling traffic roared through mart and street,
High priests were gods, his spiced-balmed kings enshrined,
　Set death at naught in rock-ribbed channels deep.
Seek Pharaoh's race to-day, and we shall find
　Rust and the moth, silence and dusty sleep.

"O World-God, give me Beauty!" cried the Greek.
  His prayer was granted. All the earth became
Plastic and vocal to his sense; each peak,
  Each grove, each stream, quick with Promethean flame,
Peopled the world with imaged grace and light.
  The lyre was his, and his the breathing might
Of the immortal marble, his the play
  Of diamond-pointed thought and golden tongue.
Go seek the sunshine race. Ye find to-day
  A broken column and a lute unstrung.

"O World-God, give me Power!" the Roman cried.
  His prayer was granted. The vast world was chained,
A captive to the chariot of his pride,
  The blood of myriad provinces was drained
To feed that fierce, insatiable red heart—
  Invulnerably bulwarked every part
With serried legions and with close-meshed Code,
  Within the burrowing worm had gnawed its home:
A roofless ruin stands where once abode
  The imperial race of everlasting Rome.

"O Godhead, give me Truth!" the Hebrew cried.
  His prayer was granted. He became the slave
Of the Idea, a pilgrim far and wide,
  Cursed, hated, spurned, and scourged, with none to save.
The Pharoahs knew him, and when Greece beheld,
  His wisdom wore the hoary crown of Eld,
Beauty he hath forsworn, and wealth and power.
  Seek him to-day, and find in every land,
No fire consumes him, neither floods devour;
  Immortal through the lamp within his hand.

—EMMA LAZARUS.

"HAD SEEN GOD FACE TO FACE"

"There was a man who saw God face to face,
  His countenance and vestments evermore
  Glowed with a light that never shone before
Saving from Him who saw God face to face.

"And men anear Him for a little space
  Were solely vexed by the unwonted light.
  They bore his body to a mountain height
  And nailed Him to a tree, then went their way,
  And He resisted not nor said them nay
Because that He had seen God face to face.

"There was a Man who saw man face to face,
  And ever as He walked from day to day,
  The deathless mystery of being lay
Plain as the path before Him face to face,
And each deep-hid inscription could He trace.

"When men had fought and loved and fought again ·
How in lone anguish souls cried out for pain,
  How each green foot of sod from sea to sea
  Was red with blood of men slain wantonly
With all the haste and rush and fever pain.

"The sordid walk and talk of squalid men,
  He saw the vision changeless as the stars
  That shone through temple gate or prison bars,
Through all the meanness of man's life that is,
The vision of man's life that is to be.

"So when anear Him for a little space ,
  Men whom the light did blind rose angrily
  And nailed His body to the cruel tree
  He did not resist them nor say them nay
  For earth's one secret plain before Him lay,
And in man's life He saw God face to face."
                                   —David Starr Jordan.

FATE

Two shall be born the whole wide world apart
And speak in different tongues, and have no thought
Each of the other's being, and no heed:
And these o'er unknown seas, to unknown lands,
Shall cross, escaping wreck, defying death;
And all unconsciously shape every act
And bend each wandering step to this one end—
That one day out of darkness they shall meet
And read life's meaning in each other's eyes.

And two shall walk some narrow way of life,
So nearly side by side that should one turn
Ever so little space to left or right,
They needs must stand acknowledged face to face;
And yet with wistful eyes that never meet,
With groping hands that never clasp, and lips
Calling in vain to ears that never hear,
They seek each other all their weary days,
And die unsatisfied. And this is Fate.

—SUSAN MARR SPAULDING.

BEAUTIFUL HANDS

As I remember the first fair touch
Of these beautiful hands that I love so much,
I seem to thrill as I then was thrilled
Kissing the glove that I found unfilled—
When I met your gaze and the queenly bow,
As you said to me laughingly, "Keep it now!"
And dazed and alone in a dream I stand
Kissing the ghost of your beautiful hand.

When first I loved in the long ago,
And held your hand as I told you so
Pressed it and caressed it and gave it a kiss,
And said, "I could die for a hand like this!"
Little I dreamed love fullness yet
Had to ripen when eyes were wet,
And prayers were vain in their wild demands
For one warm touch of your beautiful hands.

Beautiful hands! O beautiful hands!
Could you reach out of the alien lands
Where you are lingering, and give me to-night
Only a touch—were it ever so light—
My heart were soothed, and my weary brain
Would lull itself into rest again;
For there is no solace the world commands
Like the caress of your beautiful hands.

—JAMES WHITCOMB RILEY.

A NIGHT WITH A WOLF

Little one, come to my knee!
  Hark, how the rain is pouring
Over the roof, in the pitch-black night,
  And the wind in the woods a-roaring!

Hush, my darling, and listen,
  Then pay for the story with kisses;
Father was lost in the pitch-black night
  In just such a storm as this is!

High up on the lonely mountains,
  Where the wild men watched and waited;
Wolves in the forest, and bears in the bush,
  And I on my path belated.

The rain and the night together
  Came down, and the wind came after,
Bending the props of the pine-tree roof,
  And snapping many a rafter.

I crept along in the darkness,
  Stunned and bruised and blinded—
Crept to a fir with thick-set boughs,
  And a sheltering rock behind it.

There, from the blowing and raining,
  Crouching, I sought to hide me;
Something rustled, two green eyes shone,
  And a wolf lay down beside me.

Little one, be not frightened;
  I and the wolf together,
Side by side, through the long, long night
  Hid from the awful weather.

His wet fur pressed against me;
  Each of us warmed the other;
Each of us felt, in the stormy dark,
  That beast and man was brother.

And when the falling forest
  No longer crashed in warning,
Each of us went from our hiding-place
  Forth in the wild, wet morning.

Darling, kiss me in payment!
  Hark, how the wind is roaring!
Father's house is a better place
  When the stormy rain is pouring!
                                    —BAYARD TAYLOR.

WHAT HAVE WE DONE TO-DAY

We shall do so much in the years to come,
  But what have we done to-day?
We shall give our gold in a princely sum,
  But what did we give to-day?
We shall lift the heart and dry the tear,
We shall plant a hope in the place of fear,
We shall speak the words of love and cheer,
  But what did we speak to-day?

We shall be so kind in the afterawhile,
  But what have we been to-day?
We shall bring to each lonely life a smile,
  But what have we been to-day?
We shall give to truth a grander birth,
And to steadfast faith a deeper worth,
We shall feed the hungering souls of earth,
  But whom have we fed to-day?

We shall reap such joys in the by and by,
  But what have we sown to-day?
We shall build our mansions in the sky,
  But what have we built to-day?
'Tis sweet in idle dreams to bask,
But here and now do we do our task?
Yes, this is the thing our souls must ask:
  "What have we done to-day?"
                              NIXON WATERMAN.

HABIT

So, then! Wilt use me as a garment? Well,
  'Tis man's high impudence to think he may;
But I—who am as old as heav'n and hell—
  I am not likely to be cast away.

Wilt run a race? Then I will run with thee,
  And stay thy steps or speed thee to the goal;
Wilt dare a fight? Then, of a certainty,
  I'll aid thy foeman, or sustain thy soul.

Lo, at thy marriage feast, upon one hand
  Face of thy bride, and on the other—mine!
Lo, at thy couch of sickness close I stand,
  And taint the cup, or make it more benign!

Yea, hark! The very son thou hast begot
  One day doth give thee certain sign and cry;
Hold thou thy peace—frighted or frighted not—
  That look, that sign, that presence—it is I!

M. S. Anderson.

BROTHERHOOD

It's the kindly hearts of earth that make
  This good old world worth while.
It's the lips with tender words that wake
  The rare-erasing smile.
And I ask my soul this question when
  My goodly gifts I see,—
Am I a friend to as many men
  As have been good friends to me?

When my brothers speak a word of praise
  My wavering will to aid,
I ask if ever their long, long ways
  My words have brighter made.
And to my heart I bring again
  This eager, earnest plea,—
Make me a friend to as many men
  As are good, staunch friends to me.

—Nixon Waterman.

THE HOUSE BY THE SIDE OF THE ROAD.

(He was a friend to man, and lived in a house by the side
of the road.—Homer.)

There are hermit souls that live withdrawn
    In the peace of their self-content;
There are souls, like stars, that dwell apart.
    In a fellowless firmament;
There are pioneer souls that blaze their paths
    Where the highways never ran;
But let me live by the side of the road
    And be a friend to man.

Let me live in a house by the side of the road,
    Where the race of men go by—
The men who are good and the men who are bad,
    As good and as bad as I.
I would not sit in the scorner's seat,
    Or hurl the cynic's ban;
Let me live in a house by the side of the road
    And be a friend to man.

I see from my house by the side of the road,—
    By the side of the highway of life,
The men who press with the ardor of hope,
    The men who are faint with strife.
But I turn not away from their smiles nor their tears—
    Both are parts of an infinite plan;
Let me live in a house by the side of the road
    And be a friend to man.

I know there are brook-gladdened meadows ahead,
    And mountains of wearisome height;
That the road passes on through the long afternoon,
    And stretches away to night.
But still I rejoice when the travelers rejoice,
    And weep with the strangers that moan,
Nor live in my house by the side of the road
    Like a man who dwells alone.

Let me live in my house by the side of the road,
  Where the race of men go by—
They are good, they are bad, they are weak, they are strong,
  Wise, foolish—so am I.
Then why should I sit in the scorner's seat,
  Or hurl the cynic's ban?
Let me live in a house by the side of the road
  And be a friend to man.
                 —SAM WALTER FOSS.

WHILE THE DAYS ARE GOING BY

There are lonely hearts to cherish,
  While the days are going by;
There are weary souls who perish,
  While the days are going by;
If a smile we can renew,
As our journey we pursue,
Oh, the good we all may do,
  While the days are going by.

There's no time for idle scorning,
  While the days are going by;
Let your face be like the morning,
  While the days are going by;
Oh, the world is full of sighs,
Full of sad and weeping eyes;
Help your fallen brothers rise,
  While the days are going by.

All the loving links that bind us,
  While the days are going by;
One by one we leave behind us,
  While the days are going by;
But the seeds of good we sow,
Both in shade and shine will grow,
And will keep our hearts aglow,
  While the days are going by.

THE DEAD FAITH

She made a little shadow-hidden grave
  The day Faith died;
Therein she laid it, heard the clod's sick fall,
  And smiled aside—
"If less I ask," tear-blind, she mocked,
  "I may be less denied."

She set a rose to blossom in her hair,
  The day Faith died—
"Now glad," she said, "and free at last, I go,
  And life is wide."
But through long nights she stared into the dark,
  And knew she lied.

FANNIE H. LEA.

THE HEROIC AGE

He speaks not well who doth his time deplore,
Naming it new and little and obscure,
Ignoble and unfit for lofty deeds.
All times were modern in the time of them,
And this no more than others. Do thy part
Here in the living day, as did the great
Who made old days immortal! So shall men,
Gazing long back to this far-looming hour,
Say: "Then, the time when men were truly men;
Though wars grew less, their spirits met the test
Of new conditions; conquering civic wrong ;
Saving the State anew by virtuous lives;
Guarding the country's honor as their own,
And their own as their country's and their sons';
Defying leagued fraud with single truth;
Not fearing loss, and daring to be pure.
When error through the land raged a pest
They calmed the madness caught from mind to mind
By wisdom drawn from eld, and counsel sane;
And as the martyrs of the ancient world
Gave Death for man, so nobly gave they Life;
Those the great days, and that the heroic age."

—RICHARD WATSON GILDER.

THE DUST

Yea, spit on me! Yea, spurn me with your feet!
  Ye kings and seers and bards together!
For I am but the dust—the shapeless dust—
  The sport of winds and of the weather!

Yet once the lightning of the flesh I wore;
  Peal after peal like glorious thunder,
Once with the shock of being sweet as song
  The senses shook my heart of wonder!

And once in burning hush of life's high noon,
  I heard the rosy mouth of woman
Spilling love's voice of spikenard on the air—
  Divine, and yet supremely human.

Yea, spit on me! Yea, spurn me with your feet!
  Ye kings and sears and bards together!
Yet once your solemn robes of state I wore
  Who now am sport of winds and weather!
                          —EDWARD W. MASON.

HOW HE LIVED

So he died for his faith. That is fine
  More than most of us do.
But stay! Can you add to that line
  That he lived for it, too?

It is easy to die. Men have died
  For a wish or a whim—
From bravado, passion or pride;
  Was it hard for him?

But to live; every day to live out
  All the truth, that he dreamt,
While his friends met his conduct with doubt,
  And the world with contempt—

Was it thus that he plodded ahead,
  Never turning aside?
Then we'll talk of the life that he led
  Never mind how he died.   —ERNEST CROSBY.

THE HILLS OF REST

Beyond the last horizon's rim,
  Beyond adventure's farthest quest,
Somewhere they rise, serene and dim,
  The happy, happy Hills of Rest.

Upon their sunlit slopes uplift
  The castles we have built in Spain—
While fair amid the summer drift
  Our faded gardens flower again.

Sweet hours we did not live go by
  To soothing note, on scented wing;
In golden-lettered volumes lie
  The songs we tried in vain to sing.

They all are there: the days of dream
  That build the inner lives of men;
The silent, sacred years we deem
  The might be, and the might have been.

Some evening when the sky is gold
  I'll follow day into the west;
Nor pause, nor heed, till I behold
  The happy, happy Hills of Rest.
                          —Albert Bigelow Paine.

"IN THE FAR FORGOTTEN LANDS"

In the far forgotten lands,
By the world's last gulf of night,
Gasps a naked human soul,
Writhing up and falling back,
Screaming for a God who cares.

In the far forgotten lands,
By the world's last gulf of night,
Bat-like creatures vex the gloom
And whimper as they shudder by—
"Is there any God who cares?"

In the far forgotten lands,
By the world's last gulf of night,
Walks the cross-stained Nazarene,
Searching ever for his own
On the crumbling edge of hell.

In the far forgotten lands,
By the world's last gulf of night,
There He wanders all alone,
Dragging bleeding hearts from hell
With the whisper, "God does care!"
　　　　　　　　　　—L. H. Harris.

LINES ON A SKELETON

Behold this ruin! 'Twas a skull
Once of ethereal spirit full.
This narrow cell was Life's retreat,
This space was Thought's mysterious seat,
What beauteous visions filled this spot,
What dreams of pleasure long forgot,
Nor hope, nor joy, nor love, nor fear,
Have left one trace of record here.

Beneath this moldering canopy
Once shone the bright and busy eye,
But start not at the dismal void—
If social love that eye employed,
If with no lawless fire it gleamed,
But through the dews of kindness beamed,
That eye shall be forever bright
When stars and sun are sunk in night.

Within this hollow cavern hung
The ready, swift, and tuneful tongue;
If Falsehood's honey it disdained,
And when it could not praise was chained;
If bold in Virtue's cause it spoke,
Yet gentle concord never broke—
This silent tongue shall plead for thee
When Time unveils Eternity!

Say, did these fingers delve the mine?
Or with the envied rubies shine?
To hew the rock or wear a gem
Can little now avail to them.
But if the page of Truth they soiught,
Or comfort to the mourner brought,
These hands a richer meed shall claim
Than all that wait on Wealth and Fame.

Avails it whether bore or shod
These feet the paths of duty trod?
If from the bowers of Ease they fled,
To seek affliction's humble shed;
If Grandeur's guilty bribe they spurned,
And home to Virtue's cot returned—
These feet with angel wings shall vie,
And tread the palace of the sky!

—Anonymous.

SUNRISE

The somber skies a sudden brightness show,
The clouds and mist reflect a golden glow,
And far and near what tender glories flow
  As Sunrise comes!

The spreading hills upraise themselves in song,
The streams soft murmur as they move along;
What hopes and yearnings rise in rapid throng
  When sunrise calls!

The slumb'ring city wakens from its sleep,
The streets and homes no longer silence keep;
O faithful heart, forget thy sorrows deep
  With sunrise near!

The night will pass, God's dawn will come again,
Your doubt and fears will vanish like the rain,
And you will smile away the haunting pain—
  'Tis sunrise now!

—Abram S. Isaacs.

THE SONG OF LIFE'S BRIGADE

Wounded? Yes, but marching,
　And singing as we go;
Singing up to victory,
　Or death before the foe.

Weary? Yes, but marching,
　And thirsty as we cheer,
That other flagging footsteps
　May quicken as they hear.

Fainting? Yes, but marching,
　To bear a comrade slain
Beyond the glare of battle
　To friendly beds of pain.

Dying? Yes, but marching
　In spirit where they go,
Singing up to victory
　Forgetful of the foe!

　　　　　　　　　　—MARTHA BIANCHI.

IF

If you can keep your head when all about you
　Are losing theirs and blaming it on you;
If you can trust yourself when all men doubt you,
　But make allowances for their doubting too;
If you can wait and not be tired by waiting,
　Or being lied about don't deal in lies,
Or being hated don't give way to hating,
　And yet don't look too good, nor talk too wise;

If you can dream—and not make dreams your master;
　If you can think—and not make thoughts your aim,
If you can meet with Triumph and Disaster
　And treat those two imposters just the same,
If you can bear to hear the truth you've spoken
　Twisted by knaves to make a trap for fools,
Or watch the things you gave your life to, broken,
　And stoop and build 'em up with worn-out tools;

If you can make one heap of all your winnings
  And risk it on one turn of pitch-and-toss,
And lose, and start again at your beginnings
  And never breathe a word about your loss;
If you can force your heart and nerve and sinew
  To serve your turn long after they are gone,
And so hold on when there is nothing in you
  Except the Will which says to them: "Hold on!"

If you can talk with crowds and keep your virtue,
  Or walk with Kings—nor lose the common touch,
If neither foes nor loving friends can hurt you,
  If all men count with you, but none too much;
If you can fill the unforgiving minute
  With sixty seconds' worth of distance run,
Yours is the Earth and everything that's in it,
  And—which is more—you'll be a Man, my son!
           —RUDYARD KIPLING *in American Magazine.*

CLEON AND I.

Cleon hath a million acres,
  Ne'er a one have I;
Cleon dwelleth in a palace,
  In a cottage I;
Cleon hath a dozen fortunes,
  Not a penny I;
Yet the poorer of the twain is
  Cleon, and not I.

Cleon, true, possesseth acres,
  But the landscape I;
Half the charms to me it yieldeth
  Money cannot buy;
Cleon harbors sloth and dullness,
  Freshening vigor, I;
He in velvet, I in fustian,
  Richer man am I.

Cleon is a slave to grandeur,
  Free as thought am I;
Cleon fees a score of doctors,
  Need of none have I;
Wealth-surrounded, care-environed,
  Cleon fears to die;
Death may come, he'll find me ready—
  Happier man am I.

Cleon sees no charm in nature,
  In a daisy, I;
Cleon hears no anthems ringing
  In the sea and sky;
Nature sings to me forever,
  Earnest listener I;
State for state, with all attendants,
  Who would change? Not I.
                    —Charles Mackay.

WHAT I LIVE FOR

I live for those who love me,
  Whose hearts are kind and true,
For the heaven that smiles above me,
  And awaits my spirit, too;
For all human ties that bind me,
For the task by God assigned me,
For the bright hopes yet to find me,
  And the good that I can do.

I live to learn their story
Who suffered for my sake;
To emulate their glory,
  And follow in their wake
Bards, patriots, martyrs, sages,
The heroic of all ages,
Whose deeds crowd history's pages,
  And Time's great volume make.

I live to hold communion
  With all that is divine,
To feel there is a union
  'Twixt nature's heart and mine;
To profit by affliction,
Reap truth from fields of fiction,
Grow wiser from conviction,
  And fulfill God's grand design.

I live to hail that season,
  By gifted ones foretold,
When men shall live by reason,
  And not alone by gold;
When man to man united,
And every wrong thing righted,
The whole world shall be lighted
  As Eden was of old.

I live for those who love me,
  For those who know me true,
For the heaven that smiles above me,
  And awaits my spirit, too;
For the cause that lacks assistance
For the wrong that needs resistance
For the future in the distance,
  And the good that I can do.
                  —G. Linnaeus Banks.

INDEX

POEMS.

Lightning Source UK Ltd.
Milton Keynes UK
UKHW02f2305080318
319103UK00011B/506/P